OXFORD CLASSICAL MONOGRAPHS

Published under the supervision of a Committee of the Faculty of Literae Humaniores in the University of Oxford

OXFORD CLASSICAL MONOGRAPHS

The aim of the Oxford Classical Monographs series (which replaces the Oxford Classical and Philosophical Monographs) is to publish books based on the best theses on Greek and Latin literature, ancient history, and ancient philosophy examined by the Faculty Board of Literae Humaniores.

Warfare in Roman Europe, AD 350–425

HUGH ELTON

CLARENDON PRESS · OXFORD

OXFORD

UNIVERSITY PRESS

Great Clarendon Street, Oxford OX2 6DP

Oxford University Press is a department of the University of Oxford.
It furthers the University's objective of excellence in research, scholarship,
and education by publishing worldwide in

Oxford New York

Athens Auckland Bangkok Bogotá Buenos Aires Calcutta
Cape Town Chennai Dar es Salaam Delhi Florence Hong Kong Istanbul
Karachi Kuala Lumpur Madrid Melbourne Mexico City Mumbai
Nairobi Paris São Paulo Singapore Taipei Tokyo Toronto Warsaw
with associated companies in Berlin Ibadan

Oxford is a registered trade mark of Oxford University Press
in the UK and in certain other countries

Published in the United States
by Oxford University Press Inc., New York

© Hugh Elton 1996

First issued in paperback 1997

British Library Cataloguing in Publication Data

Data available

Library of Congress Cataloging in Publication Data
Warfare in Roman Europe, AD 350–425 / Hugh Elton.
(Oxford classical monographs)
Includes bibliographical references.
1. Military art and science—Europe—History.   2. Europe—History, Military.
3. Rome—History, Military—30 BC–476 AD.   I. Title.   II. Series.
U43.E95E48   1996   355'.00936—dc20   95—17531

ISBN 0-19-815241-8

3 5 7 9 10 8 6 4

Printed in Great Britain on acid-free paper by
Bookcraft (Bath) Ltd., Midsomer Norton

for my parents
Josephine and Brian

PREFACE

This book discusses aspects of Roman and barbarian military practice in Roman Europe, AD 350–425. The geographical area covers relations with all 'Germanic' barbarians as well as those from the steppes or in Britain. The chronological period is an arbitrary one, starting with the Roman Empire as the dominant power in Europe and ending before the fall was inevitable, but with all the elements for the collapse of the Western Empire in place.

Although the late Roman and early medieval periods have seen much attention in recent years, the field of military history has been somewhat neglected. Though detailed discussions of many aspects of the late Roman army are available, there is still no comprehensive modern account of the Roman army of the fourth and fifth centuries AD. This is not such an account, but instead an attempt to provide the background that will allow such a work to be written in the future. It does not attempt to be exhaustive, but tries to provide some coverage of most relevant aspects of the subject. The result is a type of 'handbook' describing the 'normalities' of warfare in the late Empire.

The approach I have taken may appear unusual. I am not as interested in how particular operations were dealt with as the principles and strategies used in different types of operations. With such broad aims, it seemed necessary to cover large geographical and chronological areas in order both to gain enough evidence and to understand the 'big picture'.

'How effective was the late Roman army?' is the underlying question running through the book, though not determining its shape. Such a question is complex and very difficult to answer for any army, even in periods where more information is available. For the late Roman army it is almost impossible. However, unless some judgement has been made on the effectiveness of the army, it is difficult to write anything meaningful about fifth-century politics and the fall of the Western Roman Empire. This is an attempt to provide at least part of the answer to the question of the army's efficiency. It does not, however, provide a complete answer. Many topics, e.g. Roman foreign policy, barbarian military equipment, and Roman fortifications, deserve considerable attention. I have done little more than skim the surface here and am well aware that more could (and perhaps should) have been written. It is hoped that the general nature of the arguments advanced here is not adversely affected by such shortcomings. I do not deal with Roman operations within Africa (as opposed to operations launched from Europe) or east of the Bosporus. This choice was made because the types of enemy faced by the Romans in these areas and their objectives were both very different from the European barbarians. Though this limits, somewhat, coverage of the Roman army itself, the inclusion of these areas would necessitate too much diversification. The book is derived from my Oxford D.Phil. thesis (1990), which originally spanned the years 350–500. While the text has been updated, and much of the material dealing with events post-425 has been excised, some remains where I felt it provided good examples. In the footnotes, references to events later than 425 have been left intact. Translations are drawn from the edition cited in the Bibliography, except for Gregory of Tours, including Renatus Profuturus Frigeridus and Sulpicius Alexander (Penguin Classics), Mauricius (Dennis), and Zosimus (Ridley), occasionally modified where I thought it necessary.

Throughout the four years I worked on the thesis and two on the book, I have received enormous assistance from many people. First and foremost are my two supervisors. John Matthews guided my initial steps into research and helped reform my prose style, though he is not responsible for its continued shortcomings. Roger Tomlin helped refine an unwieldy collection of material into something more tightly structured and has eliminated a number of careless errors. Fergus Millar has been a support and an inspiration. I have received more encouragement from John Drinkwater than I can ever repay. I am also grateful to Philip Bartholomew, Barbara Levick, and Ian Wood for reading and commenting on parts of this work and to my examiners, Peter Heather and Wolf Liebeschuetz, both of whom have been of great help, despite our frequent disagreements over many subjects. Jane Robson has been a careful copy-editor. Numerous friends have read some of my material and provided many useful comments: Roger Batty, John Curran, Phil Freeman, Guy Halsall, Peter Heather, David Jennings, Simon Loseby, and Benet Salway. Phil deserves particular mention for his support, friendship and criticism. Mark MacIntyre has been an invaluable help in using computers. These friends, and many others, in particular my wife Krista, especially those in the Late Roman seminar in Oxford, the Sheffield Gaul Conference, and outside higher education, have provided assistance and reassurance above and beyond the call of friendship. For endless chats, cups of coffee and pints of bitter I remain intensely grateful.

Houston, Texas   H.E.
February 1994

CONTENTS

List of Figures   xii
List of Tables   xiii
Abbreviations   xiv

Introduction   1
1. Barbarian Economy and Society   15
2. Barbarian Military Practices   45
3. Roman Organization, Arms, and Equipment   89
4. Finance   118
5. Recruiting   128
6. Fortifications   155
7. Foreign Policy   175
8. Strategy   199
9. Operations   234
Conclusion   265

Appendix 1. Notes on Sources   269
Appendix 2. Barbarization and the Late Roman Army   272
Appendix 3. Danubian Archaeology in Late Antiquity   278
Bibliography   282
Index   303

LIST OF FIGURES

1.	Western German tribes	20
2.	Eastern German tribes	24
3.	Barbarian social structure: a model	33
4.	Frankish and Saxon attacks on the Roman Empire, 354–78	48
5.	Alamannic attacks, 354–78	49
6.	Attacks on the Rhine Frontier, 354–78	49
7.	Distribution of Angons, Saxes, Franciscas	66
8.	Numbers of imperial provinces, 350–480	119
9.	Resources and military expenditure (West), 350–480	126
10.	Ethnicity of regimental commanders, by decade	149
11.	Ethnicity of *magistri militum*, by decade	149
12.	Ethnicity of army officers, by decade	150
13.	Roman forts in Valeria	159
14.	Late Roman fort design	162
15.	Upgraded fort design	166
16.	Information and action: a model	179
17.	*Limitanei* commands	202
18.	Valens' Gothic campaigns, 367–9	225
19.	Mursa campaign, 351	232
20.	March order of Roman army	244
21.	Line of battle	251
22.	Line of battle variations	253
23.	The battle of Strasbourg, 357	255

LIST OF TABLES

1. *Foederati* regiments in the Roman army   93
2. Geographical origins of field army soldiers by prefecture and diocese, 350–476   134
3. Tribal origins of non-Roman soldiers, 350–476   136
4. Roman army officers, 350–476   148
5. *Auxilia palatina* troops   151
6. *Scholares*   152
7. Roman army officers, 350–476 (expanded)   273
8. Other ranks, field army, 350–500   274
9. Other ranks, field army, 350–500 (expanded)   274

ABBREVIATIONS

AA	*Auctores Antiquissimi*
AE	*L'Année Epigraphique*
AJP	*American Journal of Philosophy*
AM	Ammianus Marcellinus
Anon. *DRB*	Anonymous, *De Rebus Bellicis*
Anon. *PS*	Anonymous, *Peri Strategikes*
Anon. Val.	*Anonymus Valesianus*
ANRW	*Aufstieg und Niedergang des Römisches Welt*
ASC	*Anglo-Saxon Chronicle*
Aug.	Augustine
BAR	*British Archaeological Reports*
BJ	*Bonner Jahrbücher*
BZ	*Byzantinisches Zeitschrift*
Cass.	Cassiodorus
CBA	*Council for British Archaeology*
C.Gall.452	*Chronica Galliae ad 452*
CIL	*Corpus Inscriptionum Latinarum*
CJ	*Codex Justinianus*
CP	*Classical Philology*
CQ	*Classical Quarterly*
CSEL	*Corpus Scriptorum Ecclesiasticarum Latinorum*
CT	*Codex Theodosianus*
FHG	*Fragmenta Historicorum Graecorum*
GRBS	*Greek, Roman and Byzantine Studies*
Grosse	R. Grosse, Römische Militärgeschichte (Berlin, 1920)
GT *HF*	Gregory of Tours, *Historia Francorum*
HA	*Historia Augusta*
Hoffmann	D. Hoffmann, *Das spätrömische Bewegungsheer und die Notitia Dignitatum* (Düsseldorf, 1969)
HSCP	*Harvard Studies in Classical Philology*
Hyd.	Hydatius
IHR	*International History Review*
ILS	*Inscriptiones Latinae Selectae*

J. Ant.	John of Antioch
Johnson	S. Johnson, *Late Roman Fortifications* (London, 1983)
JRA	*Journal of Roman Archaeology*
JRS	*Journal of Roman Studies*
Jul.	Julian
Lander	J. Lander, *Roman Stone Fortifications from the First Century AD to the Fourth, BAR* S206 (Oxford, 1984)
Lib.	Libanius
LRE	A. H. M. Jones, *Later Roman Empire* (Oxford, 1964)
LV	*Laterculus Veronensis*
Marc. Com.	Marcellinus Comes
MGH	*Monumenta Germaniae Historica*
ND	*Notitia Dignitatum*
NTh	*Novellae Theodosianae*
NSev	*Novellae Severianae*
NVal	*Novellae Valentiniani*
Olymp.	Olympiodorus
Pan.Lat.	*Panegyrici Latini*
PBSR	*Papers of the British School at Rome*
PG	*Patrologia Graeca*
Philost.	Philostorgius
PL	*Patrologia Latina*
PLRE	*Prosopography of the Later Roman Empire*, i, ed. A. H. M. Jones, J. R. Martindale, and J. Morris (Cambridge, 1971); ii, ed. J. R. Martindale (Cambridge, 1980)
Prosp.	Prosper
P.S.Sabae	*Passio Sanctae Sabae*
RE	*Real-Encyclopedia*
RIB	*Roman Inscriptions of Britain*
RPF	Renatus Profuturus Frigeridus
SA	Sidonius Apollinaris
SRM	*Scriptores Rerum Merovingicarum*
Symm.	Symmachus
Them.	Themistius
Theoph. *AM*	Theophanes, *Chronographia*, *Anno Mundi*
Veg.	Vegetius
Zos.	Zosimus

mille Sarmatas, mille Francos semel et semel occidimus
mille Persas quaerimus

We've killed thousands of Sarmatians, thousands of Franks
again and again; we're looking for thousands of Persians

(Historia Augusta, Vita Aureliani, 7. 2)

Introduction

In AD 350 the Roman Empire was ruled by two *Augusti*, the surviving sons of Constantine the Great, Constans (in the West except Thrace) and Constantius II (Thrace and the East). The army was divided into three major field armies, in Gaul under Constans, in Illyricum under the *magister militum* Vetranio, and in the East under Constantius. During the previous decade there had been little hostility by barbarians in Europe, with only a Frankish attack in 341/2 and an attack on Britain in 342/3 being known.

In 350 the Gallic army revolted and declared the *comes* Magnentius emperor. He killed Constans and swiftly moved into Italy, killing another usurper there, Nepotianus. Africa and Spain also came over to him, but he was prevented from occupying Illyricum by the usurpation of Vetranio. After negotiating with both Constantius and Magnentius, Vetranio surrendered to the former in December 350 and was exiled.

In 351 Magnentius entered Pannonia across the Julian Alps and pushed Constantius' forces back down the Savus valley. After skirmishes at Atrans, Siscia, and Cibalae, Magnentius attacked Mursa but failed to capture the city. Constantius then defeated him in a bloody battle outside the town and pushed him back over the Alps. While Magnentius' troops were engaged in Pannonia, Alamanni (in a confederation led by Chnodomarius) and Franks raided into Gaul and defeated Magnentius' brother, the Caesar Decentius in 351/2.

The following year, 352, Constantius crossed the Alps, defeating Magnentius at Aquileia and forcing him out of Italy and back to Gaul. In 352/3 naval expeditions were sent to recapture Spain and Africa, while in 353 Constantius' main force crossed the Cottian Alps, defeating Magnentius for a third time at Mons Seleucus in the Isère valley. Magnentius fled further into Gaul before he and Decentius committed suicide in August. The Alamanni and Franks continued to take advantage of the disruption by raiding in Gaul, leading to Constantius' appointment of Silvanus as *magister militum per Gallias*.

During 353 Silvanus campaigned against the Franks and Alamanni from Cologne and Trier, while Constantius operated against the Alamanni from Augst in 354 and 355, before moving into Italy in late summer 355. Then, as a result of court politics, Silvanus was forced into a usurpation in August. His swift murder by his troops, suborned by a negotiating mission led by the *magister militum* Ursicinus, forestalled another civil war; Constantius' cousin Julian was now appointed Caesar and placed in charge of the Gallic army.

Barbarian raids in Gaul continued, the disruption caused by Silvanus' usurpation allowed some Franks to capture Cologne, and Alamannic raiders remained active in Gaul. In 356 Julian restarted operations to clear the Alamanni from Gaul, while Constantius operated across the Rhine from around Augst again before retiring to Italy and leaving his army under the *magister militum* Barbatio. During 357 Julian defeated the Alamanni under Chnodomarius at Strasbourg and crossed the Rhine into Alamannia, though he did not co-operate in a combined operation with Barbatio in Raetia. Julian then marched north to engage the Franks.

Further attacks on Raetia and new activity on the middle Danube, led by the Quadic King Araharius, forced Constantius back into action. He delivered a swift check to the Alamanni in Raetia in 357 before moving into Pannonia and wintering in Sirmium. From here in 358 he led pre-emptive strikes against the Sarmatians and Quadi. In Gaul, Julian defeated some Franks in the north and then attacked into Alamannia again. In 359 he continued these strikes against the Alamanni. Elsewhere, the lower Danube seems to have been quiet, though the Picts raided into Britain. Constantius struck into Sarmatia again before leaving Europe to march east to engage the Sassanid Persians.

In reply to the Pictish raids, Julian detached a small expeditionary force to Britain in winter. Soon afterwards the Gallic army again revolted and declared Julian Augustus. When he heard of the usurpation, Constantius began preparations for civil war and started to disengage from the eastern frontier. Julian meanwhile crossed the Rhine in the north and defeated some Franks before marching to south Gaul to prepare for the war against Constantius. Alamannic raids during the winter were defeated and in 361 Julian moved east.

A swift advance on a broad front through north Italy and Noricum brought him into Pannonia from where he occupied Illyricum as far as the pass at Succi. Spain and Italy went over to Julian, though Africa did not. Constantius had by now reached Thrace with a large army and was preparing an assault for the following spring. Julian's position in Italy, uncertain because of the lack of corn from Africa, was undermined by the capture of Aquileia by some rebellious prisoners and the peninsula was lost to his control. Had the war continued Constantius would have had a good chance of victory, but luckily for Julian, Constantius fell ill and died in November 361.

Julian then prepared to attack Persia, to carry on the war hastily ended by Constantius. He negotiated for some allies from the Goths on the lower Danube, while refusing to deal with others who objected to the terms of their treaties. The Persian expedition was launched in 363 and, despite early successes, was forced to retreat, with Julian being killed on the return march. Jovian was elected emperor by the army and made peace with the Persians, but then died. Valentinian was then chosen as emperor and quickly declared his brother Valens as colleague. Valentinian took the western part of the Empire and departed for there immediately, not arriving in Gaul until late 365, where he found Alamanni raiding throughout Gaul.

In late 364, Valens was warned of Gothic hostility and began preparations for a campaign on the lower Danube, sending troops back from the eastern frontier to Thrace. At the same time, Julian's distant relative Procopius launched a usurpation against Valens. He took advantage of Valens' sending a field army brigade to the Danube via Constantinople, persuading it to support him in late September 365. Thrace soon fell under his control and with it the rest of the troops that Valens had been assembling for the Gothic campaign. Illyricum, under Equitius, remained loyal to Valens, blocking the passes leading westwards.

Procopius then crossed into Asia Minor and persuaded other troops of Valens to fight for him. He also summoned allies from the Goths and other barbarians beyond the Danube. Valens, moving from the east, was able to confine Procopius to the western reaches of Asia Minor until the rest of his army arrived from the eastern border, but could not prevent the fall of Nicaea and Cyzicus to Procopius. Equitius then launched an offensive in support of Valens from Illyricum into Thrace. Once Valens' main army had arrived, he defeated Procopius at Nakolia in May 366. Procopius was captured and executed. After Procopius' death, his relative Marcellus seized the purple in Thrace, hoping for Gothic support, but was soon captured and executed.

In winter 366 more Alamanni attacked across the Rhine, but were repulsed in a series of running battles. Valentinian fell seriously ill in 367, curtailing offensive operations, despite attacks by Franks and Saxons on north Gaul and Britain. Britain also came under attack from Picts, Scotti, and Attacotti, forcing the dispatch of an expedition from Gaul under Theodosius the Elder which defeated the Saxons in Britain before winter. During the following year he secured the north and put down Valentinus' conspiracy before returning to Gaul.

Back on the Danube, Valens continued preparations for the campaign against the Goths which had been aborted by Procopius' usurpation. In the next campaigning season, 367, he crossed the Danube forcing the Goths into the hills. In 368 campaigning was impossible because of floods and in 369 Valens crossed the Danube again. The Goths again avoided battle and fled for the hills before suing for peace. Valens accepted this, then departed swiftly for the eastern front where the Sassanid Persians had resumed offensive action.

During 368 Valentinian transferred troops from Illyricum and Italy to Gaul and began a series of campaigns against the Alamanni. He crossed the Rhine and defeated some Alamanni at Solicinium. The following year, 369, was one of consolidation in central Gaul, though Saxon raiders in north Gaul were also engaged. Preparations were also made for a major campaign in 370, involving an attack by Valentinian across the upper Rhine, a second Roman expedition launched from Raetia and an allied force of Burgundians entering Alamannia from the east. These preparations were upset by another Saxon attack from the north, requiring the diversion of Roman troops and the cancellation of the northern part of the operation, though the southern arm of the attack was successful. In 371 more forts were constructed, but in 372 Valentinian returned to the offensive, trying to capture the stubborn Alamannic king, Macrianus. Though he could install his own candidate for king in this area he was unable to impose his will on the Alamanni in the long term. Fort building continued in 373, though the dispatch of Theodosius the Elder to Africa with an army (drawn from Gaul and Illyricum) reduced offensive capabilities. None the less, in 374 another Roman expedition crossed the Rhine against the Alamanni.

In 374 the Quadi undertook more raids on the Danube, which in turn encouraged the Sarmatians to start raiding, both being prompted by the earlier withdrawal of troops for Theodosius' expedition. Local counter-attacks defeated the Sarmatians and reinforcements from Gaul arrived before the end of winter. Valentinian himself arrived in spring 375 and made peace with the Sarmatians before launching a large expedition against the Quadi. At the close of the campaigning season the Quadi sued for peace, but in the course of the negotiations Valentinian died of apoplexy.

In 375 the strategic situation of the Roman Empire had changed little from that of 350. The previous twenty-five years had been turbulent but no more or less so than the early years of the fourth century. Internally, usurpers had always been defeated. Externally, the barbarians had been kept at bay and Roman arms were dominant on the Rhine and Danube, able to strike across the rivers with apparent impunity. The barbarians were at their most dangerous when they combined under a capable leader, but the Romans could defeat even such combinations, and some areas, such as the lower Danube, are not known to have suffered any barbarian raids in this period. The future looked secure.

The arrival of the Huns in Europe upset all this. Their attacks on the Goths during the early 370s caused some to flee, others to submit to them. Refugees appealed to Valens and arrived on the Danube. Plans to settle the Tervingi peacefully were disrupted by the incompetence and greed of Roman officials, leading to hostilities with those Goths within the Empire. The Illyrian field army campaigned against the numerous groups, receiving Western reinforcements in the winter of 376/7; Valens himself remained at Antioch, watching the Persians. Fighting continued in 377 and by winter the Eastern army had the Goths blocked up in Scythia. The Romans were unable to maintain the blockade and had to withdraw behind the Haemus mountains.

In 378 Gratian sent further troops from the West to aid Valens. This led to an attack by an Alamannic confederation led by Priarius. Alarmed, Gratian recalled the troops marching eastwards and returned to Gaul where he defeated Priarius at Argentaria. He then crossed the Rhine and followed the Alamanni into the hills, forcing them to submit.

After this, Gratian led his troops east in person, following the course of the Danube and fighting off Alan raiders on his march. By now, Valens had left the eastern frontier and had arrived in Thrace with reinforcements. Feeling unable to wait for Gratian's army, he engaged the united Goths at Adrianople on 9 August 378. A disastrous defeat followed, with the destruction of much of the Eastern field army and Valens' death on the battlefield. Gratian's immediate response was to appoint Theodosius the Younger as *magister militum* to restore control to the middle and lower Danube. Theodosius campaigned so successfully against Sarmatians and Goths that in early 379 he was created *Augustus* for the eastern part of the Empire by Gratian. Soon after this Gratian returned to Gaul to carry out more operations where the Alamanni were still raiding.

In 380 a Gothic group led by Alatheus and Saphrax attacked Pannonia. Gratian left Gaul, reaching Pannonia in August, and came to some agreement with Alatheus and Saphrax. He stayed here until 383 when he moved to Italy, then into Raetia, preparing a strike against the Alamanni Iuthungi.

Magnus Maximus, general in Britain, seized the purple in June 383 and crossed from Britain to Gaul. Gratian aborted his campaign against the Alamanni and marched to Paris where he met Maximus. After five days of skirmishing and negotiations Gratian's army went over to Maximus. Gratian fled for Italy, but was caught and killed at Lyons in August. Maximus now controlled Britain, Spain, Gaul, and Africa. Italy continued to be held by Valentinian II (Valentinian I's young son), who blocked the Alpine passes even as negotiations between the factions began. Theodosius then recognized Maximus on Valentinian's behalf.

In 384, despite the threat of an attack from Maximus, Valentinian sent an expedition against the Alamannic Iuthungi under Bauto, continuing the aborted campaign of 383. In 386 some Sarmatians attacked Pannonia. Valentinian's army repulsed them and rejected an offer of help from Maximus.

In 386 the Greuthungi across the Danube made an attempt to cross into the Empire to escape the Huns, but the *magister peditum* Promotus destroyed the Goths as they crossed. Numbers of prisoners were taken, some of whom were recruited for use against Maximus.

In June–July 387 Maximus broke the peace with Valentinian and

Theodosius and stormed across the Alps, his army including allied Franks and Saxons. Valentinian fled first to Aquileia, then to Thessalonica, while Italy fell into Maximus' hands. After expelling Valentinian, Maximus began negotiations with Theodosius and a settlement appeared possible. But in spring 388 Maximus crossed the Julian Alps and occupied Pannonia. Meanwhile Theodosius himself left Thessalonica in June after summoning allied contingents from Goths, Alans, Iberians, and Armenians. Maximus was able to persuade some Goths to defect. Theodosius also sent out two secondary attacks, a marine assault on Sicily and Italy and an expedition from Egypt to Africa. In the Adriatic Theodosius' troops avoided Maximus' navy (under Andragathius), landed in Sicily, and defeated Maximus' troops there. In Pannonia, Maximus marched up the Savus, captured Siscia, and then defeated Maximus' main army at Poetovio. Maximus was pursued to Aquileia where, after slight resistance, he was captured and executed in late August.

In Gaul, a Frankish coalition of several cantons attacked Germania Secunda and threatened Cologne. Roman relief forces defeated the Franks and pursued them across the Rhine, though they suffered badly in confused fighting in swamps and forests. This upsurge in Frankish activity led Theodosius to send reinforcements under Arbogastes to the area, quickly restoring Roman dominance. In 389 Arbogastes exacted hostages from the Franks and in late 391 he crossed the Rhine in the winter, ravaging the territory of the Bructeri and Chamavi.

In 392, after the death of Valentinian II, Arbogastes raised Eugenius to the purple and gained control over Gaul, Spain, and Britain. A show of force on the Rhine secured peace (and probably recruits) and in 393 Eugenius advanced to Italy which now accepted him as Emperor. Theodosius had also summoned allies and left Constantinople in May 394 with a Roman army supported by fresh contingents of Gothic, Alanic, and Iberian allies. Eugenius did not advance from Italy and by September Theodosius had reached the Julian Alps. Eugenius had fortified the main pass, but was defeated in a two-day bloody battle. Theodosius entered Italy, but died a few months later, in January 395.

Later that year some Goths, under Alaric, who had been settled in Thrace started plundering in Thessaly. Stilicho led the combined Eastern and Western field armies back from Italy through the Balkans. He pinned Alaric down but could not defeat him, and

before the end of the year returned the Eastern troops to Constantinople and left for the West, leaving the Goths unsubdued.
Some Huns took advantage of this disruption to raid into Thrace.

In 396 Stilicho marched to the Rhine where he broke up a
Frankish coalition, removing both its leaders from power. He also
recruited extensively to replace the losses of 394–5, before returning
to Italy. Also in 396 Alaric entered Greece, then crossed to the
Peloponnese in 397. Stilicho sailed to the Peloponnese and dis-
embarked an army there. After fighting in Arcadia he blockaded
Alaric near Elis, but again could not defeat him. Stilicho then
returned to Italy while Alaric crossed over to Epirus where he
received some recognition in the form of the title of *magister
militum per Illyricum* from the eastern government.

Later in 397 Gildo transferred his allegiance from Rome to
Constantinople. Stilicho responded by sending a small force, 5,000
men under Gildo's brother, Mascezel, hoping to avoid political
problems and civil war. Gildo was swiftly defeated before the East
had time to react. During 398 there were some raids in Scotland,
apparently defeated without difficulty.

In 398 Eutropius led a successful campaign against Caucasian
Huns in Asia Minor. Soon afterwards, Tribigildus revolted in
Phrygia. Two Eastern armies were sent against him. One, under
Leo, was defeated; the commander of the second, Gainas, took
advantage of the crisis to win political concessions from Arcadius
in return for quelling the revolt. As a result, Eutropius was over-
thrown, but Gainas was unable to replace Eutropius until he exiled
another rival, Aurelianus. Aurelianus though was soon able to
engineer Gainas' removal from Constantinople in 400. Gainas
retreated through Thrace and across the Danube, but was killed
by Uldin's Huns.

Although the Empire appeared superficially similar in 400 to
375 there were some important differences. The first of these was
the political divergence between its two parts. Though there had
been multiple rulers of the Empire before, Honorius and Arcadius
both came to the throne as minors and soon lost control to powerful
'advisers': in the West Stilicho, Olympius, and then Constantius,
in the East Rufinus, then Eutropius, Gainas, Aurelianus, and
Anthemius. This led to the two parts co-operating less, especially
in the Balkans. Secondly, the territorial integrity of the Empire had
been damaged by the settlement of the Goths in the Balkans under

their own rulers, coupled with the repeated inability of Stilicho to destroy them in the years following Theodosius' death.

Neither of these problems was necessarily fatal. Relations between the two parts of the Empire could have been improved, Alaric could have been defeated, and the Goths destroyed. This did not occur and though the strength of the Empire remained immense, its ability to deploy all of its resources against a single enemy was now compromised.

In 401 Alaric returned to Italy, fighting inconclusive battles against Stilicho at Pollentia and Verona in 402, then retreating to the Balkans. Negotiations and an alliance with Stilicho in 405 were upset by the arrival of another Gothic force in Italy. These Goths, led by Radagaisus, crossed the Danube and reached Florence. Here, they were blockaded by Stilicho with Hun and Alan allies, starved, then destroyed in battle.

Towards the end of 406, the army in Britain raised first Marcus, then Gratian, and finally a soldier, Constantine, to the purple. At this time, in Gaul, in the winter of 406, the Asding and Siling Vandals, the Alamanni Suevi and some Alans crossed the Rhine. Constantine crossed from Britain to Boulogne in spring 407, gained the support of the Gallic army, and defeated the invaders who then joined him as allies. From Italy, Stilicho acted against Constantine by sending Sarus into Gaul with an army. Sarus besieged Constantine in Valentia, but was then forced to retire to Italy. Constantine occupied the Italian Alps, then sent troops under the command of his son, the Caesar Constans, and the *magister militum* Gerontius into Spain in 408, controlling the province by early 409.

Arcadius died on 1 May 408 in Constantinople and was succeeded by his 7-year-old son, Theodosius II. More dramatic changes occurred in the West on 13 August 408, when Olympius, *magister scrinii*, led a coup against Stilicho, leading to Stilicho's execution on 22 August. Alaric, still in Illyricum, tried to make peace again, after abortive negotiations in 407. Negotiations again broke down, and Alaric marched on Italy to besiege Rome in November 408. After negotiating a payment from the city of Rome, the Goths withdrew to Tuscany. Honorius, too involved with Alaric to risk another confrontation, recognized Constantine as his imperial colleague in January 409.

In the East, Arcadius' premier adviser, Anthemius, acted as

regent to Theodosius. Some Huns, under Uldin, raided across the
Danube in 408, but were forced to retreat after many of their allied
Sciri defected. With the departure of the Goths the Eastern Empire
seems otherwise to have come under very little foreign pressure at
this time.

From Gaul, Constantine crossed the Alps into Italy unopposed,
but was forced to withdraw by Honorius. In Spain, Gerontius
revolted when Constantine tried to replace him, raising one of his
domestici, Maximus, to the purple. Gerontius was also able to incite
some of Constantine's barbarian allies, the invaders of 406, to
revolt. Following a large attack by Saxons in 410, the British cities
revolted from the Empire and expelled their attackers, a move
emulated by some Armorican cities.

In Italy the Goths blockaded Rome again, and after some
countermarching were able to occupy the city. Here, in late 409,
Alaric organized the acclamation of Attalus as Emperor and sent
an expedition to Africa under Constans against Heraclianus, who
had remained loyal to Honorius and was withholding grain supplies
from Rome. In Italy, Attalus and Alaric besieged Honorius in
Ravenna, but Attalus' inability to capture the city or to ensure the
corn supply to Rome forced Alaric to depose him and negotiate
with Honorius again. The failure of these negotiations led Alaric
to sack Rome. He planned to cross into Africa, but before this he
died, and his brother-in-law Ataulf became king.

Temporary peace was made with the Goths in 411, allowing
Honorius to send an army into Gaul. Here, by spring 411, Maximus
and Gerontius had defeated and killed Constans at Vienne before
moving south to besiege Constantine at Arles. Honorius' *magistri
militum*, Constantius and Ulfilas, drove Gerontius back to Spain
where he was attacked and killed by his Spanish troops, though
Maximus escaped to Spain, where he continued to rule in the
mountains until 414. After Gerontius' defeat, Constantius and
Ulfilas besieged, captured, and executed Constantine in Arles.

It was only in 411, after the death of Gerontius and the flight
of Maximus, that the barbarians who had entered Spain founded
their own kingdoms. The Asding Vandals and the Suevi settled in
Galicia, the Alans in Lusitania and Carthaginiensis, and the Siling
Vandals in Baetica. Tarraconensis remained Roman. With the death
of Constantine, another usurper appeared in Gaul, Jovinus—who
was proclaimed emperor by a large force of Romans at Mainz with

the support of the Burgundian King Guntiarius, the Alan Goar, and some Franks and Alamanni. He captured Arles and forced Constantius and Ulfilas to retreat to Italy. Honorius then persuaded Ataulf to enter Gaul in 412, allowing Honorius to subdue Jovinus cheaply in 413 and also get the Goths out of Italy.

Honorius' general in Africa, the *comes Africae* Heraclianus, rebelled in 413. After delaying dispatch of the grain fleet in early April, he crossed to Italy with a large fleet, but was defeated by Marinus. This usurpation and ensuing disruption meant that the Romans could not provide the grain they had promised to the Goths. Ataulf therefore attacked Marseilles unsuccessfully, but captured Narbonne, Toulouse, and Bordeaux, creating an area for the Goths to settle, and declared Attalus Emperor again. Honorius sent Constantius with an army into south-western Gaul and blockaded the Mediterranean coast, forcing Ataulf out of Narbonne and into Spain in summer 414.

Ataulf was murdered soon after settling in Spain, by Segericus, who became king but was murdered a week later. Vallia was the next king. The Goths were still being blockaded by the Romans. Vallia tried to return to Gaul, failed, and marched south to Baetica, hoping to cross into Africa. The Goths assembled a fleet, but it was wrecked by storms. Suffering from severe food shortages, Vallia finally came to terms with the Romans, promising to campaign against the barbarians in Spain. In 416–18, the Goths destroyed the Siling Vandals in Baetica. Vallia then turned on the Alans, who fled to the Asdings in Galicia.

In 418, the Goths were ordered out of Spain and were settled in Aquitania Secunda and some other *civitates*, including Toulouse, by Constantius. Under their treaty obligations, the Visigoths (as the confederation is now known) had to supply contingents to the Roman army. All of Spain, with the exception of Galicia, was back under direct Roman control. The Suevi under their king, Hermeric, and the Asding Vandals under Gundericus occupied Galicia, but in 419 the two tribes began fighting. The Romans forced the Vandals to lift the siege of the Suevi by sending an army under the *comes Hispaniarum* Asterius to Spain. The Vandals were forced to retreat to Baetica.

During the early fifth century Franks seem to have begun moving into Germania Secunda and Belgica Secunda, with Trier being sacked in 419/20. The Roman response was to send the general

Castinus against the Franks in 420. Frankish pressure is also shown by Clodio's seizure of Cambrai, Tournai and some territory up to the river Somme, an event for which no date can be given, though perhaps it happened in the 420s.

On 21 February 421, Constantius was elevated by Honorius to Augustus. By the end of 421 the usurper Maximus had been captured in Spain, presumably by Asterius. Another Roman expedition was sent against the Vandals in Baetica in 422, under the command of Castinus. Bonifatius was also assigned to the operation, but quarrelled with Castinus and withdrew to Africa. Castinus commanded a number of Visigothic allies drawn from the recent settlement in Gaul, as well as a large Roman force. The Romans were initially successful, but then were seriously defeated by the Vandals. At this, the Visigoths deserted, forcing Castinus to return to Tarraco.

We have no reports of any action along the Danube in the Western Empire, though the Huns on the lower Danube raided Thrace again in 422, taking advantage of Roman distraction in a war on the Eastern frontier. Then Honorius, still relatively young at the age of 39, died in Ravenna in mid-August 423. At Rome, the *primicerius* Ioannes, taking advantage of the absence of the legitimate heir Valentinian in Constantinople, usurped the Western Empire, supported by the *magister militum* Castinus. Gaul, Spain, and Dalmatia supported him, but Africa, under Bonifatius, remained loyal to Valentinian. Initial attempts at negotiating a settlement in 424 failed and Ioannes turned to military efforts, sending the *cura palatii* Aetius to the Huns in Pannonia to hire allies.

Theodosius II spent most of the year assembling troops and sent an expedition into Dalmatia under the *magistri militum* Aspar and Ardabur in the autumn. In 425 they launched an attack on Italy, the army being supported by a fleet. Aquileia fell quickly and Ioannes retreated to Ravenna while the Eastern army occupied the Po valley. A final battle near Ravenna resulted in Ioannes' capture and execution. Three days later, the Huns from Pannonia arrived and an inconclusive battle was fought. The Huns were then bought off, Aetius dismissing them in return for a pardon for the rebels. Castinus was exiled, Sigisvultus and Aetius continued to serve in the army. Taking advantage of Roman preoccupations, the Goths in Gaul attacked Arles, but were beaten off by an army led by the newly promoted *magister militum*, Aetius.

The military problems faced by the Roman Empire now differed between East and West. Those faced by the Western Romans were markedly different at the beginning and end of Honorius' reign. In 395 there were no independent settlements in the West. By 425 there were independent kingdoms of Vandals, Suevi, Visigoths, and Burgundians, and the diocese of Britain had been completely lost to the Empire. Although the settlers were allied to the Romans, these treaties were not always kept, and during the remainder of the fifth century the Romans were to spend as much time defending the Empire from internal enemies as from external ones. This distinction is important, since it meant that imperial resources were frequently divided. In contrast, the Eastern part of the Empire had lost none of its territory to barbarians. In both East and West continuing Roman operational success suggests that sufficient resources were available to safeguard the Empire, provided they could be focused on the task of preserving the government.

I

Barbarian Economy and Society

In the late fourth century AD various barbarian, in the sense of non-Roman, tribes lived on the borders of the Roman Empire in Europe. The orthodox view of these barbarians, partially rejected here, sees the small Germanic tribes known from the first century combining into large confederations in the third century. Thus the Bructeri, Chatti, etc., were replaced by the Franks on the lower Rhine. These Franks were distinct socially and politically from the Saxons to the east and the Alamanni to the south. On account of their size, these confederations posed a greater danger than their predecessors to the Roman Empire. Though the first wave of attacks in the third century was eventually defeated, continuing invasions in the fourth and fifth centuries inevitably overloaded the defences of the Empire. This allowed barbarian tribes to move into the Empire, a movement encouraged by pressure from the tribes further east, such as the Huns.[1]

This chapter argues that the literary and archaeological evidence suggests that barbarian society was uniform and that no significant differences in material or socio-political culture existed between the various groups living along the frontier. Although it cannot be proved that all groups were identical, it seems reasonable to follow Roman sources and treat all as 'barbarians', in general indistinguishable from one another, except by their membership of a political grouping. 'Barbarian' is used throughout to describe all non-Roman European enemies of the Empire, including Huns and Alans. Where 'Germans' are referred to, this includes all barbarians except Huns and Alans.

A cursory examination of the archaeological evidence suggests

---

[1] e.g. E. Demougeot, *La Formation de l'Europe et les invasions barbares* (Paris, 1979); for a good discussion of the historiography of the invasions, W. Goffart, *Barbarians and Romans* (Princeton, NJ, 1980), 3–35, and 'Rome, Constantinople and the Barbarians', *AHR* 86 (1981), 275–306.

that there were no major differences in barbarian cultural levels along the frontier. The same types of artefact (pots, brooches, belt buckles, etc.) are found everywhere, suggesting a common level of technology with only local differences. Material is also found in similar quantities. No barbarians produced large quantities of glass or built whole villages of stone houses, and groups lived in small villages, not large towns. Local differences are not sufficient to distinguish between barbarian groups. Although distributions differ for specific types of artefacts, these distributions overlap to such an extent that they cannot reflect political boundaries, although they may reflect regional customs.[2]

This is, of course, to simplify matters drastically. Not all barbarians were identical and, for example, barbarians from the lower Rhine and middle Danube (admittedly on the evidence of funeral deposits) seem to have worn their brooches differently. But these sorts of distinctions do not suggest radically different societies, rather local variation. It seems likely that such features had no significance at any level other than of local fashion. The differences that did exist were very subtle and though they may have been apparent to contemporaries, they are lost to us. It is now generally accepted by archaeologists that 'archaeological cultures clearly cannot be correlated in any mechanical fashion with societal groupings such as tribes, bands or nations'.[3]

Most literary accounts of barbarians present the same picture as the archaeology, i.e. of peoples with few differences. While an appealing point of view because of its simplicity, this hypothesis cannot be immediately accepted at face value. First, the difficulties faced by many Romans in obtaining information must be taken into account. According to Cassius Dio, in the early third century,

[2] Artefact distribution is conveniently mapped in north-west Europe by H. Böhme, *Germanische Grabfunde des 4 bis 5 Jahrhunderts zwischen unterer Elbe und Loire* (Munich, 1974), e.g. Karte 15: on overlaps see P. H. Heather and J. F. Matthews, eds., *The Goths in the Fourth Century* (Liverpool, 1991), 63–6, 71–7; on rich Rhineland sites see R. Pirling, 'Ein fränkischer Fürstengrab aus Krefeld-Gellep', *Germania*, 42 (1964), 188–216; on Danubian sites see I. Ionita, 'Contributii cu privire la cultura Sîntana de Mureş-Černeahov pe teritoriul Republicii Socialistii Românâ', *Arheologia Moldovei*, 4 (1966), 189–259.

[3] B. G. Trigger, *Time and Traditions* (Edinburgh, 1978), 116 and *passim*; S. J. Shennan, ed., *Archaeological Approaches to Cultural Identity* (London, 1989); on archaeological differentiation see Böhme, *Germanische Grabfunde*, 158–65; cf. T. S. Burns, *A History of the Ostrogoths* (Bloomington, Ind., 1984), 115–17; E. James, *The Franks* (Oxford, 1988), 46.

'in Rome, for example, much is going on, and much in the subject territory, while, as regards our enemies, there something is happening all the time, in fact every day, and concerning all these things no one except the participants can easily have correct information, and most people do not even hear of them at all'.[4] These problems would have been faced by fourth- and fifth-century writers too, or at least by those who did any serious research. Most poets and orators, one suspects, would not devote much time to research, with the result that their accounts would reflect only information easily available (at court), not necessarily the truth. Thus Ammianus Marcellinus, who served in Gaul, refers to groups such as the Atthuarii, Salii, Chamavi, Lentienses, Iuthungi, and Bucinobantes, while making it clear that these were from the regions inhabited by Franks and Alamanni. However, Claudian, who seems never to have been near the frontier, refers to the Chatti, Bructeri, Sugambri, and Cherusci as though they were equivalents of the Suevi and Germani.[5]

Secondly, literary stereotypes are frequent in descriptions of barbarians, to the extent that some descriptions were repeated almost verbatim from earlier authors. The problems of stereotyping can be minimized in three ways. First, the author concerned can be checked for internal consistency. Secondly, the account can be checked against archaeological evidence. If there is a strong divergence one should be at least wary of the literary material. An attempt can be made to understand the stereotype, by analysing its source and context. These problems affect the evidence relevant to the Huns in the fifth century, usually seen as an exclusively horse-riding pastoral nomadic society. Their recorded actions are not consistent with this picture. The archaeological evidence from the region of the Theiss, controlled by the Huns in the early fifth century, shows no marked change from the fourth century in types of artefact. It is clear that the accounts of the Huns given by Jerome and Claudian are based on Ammianus Marcellinus' account and cannot be used to confirm the details Ammianus provides of the Huns.

Some Romans recognized other differences between various groups, though these distinctions too could be stereotypes of

---

[4] Dio 53. 19. 5; cf. Eunapius fr. 50, 66. 1–2.
[5] Claudian, *De 4 Cons. Hon.* 446–52, cf. *De Bello Gothico*, 419–24, *De Cons. Stil.* 3. 17–19; cf. SA, *Carm.* 5. 470–9; *Pan. Lat.* 10(4). 18. 1.

their own. The sixth-century *Strategikon* of Mauricius, a military handbook, divides the enemies of the Empire into four major groups on the basis of geography and military techniques, the Persians, the Scythians (i.e. Avars, Turks, and other 'Hunnic' types), the Western barbarians (specifically Lombards, Suevi, and other fair-haired races), and the Slavs and Antes from the lower Danube.[6]

Though stereotyping was frequent in descriptions of barbarians, it is hard not to accept the basic impression given by contemporaries. All the societies are described in the same way, as farmers or shepherds, living under kings, economically primitive, and having no roads, towns, or literature. Roman writers never strayed outside these limited alternatives. In comparison, descriptions of the Arabs stress that they lived in tents, treated their women as communal, were shepherds not farmers, did not stay in one place but moved their settlements around, and were ruled by chieftains. They are distinctly different in description from European barbarians. Roman descriptions of the Sassanid Persians and Moors are again quite different.[7]

This hypothesis that barbarian groups seemed similar to the Romans can also be tested by producing evidence which shows whether barbarians could easily be distinguished from each other. The problems in distinguishing these peoples are illustrated by a passage of Cassius Dio, describing a Roman treaty with the Quadi in the second century. 'However, the right to attend markets was not granted to the Quadi, lest the Iazyges and Marcomanni, whom they had sworn not to receive, or to allow through their territory, should be mixed up with them and, passing themselves off as Quadi, might spy on the affairs of the Romans and buy supplies.'[8] From this it is clear that the Romans could not be sure of recognizing neighbouring barbarians and distinguishing between them if they did not declare themselves. Procopius in the sixth century recorded

there were many Gothic people (ἔθνη) in earlier times, as there are now, and the greatest and most important of them all are the Goths, Vandals,

[6] Mauricius, *Strat.* 11. 1–4; see App. 1 for further discussion of the *Strategikon*.
[7] On stereotypes see B. D. Shaw, '"Eaters of Flesh, Drinkers of Milk"; the Ancient Mediterranean Ideology of the Pastoral Nomad', *Ancient Society* 13/14 (1982/3), 5–31; for descriptions of Arabs see AM 14. 4; Persians, AM 23. 6. 75–84; Mauricius, *Strat.* 11. 1; Moors, Procopius, *BV* 4. 6. 10–13.
[8] Dio 72. 11. 3.

Visigoths, and Gepids .... All these, while they are distinguished from one another by their names, as has been said, do not differ in anything else at all. They all have white bodies and yellow hair, are tall and pleasing to the eye, they use the same laws and practise a common religion. For they are all of Arian belief and have one language, Gothic. And it seems to me that of old they all came from one people and later were distinguished by the names of those leading each tribe.[9]

Procopius, who had fought against Goths and Vandals, felt there were few significant differences. This suggests that there were few distinctions visible to (made by?) most Romans between barbarian groups earlier. From this account one would expect the Romans to have difficulties in identifying peoples. It is likely that Procopius' assessment that the names of leaders determined groupings was a means often used by Romans to identify barbarians, that is, they were assumed to be of the same tribe as their leader.[10]

Having considered these points, we can now attempt to reconstruct barbarian society, using literary and archaeological evidence from different regions. It is not intended to give a full description, but to show how the structure of barbarian society influenced, if not determined, military relations with the Roman Empire. Factors which do not affect this significantly are therefore not discussed.[11]

ECONOMY

Barbarian economies can be divided into two main groups, East and West, with the dividing line coming on the Danube bend around Budapest where the Great Hungarian Plain began. Local variations would have always existed, but do not affect the overall

[9] On Gothic similarity see Procopius, *BV* 3. 2. 2–5; for Alans described as Goths see Procopius, *BV* 3. 3. 1; for other confusion see Priscus fr. 22. 3 (= Suda M. 405) showing Attila angry at Roman paintings depicting barbarians giving tribute to the Emperor, presumably because they looked like his own people.

[10] For Goths see J. Ant. fr. 206. 2; Malalas 460; cf. early Anglo-Saxon groups named after a leader, Haestingas, Oiscingas, etc., J. N. L. Myres, *The English Settlements* (Oxford, 1986), 36–44. For problems in attributing race see R. L. Reynolds and R. S. Lopez, 'Odovacer: German or Hun?', *AHR* 52 (1947), 36–53; B. MacBain, 'Odovacer the Hun?', *CP* 78 (1983), 323–7.

[11] E. A. Thompson, *The Early Germans* (Oxford, 1965); M. Todd, *The Barbarians* (London, 1972) and *The Northern Barbarians*[2] (Oxford, 1987); O. Maenchen-Helfen, *The World of the Huns* (Berkeley, Calif., 1973); see also *Reallexikon der Germanische Altertumskunde*[2] (Berlin, 1973–).

picture presented here. In 350 the major groups of Western barbarians were the Picts, Scotti, Franks, Saxons, Alamanni, and
Quadi (Fig. 1).

The Picts lived in lowland Scotland north of Hadrian's Wall.[12]
The Attacotti were also a threat to Britain. They may have been a

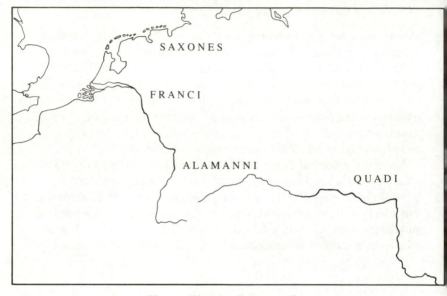

Fig. 1   Western German tribes

subdivision of the Picts, but they are hardly known, being mentioned
twice by Ammianus, once by Jerome, and not at all by other
writers.[13] The Scotti from Ireland are similarly obscure. We know
very little about them beyond the fact that they had kings. Several
Irish kings in the late fourth and early fifth centuries were famed
for raiding England (capturing St Patrick) and even for settling in
Wales.[14]

In the fourth century the Franks occupied territory bordering

[12] L. Alcock, *Arthur's Britain* (London, 1971), 270–7; 'A Survey of Pictish
Settlement and Archaeology', J. G. P. Friell and W. G. Watson, eds., *Pictish Studies*,
BAR 125 (Oxford, 1984); *LV* 13. 3–4; AM 20. 1. 1, 26. 4. 5, 27. 8. 5.

[13] On Attacotti see AM 26. 4. 5, 27. 8. 5; Jerome, *Adversus Iovinianum*, 2. 7 = *PL*
23. 308–9, *Ep*. 69; P. Bartholomew, 'Fourth-Century Saxons', *Britannia* 15 (1984),
169–85 at 173–7.

[14] For Scotti see Alcock, *Arthur's Britain*, 254–70; Bartholomew, 'Saxons', 169–
85; E. A. Thompson, *Who was St. Patrick?* (Woodbridge, 1985); *LV* 13. 2; AM 20.

the Rhine from the North Sea coast to an area south of Cologne where they had a frontier with the Alamanni. The area as a whole was known as Francia. On occasion the area was referred to as Sugambria and 'Sugambri' seems to have been used, poetically at least, as a synonym for Franks. The island of Batavia was also occupied by Franks, having been captured from the Romans in the early fourth century.[15]

To the east of Francia lay Saxonia, though the boundaries between the two are unknown and were probably not distinct. Saxons and Franks were often referred to in the same breath by Roman historians, perhaps because of uncertainty as to the origin of particular groups.[16] The Saxons lived mostly on the coast. It is possible that some did not live too far from the Rhine since Magnentius hired Saxons for use against Constantius II, though this may be an example of the lack of difference between, and Roman inability to distinguish, Franks and Saxons. From Bede we can deduce that some Saxons lived between the Elbe and the Weser rivers in the seventh and eighth centuries and they may have lived there in the fourth and fifth centuries. To their north the Angles inhabited modern Angeln.[17]

The Alamanni inhabited an area which can be divided into several regions. Their borders with the Romans ran along the river Rhine, from Mainz as far as Lake Constance, the river Iller, and the Danube as far as Regensburg. North of the Main and the Taunus mountains lay the Franks, to the west of Alamannia the Quadi.[18] Between the Alamanni and the Quadi the area of the Bohemian plateau is only sketchily known. The Marcomanni seem to have lived in this region, though they are rarely referred to. It

1. 1, 26. 4. 5, 27. 8. 5; for discussion of sources for Irish in England see D. Dumville, 'Sub-Roman Britain: History and Legend', *History*, 62 (1977), 173–92.

[15] James, *Franks*; L. C. Feffer and P. Perin, *Les Francs* (Paris, 1987) summarize and refer to all earlier work; but see also the more traditional approaches of F. Beisel, *Studien zu den fränkischen-römischen Beziehungen* (Idstein, 1987) and E. Zöllner, *Geschichte der Franken* (Munich, 1970); located between Saxons and Alamanni, Jerome, *V. Hilarionis*, 22.

[16] Bartholomew, 'Saxons', 169–85.

[17] On Saxon geography see Todd, *Northern Barbarians*[2], 82; Bede 1. 15; on marshes see Orosius 7. 32. 10; on terpen see Elder Pliny, *NH* 16. 1. 3.

[18] I have not seen L. Okamura, *Alamannia Devicta* (Michigan, 1984), for 3rd-cent. Alamanni; on 4th cent. see R. S. O. Tomlin, 'The Emperor Valentinian I', D.Phil. thesis (Oxford, 1975); W. Müller, ed., *Zur Geschichte der Alamannen*, (Darmstadt, 1975); see also the useful series *Quellen zur Geschichte der Alamannen*, ed. C. Dirlmaier and G. Gottlieb (Heidelberg, 1976).

is just possible that they were called Alamanni or Quadi by some writers during this period.[19] The Quadi lived across the Danube, bordering Pannonia Prima and the northern reaches of Valeria, from Vienna to Aquincum. Their western neighbours were the Alamanni, their eastern neighbours the Sarmatians.[20]

The Burgundians were enemies of Rome in the third century, but are hardly attested in the fourth before reappearing in the fifth. Earlier clashes occurred around the upper Rhine. In the fourth century they lived to the east of the Alamanni, but by the fifth century they were on the Rhine and had begun to cross the river.[21] The Vandals were similarly obscure in 350, living to the north of the Quadi, and they had little direct contact with Rome until the early fifth century.[22]

Most, if not all, Western barbarians were farmers. This was a subsistence economy and most people would have had to spend almost all of their time producing food. Because of this we should not expect the barbarians to have standing armies or to be available for long campaigns. Many barbarian military operations took place in winter, while summer raids tended to avoid harvest times (May–July for spring wheat, September–October for autumn crops). The most common crops were cereals, pulses, and vegetables. Meat was provided by cattle and pigs, both of which could be grazed in woodland, and sheep provided meat as well as wool.[23]

The economy of the Eastern barbarians differed significantly from that of Western barbarians. The societies from the Great Hungarian Plain as far east as Moldavia were semi-sedentary and

[19] AM 31. 4. 2; Paulinus, *V. Ambrosii*, 36.

[20] U.-B. Dittrich, *Die Beziehungen Roms zu den Sarmaten und Quaden im vierten Jahrhundert n. Chr.* (Bonn, 1984); Quadia, AM 16. 10. 20, 30. 5. 13.

[21] For Burgundians see *RGA*[2]; O. Perrin, *Les Burgondes* (Neuchâtel, 1968); on 4th cent. see AM 28. 5. 9–14; Jerome, *Chron.* sa 373; on 5th cent. E. A. Thompson, *Romans and Barbarians* (Madison, Wis., 1982), 32–7.

[22] L. Schmidt, *Geschichte der Wandalen*[2] (Munich, 1942); C. Courtois, *Les Vandales et l'Afrique* (Paris, 1955).

[23] Todd, *Northern Barbarians*[2], 100–14; for Scotti and sheep/cattle see Patrick, *Conf.* 16; for pigs see Muirchu, *V. Pat.* 11; Patrick, *Conf.* 19; for Franks as farmers see AM 17. 9. 2–3; Claudian, *De Cons. Stil.* 1. 222–7; for Saxons and fishing see Elder Pliny, *NH* 16. 1. 4; for Saxons with cattle, horses see W. A. Van Es, 'Wijster: A Native Village beyond the Imperial Frontier', *Palaeohistoria*, 11 (1967), 574; cf. A. E. Van Giffen, 'Der Warf in Ezinge Prov. Groningen und seine westgermanische Häuser', *Germania*, 20 (1936), 40–7 at 40; on Alamanni and farming see AM 16. 11. 11, 17. 1. 7, 10. 6, 9, 18. 2. 19, 27. 10. 7; Lib. *Or.* 12. 44, 48, 18. 34, 52; for Alamanni and cattle see AM 17. 1. 7, 10. 6; Lib. *Or.* 18. 45.

social groups did not remain in the same place permanently. Harsh climates, flooding, and erosion made agriculture difficult, while growing methods meant that soil exhaustion would occur within a few years, forcing occasional relocation; ploughs able to use the soil effectively were not developed until the nineteenth century. These areas were thus not as efficiently exploited as similar areas in the Roman Empire, e.g. the Thracian plain, though even these areas were less intensively exploited than, say, central Greece.[24] Hunting and fishing were also used as subsistence strategies. Sheep, much more important to these people than to Western barbarians, were herded in large numbers, together with cattle. Continual transhumance activity took place, especially in the Carpathians. Large-scale herding meant that horses also played an important (though by no means dominant or necessary) role in the culture. Though it is an argument from silence, the few accounts of Roman expeditions against the Goths do not mention destruction of fields or houses, unlike accounts of attacks on western barbarians. The relocations of these groups did not necessarily take place on an annual or even a regular basis, but settlements would move to fresh areas every few years. This, in outline, is what is meant by a semi-sedentary society. But it conflicts with what is often written about Sarmatian and Gothic society, so needs closer examination (Fig. 2).[25]

Sarmatia lay roughly opposite the Danube bend in the west and extended down the Danube as far as the Iron Gates. The western neighbours and occasional allies of the Sarmatians were the Quadi, while the Goths lived on their eastern borders.[26] The Sarmatians,

[24] R. Batty, 'The Peoples of the Lower Danube and Rome', D.Phil. thesis (Oxford, 1990), 3–13, 400–3; W. H. MacNeill, *Europe's Steppe Frontier* (Chicago, 1964), 2–14.

[25] For nomads as farmers see F. Hole, 'Pastoral Nomadism in Western Iran', in R. A. Gould, ed., *Explorations in Ethnoarchaeology* (Albuquerque, 1978), 127–67, at 152–4; for devastation of Gothia see AM 27. 5. 4, 6; for economy in mountains see Jordanes, *Getica*, 267, 273; J. H. W. G. Liebeschuetz, *Barbarians and Bishops* (Oxford, 1991), 83–5; for a more traditional view of Gothic society see P. J. Heather, *Goths and Romans* (Oxford, 1991), 89–97, a view opposed by Batty, 'Peoples', 405–14; on later regional importance of sheep and cattle see Constantine Porphyrogenitus, *De Administrando Imperii*, 2. 6–8, 7. 11–12, 17, 8. 34–5.

[26] Dittrich, *Die Beziehungen Roms*; for extent of Sarmatia see AM 16. 10. 20, 17. 12. 6, 13. 20; for mountains see AM 17. 12. 5, 13. 22, 31. 4. 13; for plains see AM 17. 13. 22; for marshes see AM 17. 13. 4, 18, 29; Priscus, fr. 12. 2. 275–6; on floods see AM 17. 12. 4, 13. 4.

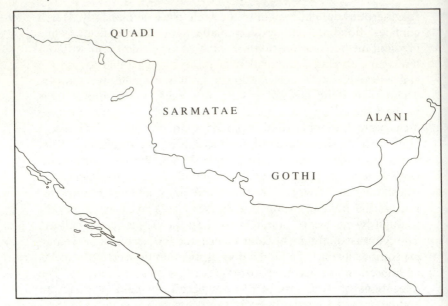

Fig. 2   Eastern German tribes

according to Ammianus, had similar customs and military equipment to the Quadi. They inhabited villages, were found in forests
and mountains and, like the Franks and Alamanni, readily took
refuge in marshes and mountains. They were also accustomed to
using boats.[27] Despite this, it is usually suggested that the Sarmatians
were pastoralists whose armies were composed solely of mounted
warriors. According to Ammianus, the Sarmatians 'travel over very
great distances chasing others or themselves turning their backs,
being mounted on swift and obedient horses and leading one or
sometimes two, so that changing may maintain the strength of their
mounts and their vigour be renewed by alternate rests'.[28] Though
a description of a raiding party, this is often taken as conclusive
proof that all Sarmatians were nomads. Ammianus mentions that

[27] Dittrich, *Die Beziehungen Roms*, 19–25; for characteristics see AM 17. 12. 1–3;
G. A. Crump, *Ammianus Marcellinus as a Military Historian, Historia Einzelschriften*,
27 (Wiesbaden, 1975), 23–4; for boats see AM 17. 13. 17, 27; for refuge see AM 17.
13. 18, 31. 4. 13; cf. Dio 72. 19. 2; for farming on Hungarian plain, cf. Priscus fr.
12. 2. 264–80.
[28] AM 17. 12. 3; for Sarmatian cavalry and infantry see AM 17. 13. 9.

the Sarmatians owned horses and used them while raiding, but he does not say that they were all mounted raiders. Nor is there any mention of horses in Ammianus' detailed descriptions of two sessions of negotiations with the Romans in 357 and 358. Lastly, Ammianus mentions the Huns and Alans as if nomads were new to Europe, describing their lifestyle in detail, which suggests that on their arrival they were markedly different from the Sarmatians he had previously mentioned.[29]

Since there is a strong body of evidence that suggests that the Sarmatians were not a nomadic society, what has suggested that they were? Four classical accounts—those of Dio, Tacitus, Pausanias, and Ammianus Marcellinus—describe the Sarmatians. Dio deals with a single battle at length and mentions nothing about the Sarmatians except that they had their own boats and horses. Tacitus, Pausanias, and Ammianus all focus on the armour of the Sarmatian cavalry, mentioning the scales made of chipped bone or horn, the same image that appears on Trajan's Column. This was obviously a characteristic of the Sarmatians in the first two centuries AD, and a stereotype on which Ammianus was drawing. But none of these writers states that the Sarmatians lived from herd animals, a characteristic of (though not one exclusive to) a nomadic society, nor do they state, or even imply, that all, or even most, were mounted warriors. If the Sarmatians had been nomads, it seems likely that they would have been described as the Huns were. A single passage from Ammianus suggests that some sections of their armies were for the most part cavalry. Other sources do mention horses frequently and they seem to have been a strong element in Sarmatian armies, but this is only to be expected in a people living, for the most part, on flat river plains.[30]

The Goths lived on similar river plains to the north of the Danube, controlling the area from the Iron Gates to Moldavia. To

---

[29] On cavalry see AM 17. 13. 9; on Sarmatian negotiations see AM 17. 12–13, 19. 11; cf. Turks, Menander fr. 10. 3.

[30] cf. Tacitus, *Histories*, 1. 79, mentioning 9,000 cavalry is often quoted, but see also 3. 5, where the Sarmatians 'offered to raise a mass levy as well as a force of cavalry, their one effective arm'; Pausanias 1. 21. 8, saying that the Sarmatians are nomads and most of their territory is forests; Dio 72. 7, 16. 2; AM 17. 12. 2–3; on minimal differences in archaeology see J. Tejral, 'Zur Chronologie der frühen Völkerwanderungszeit im mittleren Donauraum', *Archaeologia Austriaca*, 72 (1988), 223–304.

the west of the Goths lay the Sarmatians, to their east the Alans.[31] This large area can be divided into two major zones, the plains and the Carpathian mountains. North of the Danube and east of the Iron Gates, the Wallachian Plain extended up to 100 km. north from the Danube into the mountains. It was dry and generally unsuitable for farming though able to support herd animals. A sub-zone of marshy areas subject to frequent flooding lay along the river-bank.[32]

The Goths, like other communities in the Danubian basin, were semi-sedentary, their subsistence strategies including agriculture, pastoralism, hunting, and fishing. The frequent movements of groups of people in the lower Danube region meant that central authority was less powerful than in the West, while local *optimates* were stronger and more independent. Individuals and groups drifted from leader to leader according to his success. This resulted in a society in which many political groups resided.[33]

To the east of Gothia lay Moldavia, an area inhabited by the nomadic Alans. The area is a high plateau (over 100 m.), flat and inhospitable, cut by numerous watercourses. As in Gothia, the environment was generally unfavourable to agriculture using contemporary techniques. It was the European end of the steppe corridor leading to the Don and the steppes of the Ukraine. It is thus no surprise to find that the Alans hardly practised agriculture. 'Only a small part of these peoples live on the fruits of the earth; all the rest roam over deserted wastes, which never knew plough nor seeds. ... Their dear ones, their dwellings and their poor belongings they pack upon wagons covered with the bark of trees.'[34] The Alans rapidly lost their nomad characteristics once they left the steppes.[35]

It was in this area that the Huns first appeared. The Huns had migrated from east of the Black Sea and had entered Europe in

[31] Burns, *Ostrogoths*; H. Wolfram, *History of the Goths* (London, 1988); Heather, *Goths and Romans*, and with Matthews, eds., *Goths*.

[32] On Danubian plain see Procopius, *Buildings* 3. 7. 13–15; Mauricius, *Strat.* 11. 4. 5; on floods see AM 17. 13. 4, 27. 5. 5; on mountains see AM 27. 5. 3–4, 31. 4. 13; on woods see *P.S.Sabae* 4. 6; AM 31. 4. 13.

[33] Liebeschuetz, *Barbarians and Bishops*, 83–5; Batty, 'Peoples', p. viii, 'continuous discontinuity'; on the archaeology, see App. 3.

[34] AM 22. 8. 42.

[35] On Alans see AM 31. 2. 17–24; being recorded as Goths see Procopius, *BV* 3. 3. 1; on their agriculture see MacNeill, *Europe's Steppe Frontier*, 4–6.

the early 370s, crossing the lower Don and Dneister and following the coast of the Black Sea into Moldavia and Wallachia.[36] Ammianus Marcellinus describes Hun society at this date. They herded sheep for meat and wool, cattle for milk and meat. They were not tied to any particular area of land, but moved from pasture to pasture in wagons. Most Huns rode horses, easing the problems of controlling large herds over great distances. They spent so much time on their horses that their gait was often affected. Huns possessed considerable strategic and operational mobility and this was used to good effect in their early campaigns against the Goths. At this point they were similar to the Alans that they supplanted.[37]

The Huns are described in these terms for the late fourth century, and it has been accepted, following Thompson and Maenchen-Helfen, that the Huns remained as pastoralists throughout the fifth century and that their society did not change at all. There are problems with the evidence for this point of view, controversially raised by Lindner. The main evidence for the traditional view is the apparent unanimity of the sources. Almost all writers who describe the Huns in the fifth century write in terms similar to Ammianus and Eunapius. However, Jerome, Claudian, and (via Claudian) Sidonius Apollinaris used Ammianus as a source for their descriptions of the Huns, while Zosimus and Jerome used Eunapius as a source for their accounts. Once we get away from this group of late fourth-century-inspired sources and when the Huns have left Moldavia, the picture is somewhat different. Why should the fifth-century Huns be seen as a purely pastoral society, unlike all previous inhabitants of the region?[38]

There are several reasons for caution. First, in our other sources (e.g. Priscus in the fifth century), horses are rarely mentioned in

[36] Maenchen-Helfen, *Huns*; E. A. Thompson, *A History of Attila and the Huns* (Oxford, 1948); F. Altheim, *Geschichte der Hunnen* (Berlin, 1959–62).

[37] On Huns see AM 31. 2. 1–11; W. Richter, 'Die Darstellung der Hunnen bei Ammianus Marcellinus', *Historia*, 23 (1974), 343–77; on their gait see Zos. 4. 20. 4; AM 31. 2. 6; on their traditions see Procopius *BV* 3. 18. 13–14.

[38] On Ammianus as source for Claudian see A. D. E. Cameron, *Claudian* (Oxford, 1970), 333; O. Maenchen-Helfen, 'The Date of Ammianus Marcellinus' Last Books', *AJP* 76 (1955), 384–99; for Jerome see Maenchen-Helfen, ibid.; A. D. E. Cameron, review of Syme, *Ammianus and the Historia Augusta, JRS* 61 (1971), 255–67 at 259; on Claudian as source for Sidonius *Carm.* 2. 243–69, see A. Loyen, *Sidoine Apollinare*, 1 (Paris, 1960), 173 n. 38; on Eunapius as source for Zosimus 4. 20. 3–4 see F. Paschoud, *Zosime*, ii² (Paris, 1979), 372 n. 142; for Jerome see T. M. Banchich, 'Eunapius and Jerome', *GRBS* 27 (1981), 319–24; Eunapius fr. 41.

Hunnic contexts. Attila received Maximinus' embassy in 449 in a building with chairs and couches, whereas in the sixth century a Turkish leader received a Byzantine envoy both in a tent on a wagon and in a building.[39] If the Huns were a pastoral nomad society in the fifth century, one would expect accounts of their actions, especially their military exploits, to be similar to those of the fourth-century Gothic wars. Accounts of the Huns in the fourth century mention their strategic and tactical mobility, mounted archers, horses, etc., but those in the fifth century do not. Nothing that the Huns are recorded as doing after 376 is obviously the work of a mounted army, though their earlier battles with the Goths had involved such manœuvres. The only occasion where they might have been involved in long-distance high-speed movement is in 388, during Theodosius' pursuit of Maximus. The logic of many historians is succinctly described by Lindner: 'Huns were present, Theodosius seems to have brought cavalry along, the Hun auxiliaries must have been mounted (because they were Huns), so the Huns' horsemen won the battle.' This victory may have been the result of Hunnic cavalry, but the evidence does not prove this.[40]

Secondly, the archaeology of pastoral nomads differs little in type of artefact from that of more settled peoples. Although pastoral nomads can be archaeologically characterized by herd-animal remains and seasonal occupation of non-permanent dwellings (usually singly rather than multiply roomed), nomads did farm and use pottery, albeit on a small scale, so neither of these find-types can be used to identify archaeological materials as 'non-nomadic'.[41] The available archaeological evidence from the middle and lower Danube region does not show a dramatic change with the arrival of the Huns. This lack of significant artefactual change, combined with similarity in settlement structure, suggests that no major socio-economic change occurred in this region, though there was large-scale political change.[42]

---

[39] On couches see Priscus fr. 13. 1. 28–40; on Turks see Menander fr. 10. 3.

[40] On Gothic war see AM 31. 3. 6; on fighting necessarily being by mounted troops see AM 31. 3. 5–8; R. P. Lindner, 'Nomadism, Horses and Huns', *Past and Present*, 92 (1981), 1–19 at 7; cf. for 6th-cent. raiding, Agathias, *Hist.* 5. 11–13, 19.

[41] R. Cribb, *Nomads in Archaeology* (Cambridge, 1991); on problems in identifying evidence, Hole, 'Pastoral Nomadism', 127–67, is useful; Maenchen-Helfen, *Huns*, 169–71.

[42] On 5th-cent. Moldavia see G. Teodor, *The East Carpathian Area of Romania 5th–11th Centuries AD*, *BAR* S81 (Oxford, 1980), 3–56; on continuity see V.

Thirdly, much of the area occupied by the Hun Empire was not suited to pastoralism alone, as shown by the Sarmatian and Gothic way of life. If the Huns remained as pastoral nomads they would presumably not have been making the most effective use of their environment, a hypothesis hard to sustain. Such economic sacrifice would be understandable if carried out for military purposes, in order to maintain an effective cavalry force, but there is no evidence for this being done on a large scale, if at all.[43]

It thus seems more likely that Hunnic society in the fifth century was much more sedentary than was argued by Thompson and others. Hunnic villages were plentiful on the Hungarian plain and were well-supplied with millet and barley. Even in Moldavia agriculture and fixed settlements had some role, though a minor one, to play.[44]

Although the Hunnic Empire was not a pastoral nomad society in the fifth century, this is an economic judgement. It does not mean that horses did not play a major role in Hun society—their skills on horseback seem to have been preserved and many of them were excellent mounted warriors. Furthermore, Hun society was not identical in all areas and the Moldavian steppes continued to be inhabited by pastoralists throughout the fifth century.[45]

The basic conclusions drawn here, of sedentary western barbarians, semi-sedentary Goths, and Huns who were semi-sedentary in the fifth century, differ somewhat from orthodox opinions. Economic characteristics were a product of the environment, not an inherent property of a people. Therefore, as peoples moved their economies would change. Goths were only semi-sedentary while living in the

Bierbrauer, 'Zur chronologischen, sozialischen und regionalen Gliederung des ostgermanischen Fundstoffs des 5. Jahrhunderts in Südosteuropa', *Die Völker an den mittleren und unteren Donau im fünften und sechsten Jahrhundert*, (*Österreichische Akademie der Wissenschafte, Phil. Hist. Kl. Denkschriften* 145) (1980), 131–42; R. Harhoiu, 'Aspects of the Socio-Political Situation in Transylvania during the Fifth Century', in M. Constantinescu *et al.*, eds., *Relations between the Autochthonous Population and the Migratory Populations on the Territory of Romania* (Bucharest, 1975), 99–109 at 108–9; on Bratei culture see E. Zaharia, 'Données sur l'archéologie des IVe–XIe siècles sur le territoire de la Roumanie', *Dacia*, NS 15 (1971), 269–88.

[43] Priscus fr. 49; AM 31. 2. 10.
[44] On Hunnic villages and crops see Priscus fr. 12. 2. 264–80; on Moldavia see Teodor, *East Carpathian Area*, 3–55.
[45] On nomads in Moldavia see Menander fr. 2; on sedentarization see P. Anderson, *Passages from Antiquity to Feudalism* (London, 1974), 217–18; J. F. Matthews, *The Roman Empire of Ammianus* (London, 1989), 355.

Danube basin. When they settled in Aquitaine and Italy they became farmers, living in permanent settlements.

In all cases, barbarian communities were subsistence communities. This to some extent determined military relations with the Romans. There was a large pool of manpower available for military purposes, but it could be used only at certain seasons without disrupting food production and threatening famine. Military operations initiated by barbarians would therefore be of short duration, probably measurable in months. The more mobile nature of Eastern European groups meant that it was more difficult for the Romans to engage them at home or to destroy their livelihood.

BARBARIAN SOCIETY

This barbarian society, Eastern or Western, was non-urban. Most settlements were villages and though there were some small hamlets or even isolated farms, especially in uplands and remote areas, there were no larger settlements. Pictish settlements are hard to describe since only stone traces survive. Small villages seem to be most common, sometimes including sunken dwellings, and in general they seem little different from villages in western Europe.[46] Ammianus' descriptions of the villages of the Quadi and Alamanni suggest clusters of wooden huts with thatched roofs which were easily burnt and the same impression is given of Frankish villages by Sulpicius Alexander. This literary evidence is confirmed by archaeology, such as for the well-documented villages of Feddersen Wierde, Wijster, Ezinge, and, in Britain, West Stow. Sometimes one large house dominated the village site, suggesting one focus of authority in a small community. There were about fifty buildings at Feddersen Wierde, perhaps supporting a population of fewer than 500, though this cannot take into account dispersed settlement around the site. Individual houses were of 'longhouse' or Grubenhaus construction, sometimes sunk into the ground, with animals usually kept at one end of the building. A few stone constructions, similar to Roman villas, are known in Alamannia and Quadia. Most villages appear not to have been fortified, but

---

[46] Alcock, *Arthur's Britain*, 272–5, and 'Pictish Settlement', 7–48; T. Watkins, 'Where were the Picts?', *Pictish Studies*, 63–86.

some hilltop sites with stone walls are known, for example Glauberg in Alamannia, which also had some stone buildings. Other villages could be fenced or palisaded, Wijster for example. On the North Sea coast, villages were built on *terpen*, mounds increased, or created by, natural accumulations of dung and debris and deliberate accumulations of clay.[47]

The same style of building, wooden or wattle-and-daub construction with thatched roofs, was used by Eastern barbarians and is described by Ammianus for the Sarmatians and by Priscus for the Huns. There seems to have been more variety in buildings and, as well as longhouses, there were smaller structures, often single-roomed and less permanent, frequently with sunken floors. Settlements were rarely fortified. Unfortunately, the length of occupation of these temporary sites cannot be determined. In the Black Sea coastal regions similar buildings were constructed of stone.[48]

Nomad habitations, for example in Moldavia, were less permanent and some groups lived in wagons in a peripatetic lifestyle. Others lived in a semi-sedentary manner, constructing temporary villages. The precise type of settlement probably varied according to climate and the type of region currently inhabited.[49]

---

[47] On villages see Todd, *Northern Barbarians*[2], 77–100; Herodian 7. 2. 3–4; on *terpen* see Pliny, *NH* 16. 1. 3; on Franks see Sulpicius fr. 1; on Saxons see W. Haarnagel, *Die Grabungen Feddersen Wierde*[2] (Wiesbaden, 1979); Van Es, 'Wijster', 49–124; Alamanni, AM 17. 10. 7, 18. 2. 15; on their farmsteads see *RGA*[2] i. 149*d*; in general, ibid. 156*c*; AM 17. 1. 7; on their 'villas', AM 17. 1. 7; Todd, *Northern Barbarians*[2], 99; on Quadi see AM 30. 5. 14; on their 'villas' see L. Pitts, 'Roman Style Buildings in Barbaricum (Moravia and SW Slovakia)', *Oxford Journal of Archaeology*, 6 (1987), 219–36; on fortifications see G. Mildenburger, *Germanische Burgen* (Münster, 1978); for hilltop sites see map, *RGA*[2] i. 146; Todd, *Northern Barbarians*[2], 98–9; J. Werner, 'Zu den alamannischen Burgen', in Müller, ed., *Geschichte der Alamannen*, 67–90; for palisades see Van Es, 'Wijster', 44–8.

[48] On Sarmatians see AM 17. 13. 12–13; on Danubian Goths see Teodor, *East Carpathian Area*, 6–9 (7 mentions seasonal dwellings); *P.S.Sabae*, 4. 5, 5. 3 (roof beam), though reflecting Roman views of a Gothic village, not a contemporary description of a Gothic village; Heather and Matthews, *Goths*, 56–8; G. Bichir, *Archaeology and History of the Carpi*, *BAR* S16 (Oxford, 1976); A. Haüsler, 'Zu den sozialökonomischen Verhältnissen in den Černjakov-Kultur', *Zeitschrift für Archeologie*, 13 (1979), 23–65; A. V. Kropotkin, 'On the Centres of the Černjakhov Tribes', *Sovietskaya Archeologiskaya* (1984/3), 35–47; G. Diaconu, 'On the Socio-Economic Relations between Natives and Goths in Dacia', in Constantinescu, ed., *Relations*, 67–75 at 69–70; on Hun villages see Priscus fr. 11. 2. 264–80, 356–73, 551–6, 14. 1. 58–65; Jordanes, *Getica*, 178–9.

[49] Nomads: for their lack of villages see AM 31. 2. 4; wagons, AM 22. 8. 42, 31. 2. 10, 18.

SOCIAL STRUCTURE

Most villages or groups of hamlets had a dominant noble family or families, described by the Romans as *optimates, proceres,* μεγιστάνες, or λογάδες, while archaeological evidence often shows villages with a large central building. The relationship of these families to the rest of the village is unclear, but their dominant position was probably the result of wealth and tradition, not of any formal position. The Gothic μεγιστάνες mentioned in the *Passion of St Saba* were able to impose their will on Saba's village by force, but it is clear that not all aspects of village life were controlled from above, since the villagers were only prevented from concealing Saba's Christianity from the μεγιστάνες by Saba himself. Saba's village shows that the *optimates* (the term I use for barbarian nobility) were not resident in every village and suggests that some *optimates* had power over several settlements, but resided in one only. In times of war and when negotiating with the Romans *optimates* are usually found accompanying their king. They seem rarely to have acted independently, suggesting small resources of their own.[50]

A number of villages and their *optimates* formed a canton (*pagus*) under a royal family, e.g. the Brisigavi led by Vadomarius and Vithicabius. Cantons were probably formed by distinct geographical areas, perhaps one valley per canton, but their composition may not have been fixed. It seems likely that the more successful a king was, the greater his sphere of influence, and the more *optimates* who would follow him. Ammianus describes two Alamannic kings, Chnodomarius and Serapio at Strasbourg in AD 357 who 'were followed by the kings next in power, five of them, and ten *regales* and a great train of *optimates* and 35,000 armed men'. There is no evidence of anything binding one *optimas* to a particular canton, and it is probable that those on the fringes of royal authority might change allegiance from time to time, or even not belong to a canton (Fig. 3).[51]

---

[50] C. A. Smith, 'Exchange Systems and the Spatial Distribution of Elites', in C. A. Smith, ed., *Regional Analysis 2* (New York, 1976), 309–74, shows how much more we could know about social relations; A. C. Murray, *Germanic Kinship Structure* (Toronto, 1983); for Goths see *P.S.Sabae*, 3. 1, 4; on being in charge of several villages see Priscus fr. 14. 54–6; on accompanying king see AM 16. 12. 26, 17. 12. 11, 31. 5. 7; on independence see Hyd. 92.

[51] On Alamanni see AM 16. 12. 26; for individual kings gaining power see AM 29. 4. 2; Malchus fr. 18. 1, 2. 55–9.

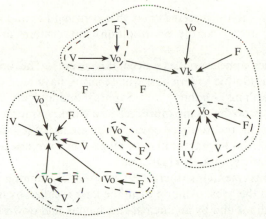

Fig. 3 Barbarian social structure: a model. V: village; F: farm; O: *optimas*;
K: king; →: dependence; - - -: *optimas* group; . . .: cantonal boundary

KINGSHIP

Each canton was ruled by a king (or kings) from an extended royal
family. The kings were described by the Romans as *reges*, φύλαρχοι,
or βασιλεῖς. Within a family some members (perhaps subordinate
branches or younger sons) had a lower status, only providing sub-
kings (*reguli* or *subreguli*). Other members of the family had royal
status (*regales*), a term which could also be used to refer to any or
all of a royal family. These distinctions were made by Roman
historians (especially Ammianus) and probably conceal a more
complicated situation. These subdivisions could be named after
individual rulers.[52]

Most cantons had one king, but multiple kingship was not
uncommon. In some cases all the heirs of the old king succeeded,
regardless of number, and it was the kingship, not the kingdom,
that was divided. Thus in the early 350s the brothers Vadomarius
and Gundomadus both ruled the Alamannic canton of the Brisigavi,
but in 357 Gundomadus was assassinated. Vadomarius remained
as sole king and after his kidnap by the Romans was succeeded by

[52] On kingship see P. H. Sawyer and I. N. Wood, eds., *Early Medieval Kingship*
(Leeds, 1977); J. M. Wallace-Hadrill, *Early Germanic Kingship* (Oxford, 1971); H.
A. Myers and H. Wolfram, *Medieval Kingship* (Chicago, 1982), 59–80; on being
named after rulers see J. Ant. fr. 206. 2; Malalas 460.

his son Vithicabius. It seems likely that personalities and supporters played as strong a role as tradition and custom in resolving successions.[53]

Minorities appear to have been rare events. The only known child king is Gothic Viderichus, who seems to have been dominated by his guardians Alatheus and Saphrax and quickly disappears from view, probably being murdered as a child.[54] Among the Quadi and Goths in the fourth century individuals called *iudices* are referred to, who appear similar to kings. They are not heard of in the fifth century, though kings are.[55]

Ammianus mentions sacral kingship once, among the Burgundians in the 370s. 'Among them the king is called by the general name Hendinos and by an ancient rite, having laid down his power, is removed, if under him fortune in war was uncertain or if the earth denied enough crops.'[56] Any sacral traditions that did exist, however, appear to have been weak and royal status seems to have been based as much on power as any tradition or hereditary nature, shown by the ability of *optimates* to become kings. Singeric, brother of the exiled Gothic *optimas* or *dux* Sarus, became king of the Goths in 415. The uncertainties of succession are probably one reason why many known kings are not linked to each other. Thus Singeric was succeeded by Vallia, no relation to him, and Vallia's heir, Theoderic, was unrelated to Vallia. It is not until the establishment of settled kingdoms in the West that we can reliably trace royal genealogies through more than two generations.[57]

The links between a people and their kings were often so weak that rulers from different tribes could be imposed on them, e.g. the

[53] On multiple kingship see Alamanni, AM 14. 10. 1, 16. 12. 17; on Burgundians see GT *HF* 2. 32; on Huns see Priscus fr. 11. 2. 241–63; on Franks see GT *HF* 2. 42; on Ostrogoths see *PLRE* ii, Theoderic 2 and children, Theoderic 5 and Anonymous 123; on 511 division, I. N. Wood, 'Kings, Kingdoms and Consent', in Sawyer and Wood, eds., *Early Medieval Kingship*, 6–29.

[54] *PLRE* i, Viderichus; cf. B. Croke, 'Mundo the Gepid: from Freebooter to Roman General', *Chiron*, 12 (1982), 125–35.

[55] *Iudices*: for Quadi see AM 17. 12. 21; for Goths see AM 27. 5. 6, 31. 3. 4; Wolfram, *Goths*², 94–6, 98; Heather, *Goths and Romans*, 97–107.

[56] AM 28. 5. 14; J. M. Wallace-Hadrill, *The Long-Haired Kings* (London, 1962), 153–8, and *Germanic Kingship*, 14–15.

[57] On *optimates* becoming kings see Singeric, Olymp. fr. 26; in this context Jordanes' list of Gothic kings is of little use, existing to legitimate a ruling family and derived almost entirely from material still available to us; P. J. Heather, 'Cassiodorus and the Rise of the Amals: Genealogy and the Goths under Hun Domination', *JRS* 79 (1989), 103–28.

Hun Ellac in the 440s ruling the Akatiri or the Visigoth Aioulfus becoming king of the Suevi in Spain in the 450s.[58] In such a situation, any royal blood was important. Royal relatives could be leaders of opposition and their frequent murder or exile may have been a king's way of dealing with threats to his power. Clovis certainly took great care to eradicate all the relations he could find.[59]

The weak social distinction between *regales* and *optimates* helps explain the frequently troubled relations between kings of cantons and their *optimates*. This was occasionally exploited by the Romans. Factional strife perhaps led to the murder of Gundomadus in 354, killed by his brother, but probably with the support of (some of) the canton. Another case of factional strife is Fraomarius, ruler of the Alamannic canton of the Bucinobantes. He was given the kingship by Valentinian I after Macrianus, the previous king, had been expelled by the Romans. After a few years Fraomarius was withdrawn by the Romans because the canton had been devastated by an unknown attacker. When we next hear of the Bucinobantes, they are again being ruled by Macrianus, and it is tempting to see him as the attacker who reclaimed his kingdom after making Fraomarius' position untenable. A third case is that of Sarus, a powerful noble in the Gothic confederation led by Alaric. At some point before 405 he had left the Goths and worked for the Romans as a military officer, though still leading his own bodyguard. He had a blood feud with Ataulf, Alaric's brother-in-law, and for both of them this took precedence over the immediate political situation. Thus in 412 Ataulf's negotiations with Jovinus, a Gallic usurper, were broken off because of the approach of Sarus to support Jovinus. The rivalry between the two was only halted when Sarus died fighting Ataulf's entire army with only his bodyguard. Throughout these disagreements, Sarus' brother Singeric remained a powerful figure among Ataulf's Goths, even becoming king in 415.[60]

The use of violence to settle political disputes was partly the result of kings and *optimates* having their own armed retinues.

[58] *PLRE* ii, Aioulfus, Edeco, Ellac, Remismund.

[59] On Clovis' persecution see GT *HF* 2. 40–2; see *V. Remigii*, 15, for a surviving relative.

[60] For kings killed by relations see *PLRE* i, Gundomadus, Viderichus?; *PLRE* ii, Atakam, Bleda, Chilpericus II, Fredericus, Maman, Recitach, Thorismodus, Theoderic 6; on them being expelled, see *PLRE* i, Athanaric, Fraomarius; *PLRE* ii, Sarus; Claudian, *De Cons. Stil.* 1. 239–45.

These were called *comitatus* by the Romans, though barbarians used their own terms, e.g. *antrustiones* among the Franks. These men were supported by their lord in return for loyalty and military service and were the closest most barbarian groups came to having any professional soldiers until the late fifth century. In 357 Chnodomarius had 200 retainers at a time when he was leading an alliance of Alamannic cantons. This suggests that larger numbers would not be found until kingdoms were established in the Empire and more wealth was available. The *comitatus* of less successful kings were probably smaller.[61]

To support their *comitatus* and to reward their equals and followers (and appease dissidents?), kings and *optimates* were expected to give gifts. These societies thus had a small, but constant, need for prestige items to distribute. Though we understand the mechanics, it is difficult to demonstrate clearly the importance of gift exchange in fourth- and fifth-century barbarian society. Later evidence is more common. The custom is shown by Hrothgar's speech to Beowulf.

> So long as I shall rule the reaches of this kingdom
> we shall exchange wealth; a chief shall greet
> his fellow with gifts over the gannets' bath
> as the ship with curved prow crosses the seas
> with presents and pledges.[62]

The importance of the gifts in stabilizing society adds significance to Roman gifts or payments to kings who had made treaties with them. Such payments allowed the dominant, Roman-supported faction to retain its position by providing gifts for distribution, without having to go to war to obtain them. If the Romans had exerted influence without payment, there would be a greater danger of an anti-establishment, and thus anti-Roman, faction arising, possibly causing more attacks on Roman territory.[63]

---

[61] AM 16. 12. 60, 17. 10. 8, 21. 4. 5, 29. 4. 5, 31. 5. 6; Malchus fr. 18. 3. 41; Olymp. fr. 6; *P.S.Sabae*, 4. 5; SA *Ep.* 1. 2. 4, 4. 20. 1–2; GT *HF* 2. 42; Wallace-Hadrill, *Germanic Kingship*, 11–15; Thompson, *Early Germans*, 51–60.

[62] *Beowulf*, 2186–2190; AM 26. 5. 7; GT *HF* 2. 42; Menander fr. 8, 12. 5; Priscus fr. 11. 2. 203–6, 244–50, 40. 1; cf. Constantine Porphyrogenitus, *De Administrando Imperii*, 1. 1.

[63] D. Braund, 'Ideology, Subsidies and Trade: The King on the Northern Frontier Revisited', in J. C. Barrett *et al.*, eds., *Barbarians and Romans in North West Europe*, *BAR* S471 (Oxford, 1989), 14–26; Thompson, *Early Germans*, 88–108.

Some cantons may have had some form of royal council since we often hear of kings discussing matters with their *optimates*. We do not know how formal this institution was, and whether kings chose to call a council, or were forced to, in order to take into consideration the views of their *regales* and *optimates*. The latter seems more likely.[64]

TRIBES

Until barbarian groups entered the Empire, there existed no political groups larger than cantons. Tribal names such as Franks or Quadi, referred to nothing more than the area from which a barbarian group came. 'Franks' meant only 'lower-Rhine Germans' and 'Quadi' meant 'middle-Danubian barbarians'. As far as most Roman writers, particularly those away from the frontiers, were concerned, the important groupings were barbarians as a whole, then regions; little notice was taken of cantons. Roman triumphal titles were of the form 'Sarmaticus', 'Gothicus', 'Francicus', 'Alamannicus', or 'Germanicus'. No cantonal victory titles are recorded from either the early or late Empire. Only major groups are represented, and there are no 'Saxonicus', 'Hunnicus', or 'Quadicus' titles. The absence of 'Hunnicus' may be connected with the fact that only Theodosius II, Valentinian III, and Marcian are recorded as having any victory titles in the period between Gratian and Anastasius; it has nothing to do with the lack of any convincing victories, as shown by Theodosius II's titles of 'Alamannicus' and 'Germanicus'.[65] This does not mean that all Romans were unaware of the subdivisions. Ammianus certainly recognized the importance of cantons as political units and the names of many Roman

[64] Malchus fr. 18. 2. 55–9; Priscus fr. 2?; Claudian, *De Bello Gothico* 479–82; SA *Carm.* 7. 452–4, *Ep.* 4. 22. 3; AM 17. 13. 21, 31. 6. 4–5; Thompson, *Early Germans*, 29–31.

[65] P. Kneissl, *Die Siegestitular der römischen Kaiser* (Göttingen, 1969); G. Rösch, Ὄνομα Βασιλεύς: *Studien zum offiziellen Gebrauch der Kaisertitel in spätantike und frühbyzantinische Zeit* (Vienna, 1978).

regiments in the *Notitia Dignitatum* are based on cantonal (as well as tribal) titles.[66]

There is nothing to suggest that any of the cantons in a region had any constituted authority over the others. When leadership over more than one canton is found, it is the product of force, not of a formal position. Among the Sarmatians in the 350s, the *regalis* Zizais was escorted by *subreguli* and is described as *potior*, 'more powerful'. In the only mention of the leadership of the combined Alamanni at Strasbourg in 357, Kings Serapio and Chnodomarius are described as 'greater than the other kings through power (*potestate*)'. Though this could also be interpreted as 'through authority', this would make the Alamanni unique among fourth- or fifth-century barbarian tribes in having some form of constituted higher authority. In the early fifth century, the Alans in Spain were described as being 'more powerful' than the neighbouring Vandals.[67] Furthermore, the Romans never negotiated treaties with any 'high king' or with groups of cantons, only with the kings of individual cantons. This was the case even after defeating a group of co-operating cantons. Thus, after Strasbourg, Julian insisted on personal attendance at negotiations by the kings of all defeated cantons. If they were not present they might not consider themselves bound by the treaty.[68]

Although co-operation between cantons was rare, it did occur. Alamannic co-operation in 352 was the result of the ambition of King Chnodomarius, taking advantage of Roman weakness and encouraging the Alamanni to settle in Gaul. At Strasbourg in 357 Alamannic co-operation was again organized by Chnodomarius, this time to recover territory lost by Alamannic cantons on the left bank of the Rhine because of Roman action. This alliance was probably a continuation of earlier co-operation against Magnentius. Alamannic cantons also allied in 359 when the Roman army under Julian threatened to cross the Rhine into the territory of Suomarius, an Alamannic king who had allied with the Romans in 357. Other

[66] For Visi see *ND* Or. 5. 61, for Tervingi see Or. 6. 61, for Salii see Or. 5. 51, Occ. 5. 177, 210, for Bucinobantes see Or. 6. 17, for Sugambri see Or. 31. 66, for Iuthungi see Or. 28. 43, 33. 31, for Chamavi see Or. 30. 61, for Gaetuli see Or. 35. 32, for Frisii see Occ. 40. 36, for Brisigavi see Occ. 5. 201, 202, for Bructeri see Occ. 5. 187.

[67] For Sarmatians see AM 17. 12. 9–11, 14; for Alamanni see AM 16. 12. 23; for Alans see Hyd. 68.

[68] AM 17. 12. 12, 18. 2. 18–19; Eunapius fr. 18. 6.

Alamannic cantons wished to stop the Romans crossing the Rhine into Suomarius' territory. According to Ammianus they warned Suomarius not to allow the Romans to cross the Rhine. Compelled to accede to their demands, he let the other Alamanni into his territory to resist the Romans. Had it not been for the intervention of the other kings, Suomarius would have allowed the Romans to enter his territory and use it as a base for offensive operations against other cantons. Like the co-operation at Strasbourg, this seems to have been for the general benefit of the Alamanni since it was known that Julian was planning to attack several cantons. This alliance seems to have recurred in the 360s, when Valentinian I launched several campaigns against the Alamanni, and suggests some tendencies towards centralization. A similar alliance occurred in the 390s when the kings of two Frankish cantons, Marcomere and Sunno, seem to have established some form of hegemony over a number of cantons, at least the Ampsivarii and Chatti, and possibly the Bructeri and Chamavi. They raided Gaul in 388 and continued to cause trouble on the lower Rhine until dealt with by Stilicho in 396.[69]

Co-operation was not limited to cantons from the same region or 'tribe'. For example, in 357 Araharius led Quadi and Sarmatians against the Romans, and Huns and Goths fought together on a number of occasions.[70] Even when co-operation occurred it did not always last long. At the siege of Bazas in 414, the Romans were able to persuade some Alans to desert the besieging Goths and join the garrison instead.

The city's boundaries are faced round with a bulwark of Alan soldiers, prepared for pledges given and taken, to fight for us ... but when [the Goths] saw themselves shorn of no small portion of their host, the encircling hordes of ravaging Goths, straightaway feeling that they could not safely tarry now that their bosom friends were turned to mortal enemies, ventured no further effort, but chose of their own accord to retire hurriedly.

There was no love lost between allied barbarian groups and the

---

[69] On co-operation at Strasbourg see AM 16. 12. 1, 9, 23–6; with Suomarius see AM 17. 10 (357), 18. 2 (359); with Franks see Sulpicius fr. 1, 4, 6; Claudian, *De Cons. Stil.* 1. 239–45; with Sarmatians see AM 17. 12. 11–12.

[70] On Quadi and Sarmatians see AM 17. 12. 11–12; on Goths and Huns see AM 31. 8. 4; Priscus fr. 49; on Franks and Saxons see AM 28. 8. 5; on Sarmatians and Suevi see Jordanes, *Getica*, 277.

Romans not only knew this, but could exploit it.[71]

Although cantons from the same region could co-operate against
the Romans, they could also fight each other, an example being the
357 attack on the Salii by another Frankish canton, the Chamavi. On
a larger scale were the wars on the lower Danube, first to create the
Hun Empire, then following the death of Attila, when numbers of
barbarian groups struggled for dominance. There was no such thing
as barbarian nationalism and barbarians would fight alongside
Romans against their own enemies. Thus in 358 the Sarmatian Liberi
were allied with the Romans against the Sarmatian Limigantes. In
this operation the Romans also persuaded another barbarian group,
the Taifali, to fight against the Limigantes. Such hostility was not
unique as the affair of Suomarius shows.[72] Hostilities also occurred
between barbarians from different regions, e.g. between cantons of
Franks and Alamanni during the late fourth century.[73]

Co-operation between cantons, though often founded on mutual
self-interest, was dependent on capable individuals. Araharius was
responsible for the co-operation between some Quadi and Sarmatians in 357 and Marcomere and Sunno for the late fourth-
century Frankish co-operation. When we know of co-operation we
often know the names of the leaders involved. Where we do not
know the names of the leaders, we should be wary about attributing
co-operation. The 'barbarian conspiracy' of 367 and the Vandal–
Suevic crossing of the Rhine in 406 are both occasions where co-
operation is not proven, and indeed seems unlikely to have taken
place. The Vandals and Suevi attacked at the same time, but over
such a wide area (most of the length of the Rhine) that co-operation
is an unlikely possibility. Barbarians did not need to co-operate to
take advantage of Roman weakness and no one has suggested that
the Goths and the Burgundians were allied in 436 when they both
took advantage of Roman involvement with bandits in Armorica—
they were merely seizing the initiative independently.

The importance of barbarian leaders is also demonstrated by
Roman action against them. To some degree this could be counter-
productive, in that Roman pressure created leaders or reinforced

[71] Paulinus of Pella, *Eucharisticus*, 372–5; RPF fr. 2; Soz. 9. 5. 1–5; Priscus fr. 49.
[72] Intra-regional hostility: for Franks see Zos. 3. 6. 2; for Huns see AM 31. 3. 3;
Jordanes, *Getica*, 259–63; for Sarmatians see AM 17. 12. 18–19, 13. 19.
[73] On Franks–Alamanni see AM 30. 3. 7; on Goths–Sciri see Jordanes, *Getica*,
129–30, 276; Priscus fr. 45.

the authority of existing kings. The potential strength of a combined tribe forced the Romans to divide and rule, dealing with the barbarians by canton. The massive operation planned by Valentinian for 370 suggests that he saw the Alamanni as a single threat, distinct from the Franks, that could be dealt with in one operation, though each canton was attacked separately. This conception seems unlikely to have been based on any differences between the Franks and the Alamanni, but on the geography of the region, north and south of the Main river.[74]

Lack of a tribal structure is also shown by the ability of groups to move from tribe to tribe. Thus Alans and Visigoths are found in the Vandal kingdom in Africa and the Ostrogoths who invaded Italy included Rugi and Heruli in their number. The ease of assimilation suggests few differences between groups and an informal political structure.[75] It was not just barbarians who could change political affiliation. Romans could also join barbarian groups: in Italy in the 400s, Alaric was joined by Roman deserters and runaway slaves. We know of other Romans joining dissident groups, both inside and outside the Empire. The anonymous Greek merchant living among the Huns is well known, but he was only the tip of an iceberg of expatriate living, also illustrated by Eudoxius, a doctor who was involved with the Bagaudae and fled to the Huns. The apparent ease of incorporating Romans into barbarian groups suggests that barbarians would be absorbed even more easily.[76]

BARBARIAN GROUPS WITHIN THE EMPIRE

In the fifth century several groups of barbarians found themselves inside the Roman Empire, but with no formal recognition of their

---

[74] AM 28. 5. 8–10, 15.

[75] For Alans see Victor Vitensis 2. 39; Hyd. 68; for Visigoths see Possidius, *V. Aug.* 28. 4; for late Goths see Jordanes, *Getica*, 283–4; for Ostrogoths 489 see Cass. *Variae*, 1. 42–4; cf. Agathias, *Hist.* 1. 6. 3–4; Liebeschuetz, *Barbarians and Bishops*, 39–40; on Ostrogoths to Visigoths see *PLRE* ii, Beremud, Vidimir.

[76] On Roman deserters see G. E. M. de Ste Croix, *The Class Struggle in the Ancient Greek World* (London, 1981), 474–88; for Alaric and deserters see Philost. 12. 3; Zos. 5. 35. 6; on slaves see 5. 42. 3; J. H. W. G. Liebeschuetz, 'Alaric's Goths: Nation or Army?', J. F. Drinkwater and H. W. Elton, eds., *Fifth-Century Gaul: A Crisis of Identity?* (Cambridge, 1992), 75–83; on the Greek see Priscus fr. 11. 2. 407–35; Eudoxius, *C.Gall.452*, 133; AM 31. 6. 5–7.

presence and no fixed home. These groups had a peripatetic existence until they were able to make an agreement with the Empire or gain permanent control over an area. Thus a Gothic group under first Alaric, then Ataulf, and lastly Vallia, wandered through the Empire between 395 and 418, with only occasional agreements with the imperial government. The Vandal and Suevic invaders of 406 wandered similarly until their settlement in 411. Radagaisus and his followers may also come into this category.

Without land to farm, these groups were in a parlous economic condition. They had to forage continuously for survival or else live off supplies negotiated from the Empire. Herd animals became particularly important in these circumstances. Lack of a homeland, a secure rear area, also meant that these groups were always accompanied by women, children, the aged, infirm, and all the tribe's possessions. These were transported by a train of wagons, a characteristic of the Gothic peregrinations. One Roman strike against some Balkan Goths in 479 captured 2,000 wagons.[77]

Apart from this peripatetic existence such groups differed little from groups beyond the borders of the Empire. *Optimates* were still present and their power was still probably based on wealth and armed followers. The small geographical area covered by these groups meant that most members would be immediately affected by most royal decisions, perhaps leading to the establishment of a form of court. This could strengthen kingship since relations with the Romans tended to be channelled through a single leader.

During the fifth century barbarian kingdoms began to emerge within the former boundaries of the Empire. This could happen quickly (for example, after the Roman settlement of the Goths in Aquitaine in 418) or slowly (Frankish infiltration into north Gaul did not produce anything resembling a kingdom until near the end of Clovis' reign). In most cases barbarians settled on the land, to farm themselves and/or to exploit the existing agricultural population. Suggestions that nomad groups continued to practise a nomadic economy once they had settled in Spain or Gaul seem

[77] On dependants see Malchus fr. 18. 2; Zos. 4. 25. 3, 39. 4; on herds see Malchus fr. 18. 2. 29–30; on wagons see Zos. 4. 25. 3; Malchus fr. 20. 113–15, 228–31, 244–8; Claudian, *In Rufinum*, 2. 129, *De 4 Cons. Hon.* 466, *De Cons. Stil.* 1. 94–5, *De Bello Gothico*, 83, 604; AM 31. 8. 1; Paulinus of Pella, *Eucharisticus* 389.

unlikely and we should expect to see no more than transhumance within the Empire.[78]

The small numbers of barbarians in these settlements, at least compared to regional populations, and their privileged status in most areas, meant that they superimposed themselves on the existing urban and rural habitations. Barbarians seem to have had no particular antipathy for urban life, but no need for it unless they were using Roman administrative institutions. Where they did employ these institutions, they adopted urban life immediately, probably being supported by revenues from their controlled estates. Otherwise they lived in rural villas like the Roman aristocracy.[79]

Barbarian use of urban centres and Roman structures gradually led to centralization of authority in one capital: Toulouse for the Visigoths, Ravenna for the Ostrogoths, Paris for Clovis' Franks, Geneva for the Burgundians, Braga for the Suevi. The creation of a court increased royal power as the king was the means by which Romans and barbarians interacted in political affairs, similar in effect to royal leadership of peripatetic barbarian groups.

Stronger kingship also meant more control over military affairs. Warfare now became more firmly subordinated to political purposes and raiding became less common as a spontaneous event, though it retained a place within a campaign. It still occurred, however, and Anaolsus' raid on Arles in 430 was probably not 'approved' by Theoderic I.[80]

The view of barbarian society outside the Roman Empire presented here is more culturally homogeneous and politically diverse than the picture often drawn by modern historians, but is based on the same evidence. Its similarity in political terms to barbarian society in the first and second centuries is interesting and suggests that some judgements concerning the third century, such as the development of permanent large tribal confederations did not occur in the same way as is often thought.

[78] Continuance of nomadism is implied by Thompson, *Romans and Barbarians*, 27, 156, 159.

[79] Details of settlements are discussed in Goffart, *Barbarians and Romans*; S. J. Barnish, 'Taxation, Land and Barbarian Settlement in the Western Empire', *PBSR* 54 (1986), 170–95; H. Sivan, 'On *Foederati*, *Hospitalitas* and the Settlement of the Goths in AD 418', *AJP* 108 (1987), 759–72; H. Wolfram and A. Schwarz, eds., *Annerkennung und Integration* (Vienna, 1988).

[80] Hyd. 92.

This discussion has concentrated on barbarian society outside the Roman Empire in the fourth century. However, society did not remain static and there were two important developments during the fifth century. One was the appearance of wandering groups within the Empire, the other was the creation of barbarian kingdoms on former imperial territory. Yet in many areas, especially where the frontier did not move, barbarian society remained similar to how it had been in the fourth century.

This brief description of barbarian society gives a guide to what should be expected in its relations with the Romans. It was extremely fragmented and only posed any danger to the survival of the Roman Empire when several groups united. Actions by single cantons were a nuisance, but in themselves unlikely to affect the long-term integrity of the Empire. These groups were divided internally and their leaders seem to have owed their positions more to ability and wealth than to tradition and respect for their office.

2

Barbarian Military Practices

A: REASONS FOR CONFLICT

Conflict between Romans and barbarians was common, but the form it took and the reasons for fighting are complicated and not clearly understood. For any attempt to understand this conflict, it is necessary to examine two features of barbarian society—its perceptions of the Empire and its martial nature—which lay behind much conflict.

Many barbarians saw the Roman Empire as a land of opportunity and were impressed by the ease of life in the Empire, the constant supply of luxuries and the high standard of living. As always we have to work through Roman sources. In Justinian's reign, one Hunnic king complained that refugees from his rule in the Empire 'will have the power to traffic in grain, and to get drunk in their wine stores, and to live on the fat of the land. Yes, and they will be able to go into the baths, and to wear gold ornaments, the villains, and will not go short of fine embroidered clothes.' Though a sixth-century report, this seems to be representative of views held by barbarians earlier. Urban life particularly impressed barbarians. As some Goths advanced on Constantinople in 378, 'their courage was further broken when they beheld the long circuit of the walls, the blocks of houses covering a vast space, the beauties of the city beyond their reach, [and] the vast population inhabiting it'.[1]

But barbarians had another impression of the Empire, that of an armed camp, full of soldiers whom the Romans continually paraded before them. Thus in 392 'Eugenius led a military expedition as far as the frontier marked by the Rhine. He renewed the old traditional treaties with the kings of the Franks and the

---

[1] On luxuries see E. A. Thompson, *Romans and Barbarians* (Madison, Wis., 1982), 3–15; for the Hun see Procopius, *BG* 8. 19. 16–17; for Constantinople see AM 31. 16. 7; cf. Priscus fr. 11. 1. 22–9; Jordanes, *Getica*, 143.

Alamanni, and he paraded his army, which was immense for that
time, before their savage warriors.' These impressions of strength
and efficiency could be reinforced by those barbarians who served
in the Roman army and kept in contact with their people, such as an
anonymous Alamannic *scutarius* who returned home 'on business' in
378.[2]

Barbarians who lived on the frontiers were less easily impressed
than those from the interior.

And indeed, Macrianus, having been admitted with his brother among the
eagles and standards, was amazed at the magnificent appearance of the
equipment and the men, which he first saw then ... But Vadomarius,
familiar with us because he lived by the frontier, admired the splendid field
equipment, but remembered that he had often seen such things since his
youth.[3]

Once barbarians were settled within the Empire, familiarity with
things Roman would diminish the wonder even more than contact
along the frontier. Thus Ataulf in the early fifth century wished to
destroy the name of 'Romania' and replace it with 'Gothia', but
realizing the impossibility of persuading Goths to obey the rule of
law, decided to use Gothic arms to support Rome instead. His
comments on 'Romania' and 'Gothia' show a desire to exploit the
Empire, even if he had originally thought of destroying it. His
ambitions do not appear characteristic of barbarian actions, but it
is the only opinion we have recorded.[4]

The martial nature of their society meant that barbarians were
accustomed to military activity. It offered warriors a chance to
display their prowess and engage in fighting. According to Ammianus, 'among the Alani a man is judged happy who has sacrificed
his life in battle'. The prestige resulting from raids could produce
a 'knock-on' effect, creating further raids. Social rivals in the same
or another canton would be forced to compete and the easiest way
to do this would be to launch a raid of their own into the Empire.
Even if a raid were a military failure, the fighting could produce

---

[2] Eugenius, Sulpicius fr. 7; for other examples see below, p. 184; *scutarius*, AM
31. 10. 3.

[3] AM 18. 2. 17.

[4] Orosius 7. 43. 4–6; J. M. Wallace-Hadrill, *The Long-Haired Kings* (London,
1962), 25–48.

some prestige for its leader and those taking part.[5]

Like many martial societies, barbarians had an unwritten military code. This could lead to acts of incredible bravery. The death of Sarus in 413, fighting Ataulf's entire army with only eighteen or twenty men, was the death of a German hero and would not have been out of place in heroic poetry.[6] Furthermore, the influence of things military meant that violence was a political tool and was mastered by those who were successful. According to J.M. Wallace-Hadrill, 'opportunism, short-sighted and ruthless, was characteristic of every barbarian who made his way in the Roman world'.[7]

This warlike spirit meant that most barbarians did not hate the Empire, but merely attacked it because it was there. If the Empire left a city ungarrisoned, it was considered reasonable to attack it. In return, it was accepted that the Romans had the right to cross the frontier and administer some rough treatment occasionally. The result was a parasitic relationship, though not a dependency, by barbarians on the Roman Empire.

Barbarians probably never thought in terms of overthrowing the Empire, except perhaps in the West in the late fifth century. It was too big and their resources were too small, as Ataulf seems to have realized. Even the strongest barbarian alliance, Attila's confederation of Danubians, was only able to challenge the Empire as a regional power, not to threaten its existence.[8]

B: TYPES OF CONFLICT

A martial society, envious of the wealth of the Empire, was likely to come into frequent military conflict with the Empire. We do not know how frequent attacks were. However, Ammianus Marcellinus' history can be used to estimate frequencies and sizes of attacks on the Rhine frontier for the period 354–378. In Figs. 4–6 attacks are divided into three sizes, attacks conducted only by one canton

[5] On prowess-based society see B. Cunliffe, *Greeks, Romans and Barbarians* (London, 1988), 89–92; on Alans see AM 31. 2. 22–3; cf. AM 17. 12. 21: Mauricius, *Strat.* 11. 3. 4; SA *Carm.* 5. 249–54.

[6] On Sarus' death see Olymp. fr. 18; cf. Agathias, *Hist.* 1. 15; Cass. *Variae*, 1. 24 and 38 for Ostrogothic Italy.

[7] *Long-Haired Kings*, 166.

[8] Orosius 7. 43. 4–6; cf. Thompson, *Romans and Barbarians*, 6–7.

(arbitrarily given a value of 1 on the y-axis), those possibly by
more than one canton (valued at 2), and those definitely by more

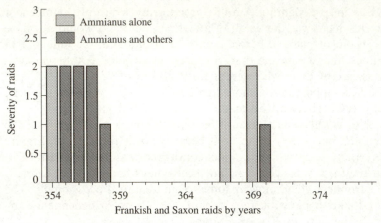

Fig. 4   Frankish and Saxon attacks on the Roman Empire, 354–78

than one (valued at 4). Figs. 4 and 5 show attacks on the North
and South Rhine separately, and separate attacks recorded either
solely by Ammianus Marcellinus or by Ammianus and other
sources. The detailed nature of Ammianus' account suggests that
he recorded all major attacks, a hypothesis supported by these
graphs. Fig. 6 shows the whole Rhine frontier. These graphs show
that recorded barbarian activity was not an annual activity, but
one that occurred in bursts. The bad times were balanced by periods
of peace, probably punctuated by minor (and thus unrecorded)
incidents. This presentation of information gives the impression
that frontier life was dangerous and that trouble could always
occur, but also suggests periods of peace. Barbarian attacks on the
Empire can be divided into three types, raids, conquests, and
defensive wars.

Raids

Raids intended to gain plunder were the most common type.
Constantius II described the problem in a speech to his army in
357: 'Our enemies in their madness were overrunning all Illyricum
... and in successive raids were laying waste our furthest borders
... They did not trust to engagements nor to arms and strength,

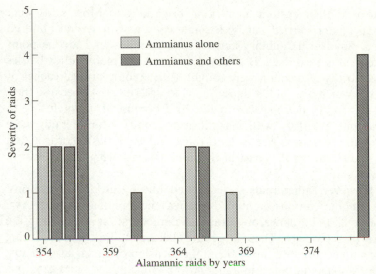

Fig. 5   Alamannic attacks, 354–78

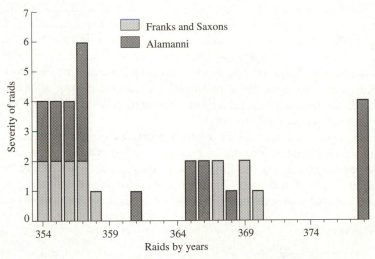

Fig. 6   Attacks on the Rhine frontier, 354–78

but as is their custom, in lurking brigandage.'[9] Most raids were
small affairs, carried out by a single canton with several hundred
men. Small-scale military activity was common and at one point
Ammianus recorded: 'Besides these [actions], many other battles
less worthy of mention were fought, throughout various reaches of
Gaul, which it would be superfluous to describe, both because their
results led to nothing worthwhile and because it is not fitting to
spin out a history with insignificant details.' Marine raids were
probably the same size as land raids and Hydatius records a raid
by the Heruli on the coast of Spain in 455 involving 400 men from
seven ships.[10]

However, other raids were carried out by groups of cantons.
Alamannic cantons combined against the Empire in 352/3, 357,
and 378, and a dangerous Frankish confederation appeared in the
late 380s and 390s. These large raids became more common during
the fifth century, examples being the invasion of Radagaisus in 405,
the Vandals and Suevi in 406, and the Huns in 422, 442, 447, 451,
and 452.

Large raids and confederations depended on effective barbarian
leadership. The Huns made major attacks against the Eastern
Empire in 442 and 447, and in 451 and 452 they attacked the
Western Empire. However, these were major attacks only because
of the unification of the Danubian barbarians under a single leader,
Attila. Before Attila, the Huns were not strong enough seriously to
threaten the Empire and after his death the Balkan provinces did
not suffer from a major attack (as opposed to raiding) until the
Bulgar attacks of the 490s. Although there were more large raids
in the fifth century, small raids also continued. Raetia and Noricum
seem never to have been disturbed in the same way as Gaul
during the fifth century, though they suffered occasionally from the
Alamanni across the Danube.

There were several reasons for the occurrence of individual raids.
The most common was to take advantage of Roman weakness.
Barbarian attacks on the Empire were more likely to occur, to be
successful, and thus attract the attention of contemporaries, at
times of imperial weakness—usually as a result of movements of

  [9] AM 17. 13. 27.
  [10] AM 22. 7. 7, 27. 2. 11; Hyd. 171; Them. *Or.* 10. 137; cf. Ine 13. 1: 'we call up
to seven men "thieves", from seven to thirty-five a "band", above that it is an
army.'

troops from one frontier to a crisis elsewhere. Thus the Hunnic attack of 442 was occasioned by the absence of the Eastern field army in Sicily, fighting the Vandals. This weakness did not need to be actual, only perceived. The 378 attack by some Alamanni was a response to the news that Gratian was marching east, not to his departure. Romans were accordingly worried about the consequences of moving troops from one area to another.[11]

The opportunities caused by Roman action elsewhere brought increasing barbarian attempts to realize these opportunities and in turn created more crises. Thus Stilicho's measures to contain Alaric in Italy in 399–401 involved weakening the defences of Gaul and Raetia, bringing about the attacks of Radagaisus in 405, then the Vandals and Suevi in 406. Similarly, the disruption caused in Gaul by the Vandal and Suevic attacks and the usurpation of Constantine III allowed the Goths (by then in Gaul) to take advantage of the disruption and set up a kingdom in south-western Gaul, while the Burgundians crossed the Rhine. And though the usurpers were defeated and the Goths finally settled (under Roman control) in Aquitaine, the diversion of Roman attention from the Rhine frontier to central Gaul allowed the Franks to make their way into the Empire in north-east Gaul. For the next twenty years Rome's military efforts were concentrated on defending what she controlled in Gaul, not on recovering what had been lost. Such a series of multiple crises was less common in the fourth century, though it almost occurred during the usurpations of Magnentius and Silvanus. If an unsubdued barbarian group had been present in the Balkans at the same time, the results would probably have been similar to fifth-century events. And from the 380s, failure to expel, destroy, or disperse the Goths in the Balkans meant that serious internal troubles were always a possibility, increasing the severity of other crises.

A second reason for raids was Roman action. When the Romans murdered the Quadic King Gabinius in 374, his canton (and others) responded by attacking the Empire. Similar in effect were Roman attempts to infringe barbarian territorial rights, for example by

---

[11] For timing, 442, Theoph. *AM* 5942; Marc. Com. sa 441; Theoderet, *HE* 5. 37. 5; 378, AM 31. 10. 3–5; for others, 352/3, Zos. 3. 1. 1; 357, AM 17. 2. 1; 360/1, AM 21. 3. 1; 374, AM 29. 6. 1; 401, Claudian, *De Bello Gothico*, 278–80; 422, Theoph. *AM* 5943; Marc. Com. sa 422; 439, Prosp. 1339; for fear of consequences see Lib. *Or.* 18. 95; AM 21. 4. 6, 31. 7. 4; Them. *Or.* 10. 136.

trying to build a fort on their territory. Attacks might also be caused by terminating or reducing subsidies. It was the reduction of subsidies in 365 that led to the Alamannic attack, though clumsy handling by the *magister officiorum* exacerbated the problem.[12] Thirdly, raids could be brought about by problems in a canton, for example a shortage of food or clothing. These resulted in Gothic attacks on Balkan provinces in the 470s.[13]

Raiders hoped to gain as much plunder as possible and then retire. This plundering meant that barbarians were often described as *latrones*.[14] Most raids did not penetrate very deep into the Empire, which meant that the frontier bore the brunt of attacks. Many of the battles fought against the Alamanni in the fourth century took place in the Rhine valley, for example, at Brumath, Strasbourg, and Argentaria. On occasion raids struck deeper, for example the Alamannic attack on Lyons in 357. Larger raids, with less immediate fear of counter-attack, might strike more deeply. Thus the Alamanni in 366 seem to have headed directly west from the Rhine, with fighting being recorded at Scarponne (on the Moselle between Metz and Nancy) and Chalons-sur-Marne, the latter more than 300 km. from the Rhine. But even these large raids usually confined their activities to frontier areas. Frankish attacks seem to have concentrated on Trier, said to have been sacked four times in the first half of the fifth century. Other Frankish raids are known against Cologne and Toxandria, but until the late fifth century the Somme seems to have been the western limit of Frankish activity in Gaul. Though the raids may not have penetrated deeply, raiding groups tended to split up and cover a wide area, albeit in small numbers.[15]

Marine raids could strike more deeply. The Heruli who attacked Spain in 455 must have sailed from as far east as the Rhine and were probably the Heruli who are mentioned by Procopius as living in Denmark. Saxons from east of the Rhine threatened the Loire

---

[12] On murder see AM 29. 6. 5–6; on infringing rights see AM 28. 2. 1–9, 29. 6. 1–16; on reducing subsidies see AM 26. 5. 7; Priscus fr. 24. 2.

[13] For food see Priscus fr. 37; Jordanes, *Getica*, 283; Procopius, *BV* 3. 3. 1; for clothing see Jordanes, *Getica*, 283.

[14] e.g. *NVal* 9 (440); AM 16. 10. 20, 17. 13. 27, 28. 5. 7; Eugippius, *V. Sev.* 4. 1; *ILS* 8913.

[15] For depth see Lyons, AM 16. 11. 4; for Trier see Salvian, *dGD* 6. 39; H. H. Anton, 'Trier im Übergang von der Römische zur frankischen Herrschaft', *Francia*, 10 (1982), 1–52.

valley and the Visigothic kingdom in Aquitaine. The long distance between marine raiders' place of origin and the areas they attacked suggests that knowledge of a short-term Roman weakness or direct Roman provocation were not likely to be motives and that raiders simply set out to plunder. Other naval raids were shorter in range, such as those of the Franks and Saxons against north Gaul and Britain.[16]

The plunder taken by the raiders tended to be confined to easily movable items. Gold, silver, and jewellery were probably preferred, though they would rarely be available in large amounts unless towns were sacked.[17] Cattle and sheep would be useful plunder in the short term, providing food for raiders and essential supplies for groups wandering within the Empire. But the capture of herd beasts would have a dramatic reduction in the mobility of the raiders, since cows and sheep cannot move more than 30 km. per day, with no more than 15 k.p.d. being recommended. Oxen have a maximum speed of 25 k.p.d. This slowing of movement sometimes contributed to raiders being caught while loaded with booty: Frankish raiders retreating in 388 were caught in the *Silvae Carbonariae*.[18] A third type of plunder was prisoners (who could be ransomed later, but were usually kept as slaves). When negotiating peace treaties, the Romans generally demanded the release of prisoners, most of whom had presumably been captured in raids. Prisoners would also slow the movement of raids and increase the logistical burden by needing to be fed.[19] Food or drink was also plundered, and often consumed on the spot. This occasionally led to unfortunate consequences where the sated barbarians were caught by surprise, as happened

[16] On Heruli see Hyd. 171; on Saxons see GT *HF* 2. 18–19; SA *Ep.* 8. 6; AM 27. 8. 5, 28. 5. 1.

[17] For luxuries see Maximus of Turin, *Sermo* 18. 3, 72. 2; Hyd. 114; AM 27. 10. 2?; Zos. 5. 5. 6; for plunder (unspecified) see AM 17. 2. 1, 19. 11. 4, 20. 1. 1, 21. 3. 1, 26. 5. 9, 31. 5. 8; Zos. 4. 33. 2, 48. 1–2, 6. 3. 1; Sulpicius fr. 1; Eunapius fr. 42. 55–78; Jordanes, *Getica*, 155, 271.

[18] For livestock see Claudian, *In Eutropium* 1. 247–8; AM 16. 5. 17, 27. 8. 7, 29. 6. 6, 8; Eugippius, *V. Sev.* 4. 1, 30. 4; Malchus fr. 18. 2. 29–30, 18. 4; Jordanes, *Getica*, 273; on being slowed by booty see Priscus fr. 9. 3. 46–55; Sulpicius fr. 1; Zos. 4. 23. 4; cf. Mauricius, *Strat.* 10. 2. 2; on sheep, goats, etc. see G. Dahl and A. Hjort, *Having Herds* (Stockholm, 1976), 240; HMSO, *Manual of Horsemanship* (London, 1937), 254.

[19] AM 27. 8. 7, 10. 2, 29. 6. 6, 8, 31. 6. 7–8; Lib. *Or.* 18. 34; Maximus of Turin, *Sermo* 18. 3; Eugippius, *V. Sev.* 4. 1, 8. 12; Claudian, *In Eutropium*, 1. 245–6; Zos. 5. 5. 6; *CT* 5. 6. 2 (409), 7. 1 (366), 2 (408); Jordanes, *Getica*, 274; Hyd. 131.

to Franks in 356, Alamanni in 366, and Goths in 377.[20]

Some destruction might take place in plundered areas and state-ments about burning, especially in poetry, suggest this was common. Thus Orientius characterized the invasion of Gaul in 406 by the line 'all Gaul smoked as a funeral pyre'. Since many structures, especially in the countryside, would be of wooden construction with thatched roofs, accidental burning was probably common.[21]

Much of this plundering is undetectable in the archaeological record and consequently we are dependent on literary accounts for this sort of activity. It has been argued that the archaeological record in Britain reflects the destruction of the 367 raids, though closer examination of the quoted record suggests natural collapse or burning of different periods. According to Evans, 'evidence of destruction deposits ... has yet to be demonstrated in the case of the "Barbarian Conspiracy" in northern England'. The plundering described here usually resulted from raiding, but similar actions could occur during wars.[22]

Conquest

The second type of attack was an attempt to settle within the Empire, by conquest if necessary. These attacks occurred in the fourth century, but became more common in the fifth. If there was an opportunity to settle in the Empire, barbarians would usually seize it. One example was the invasion of the Alamanni in 352–3, taking advantage of the removal of troops by Magnentius. This invasion probably started as a number of raids, but rapidly developed into settlement when it became apparent that there was no effective opposition. If land could be seized without fighting this would be done, for example by Franks infiltrating into north Gaul in the early fifth century. As soon as barbarians settled on any territory they began farming on it.[23]

---

[20] AM 27. 2. 2; Zos. 3. 7. 4, 4. 23. 4; Malchus fr. 20. 35–42.

[21] Orientius, *Commonitorium* 2. 184; AM 29. 6. 8, 31. 5. 8; Malchus fr. 2. 18–19, 20. 2–5, 99–100; GT *HF* 2. 6.

[22] D. Whitehouse, 'Raiders and Invaders, the Roman Campania in the First Millennium AD', C. Malone and S. Stoddart, eds., *Papers in Italian Archaeology*, 4, *BAR* S246, (Oxford, 1985), 207–13; Britain, P. Salway, *Roman Britain* (Oxford, 1981), 374–84; J. Evans, 'Settlement and Society in North-East England in the Fourth Century', *Settlement and Society in the Roman North* (Bradford, 1984), 43–8 at 44–5.

[23] On Franks see AM 17. 8. 3; on farming see Lib. *Or.* 12. 44, 48, 18. 43; Malchus fr. 20. 54–6.

These movements into Roman territory were not always vol-
untary. The Frankish Salii who settled in Toxandria in 358 were
driven into the Empire by an attack of the Chamavian Franks and
had to make the best of the situation. This was similar to the
Gothic crossing of the Danube in 376. The Goths entered the
Empire as refugees from the Huns, not as invaders. Some were
accepted by the Romans, others forced their way across the Danube.
An attack of the Greuthungi in 386 is more difficult to evaluate.
Women and children were apparently present at this attempt to
cross the Danube and it seems that this was also an attempt to
enter the Empire by a whole people. Their motivation was probably
similar to that which impelled them to try to enter the Empire in
376—to escape from the Huns.[24]

For the settlements resulting from these movements to have any
long-term security they needed to be recognized by the Romans
and have provision for the future. Almost all the agreements which
we know of between barbarians and Romans involved either supply
of grain or land for farming. Other terms included cash payments
and Roman offices for barbarian leaders.[25] Some kingdoms or
settlements were created without imperial sanction, as by the Salii
Franci in 358, other Franks around 428, and the Suevi, Alans, and
Vandals in 411. Such settlements would create tension with the
indigenous population, many of whom would have to be dis-
possessed to provide land for the new arrivals. The Romans counter-
attacked or forced the settlers to move on as soon as they could.
In the cases mentioned above, the Romans counter-attacked almost
immediately in 358 and 428 and over a number of years against
the 411 settlers.[26]

---

[24] On Salii see AM 17. 8. 3; Zos. 3. 6. 2–3; on Goths see Eunapius fr. 42; Zos. 4.
20. 5; on Greuthungi see Zos. 4. 38–9.

[25] W. Goffart, *Barbarians and Romans* (Princeton, NJ, 1980), discusses legal basis
of settlements and previous literature, but see also S. J. B. Barnish, 'Taxation, Land
and Barbarian Settlement in the Western Empire', *PSBR* 54 (1986), 170–95; H.
Wolfram and A. Schwarz, *Annerkennung und Integration* (Vienna, 1988); grain, Zos.
5. 48. 3, 50. 3; Olymp. fr. 22. 2, 30; Malchus fr. 18. 3. 5–7; Philost. 12. 4; for land see
Priscus fr. 48. 1, 49; Malchus fr. 2. 5–7, 18. 3. 5–7, 20. 48–9; Zos. 5. 48. 3, 5. 50. 3; on
no grain or land see Zos. 5. 36. 1, 42. 1; on payment see Priscus fr. 48. 1; Zos. 5. 48. 3;
Malchus fr. 18. 3. 13–14, 25–6; on offices see Zos. 5. 48. 3; Malchus fr. 2. 5–7, 22–8, 18.
4. 12–17; Claudian, *De Bello Gothico*, 535–6, *In Eutropium*, 2. 320–2.

[26] On illegal settlements see Salii, AM 18. 8. 3; Franks, Prosp. 1298; for Suevi,
Vandals, and Alans see Thompson, *Romans and Barbarians*, 152–60; Hyd. 49;
Orosius 7. 40. 10; on Visigoths in 413? see *C.Gall.452* 73; on Burgundians in 413
see Prosp. 1250; on Ostrogoths see Ennodius, *V. Epiphanii*, 132–4.

Other settlements were the result of negotiations between barbarians and Romans on something approaching equal terms. These settlements were those of the Visigoths in Aquitaine in 418, Alans in Gaul in 440–2, and Burgundians in Gaul in 443 and 456. They are to be distinguished from those imposed by the Romans on barbarians, as settlers or prisoners of war, without their own leaders.[27] These settlements were more secure than those made without imperial sanction. Problems with local landlords could be ironed out quickly by the imperial administration, reducing the effect of disruption. The government-administered settlements of the Goths in Aquitaine and the Burgundians in Savoy seem to have caused less trouble than the autonomous settlement of the Suevi in Galicia, though no writer in Gaul provided an account as detailed as that of Hydatius in Spain.[28] When negotiating these settlements, barbarian groups could carry on their relations with the Romans (and each other) by ambassadors. This seems to be a change in practice from the fourth century when the Roman Emperor tended to deal with barbarian kings in person. Some barbarian kingdoms developed diplomatic specialists, others negotiated by letter.[29]

As well as seizing opportunities, attacks could be made in an attempt to force a negotiated settlement on the Romans. If the barbarians could establish a dominant military or political position then they could force guarantees from the Romans. Thus Alaric's attacks on Rome and Ravenna in 409–10 were an attempt to compel Honorius to grant his demands. Gothic attempts to move into Africa to cut off corn supplies to Italy had the same objectives. Without a dominant position, Alaric was unable to compel Honorius to do anything and without success was himself liable to lose support through desertion.[30]

---

[27] Thompson, *Romans and Barbarians*, 23–37, 50–7, 251–5; T. S. Burns, 'The Settlement of 418', in J. F. Drinkwater and H. W. Elton, eds., *Fifth-Century Gaul* (Cambridge, 1992), 53–63; C. E. V. Nixon, 'Relations between Visigothic and Roman Gaul', *Fifth-Century Gaul*, 64–74.

[28] On trouble in Galicia see Hyd. 91, 96, 119, 123, 137, 140, 142, 168, 179?, 196, 202, 229, 233, 241; on Armorica see Constantius, *V. Germani* 28.

[29] Ambassadors; Ostrogoths, *PLRE* ii, Faustus 9, Festus 5, Senarius; Visigoths, *PLRE* ii, Leo 5; Hyd. 97, 170, 172, 192, 197, 205, 219, 233, 237; Jordanes, *Getica*, 231; Huns, Jordanes, *Getica*, 185–6, 225; Priscus fr. 2, 11. 1; for Vandals see Priscus fr. 36. 1, 2; Hyd. 192, Malchus fr. 17; Suevi, Hyd. 226, 230, 245, 251; for letters see Cass. *Variae* 3. 1–4; for personal meetings see GT *HF* 2. 35.

[30] Zos. 5. 37–6. 12; Malchus, fr. 20; P. J. Heather, 'The Emergence of the Visigothic Kingdom', Drinkwater and Elton, eds., *Fifth-Century Gaul*, 84–94.

Self-Defence

The third reason for barbarian conflict with the Romans was self-defence. The Romans often tried to destroy or coerce barbarian groups. Such action could be direct, by military force, or indirect, blockading the barbarians in an attempt to starve them into submission. Roman strategy was the same whether attacking settled kingdoms or migratory groups. To avoid defeat and possible annihilation from indirect action, barbarians would be forced to attack the Romans, sometimes in disadvantageous conditions.

The types of conflict changed somewhat with the establishment of barbarian kingdoms and their recognition by the Romans. Campaigns now tended to revolve around the capture of a town (the base from which authority could be exerted on a region), and raiding seems to have become less common. The 436–9 war between the Romans and the Visigoths, like the clashes between 395 and 415, was won by the Romans. But the aftermath was different from that of earlier defeats; the Romans did not force the Goths to leave Aquitaine and resume wandering. Instead, the Goths made a treaty with the Romans and their kingdom continued to exist.

B: BARBARIAN TROOP TYPES

Barbarian armies were composed of two troop types, infantry and cavalry. The majority of barbarian soldiers were infantry, equipped only with a spear and shield. Richer men, such as *optimates*, might add a sword. Throwing weapons such as axes and javelins were common, long-distance weapons such as bows less so. Armour and helmets were rare at all levels. This simple panoply was necessary for a number of reasons. One was a lack of skilled craftsmen and resources. Barbarian society may appear to have had a lot of metalwork, but in comparison to the Roman Empire it had very little and most of this was confined to social élites. Armour and weapons were expensive. This problem was intensified by Roman prohibition of arms exports to barbarians. Although the effectiveness of such a prohibition is uncertain, making arms sales illegal would have increased prices and decreased availability. On occasion, captured Roman equipment was used, further suggesting equipment shortages.[31]

Barbarian infantry usually fought in a dense mass, but could send out parties of skirmishers armed with distance weapons before the main bodies clashed in battle. These skirmishers seem not to have been organized as separate units and their equipment probably differed little from that of the men left in the main body.

In addition to their infantry, most cantons fielded some cavalry, their numbers varying from canton to canton. Cantons living in heavily wooded regions would obviously have fewer cavalry than those from the plains. Eastern barbarians (Goths, Sarmatians, Alans, and Huns), living along the Theiss and the lower Danube, seem to have had more cavalry available. Otherwise, except in small mounted raiding parties, no more than a third, and more probably no more than a fifth, of any force would be cavalry. The only figures we have in this period for the proportions of cavalry are for the Ostrogoth Pitzias' expedition against Sabinianus in 505, when he led 2,000 foot and 500 horse. The numbers of cavalrymen available could change over time. Thus the Goths probably possessed fewer cavalry in the period 376–418 than before their crossing of the Danube, a result of the hardship of their wanderings through Europe. Similarly, the Huns living around the Theiss in the fifth century probably had fewer cavalry than the Moldavian Huns of the same period.[32]

Because of the expense of owning and feeding a horse, cavalry tended to be an élite and was generally drawn from the richer echelons of society, the *optimates* and *regales*. This was especially true in the West, though less so in the east, particularly on the steppes. Good cavalry horses (14+ hands) were expensive and probably a mark of status. Some steppe nomads may have had more than one horse.[33] Once barbarians had settled within the

---

[31] On prohibition of arms export see *Digest* 39. 4. 11, 48. 4. 1–4; *CJ* 4. 41. 2 (455/7), 63. 2 (374?), 12. 44 (420); *CT* 7. 16. 3 (420); on shortage of weapons see Menander fr. 5. 4; J. Kunow, 'Bemerkungen zum Export römischer Waffen in das Barbaricum', *LIMES Studien zu den Militärgrenzen Roms 3* (Stuttgart, 1986), 740–6; on use of captured weaponry see Claudian, *De Bello Gothico*, 535–9; AM 31. 5. 9, 31. 6. 3, 31. 15. 11; Zos. 3. 18. 6.

[32] Dexippus fr. 24 says 40,000 of 120,000 Alamanni were cavalry, though numbers and proportions are doubtful, Thompson, *The Early Germans* (Oxford, 1965), 116 n. 2; on Pitzias see Jordanes, *Getica*, 300.

[33] On values see *Lex Ribuariae*, 40. 11 (late 6th cent.) for wergild purposes, stallion = 7 *solidi*, mare = 3, cow = 1 *solidus*, helmet = 6; for multiple horses see AM

Empire increased landholding may have given some the resources to raise more cavalry, but a revolution in the proportions of cavalry in barbarian armies seems unlikely. Wolfram's statement that 'the evidence for the far-reaching transformation of the Gothic army is clear cut: from this time [*c.*400] the cavalry set the tone and made up a larger and larger portion of the actual fighting force' is in fact not supported by the evidence.[34] In the sixth century, Merovingian and Ostrogothic armies continued to be composed of infantry for the most part.[35]

Although small in numbers, barbarian cavalry could be high in quality. Vegetius remarked that Roman cavalry had benefited from studying Goth, Hun and Alan cavalry. Even the Alamanni, whose home territory does not appear at first sight conducive to horsemanship, were described by Aurelius Victor as 'a people who fight wonderfully on horseback', and at Strasbourg in 357 they pushed back the Roman cavalry on the right flank. Marine raiders such as the Saxons are not known to have taken horses on raids, though they might commandeer horses after landing. Yet even these people would have some cavalry available if attacked at home.[36]

Most barbarian cavalry were shock troops, fighting in close formation with the primary function of defeating the enemy in mêlée. But some, especially those from the East where cavalry were more numerous and often bow-armed, would act as light cavalry, with functions of skirmishing and harassing the enemy. Both types were probably used for scouting. A last troop type, probably never used, was chariots. They apparently existed in Ireland at this date, but it is unlikely that they were ever transported to the mainland of Britain on raids. They were probably not used for military purposes.[37]

17. 12. 3; Mauricius, *Strat.* 11. 2. 9–14; for *regales* see AM 16. 12. 34–5; Olymp. fr. 26. 1; for *optimates* see AM 31. 5. 7.

[34] H. Wolfram, *History of The Goths*[2] (London, 1988), 167–8 at 168; cf. J. H. W. G. Liebeschuetz, 'Generals, Federates and Buccelarii in Roman Armies around AD 400', in P. W. Freeman and D. L. Kennedy, eds., *The Defence of the Roman and Byzantine East, BAR* S297, (Oxford, 1986), 463–74 at 464.

[35] Numbers: for Visigoths see Merobaudes, *Pan.* 1, fr. 2B, 19–21; for Merovingians see below, p. 60. Procopius, *BG* 6. 25. 2–3; for Ostrogoths see Jordanes, *Getica,* 300.

[36] On quality see Veg. 1. 20; Orosius 7. 34. 5; on Alamanni see Aurelius Victor, *Caes.* 21. 2; on Strasbourg see AM 16. 12. 21–2; on commandeering horses, cf. *ASC* E 994.

[37] Muirchu, *V. Pat.* 16; cf. Anon. *PS* 14.

D: EQUIPMENT

The evidence for barbarian equipment falls into two categories, literary and archaeological. Literary evidence gives only. a general, though consistent, impression which has to be supplemented by archaeological evidence. There was little difference between the Romans and barbarians in the quality of available equipment and captured equipment was used, on occasion, by barbarians.[38]

It is possible that literary evidence may be affected by stereotyping, with authors writing in the classicizing tradition portraying barbarians as howling half-naked savages. The consistency of the literary picture, however, especially when compared with material written in a less classical tradition from the sixth century, suggests general accuracy, as does the positive correlation with archaeological evidence. In the third century, Herodian stated that 'the [Roman] archers found the Germans' bare heads and large bodies an easy long-distance target for their arrows. But if [the barbarians] charged into close combat, they were stubborn fighters and often the equals of the Romans.' In 539, Procopius described the Franks as they invaded Italy: 'They had a small body of cavalry around their leader, and these were the only ones armed with spears, while all the rest were infantry with neither bows nor spears, but each one had a sword and shield and axe.' The descriptions of barbarians in the sixth-century *Strategikon* of Mauricius are similar. Western barbarians (Franks, Lombards, etc.) 'are armed with shields, spears and short swords slung from their shoulders. They prefer fighting on foot and rapid charges.' And the Slavs 'are armed with short javelins, two to each man. Some also have nice-looking but unwieldy shields. In addition, they use wooden bows with short arrows smeared with a poisonous drug.' These accounts are similar and do not suggest great variety in barbarians equipment.[39]

Archaeological evidence for equipment usually comes from graves or ritual deposits. These finds give an idea of the equipment available and its geographical distribution. The best way to assess

---

[38] *RGA²*: Bewaffnung; K. Raddatz, 'Die Bewaffnung der Germanen vom letzten Jahrhundert vor Chr. Geb. bis zur Völkerwanderungszeit', *ANRW* 2. 12. 3 (Berlin, 1985), 281–361.

[39] Herodian 6. 7. 8 (natural reading of context, though there are textual problems); for Franks see Procopius, *BG* 6. 25. 2–3; cf. Agathias, *Hist.* 2. 5. 3–4; for Western barbarians see Mauricius, *Strat.* 11. 3. 2; for Slavs see Mauricius, *Strat.* 11. 4. 11.

barbarian equipment archaeologically is to examine a number of
cemeteries from different regions. This geographical variation
should enable the hypothesis that 'all barbarians were the same' to
be tested. This examination is necessarily sketchy and is based to
a great extent on secondary literature.

Cemeteries present several problems. First is the small number
of burials with weapons, which indicates that weapon burial was
not practised by every family on the same site, even assuming that
weapon-holding was universal. Secondly, we do not know what
determined the presence or omission of weapons and armour in
graves. Deposition was affected by ritual, social, and economic
considerations, which makes reconstruction of typical barbarian
military equipment from graves an impossible practice. For
example, graves have been found which contain a single francisca
(throwing axe) (Hemmingen, nos. 16, 40; Heidenheim-Grosskuchen
no. 17), a weapon which would have been of little use on its own
in a battle. Regional variations also occur in the type of burial and
the grave goods deposited. The motivation for burying weapons in
Francia probably differed from that in Gothia, but we have no
idea as to why and little about how. What we do know is that
weapon burial was more common in Francia than in Gothia.
Thirdly, there is an almost total lack of body armour in graves and
helmets are rare. Lastly, the similarity of the equipment and
weaponry to that of Roman soldiers is marked and on the basis of
weaponry alone, no distinction could be made.[40]

The evidence from cemeteries can thus be used to show what
material was available (and probably used) in an area. However,
absence of material from graves cannot be used as an argument
for the lack of a certain type of equipment or its absence from a
particular area. Nor can the cemeteries be used to show weapon
combinations or proportions of one weapon to another or variations
in these from one area to another.[41]

[40] On grave evidence see G. Halsall, 'The Origins of the Reihengräberzivilisation:
Forty Years on', *Fifth-Century Gaul*, 196–207; E. James, 'Cemeteries and the
Problem of Frankish Settlement in Gaul', P. H. Sawyer, ed., *Names, Words, and
Graves* (Leeds, 1979), 55–89, discusses some of the problems in using this material;
on bog deposits see J. Hines, 'The Military Context of the *adventus saxonum*: Some
Continental Evidence', in S. C. Hawkes, ed., *Weapons and Warfare in Anglo-Saxon
England* (Oxford, 1989), 25–48.

[41] For examples of the misuse possible see James, 'Cemeteries', 55–89 at 78; Todd,
*Northern Barbarians*², 142.

The first cemetery to be examined is Perdöhl, near Wittenburg, in Mecklenburg, deep within the *barbaricum*. This was a cremation cemetery of the late third to fifth centuries. Of 429 adult cremations only ten contained weapons, perhaps 5 per cent of male graves. All of the weapons were spears and light javelins, in numbers varying from one to eight per grave. There were no swords, shield bosses, etc., though their survival may have been affected by cremation. There were no bows, armour, or helmets surviving. This site in the *barbaricum*, approximately 320 km. from the Rhine, differs little from other contemporary cemeteries in the same area and is mainly distinguished from earlier cemeteries by the presence of weaponry.[42]

The second example is a late fifth- to early sixth-century inhumation cemetery at Hemmingen, 15 km. north-west of Stuttgart and approximately 80 km. east of the Rhine, lying in Alamannia. The cemetery was small, with only fifty-seven graves excavated. Of the adult burials, sixteen were of men, thirty-one of women, and two of unknown sex. There were three male child burials, three female, and two of unknown sex. Two of the three male child graves contained weapons as did eight of the sixteen male graves. Of the latter, four contained either a single francisca or javelin, one a single *spatha*, one a sax and javelin, one a *spatha* and javelin, and the richest grave (no. 2) a *spatha*, francisca, and several javelins. Two of the graves with *spathae* (but not no. 2) also had shield bosses.

Hemmingen can be compared with another inhumation cemetery of the same date at Heidenheim-Grosskuchen, a village near Heidenheim in southern Germany. Of the twenty fifth-century burials, five were male, thirteen female, and two of unsexed children. Two graves of adult males contained weapons, one a francisca (no. 17), the other a shield, spear, and *spatha* (no. 21).[43] Both these examples had a greater variety of equipment than the cemetery at Perdöhl, possibly the result of easier access to Roman traders, though the fact that Perdöhl was a cremation cemetery is important. It is also important that peoples based in north Germany tended not to bury

---

[42] E. Schuldt, *Perdöhl* (Berlin, 1976); cf. A. Leube, 'Archäologische Formengruppen im nördlichen Elb-Oder-Gebiet während des 1. bis 4. Jhrhndrt', *Prace Archeologiczne*, 22 (1976), 355–70.

[43] H. F. Müller, *Die alamannische Gräberfeld von Hemmingen* (Stuttgart, 1976); A. Heege, *Grabfunde der Merowingerzeit aus Heidenheim-Grosskuchen* (Stuttgart, 1987), 1–125.

weapons with their dead until the early sixth century.

The third example is from the eastern fringes of the *barbaricum*, at Letçani in modern Romania, about 30 km. east of the Prut and *c.*200 km. north of the Danube. It is a late fourth-century cemetery of the Sintana de Mures-Chernjakov culture, with forty-eight graves. Sixteen burials are cremations, thirty-two inhumations. Of the latter, seventeen were female, five male, three adult and unsexable, and seven of children. It is characteristic of cemeteries east of the Danube bend in having few weapon-burials. Only two of the burials contain any military equipment. One (no. 21) contained what might be a shield boss, another (no. 25) a spearhead. No other burial contains any weaponry and even the knives so common in contemporary Western cemeteries are almost totally absent.[44]

The evidence for barbarian equipment has to be used with care, though it is adequate to show what was available to barbarian warriors. However, the distribution of equipment and weapon combinations cannot easily, if at all, be deduced from the archaeological record.

Offensive Equipment

Offensive weaponry used can be divided into missile weapons, used before contact, and hand-to-hand weapons. Missile weapons can be subdivided into two groups, long- and short-range weapons. The only long-range weapon used by the barbarians was the bow. The most common type was the longbow, constructed from a single piece of wood. Complete examples from bog deposits at Thorsberg are 1.65 m. and 1.51 m. in length, and one from Nydam measures 1.9 m. But bows of composite wood and horn construction were also used, especially among those people with steppe antecedents, the Alans, Sarmatians, and Huns. Archaeological evidence for bows is rare and they are not often found in graves. However, iron or bone arrowheads and horn stiffeners often survive if they were used (but being intrinsically undatable may not always be dated correctly). Ammianus says that the Huns used bone arrowheads, but none have survived that can be assigned to the Huns. However,

---

[44] C. Bloşiu, 'Necropola dia secolul al 4-lea e. n. de la Letçani (jud. Iaşi)', *Arheologia Moldovei*, 8 (1975), 203–80, with French summary; details of other cemeteries in same region, J. Werner, 'Dančeny und Brangstrup', *BJ* 188 (1988), 241–86; on the Sintana de Mures/Chernjakov Culture, Heather and Matthews, *Goths*, 51–101.

of 125 arrowheads from Nydam 14 were of bone, so barbarians did use bone for this purpose.[45] Bows seem not to have been widely used and were probably carried by only a few warriors, perhaps those in skirmishing roles. Though archers do occur in literary accounts, only the Huns had a reputation for numbers of bowmen. Some people even achieved the opposite reputation, Agathias stating that the Franks did not know how to use bows.[46] Barbarians are not known to have used slings, though the cheapness and simplicity of this weapon makes it unlikely never to have been used.

Short-range missile weapons were usually spears. Literary accounts stress the large number of spears thrown before contact: 'hurling weapons from all sides like hail'. Many graves contain more than one spear, some of which may have been used for throwing (as javelins) and others retained for hand-to-hand combat. Graves have been found with as many as eight of these weapons (Perdöhl no. 382) which would suggest that some individuals had considerable missile power, though the number of men so armed is unknown. No differences exist which can be used to divide the finds into throwing and melée weapons. The same weapons, or at least their heads, were probably used for both purposes, though thrown weapons may have had shorter shafts. Such javelin-heads are often described in archaeological reports as 'pfeilspitzen', although their shaft diameter, usually around 2 cm., makes most of them too large to be arrows, which usually have shafts of less than 1 cm. in diameter.[47]

[45] On bows, K. Raddatz, *Der Thorsberger Moorfund* (Neumünster, 1987), 511, 512; K. Beckhoff, 'Die eigenzeitlichen Kriegsbogen von Nydam', *Offa*, 20 (1963), 39–48; bone arrowheads, AM 31. 2. 9; K. Raddatz, 'Pfeilspitzen aus den Moorfund von Nydam', *Offa*, 20 (1963), 49–56; problems in survival of archery equipment, J. C. Coulston, 'Roman Archery Equipment', in M. C. Bishop, ed., *The Production and Distribution of Roman Military Equipment*, *BAR* S275 (Oxford, 1985), 220–366 at 222–4; M. Kazanski, 'À propos des armes et des éléments de harnachement "orientaux" en Occident à l'époque des Grandes Migrations (4ᵉ–5ᵉ s.)', *JRA* 4 (1991), 123–39 at 135–6.
[46] Use: for Alamanni, AM 27. 1. 3, 31. 10. 8; Eunapius fr. 18. 6; for Franks see Sulpicius fr. 1 (mentioning poison, cf. SA *Carm.* 5. 400–2; *Pactus Legis Salicae* 17. 2; Mauricius, *Strat.* 11. 4. 11); for Goths see AM 31. 7. 13–14; Orosius 7. 33. 14; Veg. 1. 20; for Sarmatian bows see HA *Triginti Tyranni*, 10. 12; for Huns see SA *Carm.* 2. 266; Olymp. fr. 19; AM 31. 2. 9; Jordanes, *Getica*, 128, 255; for Vandals see SA *Carm.* 5. 400–2; on lack of use see Agathias, *Hist.* 2. 5. 4.
[47] On thrown weapons see AM 27. 1. 3–5; Lib. *Or.* 59. 131; J. Werner, 'Pfeilspitzen aus Silber und Bronz in germanischen Adelsgräbern der Kaiserzeit', *Historisches*

As well as these javelins, short-range missile power could be provided by angons (Hemmingen no. 21), franciscas (Hemmingen no. 2), or saxes. Angons were spears with the upper length of the shaft protected (or formed) by a metal sheath, 1.64 m. long in an angon from Krefeld-Gellep (no. 1782), but usually shorter. These were usually carried in addition to other weapons. Angons were widely distributed, being found along the Rhine as well as deep in the *barbaricum* on the Elbe, in Britain, and along the middle Danube (Fig. 7). Agathias said that the Franks had 'axes with two edges and angones which they use for all purposes. The angones are spears, not very small, but not very big either, of a size both for throwing, if need be, and for meeting charges at close quarters.'[48] Franciscas were throwing axes. Although they are traditionally supposed to have been a Frankish weapon, their find locations do not support this theory. Large numbers occur in Francia and in Gaul, but they are also to be found (in smaller numbers) in England, Alamannia (Hemmingen nos. 2, 16, 29, 32), and further east (Fig. 7).[49] A third type of weapon was the sax, a single-edged knife with a point, c.0.3–0.65 m. in length (Hemmingen no. 15). Although the Saxons were supposed to derive their name from the sax, these weapons were found throughout the *barbaricum* (Fig. 7).[50]

In all three cases, the distribution-map of these artefacts reflects the amount of fieldwork and publication carried out, as well as the spread of material. However, the distribution is certainly wider than would be expected if angons and franciscas were characteristic of the Franks, as was suggested by contemporary writers.[51]

Jahrbuch, 74 (1955), 38–41; on volume of fire see AM 14. 10. 6, 16. 12. 46, 27. 1. 3; on multiples see Veg. 1. 20; Mauricius, *Strat.* 11. 4. 11; AM 14. 2. 7; on arrow shaft diameters see R. Hardy, *Longbow* (Cambridge, 1976), 200–1, 5/16" = 8 mm.; also Coulston, 'Archery Equipment', 220–366 at 264 n, 266–7.

[48] S. von Schnurbein, 'Zum Ango', G. Kossack and G. Ulbert, eds., *Festschrift für Joachim Werner zum 65 Geburtstag* (Munich, 1974), 411–33; Agathias, *Hist.* 1. 21. 8, 2. 5–8; *RGA²*: *Ango*.

[49] Agathias, *Hist.* 2. 5. 4; SA *Carm.* 5. 246–9, *Ep.* 4. 20. 3; Procopius, *BG* 6. 25. 2–4.

[50] D. A. Gale, 'The Seax', *Weapons and Warfare*, 71–83; Kazanski, 'À propos des armes', 123–39 at 132–4.

[51] Distributions in Fig. 7 plotted from Böhme, *Germanische Grabfunde*; W. Menghin, *Das Schwert im frühen Mittelalter* (Stuttgart, 1983); *Germanen, Hunnen, Awaren* (Nuremberg, 1987). The intention is to show that these weapons were used over a wide area and not to plot all known find spots; it also shows the lack of readily accessible syntheses of Eastern European archaeology and the rarity of weapon burials from this region.

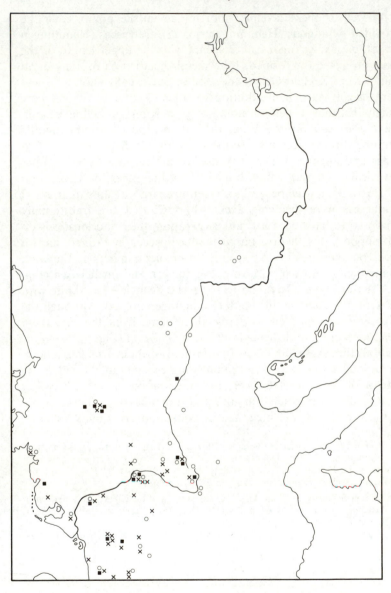

Fig. 7 Distribution of Angons, Saxes, Franciscas. Angon; o: Sax; x: Francisca: ■

The basic mêlée weapon of barbarian infantry was the spear, by far the most common weapon found in graves. Spears were simple to produce and an effective weapon when used by close-formation infantry. The functional nature of spears meant that there was little variety in the form of the spearhead. Their length appears to have been *c*.2.5–3.5 m. The angons used for throwing could also be used in hand-to-hand combat when their metal shafts would be of some value in preventing the shafts from being cut by enemy swords.[52]

Swords were much less common weapons than spears. Their production was a skilled and expensive affair and swords were therefore rare beyond the Roman Empire, though they seem to have been relatively common within it. Many barbarian graves found with swords also contain spears, which may suggest that it was a status symbol as well as a primary weapon. These swords were mostly long (*c*.0.8–1.0 m.) two-edged weapons with a point, able to be used for both thrusting and cutting. They differed little from the Roman *spatha*.

Swords may have become slightly more common during the fourth and fifth centuries, though this cannot be deduced from our evidence. Any increase in number would have been a gradual process, partly resulting from continued contact with the Romans. A small increase in the use of swords would not make any significant difference to barbarian warfare; although swords would make individual barbarian warriors more effective against armoured troops, increasing the small number of men with swords would not allow the barbarians to do anything they could not already do. The spear remained the weapon of the majority throughout this period.[53]

Saxes were also common hand-to-hand weapons throughout the *barbaricum*. They were cheap to produce and were presumably used by less well-off barbarians or as secondary weapons.[54] Axes, clubs, and war-hammers were used on occasion, but do not appear to have been common hand-to-hand weapons. No people achieved a

[52] For spears see J. Swanton, *The Spearheads of the Anglo-Saxon Settlements* (London, 1983); for length see AM 17. 12. 2; Lib. *Or.* 59. 275.

[53] Kazanski, 'À propos des armes', 123–39 at 123–32; Menghin, *Das Schwert*, though unfortunately limited to 5th–7th cent. and some of Western Europe; J. Lønstup, 'Das zweischneidige Schwert aus der jüngeren römischen Kasierzeit im freien Germanien und im römischen Imperium', *LIMES 3*, 747–9; rarity, *Beowulf*, 2047–56; on cost (7 *solidi*) see *Lex Ribuariae*, 40. 11.

[54] On saxes, see above, n. 51.

reputation for their use similar to that gained by the Franks for thrown axes. Many of the axes and hammers found in graves may have been tools rather than weapons.[55]

Cavalry weapons were similar to infantry weapons, but the rarity of archaeological evidence for weaponry that definitely belonged to cavalry blurs distinctions between the two types. Even when spurs or harnesses are found in graves (rarely in the fourth and fifth centuries, though more common later), the equipment may not have been intended for use while mounted.

Missile weapons used by mounted troops were bows and javelins. The bow seems only to have been used by individual cavalrymen in the West, not by large numbers, and was probably an extension of the hunting use of the bow. Cavalry deriving from steppe peoples, the Huns and Alans (and perhaps the Sarmatians and Goths), probably made greater use of the bow, though there is unfortunately very little direct evidence. However, Hunnic *foederati* regiments in Roman service were probably equipped with bows. Short-range missiles were probably provided by javelins, though the number of missiles carried is unknown.[56]

Mêlée weapons were the spear and sword. Cavalry spears seem (at least on the evidence of a seventh-century tombstone from Halle and late Alamannic graves) to have been the same length as infantry spears. Analogy with Roman practice and the Halle tombstone suggest they could be held underarm and used as a lance, though overarm thrusting probably continued. The use of swords was probably more widespread than among infantry, since those rich enough to afford horses could probably also afford swords, though both used the same type of sword, the *spatha*.[57] Lastly, a weapon occasionally used by cavalrymen was the lasso, though its use appears to have been confined to those cavalry deriving from the Danube basin.[58]

---

[55] For clubs see AM 31. 7. 12; for axes see AM 31. ˙3. 3; for war-hammers see Menghin, *Das Schwert*, nos. 39, 44, 45.

[56] On bows (above, n. 45) see Theoderic, SA *Ep.* 1. 2. 5; on Huns see AM 31. 2. 9; Olymp. fr. 19; Maenchen-Helfen, *Huns*, 221–32; Jordanes, *Getica*, 128, 255; SA *Carm.* 2. 266; on Hun *foederati* see Zos. 5. 45. 6 and below, p. 108; on javelins cf. 6th-cent. nomads, Procopius, *BG* 6. 1. 8–10; Mauricius, *Strat.* 11. 2. 6.

[57] On spears see Mauricius, *Strat.* 11. 2. 6; AM 16. 12. 24; on tombstone in Halle Landesmuseum see P. Brown, *The World of Late Antiquity* (London, 1971), pl. 80; on swords see Mauricius, *Strat.* 11. 2. 6.

[58] On lassoes see Olymp. fr. 18 (but see R. C. Blockley, *Fragmentary Classicising*

Defensive equipment

Although the quality of barbarian military equipment was roughly equal to that of the Romans, the quantity certainly was not. Nowhere is this more apparent than in defensive equipment: shields, body armour, and helmets. The Romans themselves remarked on this shortage, which is also very visible in the archaeological record.

Shields were the most common type, complementing the spear and probably used by most warriors. There are fewer surviving examples than there are of weapon graves or spears, though most of the (earlier) pictorial evidence shows barbarians with shields. No late antique author suggests that shields were lacking, though they do mention the lack of armour. Shields were either rarely placed in graves or preservation was affected by their construction. Shields were made from wood or hide with a metal boss, though some first-century AD shields recovered from bog deposits were constructed from wood alone. Some third-century shields had metal bindings around the rim and this may have been common, with a fifth-century example being known from Skedemosse in Denmark. Surviving shields are circular and a third-century example from Thorsberg is around 1.0 m. in diameter, though oval shields similar to Roman examples were probably also common. One Hun is described as having a habit of leaning on his shield, suggesting a height in excess of 1.0 m. (or a very short Hun). Spiked shield bosses have frequently been found, suggesting a function as a secondary weapon.[59]

Though shields may have been plentiful, armour is not common in either the literary or archaeological evidence. Literary evidence suggests that very little armour was available and in all Ammianus' descriptions of the Alamanni, only one man is mentioned who wore armour and a helmet, King Chnodomarius at the battle of Strasbourg.[60] Archaeologically, an idea of the rarity of armour can be provided by Böhme's synthesis of Germanic grave-material of the fourth and fifth centuries between the Elbe and the Loire. In a

Historians of the Later Roman Empire (Liverpool, 1983), vol. ii for text note); AM 31. 2. 9; Soz. 7. 26. 6; Malalas 364.

[59] Shields for bindings see Raddatz, *Thorsberger Moorfund*, nos. 298–309, 311, 313, Taf. 29; SA *Ep.* 4. 20. 3 (?); U. E. Hagberg, *The Marsh of Skedemosse* (Stockholm, 1967), no. 847, pl. 19; for the Hun see Soz. 7. 26. 6; cf. *PLRE* ii, Zerco; for spiked bosses see Menghin, *Das Schwert, passim*.

[60] Chnodomarius, AM 16. 12. 24; Lib. *Or.* 18. 61; SA *Ep.* 4. 20; cf. Herodian 6. 7. 8.

list of over 100 weapon graves, *none* of these beyond the Rhine contain either a helmet or body armour. This point is reinforced by Menghin's study of early medieval swords, which lists only two helmets and no body armour in a sample of 100 *spathae* finds, mostly from graves, of the fifth and early sixth centuries. Owners of *spathae* would tend to be rich and most likely to own any defensive equipment available. Even the grave of Childeric I, the Frankish king buried at Tournai in 481, seems not to have contained any defensive armour, though it is one of the richest barbarian graves from the fifth century.

But there is some archaeological evidence for armour. Mail-shirts are known, but this is mostly confined to the Baltic coast, and as far as is known there are none attributed to the fourth and fifth centuries close to the Empire. Even the rich bog deposits of the late second and early third century at Thorsberg contained only four small pieces of mail.[61] Finds of armour and literary mentions are usually mail. The only other type mentioned is the scale armour of the Sarmatians. The manner of Ammianus' description, in a clearly derivative passage, suggests this is a topos, and similar armour is mentioned by Pausanias. Scale armour is known from eastern Europe, however, and though uncommon it was not totally unknown.[62]

Once barbarian groups had settled within the Empire armour may have become more common, though its expense meant that it was still usually confined to the nobility. Among the Ostrogoths in the sixth century only their nobles had armour and Agathias could describe the Franks at the same time as totally lacking body armour.[63] The rarity of armour can be shown by evidence from a slightly later period. The (probably) eighth-century poem *Beowulf* gives the impression, unique among literary sources, that armour was widespread. However, its constant stress on the armour worn by protagonists suggests that armour was rare. Beowulf himself

---

[61] Böhme, *Germanische Grabfunde*; Menghin, *Das Schwert*; Raddatz, *Thorsberger Moorfund*, nos. 407. 1, 408, 415, 416.

[62] AM 17. 12. 2; Pausanias 1. 21. 8; Maenchen-Helfen, *Huns*, 241–51.

[63] On value see *Lex Ribuariae*, 40. 11 (mailshirt, 12 *solidi*, helmet, 6 *solidi*); for armour see Mauricius, *Strat.* 11. 2. 6; GT *HF* 5. 48; Agathias, *Hist.* 2. 5. 3; Paul the Deacon, *Historia Langobardorum*, 1. 20; for nobles only see Procopius, *BG* 5. 23. 9, 7. 4. 21; on lack of armour see Procopius, *BP* 2. 25. 27, *BG* 7. 14. 26; Mauricius, *Strat.* 11. 4. 15–16.

was equipped with a mail-shirt, but his request to Hrothgar before
fighting Grendel shows its value:

> But if the fight should take me, you would forward to Hygelac
> This best of battle-shirts, that my breast now wears,
> The queen of war-coats, it is the bequest of Hrethel
> And from the forge of Wayland.

A tradition of handing down armour may account for its rarity in
graves. Armour could also be burnt on the pyre of a dead hero.

> The pyre was erected, the ruddy gold
> brought from the hoard, and the best warrior
> of Scylding race was ready for the burning
> displayed on his pyre, plain to see
> were the bloody mail-shirt, the boars on the helmet

The same poem describes the death of King Hygelac, 'the king's
person passed into Frankish hands, together with his corselet'. Its
loss was worth mentioning. These two mechanisms could account
for the lack of armour in the archaeological record, but they would
only have evolved if there had been a shortage of armour.[64]

Helmets were also rare, though they appear to have been more
common than body armour. Some have been found in graves
beyond the Rhine and Danube and a few examples are known
from cemeteries within the Empire. Nevertheless, they were probably owned mostly by the rich. Like swords and body armour,
helmets probably became more common as barbarians settled in
the Empire. The helmets known are metal, but it is possible that
some men wore leather helmets which would be unlikely to survive
archaeologically.[65]

Although reference to earlier sources has generally been avoided,
Tacitus' description of barbarian equipment in the first century is
particularly illuminating.

Only a very few [barbarians] have swords or spears. The spears that they
carry, 'frameae' is the native word, have short and narrow heads, but are
so sharp and easy to handle that the same weapon serves for fighting hand-
to-hand or at a distance. The horseman demands no more than a shield

[64] On handed-down armour see *Beowulf*, 452–6, 2615–24, 2809–12; cf. Maenchen-
Helfen, *Huns*, 241; for destruction on pyre see *Beowulf*, 1107–13, 3136–9; Hygelac,
Beowulf 1210–11.
[65] Literary references are rare, AM 16. 12. 24.

and spear, but the infantry has also javelins for throwing, several to each
man, and can hurl them to a great distance ... Few have breastplates
[*loricae*], and only here or there a helmet of metal or hide ... Their strength
lies in their infantry rather than cavalry.[66]

There was no significant change in barbarian equipment from
Tacitus' time until the sixth century.

E: OPERATIONS

Deployment and mustering

In the fourth century, the only bodies of standing troops among
the barbarians were *comitatus*, so before fighting an army had to
be mustered. Though small numbers of men could be brought
together swiftly, assembling warriors from a number of cantons
would take longer and if the Romans could catch barbarians at
home by surprise then they might be able to defeat them in detail.

Evidence for the size of attacks is extremely sketchy and there is
not enough evidence from which to draw firm conclusions. The
majority of raids seem to have been conducted by a single canton
and appear not to have been much bigger than 2,000 men, but
most raids were smaller than this. Raiding groups seem to have
remained roughly constant in size over the fourth and fifth centuries.
In the winter of 357, a group of Franks occupied a deserted fort
on the river Meuse. This band was recorded by different sources as
600 and 1000 strong. A century later, Majorian defeated a band of
900 Alamanni who had crossed the Alps. In 378 raiders of the
Lentienses, having broken through the border troops, were defeated
by an *auxilia palatina* brigade, a force no more than 2,500 strong.[67]
Estimating the size of larger attacks is impossible. Many figures
given by our sources are impossible on logistical grounds (e.g.
armies over 100,000 men), but occasionally we hear of smaller
totals which may be accurate. At the battle of Strasbourg in 357
the kings of four to six Alamannic cantons led 35,000 men, who
included some mercenaries and some lent (by other kings?) as a

---

[66] Tacitus, *Germania*, 6. 1–2.
[67] Sizes: for Meuse see Lib. *Or.* 18. 70; AM 17. 2. 1; for Majorian see SA *Carm.*
5. 373–80; for Lentienses see AM 31. 10. 4; cf. Eugippius, *V. Sev.* 4. 2–4, 27. 2–3.

favour. These groups seem not to have been organized in any formal manner and leadership was the duty of kings and *optimates*.[68]

Estimating tribal strength, the number of barbarians in a region, is obviously difficult, given the problems with estimating cantonal size and numbers of cantons. The best evidence for the size of tribes is provided by the Alamanni. The three largest Alamannic armies that we have evidence for in this period are recorded by Ammianus Marcellinus. Of these, one was 35,000 in 357, another 40,000 strong in 378. A third was in three divisions in 366, of which one was over 10,000 strong. Comparisons with earlier barbarian tribes such as the Helvetii and their allies in 58 BC would suggest that approximately 25 per cent of the population were able to fight as warriors. This would give the Alamanni a minimum population base of around 150,000. This figure is roughly comparable with the strength of the Tervingi in 376 who are recorded by Eunapius as having a population of 200,000 when they crossed the Danube.[69]

Planning

The amount of planning involved in raids appears to have been minimal since they were simply intended to gain plunder. If there was no Roman opposition as when troops had been removed from Gaul in 351, then raids might take place at any time. If they were responding to a Roman weakness this inevitably determined their timing, though no season seems to have been avoided. Raids frequently occurred in winter, for example, the attack by a group of Franks in 357 or the raid of Beorgor, defeated near Bergamo in early February 464.[70]

Once it had been decided to launch a raid, it was necessary to choose an area to attack and keep an eye out for the Roman army. Both choices depended on local intelligence, though it does not seem likely that raiders planned their attacks in great detail. One exception is the attack of Rando on Mainz in 368.

An Alamannic *regalis*, by the name of Rando, after a long preparation for his plans, made his way in secret into Mainz, which had no garrison, with

---

[68] Goffart, *Barbarians and Romans*, 231–4; Strasbourg, AM 16. 12. 4, 24–6.
[69] For Alamanni, 357 see AM 16. 12. 26; 378, AM 31. 10. 5; 366, AM 27. 2. 4 and 7; on population size see Caesar, *De Bello Gallico* 1. 29, 92,000 warriors from a population of 368,000, a suspiciously exact ratio of 1:4; for Tervingi see Eunapius fr. 42. 4–5; cf. Dexippus fr. 24 mentioning 120,000 Iuthungi in the 3rd cent.
[70] AM 16. 4. 1–4, 17. 2. 1–4, 19. 11. 4, 27. 1. 1; Marc. Com. sa 464; Hyd. 140.

soldiers lightly equipped for plundering. And since he found a Christian festival being celebrated, he was unhindered in carrying off defenceless men and women of all classes together with no small amount of domestic goods.

While in the field, raiders were self-sufficient, so supplies would not affect planning. Many raids may not have been planned or controlled by kings, but took place without their knowledge. Kings could at least claim this, even if it was not always true.[71]

Invasions were similarly badly planned. The frequent lack of a single leader made control and organization more difficult and it was only with a capable leader that any centralized activity could take place. Alamannic operations in the late 350s under Chnodomarius' leadership contrast markedly with the confused Gothic actions of the 370s–380s. Supply considerations were rarely taken into account and hardship was frequent in these situations.[72] These large attacks could also take place in winter. Thus Alaric crossed the Julian Alps and threatened Milan in winter 401, while the Vandals, Alans, and Suevi crossed the Rhine on the last day of 406.[73]

The development of stronger kingship in the fifth century meant that more planning took place before attacks on the Romans. The clashes between the Hun Empire and the Romans involved some planning, possibly because of Attila's autocratic position. In 451 Attila made a deliberate decision to attack the Western rather than the Eastern Empire since 'it seemed best for him first to undertake the greater war and march against the west', though his strategic objectives are unclear to us.[74]

Strategic Intelligence

The success or failure of attacks was often determined by the available intelligence. This intelligence could be extremely accurate. Rando's attack on Mainz in 368 took advantage of the absence of its garrison, as well as attacking on a Christian feast-day. Likewise good intelligence led to the attack on and siege of Julian at Sens

---

[71] AM 16. 12. 17; Rando, AM 27. 10. 1–2; Hyd. 192?
[72] RPF fr. 2.
[73] Winter attacks: for 401 see *Fast. Vind. Prior.* sa 401; Claudian, *De 6 Cons. Hon.* 442–4; for 406 see Prosp. 1230.
[74] Priscus fr. 20. 1; F. M. Clover, 'Geiseric and Attila', *Historia*, 22 (1973), 104–17, over-estimates the planning carried out by Attila.

in winter 356–7, when the Alamanni knew he had only a few troops
with him. In 409 Alaric was able to ambush 6,000 Romans marching
from Dalmatia into Italy, because he had already learnt of their
approach.[75] But where good intelligence was lacking, disasters could
occur. In 378 the Alamannic King Priarius organized an attack on
Gaul in the knowledge that Gratian and some of the field army
had left for Illyricum, but was caught by surprise when Gratian
returned to fight at Argentaria. And the failure of the Greuthungi
to discover Promotus' deception in 386 was catastrophic.[76]

There were several ways in which the barbarians could obtain
their intelligence. They used spies, though the professionalism of
some of these men was minimal, if the behaviour of a Gothic spy
in 391 is anything to go by: the Emperor Theodosius 'was lying in
a room of the lodgings when he saw a man who said nothing and
looked as if he wished to escape notice'. Information was often
received from Romans, usually civilian criminals or deserting soldiers, generally men facing punishment rather than hoping for a
better life with the barbarians. Information could also be transferred
through events of everyday life, since merchants crossed the frontier
regularly and there would also be frequent contact in the major
cities along the frontier. To be included in this category is the
information gained by Priarius and the Lentienses from an Alamannic soldier home on leave ('for business') in 378, though it
would seem unlikely that the Lentienses were not already aware of
the troop withdrawals. Lastly, envoys to the Romans for whatever
reasons could also collect information.[77]

Overall, barbarian intelligence seems good. J. F. Matthews has
suggested that 'there was little of importance that did not somehow
come to their attention'. However, the interpretation of information
received seems sometimes to have been at fault. There were no
mechanisms for checking intelligence and in some cases barbarians
acted on the first piece of information received. Thus the Frankish
raiders encountered by Severus in 357 thought the Romans were

---

[75] For Rando see AM 27. 10. 1–2; for Sens see AM 16. 4; for Alaric see Zos. 5.
45. 1–2; on 442 see Theoph. *AM* 5942; on 459 see Priscus fr. 36. 1.

[76] For 378 see AM 31. 10. 5–12; for 386 see Zos. 4. 38–9; for 440s see SA *Carm.*
5. 211–30; AM 17. 12. 4.

[77] On spies see Zos. 4. 31. 3, 48. 4–6; SA *Ep.* 4. 22. 3; on deserters see AM 16. 4.
1, 12. 2, 31. 7. 7; A. D. Lee, *Information and Frontiers* (Cambridge, 1993), 170–82;
on casual transfer see AM 27. 5. 2?, 31. 10. 3; Malchus fr. 11; on envoys suspected
of spying see Lib. *Or.* 18. 52–3.

still engaged with the Alamanni to their south and the Alamannic raiders of 378 also seemed surprised to meet Roman resistance and presumably thought that most Roman troops in the area had marched east.[78]

Supply

When barbarian raiders left their home territory, they ceased to be supplied with food from their homes and were dependent on what they carried with them initially and what they could find. Supply was rarely a problem for groups that kept moving and foraged in new areas, but a prolonged stay in the same area could lead to an eventual exhaustion of available forage. This in turn led to a reduction in the fighting ability of the barbarians because more time and manpower would be spent in foraging.[79] Barbarians often split up into numbers of smaller groups, covering a wider area and thus finding more food (and plunder). This dispersal would slow down their movement and would also make them vulnerable to defeat in detail, since barbarian command systems did not allow them to concentrate rapidly. However, dispersal also made it difficult for the Romans to inflict a convincing defeat on barbarian groups.[80]

Barbarians seem not to have suffered especially from supply shortages in raids occurring in winter. For a month in 356–7 Julian was besieged by some Alamanni at Sens while he was wintering there. This shows a capability of supplying men in winter in the same place for a month, though the surrounding area is mentioned as afterwards being denuded of food. The Franks that Julian besieged on the Meuse in 358 held out for fifty-four days, suggesting that they had a large amount of food with them. It was only when raiders were prevented from foraging that they suffered from starvation, otherwise they seem to have been able to support themselves from the land even in winter. Starvation was usually the result of Roman action, not natural shortages.[81]

The supply requirements of peoples on the move were somewhat

---

[78] Matthews, *Roman Empire*, 317; for hasty action see AM 17. 2. 1, 31. 10. 3–6.

[79] AM 16. 4. 4, 5. 17; Zos. 3. 7. 4; above, p. 53.

[80] AM 16. 2. 2, 7, 11. 3, 17. 12. 1, 19. 11. 1, 21. 3. 1, 27. 1. 1, 2. 1–2, 8. 7, 9, 31. 5. 8, 10. 21, 11. 4–5; Zos. 3. 7. 4; cf. Menander fr. 15. 2.

[81] On winter supply see AM 16. 4, 17. 2; on blockade, 416 see Olymp. fr. 29. 1; Jordanes, *Getica*, 281.

different. Any supply problems faced were greatly exacerbated as a result of the large numbers in these groups. Like raiders they were usually dependent on foraging, though this could be eked out by using their accompanying livestock as food supplies. Because of their high rate of food consumption they found it more difficult than raiding parties to remain in the same place for a long time. Supply problems probably account for Radagaisus' division of his army into three parts in 406. On some occasions these peoples were able to supplement foraging by purchase from local inhabitants or merchants, as the Visigoths did in 416, at least until Constantius blockaded them. Normally, livestock, forage, and purchase were sufficient for supply, even in winter—Alaric invaded Italy in winter 401 with no apparent supply problems. But if the Romans could impose a blockade on the barbarians then serious shortages could occur.[82]

On the March

Raiding parties were lightly loaded and fast moving. Some Goths and Alamanni are known to have carried tents, but with no body armour overall loads were lighter than those of Roman troops. They usually remained dispersed, but often concentrated if a Roman army entered the area. As they acquired booty these groups would move more slowly, and were on occasion caught by the Romans because of their reduced speed.[83]

The main characteristics of migratory peoples were the large number of wagons carrying their possessions, children, seed corn, etc., and the herds of sheep, cattle, and other animals. During the 470s, an Ostrogothic wagon train in the Balkans contained 2,000 wagons. The number of wagons and their inherent low speed meant that these groups had little freedom of manœuvre. Sometimes attempts were made to escape from this restriction, as in 479 when Theoderic the Amal detached the wagon train from his army in an

---

[82] For merchants see Malchus fr. 25; cf. Maximus of Turin, *Sermo* 18. 3; AM 31. 4. 11; Orosius 7. 43. 1; on foraging see AM 31. 6. 5; Claudian, *De 6 Cons. Hon.* 239–241; Malchus fr. 18. 4, 20. 35–42.

[83] On speed of movement see AM 16. 11. 14; on tents see AM 27. 2. 9, 31. 15. 15; on being slowed by booty see Zos. 4. 23. 4; AM 27. 8. 7, 29. 6. 12; Sulpicius fr. 1; Priscus fr. 9. 3. 39–53?; on reconcentrating see AM 31. 7. 7; smoke signals were used in other periods, e.g. by Magyars in 933, 'more suo igne fumoque ingenti agmina diffusa collegerunt', Widukind, *Res Gestae Saxonicae*, 1. 38, a reference I owe to C. Leyser, 'The Battle at the Lech, 955', *History*, 50 (1965), 1–25 at 16.

attempt to capture Lychidnus and the neighbouring towns by surprise. If he had been accompanied by a wagon train, news of his arrival would probably have preceded him.[84]

We know little of the march formations used in this period, though we hear of scouts, advance guards (sometimes of cavalry), and divisions into multiple bodies. Rearguards are almost unknown. Armies tended to remain concentrated as one body when in the vicinity of the enemy and we do not hear of barbarian forces splitting up for strategic purposes, though detachments might be thrown out for foraging or scouting purposes. They seem rarely to have imitated the Roman practice of building a camp at night, perhaps because of a lack of the required tools, though examples are known of fortified barbarian camps in 395, 451, and 491.[85]

River crossing

Entering the Roman Empire involved crossing the Rhine or the Danube in most cases, at least until settlements were made in the Empire. Movement within the Empire frequently necessitated river crossings too. The Danube and Rhine often froze, presenting few problems in crossing. According to the Admiralty in 1945, 'it is rare for it [the Danube] to freeze twice in one winter, and in exceptionally mild winters it may not freeze at all'. The frozen Danube appears regularly in poetry and Mauricius' *Strategikon* in the sixth century assumes that rivers in the region usually froze in winter. Freezing was most severe on the upper reaches of the Danube. The Rhine also froze occasionally, though not, as far as is recorded, in 406 or at any other time between 350 and 425. Even today, the upper Rhine can freeze in winter, leading to lower water levels in the lower Rhine, though it is now less prone to freezing as it is canalized and thus flows even faster than in antiquity.[86]

Fords could be used to cross rivers, especially when they were

---

[84] Malchus fr. 20. 113–16, 226–32.

[85] For advance guard see AM 31. 3. 5; Malchus fr. 20. 102–4; for three divisions see AM 17. 12. 7; Malchus fr. 20. 110–13; for rearguard see Malchus fr. 20. 230; for camps see Claudian, *In Rufinum*, 2. 127–9; Jordanes, *Getica*, 210; *Anon. Val.* 54?

[86] Prone to freeze: see Herodian, 6. 7. 6–7; AM 16. 1. 5, 27. 6. 12; Jordanes, *Getica*, 280; Lee, *Information and Frontiers*, 95–8; for Danube see Admiralty Handbook, Naval Intelligence Division, *Yugoslavia* (London, 1945), iii., 452–78; AM 17. 12. 4, 19. 11. 4; for Rhine see AM 31. 10. 4 but text is lacunose; Admiralty Handbook, Naval Intelligence Division, *France* (London, 1942), iv. 404–8; I know of no ancient evidence for the Rhine freezing in 406 and Gibbon says only 'most probably frozen'.

running low. Today the Danube runs low in summer above Belgrade, in autumn below it, while flooding in spring and summer. The Rhine tends to be low in late summer and early autumn, a pattern followed by most smaller rivers. These patterns were probably similar in antiquity.[87] Other crossings were accomplished by boats, usually if the crossing forces lived in the area. Thus some Alamanni crossed the Rhine by boat after the battle of Strasbourg in 357.[88] Crossings could also be improvised. This might involve rafts and rough log-built boats, as in 386 when the Greuthungi attempted to cross the Danube. Rivers could also be swum, as during the rout after the battle of Strasbourg.[89]

Tactical intelligence

The sophistication of barbarian tactical intelligence varied widely. Many barbarian groups were attacked by surprise, which suggests that their scouts (if any) had not detected the Romans. At Adrianople the Goths did not expect to engage the Romans and so their cavalry was absent foraging. Even when barbarians were being engaged by the Romans they were not always able to discover what the Romans were doing: at Solicinium in 368 the Alamanni did not detect a Roman flanking march until it reached their rear areas.[90]

On the other hand, barbarians carried out a number of successful ambushes against Roman forces. In 356 a marching column of Romans was ambushed at a crossroads by Alamannic raiders and in 409 6,000 Romans were defeated by Ataulf in Italy; as there were only 100 Roman survivors this was probably an ambush. This suggests there was some successful scouting and barbarian scouts are frequently attested.[91] Barbarian groups seem rarely to have got lost or been trapped in (as opposed to being forced into) unfavourable terrain. This may have been partly the result of obtaining Roman guides, for example the gold miners who led some Goths

[87] AM 16. 11. 9, 17. 13. 27.
[88] AM 16. 11. 9, 12. 58, 17. 13. 17, 31. 4. 5; Them. *Or.* 10. 137A.
[89] For rafts see AM 31. 4. 5; Zos. 5. 21. 2–4; Priscus fr. 11. 2. 275–6; for log dugouts (μονοξυλοι), see AM 17. 13. 27, 31. 4. 5; Zos. 4. 38. 5–39. 3; Priscus fr. 11. 2. 71–6, 273–5; on swimming see Zos. 4. 39. 3; AM 16. 12. 55–7, 17. 13. 15, 31. 4. 5.
[90] Zos. 3. 7. 2, 4. 23. 4, 25. 2; AM 17. 8. 3, 27. 2. 1–3, 31. 11. 4; SA *Carm.* 5. 211–30.
[91] On barbarian ambushes see AM 28. 2. 8; Zos. 4. 31. 3–4, 4. 49. 1–2, 5. 45. 1–2; Lib. *Or.* 18. 45; Sulpicius fr. 1, 6; Mauricius, *Strat.* 11. 4. 9; on scouts see Malchus fr. 18. 3. 40; AM 16. 11. 9, 12. 19.

in Thrace in 377. It is probable that the varying levels of scouting effectiveness reflected the ability of the barbarian leaders.[92]

At its best, the ability of barbarians to know what was going on was impressive and forced the Romans to take special measures to surprise or even engage barbarians. Roman expeditions were often forced to reach into the uplands since barbarians could remove themselves, their families, and possessions from the initial Roman area of operations. Barbarians could predict attacks and their objectives. They probably accepted this as part of the 'game'.

Tactics

Barbarians preferred to avoid pitched battles against the Romans as much as possible. Their almost invariable defeat when engaged in open battle makes this understandable. Even before Adrianople there was a great reluctance to fight on the part of the Goths; they did not expect to win. If a pitched battle had to be fought the barbarians tried to negate Roman superiority in open battle. One way of doing this was by fighting in difficult terrain such as mountains, forests, and marshes. This would reduce the Roman advantages of planning and control and made the use of cavalry and missile weapons by the Romans difficult or even impossible, turning the struggle into a series of hand-to-hand combats. The difficulties presented by the terrain were sometimes increased by deliberately blocking paths with fallen trees, a tactic not confined to battles in home territory. The advantages of fighting in difficult terrain can be seen by the frequent Roman refusal to fight in such conditions, and occasional defeats if they did so, such as the annihilation of a Roman force pursuing Franks into marshes in 388.

At first light [the Romans] marched out into the woods, with Quintinus to lead them in battle. By about mid-day they had lost themselves completely in a maze of pathways and had no idea where they were. They ran up against an endless barricade solidly constructed from huge tree-trunks and then they tried to break out over the marshy fields which bordered the forests. Here and there enemy troops showed themselves, standing on the boles of trees or climbing about the barricades as if on the parapets of turrets ... Then the Roman army, now surrounded by the main force of the enemy, rushed desperately into the open meadows, which the Franks

[92] AM 31. 6. 5–7; Zos. 1. 31, 34. 2.

had left unoccupied. There the cavalry was bogged down in marshland and the bodies of men and animals, all mixed up together, were borne to the ground in one common catastrophe.[93]

When a battle was fought, most barbarians usually formed up in a line ('by tribes, kinship, and common interest': φυλαί, συγγήνεια, προσταθεία). Cavalry deployed on the flanks of the infantry. If there was a convenient hill the battle line would be drawn up on it. Missile troops could be deployed in front of the main line and some preliminary skirmishing usually took place before the main body of the enemy was engaged.[94] If deployed on a hill, barbarians would wait until the enemy came close before charging. Their attack usually took the form of a fierce charge, occasionally in wedge formation (*cunei*), accompanied by a loud war cry. Though crude, the charge's shock value could lead to victory. But if the charge failed, superior Roman training and protection tended to win the prolonged mêlée.[95] Cavalry could be used offensively and they played this role at Adrianople. On other occasions, cavalry was used simply to protect the flanks of the infantry. They appeared on the Alamannic left flank at Strasbourg and were given close support by light infantry. This practice could have been followed by other tribes. Cavalry might also dismount to fight, though they are not attested as doing this in our period. Steppe peoples preferred to fight in a looser formation, continually harassing their enemies with barrages of missiles and avoiding hand-to-hand combat.[96] A

[93] On fighting in difficult terrain see Sulpicius fr. 1; AM 17. 1. 8, 27. 10. 9, 31. 10. 12–16; Zos. 3. 6. 3, 4. 11. 2, 45. 3; Eunapius fr. 55; Them. *Or.* 10. 137; cf. Herodian 7. 2. 5–6; Theophylact, *Hist.* 6. 8. 10–11; Mauricius, *Strat.* 11. 4. 13; on obstructing cavalry see cf. Zos. 5. 15. 5; Frontinus, *Stratagems*, 2. 3. 23; on obstacles see AM 16. 11. 8, 12. 15, 17. 1. 9, 10. 6; Sulpicius fr. 1; cf. GT *HF* 3. 28; on Roman refusal to engage see AM 16. 12. 59, 17. 1. 8; Anon., *DRB* 19. 2; on Roman defeats see Sulpicius fr. 1; cf. Zos. 1. 23. 2–3.

[94] On tactics see H. G. Gundel, *Untersuchungen zur Taktik und Strategie der Germanen nach den antiken Quellen* (Marburg, 1937), 1–60; on deployment see Mauricius, *Strat.* 11. 3. 4; Anon. *PS* 34; for cavalry on flanks see AM 16. 12, 31. 12; on defending hills see AM 17. 1. 5, 27. 10. 9, 31. 7. 10; Sulpicius fr. 6; on skirmishers see AM 16. 12. 36, 27. 1. 3, 31. 7. 12, 10. 8.

[95] For speed of attack see AM 16. 12. 36, 27. 1. 4, 10. 13, 29. 6. 14, 31. 2. 8, 5. 9; Lib. *Or.* 69. 130; Urbicius, *Epitedeuma* 7; Mauricius, *Strat.* 11. 3. 3, 6; for wedges see AM 16. 12. 20, 31. 2. 8; Agathias, *Hist.* 2. 8. 8–9; Mauricius, *Strat.* 11. 2. 14; for war cry see AM 17. 13. 10, 19. 11. 10, 31. 7. 11, 13. 10. 8, 13. 12. 11.

[96] On offensive cavalry see AM 31. 12. 17; on defensive see AM 16. 12. 21–2, 37–42; on light infantry, cf. Caesar, *De Bello Gallico* 1. 48; Veg. 3. 16; on dismounting, cf. AM 16. 12. 34; Mauricius, *Strat.* 11. 2. 19; for steppe peoples see AM 31. 2. 8–9; Mauricius, *Strat.* 11. 2. 15–31.

cutting edge to the army could be provided by grouping *optimates* and their *comitatus* together into a single unit. On account of their experience and concentration of better weaponry and armour they would give the Romans a much harder fight than the normal troops. Royal *comitatus* would have the same effect.[97]

When fighting occurred in difficult terrain the barbarians could use ambushes. The surprise effect of an ambush might shake the Romans and give the barbarians a greater chance of breaking them. At Strasbourg in 357 part of the Alamannic right wing was anchored on a canal or drainage channel, where troops were in ambush in the reeds and in ditches dug specially.[98] The extensive wagon trains of migratory people were used as bases for fighting and as refuges for women, children, livestock, etc. Such wagon laagers were used at Ad Salices in 377 and Adrianople in 378. They were also used by the Goths to fortify their camp (along with a ditch and palisade) in Greece in 395 and by the Huns at the Catalaunian Plains in 451.[99]

Barbarians seem to have been reluctant to attack or march at night, probably a reflection on their poor command skills and lack of formal organization.[100] Though the tactics used were simple there was no realistic alternative. Barbarian command systems were not sufficiently sophisticated to be able to control more than a single body of soldiers. The use of reserves, as opposed to a second line of troops, is unattested.[101]

F: SIEGE ABILITY

Barbarian siege ability was limited, though their capabilities should not be ignored. If confronted with walls, barbarians would often sit around outside for a few days, then give up in disgust. At the

[97] AM 16. 12. 49.

[98] Zos. 4. 22. 2; AM 15. 4. 7–8, 16. 12. 23 and 27, 17. 1. 6 and 8, 28. 2. 8, 30. 3. 7; Sulpicius fr. 1, 6; Lib. *Or.* 18. 56; Mauricius, *Strat.* 11. 4. 9; H. G. Gundel, 'Die Bedeutung des Geländes in der Kriegkunst der Germanen', *Neue Jahrbücher für Antike und Deutsche Bildung*, 3 (1940), 188–96; cf. Frontinus, *Stratagems*, 1. 3. 10.

[99] AM 31. 2. 18, 7. 5 (377), 12. 11, 15. 5 (378); Claudian, *In Rufinum*, 2. 127–9; Theophylact, *Hist.* 7. 2. 4–9 (Slav); Jordanes, *Getica*, 210; Veg. 3. 10; Urbicius, *Epitedeuma*, 14.

[100] Marc. Com. sa 493 could be an exception, but we do not know who initiated the battle; AM 31. 3. 6 may not be reliable; Mauricius, *Strat.* 11. 4. 9; Lib. *Or.* 18. 43.

[101] AM 16. 12. 49.

siege of Sens, 'at last on the thirtieth day the barbarians sadly departed, muttering that they were stupid and foolish to have contemplated the siege of a city'. This sort of inability led Fritigern, a Gothic leader, to remind his men that he was 'at peace with walls'. Even after their victory outside Adrianople in 378, the Goths were unable to capture the city, despite several attempts, and after a few days moved elsewhere. When barbarians did undertake sieges, they were long. The Huns besieged Aquileia for three months in 452 and Theoderic spent three years besieging Ravenna from 490.[102] This inability to capture walled sites, whether military forts or defended urban centres, was common to all barbarians. There were two main reasons for their lack of success: lack of technical expertise and logistical inadequacy.

As a rule, barbarians did not know how to build or use sophisticated machinery such as siege towers or catapults. The limit of their achievement was scaling ladders and battering rams, crude devices, though occasionally effective. These could be quickly improvised from trees, and in the third century we hear of the walls of Trapezus being scaled by improvised ladders made from trees. Countermeasures to these weapons, in the form of large ditches or moats and recessed, angled, or enfiladed gateways were simple and were present on most Roman fortified sites.[103] However, on a very few occasions barbarians involved in sieges did have more sophisticated equipment such as siege towers. In the third century the Goths used siege equipment in the sieges of Thessalonica, Philippopolis, and Side, but in both the fourth and fifth centuries such equipment is rarely recorded. In the mid-sixth century, at the siege of Rome, Goths again used siege towers. Trans-Rhenane barbarians in the third century are supposed to have used siege towers as well, but are not recorded as having such devices in the fourth or fifth centuries. In all these cases the barbarian siege equipment was ineptly used.[104]

---

[102] On siege inability see Thompson, *Early Germans*, 131–40 and *Romans and Barbarians*, 6–10; AM 16. 4. 1–2, 11. 4, 17. 6. 1, 29. 6. 12, 30. 3. 3, 31. 6. 4, 15. 15; GT *HF* 2. 7; Eugippius, *V.Sev.* 30. 3; Priscus fr. 39. 21–4; for outside Europe see AM 14. 2. 13, 28. 6. 15.

[103] On scaling ladders see Lib. *Or.* 18. 43; AM 31. 15. 13; Priscus fr. 6. 2; improvised, see Zos. 1. 33. 2; on battering rams see GT *HF* 2. 7; Priscus fr. 6. 2.

[104] Siege capability: for 3rd cent. see Eusebius, fr. 2. 2, 5; Dexippus, fr. 20, 22; for 6th cent. see Theophylact, *Hist.* 2. 16. 10–11; Procopius, *BG* 5. 21. 3–13, 24. 4, 6. 9. 12, 12. 1–5, 8. 35. 9; Agathias, *Hist.* 1. 9.

The only occasion in the fourth and fifth centuries where barbarians seem to have acquired significant siege technology was
during Attila's domination of the Huns. The Huns used siege
equipment at Naissus in 442, including shields to protect archers
and battering rams. This equipment was not of great sophistication
and it would only slightly increase the ability of barbarians to
attack towns. However, it did allow Naissus to be stormed. Similar
siege equipment was used at Aquileia in 452. This ability seems to
have been lost after Attila's death and it is not until the time of
the Avar Chagan Baian that Danubian barbarians again demonstrated a strong capability in siege warfare.[105]

It seems unlikely that some barbarians had the knowledge of
how to build siege equipment but used it only during limited
periods. It seems more likely that this equipment was built by
Roman prisoners or deserters, as happened at the siege of Vetera
during Civilis' revolt in AD 70. This hypothesis would account for
its rarity of use and tactical misdeployment. Without this equipment
the chances of storming a defended site were low and instances
of garrisoned Roman sites being successfully assaulted are very
rare.[106]

The second problem faced by barbarians was logistical inadequacy. Since they could not storm fortified sites they were compelled to starve them out. For this they had to have supplies for
the length of the siege. But if besiegers remained in the same place
for any length of time, the countryside would soon be stripped bare
of forage. This shortage would be exacerbated by the Roman
practice of removing as much foodstuff as possible into their forts.
In addition, by remaining in the same area to blockade a site, the
barbarians made it more likely that they would be attacked by a
Roman relieving force since their location would be known. Such
an attack could be especially effective if some of the barbarians
were dispersed around the countryside in foraging parties. This

---

[105] Naissus, Priscus, fr. 6. 2; however, see the cautionary note of A. D. E. and A.
M. Cameron, 'Christianity and Tradition in the Historiography of the Late Empire',
CQ NS 14 (1964), 316–28 at 321–2; K. Tausend, 'Hunnische Poliorketik', *Gräzer
Beiträge*, 12–13 (1985–6), 265–81; R. C. Blockley, 'Dexippus, Priscus and the
Thucydidean Account of the Siege of Plataea', *Phoenix*, 26 (1972), 18–27; E. A.
Thompson, 'Priscus of Panium, fr. 1b', *CQ* 39 (1945), 92–4; on Aquileia see Priscus,
fr. 22. 1; cf. siege of Arcadiopolis, Malchus fr. 2.

[106] On Vetera see Tacitus, *Histories*, 4. 23; Theophylact, *Hist.* 2. 16. 10; on
storming see AM 15. 8. 19 *reseratam* seems unlikely; Naissus, Priscus fr. 6. 2.

probably helps account for the defeat of Radagaisus while besieging Florence in 406.

Because of the lack of siege equipment, blockade was the usual way for barbarians to capture cities. To be able to operate a successful blockade the wall circuit had to be watched and the defenders stopped from obtaining supplies. Small groups of barbarians would be unable to do this successfully, leading to ineffective sieges such as that of Clermont in the 470s, a city which seems never to have been seriously invested or attacked. In 473 Arcadiopolis fell to Theoderic Triarius: 'He took the city not by storm but through severe starvation which wore down those within. For, as they held out in the hope that help would come to them from some quarter, they ate horses, pack animals, and corpses, and only despaired when this did not arrive.'[107] But there were other means of capturing fortified sites—treachery, ruse, surprise, or infiltration. Thus in 441 the bishop of Margus betrayed the city to the Huns. Treachery was usually carried out by disaffected civilians rather than by military personnel.[108] One example of barbarians trying to capture a city by ruse is in 378. Here the Goths sent Roman deserters into Adrianople, in an unsuccessful attempt to provide a diversion while they themselves attacked the gates.[109] Surprise attacks were sometimes successful, focusing on the gates of the city, since these tended to be the weakest point. In 479, Theoderic the Amal successfully surprised the defenders of Nova Epirus by his swift advance and the city fell.[110] Cities might be taken by infiltration if a concealed entrance could be found or if it were possible for barbarians to enter the city in disguise. This is not attested in Europe in this period, but in the sixth century some of the Goths besieging Rome tried to infiltrate through an aqueduct.[111]

The effectiveness of barbarian siege techniques is shown by Alaric's attempts to capture Rome. Between 408 and 410 Alaric laid siege to the city of Rome three times. He was unsuccessful

---

[107] Blockaded cities: for Arcadiopolis see Malchus fr. 2; Philost. 12. 3; for Cologne see AM 15. 8. 19.

[108] On civilian treachery see Priscus fr. 6. 1; Soz. 9. 9; Hyd. 201, 246; Olymp. fr. 11. 1, 3; on military treachery see AM 31. 15. 8–9.

[109] AM 31. 15. 8–9; Hyd. 115?

[110] Malchus fr. 20. 102–9, 113–16; AM 16. 11. 4; Julianus, *Historia Wambae*, 12, 18; on gates, AM 16. 11. 4; Lib. *Or.* 18. 43; Malchus fr. 20. 102–9.

[111] On infiltration see AM 19. 5. 5, 28. 2. 13; for Rome see Procopius, *BG* 6. 9. 1–11.

once, but was able to force negotiations with the senate; he was able to force Rome to capitulate once by a fortuitous capture of vital foodstuffs; and he was allowed into the city once through treachery. He was never able to storm it.[112] Although the above arguments make it clear that barbarians had great difficulties in capturing towns, there were occasions when barbarians apparently captured large numbers of cities. Examples are the Alamannic attacks of the early 350s, the invasion of Gaul in 406, and the Hun raids on the Balkans in the 440s. But our sources rarely tell us how the cities fell. It seems unlikely that the captured towns were garrisoned and it is probable that many of the towns were unwalled or ungarrisoned. Of the eight towns listed by St Jerome as falling to the attackers of 406, two (Arras and Speyer) seem not to have been walled and we do not know if any were garrisoned.[113]

Confirmation of the weakness of barbarian siege capability can be provided in two ways. One is the destruction of captured town or fort walls by barbarians. This occurred in Africa in the fifth century and in Italy in the sixth century. Our (Roman) sources justify this on the grounds of the difficulties the barbarians might face if the Romans recaptured them. It is difficult to think of another reason.[114] Secondly, the Romans continued to build and use fortified sites, throughout the fourth and fifth centuries, suggesting that they considered the effort expended in building them was worthwhile.

G: NAVAL WARFARE

Barbarian naval activity was confined to raids, usually of a few ships delivering a raiding party to Roman territory. Ships gave raiders greater mobility than on land, but the process of raiding was otherwise similar. This mobility allowed Saxons to raid as far as the Atlantic coast and Franks and Heruli as far as Spain. Britain

---

[112] Rome: unsuccessful, Nov.–Dec. 408, see Zos. 5. 38–42; on capitulation, late 410, see Zos. 6. 6; Olymp. fr. 10; Philost. 12. 3; on treachery see Olymp. fr. 11. 1, 3.

[113] Jerome, *Ep.* 123. 16.

[114] Thompson, *Romans and Barbarians*, 84–6; Procopius, *BV* 3. 5. 8, 3. 16. 9, *BG* 7. 6. 1, 8. 10–11, 7. 11. 32, 7. 22. 7, 7. 23. 3, 24. 29 and 32–3, 25. 7 and 11; Jul. *Ep. ad Ath.* 279A.

also suffered from Saxon raids. No barbarian naval activity is known from the Black Sea region. It was not until the establishment of barbarian kingdoms in the Empire, especially that of the Vandals in Africa, that the Romans faced a significant barbarian naval threat in the Mediterranean.[115]

The boats used by barbarians living by the North Sea were probably similar to the clinker-built longboats of Scandinavia, such as the contemporary Nydam boat, as well as the similar Sutton Hoo (seventh-century) and Gokstad (ninth-century) ships. These longboats were oar driven, having no keels and thus probably no mast, although Sidonius suggests that Saxon ships had sails. Such longboats had a shallow draught and could manœuvre in shallow waters and up rivers, as well as being easy to beach. We do not know whether these boats could carry horses, though the eighth-century vessels recorded in *Beowulf* could, suggesting that small numbers might have been transported at this period. The boats used by the Scotti to raid Britain were probably similar.[116]

H: DEVELOPMENT

As a whole, barbarian warfare changed little during this period. Those changes that did occur seem only to have made armies more organized, but not able to do what they could not do before. Political developments made larger armies more common, but tactical sophistication and individual equipment hardly changed. There seems to have been little need for Roman generals to change the way in which they fought battles, and the tactics of Julian and Constantius II in the 350s would have served the armies of Romulus Augustulus and Anastasius almost as well. What Herodian wrote in the third century was applicable to the fourth and fifth centuries

[115] Naval raids: for Saxons see Vegetius 4. 37; Claudian, *De Cons. Stil.* 2. 247–55; GT *HF* 2. 18, 19; SA *Ep.* 8. 6; for Franks see *Pan. Lat.* 10(4). 17. 1; for Heruli see Hyd. 171, 194.

[116] On boats see O. Crumlin-Pedersen, 'The Boats and Ships of the Angles and Jutes', in S. McGrail, ed., *Maritime Celts, Frisians and Saxons*, CBA *Research Report* 71 (London, 1990), 98–116; J. Haywood, *Dark Age Naval Power* (London, 1991); R. Hodges, *Dark Age Economics* (London, 1982), 94–7; on Nydam boat see H. Shettig, 'Das Nydamschiff', *Acta Archaeologia Copenhagen*, 1 (1930), 1–30; SA *Ep.* 8. 6. 15; Procopius, *BG* 8. 20. 31; Scotti, Alcock, *Arthur's Britain*, 265–6; for horses see *Beowulf*, 1896–8.

and could as easily have been written by Procopius in the sixth.

Barbarians are bold when others retreat or hesitate, but put up a very different fight if met by resistance. The reason for this is that it is not from set battles that they expect success against an enemy. They believe it is from hit and run tactics that they gain what plunder they get. We [Romans] believe in properly disciplined battle tactics and we have learned to defeat them every time.[117]

[117] Herodian 6. 3. 7.

3

Roman Organization, Arms, and Equipment

A: ORGANIZATION

The late Roman armed forces were divided into two parts, the field army troops (*comitatenses*) and the border troops (*limitanei*), which both had land and marine components. This section examines the organization of both groups together with various support services and militias.[1]

The comitatenses

The basic unit of the field army was the regiment. Infantry regiments were *legiones* or *auxilia*, cavalry regiments *vexillationes*. These technical terms are preserved in the *Notitia Dignitatum*. In other sources regiments were also referred to as *numeri*, ἀριθμοί, κατάλογοι, τάγματα, or τάξεις. Many references to military units are to 'legions', 'maniples', or 'cohorts' and have as much, if not more, to do with style and metre as technical usage. Regiments existed permanently and a number of units are attested both in the *Notitia Dignitatum* and under Justinian.[2] The evidence for the size of these units is limited. What there is suggests that establishments for *vexillationes* were c.600 strong, and establishments for *auxilia* and *legiones* c.1200. On the other hand, many recorded strengths were somewhat lower: c.400 for cavalry and c.800 for infantry regiments might have been normal. There appear to have been no major changes in unit sizes between 350 and 425. Regiments were commanded by a

---

[1] *LRE*, ch. 17, remains indispensable, as do R. Grosse, *Römische Militärgeschichte* (Berlin, 1920) and D. Hoffmann, *Das spätrömische Bewegungsheer und die Notitia Dignitatum* (Düsseldorf, 1969).
[2] For unit descriptions see A. D. E. Cameron and A. M. Cameron, 'Christianity and Tradition in the Historiography of the Late Empire', *CQ* NS 14 (1964), 316–28 at 326; e.g. AM 17. 13. 10 (*cohors praetoria*), 18. 8. 2 (*turma* for cavalry regiment), 25. 6. 3; cf. Zos. 6. 8. 2, τάγματα; Soz. 9. 8. 6, ἀριθμοί, both drawing on Olympiodorus; on continuity see *LRE* 654–5.

tribune, who could also be referred to as a *praepositus*.[3]

In addition to the fighting personnel, a number of 'service' troops were attached to army regiments, such as doctors, chaplains, and staff-officers. We know virtually nothing about military medical services save the fact that they existed. In the sixth century doctors were attached to regiments and this practice probably existed earlier.[4] Regimental chaplains are first heard of in the mid-fifth century in the East, though they may have appeared earlier, with Sozomen suggesting they were part of every regiment from the time of Constantine onwards. They probably replaced pagan priests (who may not have been attached to regiments), though these still appeared occasionally in connection with the army: Litorius consulted soothsayers in 439 before attacking the Visigoths at Toulouse.[5] The regimental staff would have kept the voluminous amounts of paperwork the army produced. We know that individual soldiers had enrolment papers (*probatoriae*) and dogtags (*bullae*) and that units had troop rosters and theoretically produced daily ration indents.[6]

[3] On cavalry *vexillationes* see AM 18. 8. 2 (359), 2 *turmae* totalling 700; Zos. 3. 3. 4 (Julian), ἴλη of 600, probably one unit, though AM 16. 12. 38 suggests that more than one regiment was involved; *P. Cairo*, 67321 (Justinian), *Numidae Justiniani* 508 strong; concerning infantry, there appears to be no difference between *legiones* and *auxilia*; on levies of 300 from units see AM 20. 4. 2 (360), 31. 11. 2 (378); on levies of 500 from legions see AM 31. 10. 13 (378); Zos. 5. 45. 1 (409), 5 τάγματα totalling 6,000; F. Paschoud, *Zosime* (Paris, 1986), v. 292 n. 102, considers them cavalry but does not explain why; Zos. 6. 8. 2 (410), 6 τάγματα totalling 4,000 = Soz. 9. 8. 6, 6 ἀριθμοί of 4,000; cf. Malalas 330, 1,500 scouts from Lanciarii and Mattiarii in 363; on 398 campaign vs. Gildo, 3 *legiones palatinae*, 3 *auxilia palatina*, see Claudian, *de Bello Gildonico*, 418–23; 5,000 men, Orosius 7. 36. 6; *auxilia* units could have been 600 strong using the same evidence; cf. AM 19. 2. 14, 7 legions and population of Amida totalled 20,000; *LRE* 680–2; R. MacMullen, 'How Big was the Roman Imperial Army', *Klio*, 62 (1980), 451–60; R. P. Duncan-Jones, *Structure and Scale in the Roman Economy* (Cambridge, 1990), 105–17, 214–17; for command see Grosse, 143–50.

[4] For medics see Veg. 3. 2; Ausonius, *Grat. Act.* 17; AM 16. 6. 2, 19. 2. 15, 25. 3. 7, 30. 6. 4–5; *ILS* 7797?; later, see Mauricius, *Strat.* 2. 9; *P. Monac.* 9; cf. *PLRE* i, Apsyrtus, Arcadius 2?; Procopius, *BG* 6. 2. 25–32.

[5] On chaplains see Cyril of Scythopolis, *V. Sabae* 9; Soz. 1. 8; Theoderet, *Ep.* 2; *P. Nessana* 35; A. H. M. Jones, 'Military Chaplains in the Roman Army', *Harvard Theological Review*, 46 (1953), 249–50; on pagans see Prosp. 1335.

[6] For *probatoriae* (enlistment papers) see *CJ* 12. 35. 17 (472); for dogtags see *Acta Maximiliani*, 2. 6; for tattoos see Veg 1. 8, 2. 5; *Acta Maximiliani*, 1. 5; *CT* 10. 22. 4 (398); Aug. *C. Ep. Parm.* 2. 29; Ambrose, *De Ob. Val.* 58; C. P. Jones, '*Stigma*: Tattooing and Branding in Graeco-Roman Antiquity', *JRS* 77 (1987), 139–55 at 149; for troop rosters see AM 18. 5. 1; Evagrius, *HE* 2. 1; Procopius, *BV* 4. 16. 3; Zos. 4. 31. 1; *CT* 6. 24. 2 (365), 5 (393); for ration indents see *CT* 7. 4. 13

Many infantry and cavalry regiments operated in pairs, forming a brigade under the command of a *comes*. These brigades seem to have been permanent entities, though no trace survives of any brigade staffs. The brigade of the Celtae and Petulantes served in Gaul with Julian, then marched east with him to Persia. They returned to the West, probably under Valentinian I, and fought in Raetia in 378. According to the *Notitia* they were in the Italian field army in the early fifth century. In the *Notitia* they are recorded next to each other, suggesting that this reflects their tactical relationship. Mentions of a single regiment from a brigade acting alone are rare. There are no cases in Ammianus' narrative where brigades are definitely split and though regiments are occasionally recorded without their partners, there is no reason to assume that the other regiment was not in the area. New units could be raised as a brigade or singly. These brigades seem to have fallen out of use by the sixth century, though a brigade of *scholae* may be recorded in 478. However, the μοῖραι described by Mauricius, consisting of several τάγματα, may be their successors.[7]

As well as Roman units, the *comitatenses* included regiments of barbarians. Contemporary terminology used to describe the various barbarian groups who fought for the Romans is confusing. The difficulties are compounded by changes in the meanings of the words used over the period studied. The troops described here as *foederati* had acquired this title by the sixth century, before which it was applied to the group referred to here as 'allies'. By Justinian's time the term σύμμαχοι was being used for the allies, though in the fourth and fifth centuries it may have been used to describe the

(365); for lodging rosters see Procopius, *BV* 3. 21. 10; R. Watson, 'Documentation in the Roman Army', *ANRW* 2/1 (Berlin, 1974), 493–507; for other records see Veg. 2. 5, 7, 19; Eunapius fr. 84.

[7] For brigades see Zos. 2. 42. 2; AM 20. 2. 5?, 21. 3. 2, 27. 1. 2; Malalas 330; Malchus fr. 18. 4 (otherwise why two *scholae*?); Hoffmann, 11–15, 384–6, 505–7, ch. 10 n. 181, but caution is necessary using his reconstructions since some (13–14) depend on the shield emblems which cannot be used as evidence; for discussion of shield emblems see R. Grigg, 'Inconsistency and Lassitude: the Shield Emblems of the *Notitia Dignitatum*', *JRS* 73 (1983), 132–42; R. S. O. Tomlin, '*Seniores-Iuniores* in the Late Roman Field Army', *AJP* 93 (1972), 253–78, app. 5; for Celtae-Petulantes see AM 20. 4. 2, 21. 3. 2, 22. 12. 6, 31. 10. 4; Jul. *Ep. ad Ath.* 282D; *ND* Occ. 5. 160–1, 7. 11–12; for details of other brigades see Hoffmann, under unit name; for regiments without partners, as reserves, see AM 16. 12. 45, 27. 10. 10, 31. 13. 9; on leading tunnel assault see AM 24. 4. 3; on boat raid see AM 16. 11. 9; on μοῖραι see Mauricius, *Strat.* 1. 4. 2, 12. 8. 8 and 11.

units here called *foederati*. These terms were never used dogmatically by contemporaries and descriptions of groups as *foederati* or allies need not be prescriptive. In some circumstances the terms might even be synonymous. *Foederati* was not a technical term with only one definition and there is no need to expect all *foederati* or allies to have identical relations with the Romans, or for their relations to remain identical over time. The definitions here are made on the basis of status and activity, not the terms used to describe them. Even so, great uncertainty remains.[8]

During the late fourth and fifth centuries *foederati* regiments were permanently established units of the Roman army, paid and equipped by the government (Table 1). They may have differed visually from regular Roman regiments, but if so, we do not know how. For the most part they were deliberately recruited from barbarians and seem to have had an intense *esprit de corps*. Olympiodorus in the early fifth century describes them as mixed Romans and barbarians. Some units are identifiable because they had an ethnic identity—the Saracens used against the Goths in 378, the Alans in the 401–2 campaign, or the Huns led by Olympius in 409. This ethnic identity was the result of their recent recruitment and would have become weaker over time as casualties were replaced by men of different origins. Once any special character was lost they would be similar to regular Roman units and become invisible to us.[9]

Unfortunately we do not know how large these units were or how many of them there were. When we have any details they are described as *numeri* or ἶλαι, terms similar to those used for regular regiments. From this evidence there is no reason to suppose that they differed from Roman units and as they were part of the regular army they might be expected to be similar in size. We know the size of only two units. The Unnigardae recorded by Synesius were

---

[8] On terminology see *LRE* 199–200, 663–6; for the 6th cent., J. Teall, 'The Barbarians in Justinian's Armies', *Speculum*, 40 (1965) 294–322; for discussion of meanings of *foederati*, H. Sivan, 'On *Foederati*, *Hospitalitas* and the Settlement of Goths in AD 418', *AJP* 108 (1987), 759–72; unfortunately J. H. W. G. Liebeschuetz, *Barbarians and Bishops* (Oxford, 1991), 32–47, conflates all barbarians in the Roman army as 'federates'.

[9] On *foederati* see Olymp. fr. 7. 4; Procopius, *BV* 3. 11. 2–4, *BG* 5. 5. 2; on Alans see Claudian, *De Bello Gothico*, 400–3, 580–9, *De 4 Cons. Hon.* 487; assuming that the Alans of Zos. 5. 26. 4 (405) are the same, otherwise they could be allies; on supplies and pay see Zos. 4. 40. 1–2.

Table 1. Foederati *regiments in the Roman army*

Regiment	Area of operations	Date	Reference
?	Thrace	365	Zos. 4. 7. 1
Alamanni	Britain	378	AM 29. 4. 7
Saracens	Thrace	378	AM 31. 16. 5–6; Eunapius fr. 42. 81–2; Zos. 4. 22. 1–3
Alans	Gaul	383	Zos. 4. 35. 2, 5? = *ND* Occ. 6. 50
?	Thrace	380s	Zos. 4. 40
Goths	Italy	386	Ambrose, *Ep.*20
Cavalry	Phrygia	399	Zos. 5. 13. 2–3
?	Asia Minor	399	Zos. 5. 17. 1–2
Alans	Italy	401	Claudian, *De Bello Gothico* 400–3, 580–9, *De 4 Cons. Hon.* 487
Alans	Italy	405	Zos. 5. 26. 4
?	Italy	408	Zos. 5. 33. 1–2
?	Italy	408	Philost. 12. 3; Zos. 5. 35. 5–5. 42. 3
Huns	Italy	409	Zos. 5. 45. 6
Honoriaci	Spain	409	Orosius 7. 40. 7
?	Italy	410	Zos. 6. 13. 2?
Unnigardae	Cyrenaica	411	Synesius, *Ep.* 78
Huns	Africa	420s	Ps. Aug. *Ep.* 4
?	Africa	420s	Olymp. fr. 40
?	Africa	427	Aug. *Ep.* 220. 7
?	West	437	Prosp. 1330
?	Italy	440	*NVal* 9. 1

40 strong, almost certainly a subdivision of a regiment, and the regiment led by Olympius in 409 was 300 strong. At least two of these regiments acquired a title similar to that borne by Roman units, the Honoriaci recorded in Spain in 409 by Orosius and the Unnigardae in Africa in 411. The similarity of these titles to those recorded in the *Notitia* suggests that the latter recorded both regular and *foederati* regiments and did not distinguish between them. As a list of unit commands it had no need to. This is also suggested by Gratian's creation of a favoured regiment of Alani in the early 380s and the high status given to a regiment of *comites Alani* in the western field army in the *Notitia*.[10] As regiments of the *comitatenses*,

[10] For Honoriaci see Orosius 7. 40. 7; for Unnigardae see Synesius, *Ep.* 78; for

foederati were commanded by tribunes. One Roman officer, Bonifatius, was recorded as 'tribune with a few *foederati*' in 417.
Regiments were also assigned to tasks in the same way as regular
regiments, for example, garrisoning Italy against the Vandals, or
sent to reinforce areas on request, such as a Hun regiment sent to
Africa in the 420s. Unlike allies, they appear to have been used in
small numbers.[11]

Of the few *foederati* regiments of which we know anything, the
Unnigardae were mounted archers and the Huns of Olympius were
probably cavalry. Tribigildus' regiment and the Alan regiment of
the fifth century were also cavalry. This suggests that the Romans
may have deliberately recruited some units from barbarians with
mounted combat skills. Individual *foederati* had wives and children
living within the Empire, often in distinct communities. All this
was similar to regular regiments. Although none of this evidence is
conclusive in itself, the similarities to regular regiments appear
more apparent than the differences.[12]

The units of the field army, both regular and *foederati* regiments,
were divided into two precedence grades, *comitatenses* and *palatini*,
though they were often referred to together as *comitatenses*. *Palatini*
ranked higher than *comitatenses*, but both were found in all field
armies. When first instituted under Diocletian and Constantine
palatini were probably confined to praesental armies accompanying
emperors, but transfers brought about the situation recorded in the
Notitia. Precedence differences could have been reflected in pay,
uniform, or morale, but we have no details. Within each grade,
units were ranked separately as infantry and cavalry, cavalry taking
precedence over the infantry. Some units had titles *seniores* and
iuniores and in identically named pairs *seniores* outranked *iuniores*.
There also existed an honorary cavalry title, *comites* (probably
derived by extension from the senior *vexillatio palatina*, the *comites*),
though this seems not to have affected precedence. The precedence
of *scholae* is unknown, but they presumably ranked above cavalry

Huns see Zos. 5. 45. 6; for Alans see Zos. 4. 35. 2, 5; *ND* Occ. 6. 50; it is often
suggested that the *Notitia Dignitatum* does not include *foederati*, e.g. Liebeschuetz,
Barbarians and Bishops, 33–4.

[11] On commanders see Olympius, Zos. 5. 45. 6; on Tribigildus see Philost. 11. 8;
Zos. 5. 13. 2; on Drumas see Zos. 6. 7. 6; on Bonifatius see Aug. *Ep.* 220. 7; on
Italy see *NVal* 9. 1 (440); on Africa see Ps. Aug. *Ep.* 4.

[12] Zos. 5. 34. 2, 5. 35. 5; Philost. 11. 8.

and infantry. Newly raised units were placed at the bottom of each rank of precedence, suggesting that the precedence system might have been based on seniority by date of formation. Demotion in precedence could be used as punishment and we hear of a unit of cavalry in Africa being downgraded in the 370s.[13]

Units could also be promoted into the field army from the *limitanei*, in this case receiving the title *pseudocomitatenses*. These regiments ranked below *comitatenses* in precedence. They are first recorded in 365. These transfers reflected field conditions, thus the legions I and II Armeniaca probably became *pseudocomitatenses* after the Persians captured their base at Bezabde in 360 and the I Armeniaca served in Julian's 363 expedition. Other transfers—those of Rhine frontier *limitanei* into the Gallic field army in the early fifth century—may reflect this or they may be the result of the centralization of Western military affairs under the *magister peditum*. Units could also be transferred out of the *comitatenses* into the *limitanei* as the Unnigardae were threatened in the early fifth century.[14]

Many *comitatenses* regiments seem to have been divided into *seniores* and *iuniores* at an unknown point. Numerous divisions of the army between emperors are known, and the earliest unit with such a title currently known is from 356, the Iovii (or Ioviani) Cornuti Seniores.[15] A number of guard units attended emperors and often participated in operations. There were five *scholae* regiments in the West at the date of the *Notitia*, seven in the East. These units were cavalry regiments and, under Justinian at least and probably earlier, were 500 strong. During the fourth century these were élite combat formations and are frequently found in Ammianus' battle narratives. In the fifth century the lack of campaigning by the Emperor meant that they saw less action, though they still served if the Emperor took to the field. By Zeno's reign in the East they seem to have become a ceremonial unit with places being sold. A similar process probably took place in the West and they were

---

[13] On precedence see AM 25. 6. 3?; on promotion see Veg. I. 17; on demotion see AM 29. 5. 20, cf. 24. 5. 10.

[14] On *pseudocomitatenses*, differing pay scales, see *CT* 8. 1. 10 (365) (not mentioned in Ammianus); on I and II Armeniaca see *ND* Or. 7. 49, 50; AM 20. 7. 1; Malalas 332; on transfer to *limitanei* see Synesius, *Ep.* 78.

[15] T. Drew-Bear, 'A Late-Fourth Century Latin Soldier's Epitaph at Nakolea', *HSCP* 81 (1977), 257–74, superseding Tomlin, '*Seniores-Iuniores*', 253–78.

pensioned off by Theoderic in 493.[16] The *candidati* were the personal bodyguard of the emperor selected from the *scholae*. In the sixth century the unit was forty men strong and this may have been its strength earlier. They were always in close attendance on the emperor.[17]

In addition to the regular army, the Romans often used groups of barbarians to fight for them as allies. They differed from *foederati* in two ways. Firstly, they were not a permanent part of the army, but were summoned by the Romans for a particular campaign, often through treaty obligations, and were then dismissed at the end of it. Thus the Goths used against Eugenius in 394 had dispersed back to their settlements by the end of the year. Secondly, they were not formed into regular regiments, but were used as single large units, suggesting that they could not be easily subdivided. These troops were known to contemporaries as *foederati*, *auxilia*, συμμάχοι, μισθωτοί, or ὁμαιχμίαι. Here they are referred to as 'allies'.[18]

Allies came under Roman strategic command, being subordinate to the highest ranking Roman officer present. At a lower level they were led by their own leaders. In 394 the Roman officers Bacurius (*dux* or *magister militum*), Gainas (*comes*), and Saul (rank unknown) commanded the allied contingents, while at a lower level Alaric led some of the allied Goths and the Huns had their own chieftains.[19] These contingents fought in their own fashion, though they were

---

[16] On *scholae* see *ND* Occ. 9. 4–8, Or. 11. 4–10; R. I. Frank, *Scholae Palatinae* (Rome, 1969) and the r ͘ ͘w by A. H. M. Jones, *JRS* 60 (1970), 227–9; on being with emperor see AM 16. 4. 1; cavalry, Frank, *Scholae Palatinae*, 52; Jul. *Or.* 2. 97c; for strength of 440 men in 404 see Palladius, *Dialogus* 9; Procopius, *HA* 24. 15, 19; for field army see *CT* 7. 4. 22–3 (396); on late fifth-cent. service see Malchus fr. 18. 4?; cf. Procopius, *HA* 24. 21; on places sold see Agathias, *Hist.* 5. 15. 1–6; Procopius, *HA* 24. 18–20; on disbanding see Procopius, *HA* 26. 27–8; but cf. Cass. *Variae*, 6. 6.

[17] On *candidati* see Frank, *Scholae Palatinae*, 127–42; AM 15. 5. 16, 25. 3. 6, 31. 13. 14–16; on individuals see App. 1; on strength see Constantine Porphyrogenitus, *De Caer.* 1. 86.

[18] On allies see J. H. W. G. Liebeschuetz, 'Generals, Federates and Buccelarii in Roman Armies around AD 400', in P. W. Freeman and D. L. Kennedy, eds., *Defence of the Roman and Byzantine East* (Oxford, 1986), 463–74; Anon., *PS* 6; on dismissal see RPF fr. 1; J. Ant. fr. 203; evidence for dismissal is minimal, but if it did not occur then these barbarians must have remained in Roman service, a hypothesis for which there is even less evidence, cf. Liebeschuetz, *Barbarians and Bishops*, 33–4; for mercenaries see Philost. 12. 14; on contrast with regulars see AM 23. 2. 7.

[19] *PLRE* i, Bacurius, Gainas, Saul; J. Ant. fr. 187; *PLRE* ii, Patriciolus, Vitalianus 2.

supplied and paid by the Romans. Nothing is known of their organization, but it may have been the same as that of barbarians outside the Empire, that is by family.[20]

The late Roman navy consisted of a number of fleets based at various ports, each composed of warships (for fighting) and merchantmen (for supply and transport of troops).[21] Nothing is known about the normal command structure, though several prominent generals are found commanding fleets as well as armies, suggesting that the navy was seen as part of the army, not as a separate service. Magnus Maximus' *magister equitum* commanded a fleet in the Adriatic in 388 and the otherwise unknown Constantius had victories on both land and sea in the fifth century. In the 450s–470s the *magister militum* Ricimer also commanded on both land and sea. Individual fleets were commanded by *praefecti* according to the *Notitia* and several of these small fleets were probably combined under a *magister militum* for major operations.[22]

We know nothing of the size of individual fleets. However, we have some data which indicate total fleet size (transports and warships) or lift capacity at certain dates. In 398 Stilicho sent 5,000 infantry to Africa from Pisa and in 410 4,000 men sailed into Ravenna. These figures are of the same order of magnitude as two expeditions to Britain, in 360 and 367, each of four regiments (2,000–5,000 men). In 413 Heraclianus sailed from Africa to Italy with a fleet, according to the manuscripts, of 3,700 ships. If the total is correct, it probably includes cargo vessels for transporting grain to Rome. The 468 expedition against the Vandals apparently totalled 1,100 ships and in 508 a naval expedition against Italy was composed of 100 (transport?) ships, 100 galleys (*dromones*), and 8,000 men.[23]

---

[20] On payment see Them. *Or.* 10. 135B; on Huns see 425, Philost. 12. 14, RPF fr. 1; on Goths in 470s see Malchus fr. 2, 16, 17; supplies, J. Ant. fr. 203 and 214. 5. 1, but see note under *PLRE* ii, Vitalianus 2.

[21] D. Kienast, *Untersuchungen zu den Kriegsflotten der römischen Kaiserzeit* (Bonn, 1966); J. R. Moss, 'The Effects of the Policies of Aetius on the History of Western Europe', *Historia*, 22 (1973), 711–31; M. Reddé, *Mare Nostrum* (Rome, 1986) and review by Y. Le Bohec, *JRA* 2 (1989), 326–31.

[22] Commanders, individual fleets, *ILS* 5902?; operations, *PLRE* i, Andragathius 3, Maximinus 4; *PLRE* ii, Ardabur 3, Constantius 9, Ricimer 2.

[23] For 398 see Claudian, *De Bello Gothico*, 418–23; Orosius 7. 36. 6; for 410 see Zos. 6. 8. 2; for 360 see AM 20. 1. 3; for 367 see AM 27. 8. 7; for 413 see Orosius 7. 42. 13; for 468 see Priscus fr. 53. 1 (Blockley, ii, n. 183); for 508 see Marc. Com. sa 508.

These fleets were based in a number of ports. In the West, Ravenna is recorded as being used by Honorius to receive convoys and with Misenum is mentioned as a fleet base by Vegetius and in the *Notitia*. Arles was used as a departure point for Theodosius' expedition against Firmus in 373. The *Notitia* also records fleets at Aquileia, Como, Ravenna, Misenum, Arles, and the mouth of the Somme.[24] No fleets are recorded in the East in the *Notitia*, but this must be a textual omission, not proof that there was no fleet, since numerous naval actions are known from the east. A law of Theodosius II in 409 mentions fleets based at Alexandria and in the Crete–Rhodes region. In 365 Cyzicus was stormed from the sea and in 388 an Eastern fleet sailed into the Adriatic and landed in Sicily. In 400 Fravitta was using a fleet in the Hellespont, and in 425 Aspar led one against Italy. Constantinople was the major Eastern base, containing (military ?) docks.[25]

Fleets consisted of two types of ships, warships and transports. Warships were oared galleys, with sails and equipped with rams. The number of banks of oars varied, but references to triremes suggests three to be typical, though Vegetius suggests as many as five. Some carried bolt-throwing artillery. Transports had sails only and would be almost defenceless if attacked. Both cavalry and infantry were transported, the mounts for the cavalry being carried in specially designed ships.[26] Though there was a standing fleet, on a number of occasions when the Romans needed a fleet frantic construction took place, as in 459 for Majorian's expedition against the Vandals. Some sources also state that the Romans had no fleet. From this it seems that fleets were not in commission permanently. Triremes could be left as hulls in dockyards when not in use, with stores kept elsewhere. In this case ships had a life of up to twenty years. In addition, fleets were not needed for day-to-day defence,

[24] Bases: for Somme see *ND* Occ. 38. 8; for Como see *ND* Occ. 42. 4; for Aquileia see *ND* Occ. 42. 9; for Ravenna see Zos. 6. 8. 2; Veg. 4. 31; *ND* Occ. 42. 7; *AE* 1975. 402; for Misenum see Veg. 4. 31; *ND* Occ. 42. 11; for Pisa see Claudian, *De Bello Gildonico*, 1. 483; for Arles see AM 29. 5. 5; *ND* Occ. 42. 14.

[25] On Fravitta see Zos. 5. 20. 3–5. 21. 4; on Constantinople see Evagrius, *HE* 2. 13; Claudian, *In Rufinum*, 2. 59–60; on Alexandrian and Carpathian (Crete–Rhodes area) fleets see *Corpus Papyrorum Raineri*, ed. C. Wessely (Vienna, 1895), 5. 10 (337/47), my thanks to Peter Brennan for this reference; *CT* 13. 5. 32 (409).

[26] On ship types see Procopius, *BV* 3. 11. 15–16; Veg. 4. 37; on triremes see Philost. 12. 13–14; Zos. 5. 20. 3, 5. 21. 3; *Ilias Ambrosiana* (Berne, 1953), pl. 11; on horse transports see Menander fr. 23. 1; on artillery see Mauricius, *Strat.* 12. 8. 21; Veg. 4. 44; Agathias, *Hist.* 3. 21. 4.

at least not until the Vandal kingdom emerged in Africa, so would naturally decline when out of use.[27]

Limitanei

The border troops are referred to here as *limitanei*, but were also known as *riparienses*, *ripenses*, *castellani*, or *burgarii*. These terms seem to be synonymous, but there may have been differences between them of which we know nothing. Apart from their organization, deployment, and use, they differed from the field army only in minor ways such as physical standards, length of service, and tax benefits on retirement.[28]

The *limitanei* contained a greater variety of units than the *comitatenses* as a result of their long period of evolution. These were *cohortes* and *legiones* for the infantry and *alae* and *equites* for the cavalry, as well as units vaguely titled *limites*, *milites*, *auxilia*, *gentes*, and *numeri*, which were all probably infantry. This terminology was not always used precisely and the *Notitia Dignitatum* described both full legions and legionary detachments in the same way.[29]

As with the *comitatenses* it is difficult to estimate unit sizes. In the third century *cohortes* and *alae* had a nominal establishment of 480, though John Lydus in the sixth century records *alae* as 600. The few milliary units recorded in the *Notitia* may have been around 750 strong, as in the third century. Border *equites* and *auxilia* were probably the same size as *cohortes* and *alae*. *Legiones* were often broken up into detachments for garrisoning a province,

---

[27] For standing fleet see Veg. 4. 31; for construction when needed see SA *Carm.* 5. 441–8; Jul. *Or.* 1. 42CD, *Ep. ad Ath.* 280A; J. Ant. fr. 214. 2; Zos. 3. 5. 2; for lack of fleet see SA *Carm.* 2. 384–6; Priscus fr. 39. 1; Jul. *Or.* 1. 42CD, *Ep. ad Ath.* 280A; for ship life see L. Casson, *Ships and Seamanship in the Ancient World* (Princeton, NJ, 1971), 90, 119–20.

[28] *Limitanei*: see H. I. Bell *et al.*, eds., *The Abinnaeus Archive* (Oxford, 1962) for the papers of a *limitanei* officer of the mid-4th cent.; on term *limitanei* see B. Isaac, 'The Meaning of the Terms *Limes* and *Limitanei*', *JRS* 78 (1988), 125–47; for first appearance of *limitanei* see *CT* 12. 1. 56 (363); on synonymity see *CT* 7. 20. 4 (325); on differentiation see D. Van Berchem, *L'Armée de Dioclétien et la Réforme Constantinienne* (Paris, 1952); on rations see *CT* 7. 4. 14 (365), 8. 1. 10 (365); on physical standards see *CT* 7. 22. 8 (372); Synesius, *Ep.* 78; on length of service see *CJ* 10. 55. 3 (284/305); on tax benefits see *CT* 7. 13. 7 (375), 20. 7 (375); on retirement benefits see *CT* 7. 20. 4 (325).

[29] At some point before the drawing up of the *Notitia*, *cunei equites* and *cunei* apparently became synonyms for *equites* and should not be considered as different types of unit; cf. *CT* 5. 6. 1 (347), 7. 13. 1 (353).

in some cases as many as six from the same legion. These varied in size and had up to five cohorts. Full-strength legions may have been the same strength as field army legions. If they were this small, some of their detachments would have been very small indeed. These guesses are establishment strengths and the real strengths would have been somewhat lower.[30]

Classes (flotillas) were also part of the *limitanei*. Each flotilla had its own base at a fort on the Rhine or Danube which was garrisoned by an infantry or cavalry unit. We do not know how big these flotillas were, though in 359 Julian assembled forty boats while campaigning on the Rhine. In 412 the border command of Moesia Secunda had 100 *lusoriae* (light boats) while Scythia had 125 *lusoriae* of two types, *iudicariae* and *agrarienses*, the latter outnumbering the former by approximately two to one. Some of these boats could be equipped with bolt-shooters, but most were small. Fourth-century Roman longboats found at Mainz (*c.*10 m. long and *c.*4 m. in width with a shallow draught) were probably the same type as Julian's forty *lusoriae* which carried 300 men.[31]

There were a number of sites on both sides of the Rhine and Danube which combined small towers with harbour areas, so-called fortified landing places. As well as providing safe docking sites for elements of a flotilla, these would also serve as harbours for the small boats probably used by land regiments for communication and supply purposes (and perhaps patrolling), providing shelter in bad weather.[32]

Precedence probably did not exist among *limitanei* regiments

---

[30] *LRE* 680–2; Duncan-Jones, *Structure and Scale*, 105–17, 214–17; the reduction in size of late Roman forts does not automatically mean a reduction in the size of units. The increased number of forts and known outposting suggest a more spread out army. In addition, many large forts continued to be used; C. Zuckermann, 'Legio V Macedonica in Egypt', *Tyche*, 3 (1988), 279–87, suggests strengths of either 400 or 800; for *ala* see Lydus, *De Mag.* 1. 46; MacMullen, 'Roman Imperial Army', 451–60.

[31] For flotillas on Danube see *CT* 7. 17. 1 (412), possibly a shake-up after the attack of the Sciri in 411; *ND* Occ. 32. 50–2 and 55–6, 33. 58, 34. 26–8, 37, 40, 42–3; AM 17. 13. 17, 19. 11. 8; Zos. 4. 39. 1–2; Veg. 4. 46; W. W. Gauld, 'Vegetius on Roman Scout-Boats', *Antiquity*, 64 (1990), 402–6; for Rhine see AM 16. 11. 8, 17. 1. 4 (800 men), 2. 3, 18. 2. 11–12 (300 men); Symm. *Laud. in Valent.* 2. 28; Gaul, *ND* Occ. 42. 14, 15, 21, 23; on ships see O. Höckmann, 'Rheinschiffe aus der Zeit Ammians: neue Funde in Mainz', *Antike Welt*, 133 (1982), 40–7; G. Rupprecht, ed., *Die Mainzer Römerschiffe* (Mainz, 1986); on artillery see Mauricius, *Strat.* 12. 8. 21. 2.

[32] cf. *ND* Occ. 34. 26–7, 37, 40, 41, 42. 16; Or. 39. 20 and 35, 40. 22, 28 and 36.

because of their static nature. Only a few *seniores-iuniores* are attested among *limitanei* and these are probably demoted *comitatenses* regiments. Similarly, there was no need for a brigade structure. Cohorts were commanded by *tribuni*, legions and their detachments, *vexillationes, alae, numeri*, and classes by *praefecti*. Both *tribuni* and *praefecti* were also described as *praepositi*, itself not a rank. In an official letter Abinnaeus, commander of an *ala* in Egypt, is referred to as *praepositus* in the address and *praefectus* in the text. The *Notitia* refers to the commanders of *milites, gentes*, and some other types of unit as *praepositi*.[33]

Protectores *and* Domestici

In the mid-fourth century the *protectores* and *domestici* could be described as staff colleges, since all tribunes and *praefecti* (unless directly commissioned) served in them before commanding their own units. The *domestici* were attached to the Emperor and usually accompanied the *comitatus* on campaign. Administratively, they were divided into *domestici peditum* and *equitum* and the *Notitia* records these regiments in both parts of the Empire, commanded by the *comes domesticorum*. Groups of *protectores* were attached to each *magister militum*. Precise duties for *protectores* and *domestici* are hard to define, though they seem never to have had a function as combat regiments. Individuals performed functions such as rounding up deserters, planning, and supervising exports from the empire. Both groups performed the same types of work, often together, accounting for some of the confusion as to their status. After a variable period (averaging five years), they were promoted to *tribuni* or *praefecti*.

By the early fifth century the character of the *domestici* and *protectores* had changed. Instead of having a transitory composition, members were attached permanently and the units became more ornamental, a part of the palace rather than of the field army. The process appears to have affected *protectores* as much as *domestici*. In the west they were both pensioned off by Theoderic in 493, though the units continued to exist in the East.[34]

---

[33] For *seniores-iuniores* see *ND* Occ. 35. 14–16, 42. 6; Tomlin, '*Seniores-Iuniores*', 253–78 at 254 n. 3; for command see Grosse, 143–51; for titles see *P. Abinn.* 3.

[34] On *protectores* and *domestici* see *ND* Or. 15, Occ. 13; Frank, *Scholae Palatinae* and the review by Jones, 227–9; for duties see Matthews, *Roman Empire*, 75–6; on pensioning off see Procopius, *HA* 26. 27–8.

Bucellarii

Many generals in the late ourth and fifth centuries had private bodyguards known as *bucellarii*. According to Olympiodorus 'in the days of Honorius, the name *bucellarius* was borne not only by Roman soldiers, but also by some Goths'. The term is not found in the fourth century though the institution may have existed then.[35] Such men would have had little impact on the army and probably saw little action in the field. They are not attested as being involved in any field battles in the fifth century. Bucellarii were few in number and we hear of no groups larger than 200–300 strong and usually fewer. They were probably mounted.[36]

Militia

It seems unlikely for several reasons that there was a universal official militia in the late Roman empire. Most importantly, there is no explicit mention of such an organization in our sources. It seems unlikely that it would be omitted from legal sources, since militia membership would require weapon ownership, which was frowned on, if not illegal.[37] On many occasions when we would expect to hear of militias, none are recorded. When there were no troops present, urban defence was carried out by various groups, armed citizens, and slaves, or occasionally veterans. In such cases the defence seems to be an *ad hoc* affair, put together on the spur of the moment, as would not be the case if there was a militia, and

[35] *Bucellarii*: Olymp. fr. 7. 4, 12; H.-J. Diesener, 'Das Buccelariertum von Stilicho und Sarus bis auf Aetius', *Klio* 54 (1972), 321–50; neither the *Thesaurus Latinae Linguae*, nor Lewis and Short's *Latin Dictionary* record the word before the 5th century; it is common to associate the *bucellarii* with the Germanic *comitatus*, *antrustiones*, etc., but fact that some of the men in the bodyguard were German does not make it a Germanic institution; Liebeschuetz, *Barbarians and Bishops*, 43–7.

[36] Eusebius, *HE* 7. 30. 8, 8. 9. 7, 14. 9; for Rufinus see Claudian, *In Rufinum*, 2. 76–7; for Stilicho see Zos. 5. 11. 4, 34. 1; for Sarus see Zos. 6. 13. 2 (300 men), Olymp. fr. 18 (18/20); for Gerontius see Soz. 9. 13. 1; for Bonifatius see Aug. *Ep.* 220. 6; for Aspar see Malalas 371; for Ricimer? see J. Ant. fr. 209. 1; for Titus see *V. Danielis Stylitae*, 60–1; for Trocundes see J. Ant. fr. 214. 5. 12; for Sabinianus see Malchus fr. 20. 131–2; for Belisarius see Procopius, *BG* 7. 1. 18–20 (7,000), cf. Africa, *BV* 3. 17. 1 (300) + 3. 19. 24 (800) = 1,100 men; Leo, *CJ* 9. 12. 10 (468).

[37] G. Webster, 'The Function and Organisation of Late Roman Civil Defences in Britain', in J. Hobley and B. Maloney, eds., *Roman Urban Defences in the West*, *CBA* 51 (London, 1983), 118–20; E. Birley, 'Local Militias in the Roman Empire', *The Roman Army*, *MAVORS* 4 (Amsterdam, 1988), 387–94; R. MacMullen, *Soldier and Civilian in the Later Roman Empire* (Cambridge, Mass., 1963), 132–9; for prohibition on arms see *CT* 15. 15. 1 (364); cf. Synesius, *Ep.* 107.

the leaders of these defenders have no special titles. Thus when Alaric approached Rome in 408, the citizens claimed to have formed a militia, suggesting there was not one already in existence.[38]

Where there was a threat, many areas did have some form of local defence. We hear of 'farmers and slaves' trained to fight robbers in Bithynia in 399, and similar groups existed elsewhere, for example the men levied in emergencies by Bishop Synesius in Cyrenaica. The equipment of these militias was always basic or improvised. Slings and spears were most common and swords, bows and armour seem rare to non-existent. Their effectiveness is uncertain. Outside Rome in 408, 'when Alaric heard that the people were trained and ready to fight, he said "thicker grass was easier to mow than thinner" and guffawed at the ambassadors'.[39]

B: TROOP TYPES

The troops of the army can be divided into infantry and cavalry, of whom the former greatly outnumbered the latter. From the *Notitia Dignitatum* we can suggest a ratio of two infantry units to one cavalry unit, and cavalry regiments were smaller than infantry regiments. We know of no differences in troop types between *comitatenses* and *limitanei* or of any change in practice in this period. As far as we can tell, the status of a regiment, auxiliary or legionary, *palatina*, *comitatenses*, or *pseudocomitatenses*, seems not to have affected its type. The only possible exception is that of the higher precedence *vexillationes palatinae* which seem to have been composed mostly of heavy cavalry with only two light cavalry units (*sagittarii*) recorded out of twenty-four regiments.

Infantry

The majority of Roman infantry regiments fought in close order in the main line of battle. Few units had special roles and although a

[38] For *ad hoc* groups of citizens see Zos. 2. 43. 3, 5. 40. 3, 6. 4. 3; Malchus fr. 20. 17–19; Claudian, *De Bello Gothico*, 463–8; SA *Ep.* 3. 3, 7; Dexippus fr. 21; AM 31. 6. 2; cf. Synesius, *Ep.* 104, 122, 125; on veterans see AM 16. 2. 1; Lib. *Or.* 18. 43; for *urbani milites* = garrison? see *CT* 4. 13. 3 (321); for slaves see Zos. 6. 4. 3.

[39] On militias see Zos. 5. 15. 5, 5. 16. 1–5; AM 27. 9. 6?; on equipment see J. Chrysostom, *Ad Stagyrum*, 6 (= *PG* 47. 458); on spears, swords, clubs, axes, shields, see Synesius, *Ep.* 108; on slings see Zos. 5. 16. 1, 3; on bows see Synesius, *Ep.* 133; on Alaric see Zos. 5. 40. 3.

number of regimental names such as *exploratores* or *lancearii* point to units having specialized functions of some sort, there is no evidence for them being carried out and these titles probably reflect special functions during an earlier period.[40] Hand-to-hand troops were supported by specialist missile regiments. Missile fire would be highly effective since few barbarians wore armour. Some units were composed totally of archers (*sagittarii*) and most infantry units seem to have had their own missile-armed contingent. Vegetius recommended that between a quarter and a third of recruits should be trained to use bows, possibly reflecting proportions within units. The inclusion of missile troops with mêlée troops on most occasions is shown by an action in 351: 'Constantius immediately sent out Scudilo and Manadus, military tribunes. They chose the best infantry and bowmen that they had under their command.' In Ammianus' account of Procopius' usurpation in 365, a skirmish between two *auxilia palatina* and a single legion was interrupted while 'they were exchanging missiles (*missilia*) between themselves'. Since the interruption was caused by Procopius rushing between the opposing battle lines the fire was probably from bows; javelins were generally thrown immediately before contact and Procopius could not have stopped fighting at this stage. There is also some weak archaeological evidence. At Housesteads on Hadrian's Wall a late fourth-century deposit of more than 800 arrows has been found and no *sagittarii* are known from the fort, a pattern repeated elsewhere.[41]

Some battle accounts show operations by 'light armed' units (*expediti, velites, leves armaturae, exculcatores, ferentarii,* or ψιλοί), e.g. an operation against Sarmatians hiding in marshes in 357, when 'light-armed troops were put into skiffs, and taking the course which offered the greatest secrecy, came up to the lurking places of the Sarmatians'. Legionaries, *auxilia*, and cavalry could all be referred to as 'light-armed'. In the sixth century these light-armed troops are always defined as being equipped with missiles and it is

[40] J. C. Balthy, 'Apamea in the Second and Third Centuries AD', *JRS* 78 (1988), 91–104 at 101; Hoffmann, 218–20.

[41] On missile troops see Veg. 1. 14–17; on mixed unit see Veg. 1. 15, 3. 14; Zos. 2. 50. 2–3; A M 26. 7. 15; cf. *CIL* 6. 32994; D. Welsby, *The Roman Military Defence of the British Provinces in its Later Phases, B A R* 101 (Oxford, 1982), 118; Coulston, 'Archery Equipment', 227–9, 232–3, 265; on training see Veg. 1. 15.

likely that this was its meaning in the fourth century.[42]

There were also regiments of *balistarii* which appear to be artillery units. There were seven regiments of *balistarii* recorded in the *Notitia Dignitatum* (three *legiones comitatenses*, three *pseudo-comitatenses* units, and one *limitanei* regiment). In addition, artillery may have been integral to infantry regiments, similar to earlier attachments to legionary centuries, though there is no direct evidence from this period.[43]

The existence of these *balistarii* regiments, together with *sagittarii* brigades (or detachments from them), suggests an ability to concentrate large volumes of firepower in one place. But these units are not conspicuous in battle accounts and we know little of their role. However, the frequent appearance of artillery in sieges suggests that they may have been integral to (*limitanei?*) regiments, or at least to units forming town garrisons. Though other missile weapons such as slings, staff-slings, and crossbows were used, they seem not to have made up entire units, with the possible exception of a regiment of *funditores*, but were part of infantry regiments.[44]

Cavalry

It is often suggested that the army was increasingly composed of cavalry during this period, though there is little evidence for this in the fifth century. Dennis presents the orthodox view of the fifth-century army. 'More emphasis was placed on mobility and thus in cavalry, who could move from one threatened sector to another. The enemies of the Romans were also depending more and more on horses in their attacks.' Against this, in 478, an Eastern field army was composed of 8,000 cavalry and 30,000 infantry. These

[42] Veg. 2. 2, 15; Zos. 4. 25. 2; AM 17. 13. 17, 19. 3. 1, 19. 11. 8 (legionaries), 20. 1. 3 (*auxilia*), 20. 4. 5, 21. 4. 8 (*auxilia*), 7. 4 (skirmishers), 9. 6, 12. 9 (skirmishers), 13. 8, 16, 24. 1. 13 (skirmishers), 2. 8 (*auxilia*), 4. 3, 5. 5 (skirmishers), 6. 9 (*auxilia*), 7. 2, 25. 6. 9 (cavalry), 30. 1. 11 (archers), 31. 11. 6; Mauricius, *Strat.* 10. 1. 4 and 16, 12. 8. 3, 5, 8, 9, and 12.

[43] On *balistarii* see *ND* Occ. 7. 97, 41. 23, Or. 7. 43, 57, 8. 46, 47, 9. 47; AM 16. 2. 5; *CIG* 8621; AM 16. 2. 5 cannot refer to a regiment of field artillery; on regiments without artillery see probably AM 19. 5. 2; integral? see Veg. 2. 25; E. W. Marsden, *Greek and Roman Artillery: Historical Development* (Oxford, 1969), 195–8; I am not convinced by P. Brennan, 'Combined Legionary Detachments as Artillery Units in Late Roman Danubian Bridgehead Dispositions', *Chiron*, 10 (1980), 553–67; no special skills were necessary for use of *ballistae* (as opposed to maintenance) according to the Ermine Street Guard who regularly use a reconstruction.

[44] *ND* Or. 7. 52; Mauricius, *Strat.* 12. 8. 4.

proportions were probably similar in the fourth century although precise figures are lacking. However, it can be roughly calculated that at Strasbourg in 357 Julian had 10,000 infantry and 3,000 cavalry. By the time of Justinian cavalry had become much more important, but precisely why or when this change occurred is unknown.[45]

There seems to have been more variety in types of cavalry than of infantry. Cavalry formed a third of the units of the army, in numbers less, as their units were smaller. The proportion of cavalry to infantry units appears to have been higher in the *limitanei* than in the *comitatenses*, possibly because they were of more use for patrolling.[46] The majority of *comitatenses* cavalry regiments were shock cavalry (61 per cent *scutarii*, *promoti*, and *stablesiani*), lance- or spear-armed and intended to defeat enemy infantry or cavalry in mêlée.[47] The *cataphracti* and *clibanarii* (15 per cent) were more heavily armoured shock cavalry. Some may have had bows, but most were armed for mêlée. These seem to have been concentrated in the Eastern armies, especially on the Eastern frontier, though many of them had served in the West, particularly in Gaul, at some point in their history, having acquired the names of their stations. These cavalry were concentrated in the field armies.[48] *Equites sagittarii* (15 per cent of *comitatenses* cavalry) and probably *Mauri* and *Dalmatae* (2 and 7 per cent respectively) were light cavalry,

---

[45] *Maurice's Strategikon*, ed. G. T. Dennis (Philadelphia, 1984), p. viii; 478, Malchus fr. 18. 2. 14–18; the change in the 6th-cent. appears to have been one of emphasis, not of numbers; J. F. Haldon, 'Some Aspects of Byzantine Military Technology from the Sixth to the Tenth Centuries', *Byzantine and Modern Greek Studies*, 1 (1975), 11–47 at 12–13.

[46] On limited recruiting see e.g. Liebeschuetz, *Barbarians and Bishops*, 33 n. 15; on training see Veg. 1. 18.

[47] M. Speidel, 'Stablesiani: The Raising of New Cavalry Units during the Crisis of the Roman Empire', *Chiron*, 4 (1974), 541–6 (= *MAVORS* 1 (Amsterdam, 1984), 391–6); some 6th-cent. cavalry were armed with lance and bow, an innovation, although we do not know the date of introduction; Procopius, *BP* 1. 1. 8–15, *BG* 5. 27. 20 and 27; Mauricius, *Strat*. 1. 2, 2. 8.

[48] J. C. Coulston, 'Roman, Parthian and Sassanid Tactical Developments', in P. W. Freeman and D. L. Kennedy, eds., *Defence of the Roman and Byzantine East* (Oxford, 1986), 59–75; J. W. Eadie, 'The Development of Roman Mailed Cavalry', *JRS* 57 (1967), 161–74, asserts (p. 170) that *cataphracti* and *clibanarii* were not synonymous: M. Speidel, 'Cataphractii Clibanarii and the Rise of the Later Roman Mailed Cavalry', *Epigrafica Anatolica*, 4 (1984), 151–6, is probably correct in equating the terms, though he attributes a degree of 'officialness' to the tombstone it probably does not possess. *Cataphracti* and *clibanarii* are here treated as identical.

used primarily for skirmishing and scouting.[49] The *scholae* were all cavalry regiments. In the West there were five shock units, in the east one *clibanarius*, one *sagittarius*, and five shock units.[50] The proportions among European *limitanei* were different. Light cavalry totalled 47 per cent (*sagittarii* 9, *Mauri* 2, *Dalmatae* 36 per cent), shock cavalry 51 per cent, and cataphracts 2 per cent. This suggests a troop mix with less emphasis on fighting field battles and lacking the units of very heavy shock cavalry.

As the *foederati* were equipped by the Romans, types of regiment would follow those outlined above and the proportions of cavalry mentioned above include *foederati*. The only regiment of *foederati* for which we know type of weaponry is the Unnigardae of Synesius who were mounted archers, though the unit of Huns led by Olympius was probably composed of horse archers. The troops provided by allies would have been similar to those fielded in barbarian armies. This means that they would have been infantry for the most part, with only a few cavalry.[51]

C: EQUIPMENT

During this period there seems to have been no major change in equipment and Roman troops were similarly armed between 350 and 425. In general terms, equipment in the ancient world hardly developed and the basic equipment of a legionary in the mid-fourth century AD (sword, spear, shield, helmet, metal body armour) was identical to that of a legionary of the mid-second century BC. It also differed little from that of a fifth-century BC Greek hoplite or a tenth-century AD Byzantine infantryman. Without significant technological development, any major change in equipment, and therefore in tactics, would be unlikely. Only internal reasons could have induced change during this period.[52]

---

[49] For Dalmatae see Zos. 1. 52. 3–1. 53. 1, cf. 1. 50. 3–4; there is no evidence for *equites Mauri* having Moorish connections at this period; for *sagittarii* in 367/9 see Them. *Or*. 8. 116.

[50] *ND* Occ. 9. 4–8, Or. 11. 4–10; Frank, *Scholae Palatinae*, 52; Jul. *Or*. 2. 97C.

[51] On Unnigardae see Synesius, *Ep*. 131; on Huns see Zos. 5. 45. 6.

[52] The best survey of equipment is T. Kolias, *Byzantinische Waffen* (Vienna, 1988); P. Couissin, *Les Armes romaines* (Paris, 1926), 471–518; Grosse, 321–38; for later developments see Haldon, 'Byzantine Military Technology', 11–447; on reasons for development of equipment and tactics see Coulston, 'Tactical Developments', 59–75 at 59.

Missile weapons

Roman weaponry can be divided into distance and hand-to-hand weapons. Most troops with distance weapons were armed with bows, usually of composite type similar to those used by the Sassanids and nomads like the Huns and Bulgars. Though Roman bows may have differed somewhat in form, infantry bows being larger than the compact reflex bows favoured by nomads, there would have been little difference in battlefield performance.[53] Some infantry may have been armed with crossbows (*manuballistae*), but these do not seem to have been common.[54] Slings (*fundi*) and staff slings (*fustibuli*, a sling attached to a long rod) were rarely used and seem more common in descriptions of sieges and irregular troops than in field battles, although Vegetius recommends that recruits in every unit be trained to throw stones by hand or with slings.[55]

In addition to these long-range weapons, an assortment of shorter range throwing weapons was used. These can be divided into two groups on the basis of range. The shorter, lighter, darts (*martiobarbuli* or *plumbatae*) were carried in numbers by (some) infantry, though they are not recorded as being used by cavalry. Vegetius recommended that they be attached behind shields in groups of five and thrown in the first charge. Reconstructions have a range of 30–65 m., which would suggest that they were thrown before charging.[56] The second group was javelins, described as

[53] On bows see Coulston, 'Archery Equipment', 220–366; cf. M. I. Rostovtzeff *et al.*, eds., *Excavations at Dura Europos, Sixth Season* (London, 1936), 453–6; on composite bow see E. Rosenthal, *The Illustrations of the Virgilius Romanus* (Zürich, 1972), pl. 14; Grosse, 335–6.

[54] Coulston, 'Archery Equipment', 259–63; Veg. 2. 15, 3. 14, 4. 21; Mauricius, *Strat.* 12. 8. 5; Anon. *DRB* 16. 5; G. T. Dennis, 'Flies, Mice and the Byzantine Crossbow', *Byzantine and Modern Greek Studies*, 7 (1981), 1–5; D. B. Campbell, 'Auxiliary Artillery Revisited', *BJ* 186 (1986), 117–32 at 126–32.

[55] For slingers see AM 19. 5. 1, 31. 15. 13; Jul. *Or.* 2. 57D; Veg. 1. 16, 2. 23, 3. 14; for irregulars see Zos. 5. 16. 1; W. B. Griffiths, 'The Sling and its Place in the Roman Imperial Army', in C. van Driel-Murray, ed., *Roman Military Equipment: The Sources of Evidence*, *BAR* S476 (Oxford, 1989), 255–79; for staff-slings see Veg. 1. 16, 2. 15, 3. 14; Mauricius, *Strat.* 12. 8. 3–4; stones, Veg. 1. 16, 2. 23; AM 20. 7. 10.

[56] Veg. 1. 17, 2. 15, 3. 14; Anon. *DRB* 10–11; Mauricius, *Strat.* 12. 8. 2, 4–5, 12, and 20; J. Bennett, 'Plumbatae from Pitsunda (Pitsyus), Georgia', *Journal of Roman Military Equipment Studies*, 2 (1991), 59–63; J. Mackay and P. Barker, 'Three Plumbatae from Wroxeter', *Antiquaries Journal*, 54 (1974), 275–7; P. A. Barker, 'The Plumbatae from Wroxeter', in M. W. Hassall and R. I. Ireland, eds., *De Rebus*

spicula, verruta, hastae, pila, iacula, or even *tela,* thrown immediately before contact. There were several types, though the differences are obscure. Vegetius suggested one *spiculum* (a heavy, armour-piercing weapon about 1.65 m. long) and one *verrutum* (lighter, about 1.0 m. in length) per man. They were carried by both infantry and cavalry. Some mosaics and wall-paintings show two javelins carried in the shield hand by both infantry and cavalry.[57]

Mêlée weapons

The standard mêlée weapon of the infantry was the spear. From surviving artistic evidence, spears seem to have been c. 2–2.5 m. in length.[58] As with the infantry, the major weapon of shock cavalry units was the spear. It was either used overarm to thrust or underarm (one or two-handed) as a lance. Unless all contemporary artists and graffitists were mistaken, it was used in this way despite the lack of stirrups. This suggests that the lack of stirrups was not important, a hypothesis supported by the apparent lack of change in cavalry tactics after their introduction in the late sixth century. The cavalry spear seems to have been the same length as the infantry spear.[59]

Bellicis, BAR S63 (Oxford, 1979), 97–100; B. Sherlock, 'Plumbatae, a Note on the Method of Manufacture', ibid. 101–2; Grosse, 334–5.

[57] On javelins see Veg. 2. 15; Mauricius, *Strat.* 12. 8. 2, 3, 5, 12 and 20; on multiples, infantry, see Grosse, 332–4; K. M. Dunbabin, *The Mosaics of Roman North Africa* (Oxford, 1978), nos. 29, 201; A. Ferrua, *Le pittura della nuova Catacomba di Via Latina* (Vatican, 1960), pl. 84; C. Cecchelli, *I mosaici della basilica di S. Maria Maggiore* (Turin, 1956), pl. 42; Anon. *DRB* 15. 4; cf. Balthy, 'Apamea', 91–104, pl. 14.2, for a 3rd-cent. example; on cavalry see Veg. 2. 15; *ILS* 9134; Dunbabin, *Mosaics*; for late 2nd/early 3rd cent. see M. Schleiermacher, *Römische Reitergrabsteine* (Bonn, 1984), no. 114.

[58] The Monza Diptych shows a spear just longer than Stilicho was tall, but it may be shortened to fit the diptych. It is approximately the same length as spears depicted on plates, coins, monuments, and mosaics; for a discussion of some of the factors influencing depiction of soldiers on monuments, J. C. Coulston, 'Roman Military Equipment on Third-Century Tombstones', in M. Dawson, ed., *The Accoutrements of War, BAR* S336 (Oxford, 1987), 141–56; I. R. Scott, 'Speaheads of the British *Limes*', in W. S. Hanson and L. J. F. Keppie, eds., *Roman Frontier Studies 1979* (Oxford, 1980), 333–43, demonstrates the lack of major change.

[59] Cavalry spears for overarm, late 3rd/early 4th cent. see Speidel, 'Cataphractarii Clibanarii', 151–6, pls. 15, 16; underarm, one-handed, late 3rd/early 4th cent. see Schleiermacher, *Reitergrabsteine*, no. 49; two-handed, mid-3rd cent. in M. I. Rostovtzeff *et al.*, eds., *Excavations at Dura Europos, Fourth Season* (London, 1933), 216–17; detailed discussion of the stirrup is obviously out of place here, but nothing could be done with stirrups that could not be done without them, though it might be done better or more easily; the Roman horned saddle allowed great flexibility

Many troops also carried the *spatha*, a straight two-edged sword
c.0.7–0.9 m. long, used by both infantry and cavalry. It had a point
so could be used for thrusting as well as cutting. Spearmen fought
in close formation where there would be little room to cut with a
spatha (though it might be used to thrust), suggesting it was a
secondary weapon. It may have been used more often by officers
than by rankers.[60] Other weapons such as lassoes, axes, and maces
were used, though we know nothing of their distribution. Their
rarity suggests that they were not primary weapons.[61]

Armour

In 350 most Roman infantry and cavalry wore armour, giving them
a distinct advantage over their barbarian enemies. This armour
seems mostly to have been mail, though some scale was also used.
Later in the fourth century, from the reign of Gratian, Vegetius
says that all regiments dispensed with armour and helmets, because
of the weight of their equipment. This may refer to the abandonment
of armour by some troops, but it seems unlikely that the whole
army did so, for several reasons. First, heavy armour was not new
to this period. Secondly, it is difficult to think of any tactical reason
by which *all* the infantry would benefit from its abandonment.
Thirdly, Vegetius' remark that unprotected soldiers suffered from
Gothic archers reinforces the likelihood that this abandonment
would not have been widespread. It seems likely that Vegetius
misinterpreted a source such as that which Zosimus had (probably
Eunapius) for the Gothic wars of the 370s, recording that Modares
'ordered his men, armed only with swords and shields and disdaining
heavier armour, to abandon the usual fighting in close order'. But
because of Vegetius' explicit statement, a suggestion that most late
Roman infantry wore armour needs some qualification. There

(for throwing) and support (for mêlée), A. Hyland, *Equus* (London, 1990), 130–6;
archaeological finds show horses from military sites as averaging 14 hands, easily
sufficient for military purposes, including carrying horse-armour, R.-M. Luff, *A
Zooarchaeological Study of the Roman North-Western Provinces*, BAR S137 (Oxford,
1982), 252–7.

[60] On *spatha* see Grosse, 330–2; for thrusting see Veg. 1. 12; cf. AM 24. 6. 11,
31. 7. 14, implying thrusting use; on secondary use see AM 31. 13. 5.
[61] For lasso see Mauricius, *Strat.* 1. 2. 7; Malalas 364; for axes see AM 19. 6. 7;
Procopius, *BP* 2. 21. 7; for their insignia see *ND* Or. 11, Occ. 9; being carried in
baggage see Mauricius, *Strat.* 2. 2. 10, 12. 8. 6; for maces (διστρία) see Theophylact,
Hist. 8. 4. 13.

are several reasons to suggest that armour was used by infantry throughout this period.[62]

During the mid- and late fourth century there appear to have been three types of armour in use. The most common was mail, found as a corselet covering the body to below the waist and over the shoulders, sometimes with leather *pteruges* attached to the skirt and sleeves, and (much less common) as a hauberk extending below the knees, to the wrists, and sometimes including a coif protecting the head. Helmets were not worn if a coif was attached to the hauberk.[63] The second type of armour was a scale corselet, similar to the mail corselet, again with and without *pteruges*. Bronze scales dating to the fifth century have been found at Nicopolis in Moesia Secunda. A third type was the cuirass, of bronze or iron, usually found with *pteruges*. Most officers seem to have worn this. Lastly, lamellar armour is known from before and after this period, but is not known in the fourth and fifth centuries.[64]

Evidence for continued use of armour by infantry is widespread. First, the mid-sixth century Byzantine army is known to have had large numbers of armoured infantry. Illustrations of these men and literary descriptions are similar to fourth-century illustrations. It seems unlikely that identical equipment was reintroduced in the sixth century after falling out of use in the fourth.[65] Secondly, armour continued to be produced. The *Notitia Dignitatum* records

---

[62] Veg. 1. 20; accepted by Liebeschuetz, *Barbarians and Bishops*, 25; rejected by N. P. Milner, 'Vegetius', D. Phil. thesis, Oxford University, 1991; Zos. 4. 25. 3; cf. Eunapius fr. 45. 1; J. C. N. Coulston, 'Later Roman Armour, 3rd–6th Centuries AD', *Journal of Roman Military Equipment Studies*, 1 (1990), 139–60.

[63] On mail see AM 16. 10. 8; SA *Carm.* 2. 143, 321–2, *Ep.* 3. 3. 5; on corselet see *ND* Occ. 9, Or. 11, insignia; on hauberk see C. H. Kraeling, *The Synagogue* (New Haven, Conn, 1956), pl. 54; *Fragmenta Virgiliana*, Cod. Vat. Lat. 3225 (Vatican), fo. 73ᵛ, pl. 49; cf. Mauricius, *Strat.* 10. 1. 4, possibly referring to detachable books, and Agathias, *Hist.* 2. 8. 4; without coif, see Kraeling, *Synagogue*, pl. 54, 55; Ferrua, *Le pittura*, pls. 84, 115; relief from the Vatican dated by R. S. O. Tomlin (pers. comm.) to 4th cent. G. M. Köppel, 'Die historischen Reliefs der römischen Kaiserzeit, IV', *BJ* 186 (1986), 1–90, no. 48 (= Vatican Inv. 1671); Cecchelli, *I mosaici*, pls. 14, 35.

[64] On scale see SA *Carm.* 7. 242, 15. 13; A. Poulter, 'Nicopolis Interim Report 1989', 9; on cuirass see *ND* Or. 11, Occ. 9; AM 29. 3. 4; *Ilias Ambrosiana*, pl. 12; a relief in the Vatican shows a suit of scale extending to the wrist; Rosenthal, *Vergilius Romanus*, pl. 14.

[65] Haldon, 'Byzantine Military Technology', 11–47 at 13–20; Procopius, *BP* 1. 24. 51; Anon. *PS* 16; Mauricius, *Strat.* 12. 8. 4; Agathias, *Hist.* 2. 8. 4; 'David' plates, J. P. C. Kent and K. S. Painter, eds., *Wealth of the Roman World* (London, 1977), nos. 179, 181–2, 185.

numbers of *fabricae* producing *scutaria et armorum*, with *armorum* here probably meaning armour rather than weapons. Two factories are also recorded as producing *loricaria*. Though production of armour continued, this does not prove it was used by infantry. The illustrations, postdating Gratian's reign (for Eastern and Western *fabricae*), in the *Notitia* show mail shirts, muscle cuirasses, and jointed-plate limb defences. Finally, a law of Marcian prohibited export of body armour (*loricae*).[66]

Lastly, artistic evidence shows many fifth-century soldiers wearing armour. The representations may be stylized, but the consistency of representation and the differences from illustrations of the early empire suggest little distortion occurred. This evidence can be divided into four groups: manuscript illustrations, official monuments, mosaics and wall-paintings, and plates, dishes, wood-carvings, etc. Western manuscript illustrations from this period show some figures with armour, though many without. The lack of illustrations of armoured soldiers does not prove a lack of armour, but should be compared with epigraphic depictions from the third century, where soldiers are almost always shown unarmoured, though fully armed. Similarly, most soldiers on the early fourth-century Arch of Constantine are shown unarmed, though most of the figures in combat are wearing armour. The Vatican Virgil, a manuscript from the early fifth century with contemporary illustrations, shows some soldiers wearing mail (including some with hauberks and coifs) and others with muscle cuirasses.[67] Official monuments show a similar picture. Some drawings of the (now lost) Column of Arcadius (386/408) in Constantinople depict armoured infantry (most in muscle cuirasses with *pteruges*, some in mail or scale). Similar figures are shown on the fourth-century panels on the Arch of Constantine. This also shows scale or mail. Such detail was time-consuming (and therefore expensive) to carve, and may have been painted. A comparison with the depiction of mail on Trajan's Column is relevant here. Many of the figures on the

[66] On *fabricae* see *ND* Or. 11. 18–39, Occ. 9. 16–39 (Paris MS best for details of armour); on production of armour see S. James, 'The *Fabricae*', in J. C. Coulston, ed., *Military Equipment and the Identity of Roman Soldiers*, *BAR* S394 (Oxford, 1988), 257–331 at 261; *CJ* 4. 41. 2 (455/7).

[67] Vatican Virgil, J. De Wit, *Die Miniaturen des Vergilius Vaticanus* (Amsterdam, 1959); cf. Ambrose Iliad, *Ilias Ambrosiana*; R. Bianchi Bandinelli, *Hellenistic-Byzantine Miniatures of the Iliad* (Olten, 1955); Rosenthal, *Vergilius Romanus*; on 3rd-cent. soldiers see Coulston, 'Roman Military Equipment', 141–56.

column were depicted as wearing mail, but the chisel marks were very shallow and are often lost or only visible to the naked eye. Any similar representation would probably be lost on sketches of the Column of Arcadius and the heavily weathered Column of Theodosius.[68] Fifth-century mosaics, such as those in the basilica of St Maria Maggiore, also illustrate soldiers with body armour and helmets. Wall-paintings of the same date often show soldiers, frequently in biblical scenes such as the Crossing of the Red Sea.[69] Finally, armoured infantry are shown in other artwork. The early seventh-century 'David' plates show Byzantine infantry wearing mail corselets with *pteruges* and an Egyptian wood-carving, probably fourth-century, shows infantry wearing mail corselets.[70]

The argument for large numbers of armoured infantry is complicated by the lack of archaeological evidence. There is very little surviving armour dating from this period. According to Robinson, 'actual Roman mail has survived in rare instances'. Since it is composed of intrinsically undatable iron rings, vulnerable to corrosion, this is not surprising. Archaeological evidence for *lorica segmentata* in the first and second centuries is much more common, but only because of the survival of the easily broken bronze hinges and fasteners, and there are only a few surviving iron plates in exceptional cases such as Corbridge. Before *lorica segmentata* was introduced, from the second century BC to at least the mid-first century AD, the entire Roman army wore mail. After this, though *segmentata* was used by most legionaries, auxiliaries, cavalry, and some legionaries continued to wear mail. However, there is little

---

[68] Column of Arcadius, two main sources: (1) Louvre MS inv. 4951, illustrated in G. Becatti, *La Colonna Coclide Istoriata* (Rome, 1960) and G. O. Giglioli, *La colonna di Arcadio a Constantinopoli* (Naples, 1952); (2) Trinity College Cambridge MS, illustrated in G. H. Freshfield, 'Notes on a Vellum Album', *Archaeologia*, 62 (1921–2), 87–104; Bibliothèque Nationale Inv. 6514, J. Kollwitz, *Oströmische Plastik der theodosianisch Zeit* (Berlin, 1941); Liebeschuetz, *Barbarians and Bishops*, 120–1, 273–8; the iconography of the column base is very similar to that of the *magister officiorum* in the *Notitia*, Occ. 9, Or. 11; Trajan's Column, J. C. Coulston, 'The Value of Trajan's Column as a Source for Military Equipment', *Roman Military Equipment*, 31–44; Arch of Constantine, H. P. L'Orange and A. Von Gerken, *Der spätantike Bildschungen des Konstantinsbogens* (Berlin, 1939).

[69] W. Dorigo, *Late Roman Painting* (New York, 1971), pl. 210; on early-mid-4th cent. catacomb paintings see Ferrua, *Le pittura*, pls. 5. 84, 115; Cecchelli, *I mosaici*, pls. 14, 34, 35 among others.

[70] 'David' plates, Kent and Painter, *Wealth*, nos. 179–87; carving, K. Weitzmann, ed., *Age of Spirituality* (New York, 1979), no. 69, and *Archaeology*, 30 (1977), front cover, Nov.

archaeological evidence for mail armour throughout this period and the only surviving complete coats come from a collapsed mine at Dura Europos. This scarcity suggests that a lack of surviving late Roman armour is not conclusive.[71]

Shock cavalry were armoured similarly to infantry and wore body armour, shields, and helmets. The armour of the *cataphracti* and light cavalry was slightly different. *Cataphracti* wore either a cuirass or mail body armour and their limbs were protected by segmented plate armour. They also had face masks on their helmets. They are not described as carrying shields, though an early fourth-century relief shows a cataphract with a shield.[72] Some cataphracts, though probably not all, rode armoured horses. Horse armour was made of scale (third-century examples of which have been found at Dura Europos) or mail, though leather or felt barding or cloth caparisons may also have been used. Caparisons would have considerably reduced the effect of missile fire, but would be unlikely to survive in the archaeological record.[73] Light cavalry were probably armoured, though there was no need for them to have been and they could have carried out their duties effectively with little armour. Their shields, if any, may have been smaller than those of the shock cavalry. Some may not have worn any protection at all.[74] Overall, continued use of body armour by late Roman troops, both infantry and cavalry, seems likely.

Vegetius also claims that helmets were abandoned under Gratian, though this seems unlikely for reasons similar to those just adduced for the lack of abandonment of armour. Furthermore, a number have actually survived, dating to the late fourth and early fifth centuries (i.e. past Gratian's reign). Helmets also appear frequently

[71] H. R. Robinson, *The Armour of Imperial Rome* (London, 1975), 164–73 at 171; Rostovtzeff, ed., *Dura Europos, Sixth Season*, 194–7; A. Poulter (pers. comm.) has seen 5th-cent. scale armour in a private collection in Bulgaria.

[72] On cataphracts see AM 16. 10. 8; Jul. *Or.* 1. 37D–38A, 2. 57B–C; Claudian, *De 6 Cons. Hon.* 569–77; Lib. *Or.* 18. 206; illustrations in *De Rebus Bellicis*, pls. 5, 6, 10–15; on segmented limb defences see *ND* Or. 11, Occ. 9; most recently, see Coulston, 'Tactical Developments', 59–75; see also Hoffmann, 69–72, 265–77; on cataphract with shield see Schleiermacher, *Reitergrabsteine*, no. 49; on lamellar see Rostovtzeff, ed., *Dura Europos, Sixth Season*, 450–2.

[73] Horse armour see Claudian, *De 6 Cons. Hon.* 569–77; Lib. *Or.* 18. 206; Anon. *PS* 17. 12–16; Mauricius, *Strat.* 1. 2. 6; for 3rd-cent. see Robinson, *Armour of Rome*, 194; Rostovtzeff, ed., *Dura Europos, Sixth Season*, 439–52; for leather (Persian) see AM 24. 6. 8; for felt (Hunnic) see Mauricius, *Strat.* 11. 2. 7.

[74] Rostovtzeff, ed., *Dura Europos, Fourth Season*, 215–16.

in later illustrations. Their simplicity and similarity suggest mass production in the *fabricae*. Two distinctive types are known and it is possible that the helmets worn by cavalry may have been different from infantry helmets or that officers' helmets differed from those worn by other ranks.[75] Greaves seem to have been worn occasionally by infantry, though they do not seem common. Third-century cloth and metal greaves have been found at Dura Europos. Only one illustration exists, of Hector outside Troy in the illustrations of the Ambrose *Iliad*.[76]

Most troops carried large oval shields. The examples on the 'David' plates, the Monza Diptych, the column of Arcadius and the Missoria of Theodosius and Valentinian are all similar in size, *c.*1–1.2 m. high, 0.8 m. wide. This is slightly smaller than the 1.6 m. height suggested by the sixth-century Anonymous Byzantinus. These shields were used by both infantry and cavalry. Round shields also existed, though they seem only to have been used by those in close attendance on the Emperor and may have been confined to the *candidati*. According to Vegetius, shields had the owner's name, cohort, and century written on the back. The terminology may be anachronistic but the practice of identifying the owner and unit probably continued.[77]

In addition to arms and armour, soldiers also carried other equipment. Every man should have carried a water-bottle, blanket, twenty days' rations and probably a pickaxe, tent quarter, and

[75] For helmets S. James, 'Evidence from Dura-Europos for the Origins of Late Roman Helmets', *Syria*, 63 (1986), 107–34, is a good summary; for details see H. Klumbach, *Spätrömische Gardehelme* (Munich, 1973); S. Johnson, 'A Late Roman Helmet from Burgh Castle', *Britannia*, 11 (1980), 303–12; for crests (of coloured feathers?) see *Ilias Ambrosiana*, pl. 25; C. Cecchelli, *I mosaici*, pl. 41; AM 24. 6. 10.

[76] For greaves (*ocreae*, κνημιδες) see Grosse, 327–8; Veg. 2. 15, 4. 44; SA *Carm.* 7. 264, *Ep.* 3. 3. 5; Lib. *Or.* 18. 280; Anon. *PS* 16. 14 and 55, 39. 31–3; Mauricius, *Strat.* 12. 8. 1, 4, and 16; Lydus, *De Mag.* 1. 46; Procopius, *BP* 1. 1. 12; for Dura Europos, cloth, see R. Pfister and L. Bellinger, *Excavations at Dura-Europos, Final Report 4.2: Textiles* (New Haven, Conn., 1945), 9; metal, unpubl. (pers. comm. S. James); *Ilias Ambrosiana*, pl. 54.

[77] For size of shields see Anon. *PS* 16. 1–13; Missorium of Valentinian, R. Delbrück, *Spätantike Kaiserporträts* (Berlin, 1933), inf. 79; cf. Couissin, *Les Armes romaines*, 197; for round shields see Constantius II plate, Kent and Painter, *Wealth*, no. 11; round shields are shown in the *Notitia* possibly because they were easier to draw with compasses; oval shields are shown on Column of Arcadius, Honorius and Valentinian's missoria, the Column of Theodosius, Delbrück, *Kaiserporträts*, inf. 94, 79, 86, and at San Vitale (6th cent.), F. W. Deichmann, *Frühchristliche Bauten und Mosaike von Ravenna* (Baden-Baden, 1958), pl. 368; for name, etc. see Veg. 2. 18.

stake. Uniform items included dogtags, boots, woollen tunic, military cloak (*chlamys*), and trousers. To this load must be added any spare clothing, boots, etc., as well as personal items. The basic fighting load would have been in the range of 25–30 kg.[78]

Remounts

Horses could be provided by troopers in cavalry regiments when enlisting, but were usually supplied by the government. They came from two sources: levies from provincials (sometimes commuted) and *honorati*, and imperial horse farms. Their supply was the duty of the *tribunus* (later *comes*) *stabuli* who was responsible for supplying all government horses.[79]

Equipment Production

The state provided equipment for troops by production from arms factories (*fabricae*). State production also eased control of weaponry, since any production that was not carried out in a *fabrica* was clearly illegal, and perhaps hindered (illegal) export beyond the frontiers.

The production seems to have been related to the administrative network of the Empire, at least as it appears in the *Notitia*. Each frontier province in Europe had a *fabrica scutaria*, while each frontier diocese had two general factories, producing body armour and other equipment. We do not know when this system was created or how it developed after the time of the *Notitia*. Specialized factories produced swords, bows, arrows, cataphract equipment, and artillery. The *fabricae* themselves were set back from the frontiers for security, and were placed on major road networks to avoid delays in transporting their products. They were probably

[78] For loads see Veg. 1. 19; for water-bottle see Suda E. 2310; for pickaxe see Anon. *PS* 18. 42–6; for rations see *CT* 7. 4. 5 (359); AM 16. 2. 8, 17. 8. 2, 17. 9. 2; Procopius, *BV* 3. 13. 15; for tents see AM 17. 13. 33, 18. 2. 10, 19. 5. 8, 20. 11. 6, 24. 1. 11, 24. 4. 2, 25. 1. 18, 29. 4. 5; *Pan. Lat.* 12(2). 10. 2; *Ilias Ambrosiana*, pl. 27; Procopius, *BV* 3. 17. 10; for stakes see AM 18. 2. 11; for blankets see AM 29. 4. 5; for dogtags see *Acta Maximiliani*, 2. 6; cf. 6th-cent. loads, Mauricius, *Strat.* 5. 4, 7. 11.

[79] Hyland, *Equus*, 71–86; on enlisting with horses see *CT* 7. 22. 2 (326); on levied horses see *CT* 11. 11. 1 (323), 16. 12 (380), 13. 5. 14 (371); on commutation see *CT* 11. 17. 1 (367), 11. 17. 2–3 (401); *Pan. Lat.* 11(3). 9; from *honorati* see *LRE* 1259 n. 37; on horse farms see *ND* Or. 14. 6; Thrace, Procopius, *BV* 3. 12. 6; Sardinia, AM 29. 3. 5; Asia Minor, Theophylact, *Hist.* 3. 1. 13; Justinian, *Nov.* 30. 5. 1; Phrygia, *CT* 6. 4. 19 (372)?; on horse quality see *CT* 6. 31. 1 (365/73).

placed within wall circuits, though we have no idea what a *fabrica* looked like and none has yet been identified archaeologically.[80]

Though production seems highly centralized, it is probable that all factories produced some other equipment in small quantities, and that units could produce and repair some of their own equipment. Arrows, javelins, and spears were simple to make and/or repair and regimental armourers probably existed. They are mentioned in Vegetius' list of members of the legion and also in Mauricius' *Strategikon*.[81]

[80] James, '*Fabricae*', 257–331, discusses the *fabricae* in depth; on archaeological assertion of *fabrica* see D. Bayard and D. Piton, 'Un bâtiment public du bas-Empire à Amiens', *Cahiers Archéologiques du Picardie*, 6 (1979), 153–68 at 162–5.
[81] Veg. 2. 11; Mauricius, *Strat.* 12. 8. 7.

4

Finance

The Roman army in the fourth century employed at least 300,000 individuals. According to an anonymous sixth-century Byzantine writer, 'expenditure on the army is the biggest item of state expenditure every year'. Paying for this organization consumed most of the imperial budget and became more difficult during the fifth century, especially in the West. The Byzantine 'Anonymous' was not alone in his views. For the fourth-century author of the *De Rebus Bellicis*, the army was a great consumer: 'let me turn to the vast expenditure on the army . . . . Because of this expenditure the whole mechanism of tax collection is collapsing'. In the 470s the Senate remarked to Zeno that 'we cannot supply our own soldiers alone without difficulties' when consulted on additional pay for allies. Military finance seems to have been a major concern throughout the period.[1]

Many contemporaries objected to this massive military spending. There was much hostile reaction to Leo's expenditure on the Vandal expedition of 468, 130,000 lb. of gold according to some sources, though one suspects that this criticism would have been less strident if the expedition had been successful. These complaints cannot be assessed statistically, but seem to be more common in the fifth century than the fourth. Complaints were made in both East and West.[2]

---

[1] Anon. *PS* 2. 19–21; Anon. *DRB* 5. 1; Malchus fr. 15; AM 20. 11. 5; Them. *Or*. 18. 222A; Gregory Nazianzus, *Or*. 19. 14; M. F. Hendy, *Studies in the Byzantine Monetary Economy, A D 300–1453* (Cambridge, 1985), 157; cf. R. MacMullen, 'The Roman Emperor's Army Costs', *Latomus*, 43 (1984), 571–80; C. R. Whittaker, in C. E. King, ed., *Imperial Revenue, Expenditure and Monetary Policy* (Oxford, 1980).
[2] Procopius, *BV* 3. 6. 2; Theoph. *AM* 5961; cf. Lydus, *de Mag*. 3. 43, 65,000 lb. gold, 700,000 lb. silver; Candidus fr. 2, 64,000 lb. gold, 700,000 lb. silver; other complaints, Valentinian I, Zos. 4. 16, 1; Theodosius I, Zos. 4. 27. 2–3; Valentinian III, *NVal* 15 (445); Avitus, J. Ant. fr. 202; Anthemius, SA *Ep*. 2. 2. 4; Eugippius, *V. Sev*. 20; Zeno, Suda E. 3100 = Malchus fr. 7, 15.

A: IMPERIAL INCOME

Any attempt to produce a detailed calculation of imperial income in the period 350–425 would be out of place here, even if it were possible. The intention is simply to show that the income of the Empire was decreasing, a trend which can be shown in a number of ways. Jones estimated that 95 per cent of imperial income came from land.[3] Some estimate of income from land taxation, though very approximate, can be made. We know the income received annually from the provinces of Numidia and Mauretania Sitifensis in the mid-fifth century, 78,200 and 41,000 *solidi* respectively. These were poor provinces. Egypt, an extremely rich diocese, of six provinces, produced approximately 20,000 lb. of gold (1,440,000 *solidi*) annually under Justinian. If the approximate 1,000 lb. of gold received from Numidia is taken as an average income then annual state income from land taxation can be reckoned as:

$$\text{Provinces } (120) \times 1,000 = 120,000 \text{ lb. gold}$$

Since the poor province of Numidia is used, this is a minimum and the real figure was probably higher. This estimate represents income of the area controlled by the Empire in the 350s, though it declined

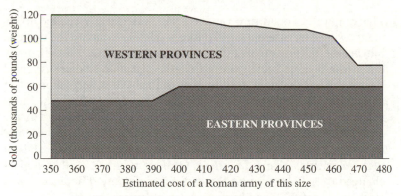

Fig. 8   Numbers of imperial provinces, 350–480

as the Empire lost territory (Fig. 8). Here, a simple method is used to assess territorial losses, merely counting the number of provinces of the Empire. Though this is a drastic over-simplification, it

---

[3] *LRE* 462–5; followed by Hendy, *Byzantine Economy*, 157–60.

provides a clear picture and, since state income was based almost totally on land, it should not be wildly inaccurate. With the available evidence, no realistic attempt can be made to take into account variations in local productivity or of different values of different provinces, though the West was always poorer than the East. The Western Empire did not suffer initially because of its weaker financial base, but after 395 it was less able to deal with already existing problems. These diagrams mask reality, in that little account is taken of the disruption caused by barbarian attacks and the wandering peoples in the Empire (e.g. the Goths in the Balkans, Italy, and Gaul between 395 and 418), but they do provide some insights, for example showing that the impact of the Vandal conquest of Africa was delayed by their non-occupation of several African provinces until Valentinian III's death in 455. These estimates also concern land area only, and do not take into account reductions in revenue from land held. Like variations in provincial wealth, this is impossible to assess, though it did occur and was a factor in reducing imperial income.[4]

B: PAYING FOR THE ARMY

The Empire's expenditure on the army was directly related to its manpower. Any attempt to produce a reliable estimate is hopeless, but an establishment of 450,000 seems reasonable, though many units would have been under-strength.[5] Regular soldiers received payment from the state in a number of forms: a miserly amount of annual pay, donatives at imperial accessions and at five-year intervals thereafter, rations, fodder, and equipment. When they left the army, they received a discharge bounty. To establish the cost of the army it is necessary to calculate the monetary cost of each of these elements. Some of these were commuted, and practices changed over time, though this did not make any difference to the Empire as it still had to buy the rations, horses, etc.

Annual pay (*stipendium*) is a difficult subject to assess since it seems to have been only a nominal sum and therefore little evidence

---

[4] On Western poverty see *LRE* 1064–8; on decline in income see *LRE* 812–23, 1039–40.

[5] *LRE* 679–83; R. MacMullen, 'How Big was the Roman Imperial Army?' *Klio*, 62 (1980), 451–60; see below Ch. 5 n. 1.

survives. Annual pay may have existed in 360 when Julian complained that Constantius II had not given the necessary money for wages for several years. It is not directly recorded after this date and had probably been discontinued by the fifth century when its low value could account for the lack of protest at its disappearance. The only idea of its value comes from papyri dating to 299 and 300. At this period legionaries and some auxiliaries received 1,800 *denarii* per annum, other auxiliaries less, small sums even then.[6]

Donatives were of greater value. A donative was received on the accession of an emperor as Caesar or Augustus and at five-year intervals thereafter, coinciding with imperial *vota*. We do not know whether the occasion for granting a donative in the East was cause for granting one in the West. Though the accession of new junior colleagues to a college of emperors was cause for donatives, we do not know if their *quinquennalia* and subsequent celebrations were.[7] The accession donative was a fixed sum of 5 *solidi* and a pound of silver, apparently the same for all ranks. The large number of *solidi* required for this gift required special minting of coins. The pound of silver was worth 4 *solidi* until 397, after which it was revalued to be worth 5 *solidi*.[8] Quinquennial donatives were of five *solidi*.[9]

Rations (*annonae*) were provided by the state either in kind (according to a fixed tariff) or commuted to money payment, universal by the fifth century. Valentinian III valued an *annona* in Numidia and Mauretania in 445 as being worth 4 *solidi* per annum. By the time of Justinian it seems to have been worth 5 *solidi* in Africa, but remained at 4 *solidi* in Egypt. Local variations in price should be expected because of different production specialities, so that wine was more expensive in Egypt than in Italy. For purposes

---

[6] On *stipendium* see *LRE* 623–4; not received, but no mention of value, see AM 20. 8. 8; Ammianus also refers to *stipendia* in 366 (26. 8. 6) and 370 (28. 6. 12) which were probably donatives; on value of *denarius* see *LRE* 438–41; here I follow the amendments of R. P. Duncan-Jones, *Structure and Scale in the Roman Economy* (Cambridge, 1990), 105–17.

[7] Hendy, *Byzantine Economy*, 175–8, 187–90, 481; *LRE* 624; *RE* 5. 1542–5; on value of silver see *LRE* 439; Hendy, *Byzantine Economy*, 480–2.

[8] Julian, AM 20. 4. 18; Procopius, AM 26. 8. 6?, Leo I, Constantine Porphyrogenitus, *De Caeremoniis*, 1. 91; Leo II, Constantine Porphyrogenitus, *De Caeremoniis*, 1. 94.

[9] Constantius II, 355 (delayed from 353?), AM 15. 6. 3; Valentinian I, 370, AM 28. 6. 12; Maximus, 388, Zos. 4. 16. 2?; Anastasius, 496, Marc. Com. sa 496; 500, Marc. Com. sa 500.

of calculation, *annonae* are taken to be worth 4 *solidi* throughout the Empire.[10] Fodder allowances (*capitus*) were likewise commuted, and in sixth-century Africa were valued as 4 *solidi*.[11]

As well as feeding troops and their horses the state also clothed them. A law of Valens assessed the cost of clothing and other expenses of a new recruit as 6 *solidi*, a sum which seems to have remained constant throughout the period. We do not know whether equipment was included in this sum or provided separately, nor do we know whether the state or the recruit paid for equipment. Manufactured items were expensive (a military cloak (*chlamys*) was costed as 1 *solidus* in 396, as 2 *tremisses* before this), and had to be replaced from time to time. The state probably paid for equipment and its replacement since salaries do not appear to have been high enough to allow for it and there was no other regular cash income.[12]

Cavalry troopers also received from the state the sum of 7 *solidi* to buy a horse. It is not known how long the Romans used cavalry horses before replacing them, though modern practice suggests twelve years as an average. The cost was high enough for those recruits joining with horses to be automatically posted to cavalry regiments.[13]

An added difficulty in calculating the value of these payments is the regularity with which they were paid. An initial clothing and horse grant would be made to each trooper, but we do not know how often they would require new clothing or horses, nor do we know how many recruits would be required every year. A minimum would be one-twenty-fourth of the numbers of soldiers in the army, but this assumes that all troops lived to serve twenty-four years, an obviously unrealistic assumption.

Finally, discharge bounties were paid to men retiring from the service. From Valentinian I onwards these consisted of an allotment of land, four oxen (3 *solidi* each?), 200 *modii* of seed corn (5 *solidi*), and 25 *folles* (a nominal sum in bronze, approximately equal to 1/60 *solidus*). Before Valentinian the alternative of a cash grant

[10] *LRE* 629–30, 670; Valentinian III, *NVal* 13. 1. 3–4 (445); Justinian, *CJ* 1. 27. 2. 20–33 (534); *Edict*, 13. 18.

[11] *LRE* 629–30; *CT* 13.7.2 (375); *CJ* 1. 27. 2. 20–33 (534); Hendy, *Byzantine Economy*, 166.

[12] *LRE* 624–5; on cloak see *CT* 7. 6. 4 (396), *P. Lips.* 34–5, 61–2.

[13] *LRE* 625–6; on length of horse use see K. R. Dixon and P. Southern, *The Roman Cavalry* (London, 1992), 173–4; *CT* 7. 22. 2 (326).

existed, worth 100 *folles* (approximately 1/15 *solidus*), or an allotment of land, two oxen, 100 *modii* of seed corn, and 25 *folles*.[14]

So far the discussion has been confined to private soldiers. Our knowledge of the rewards of officers and non-commissioned officers is sporadic. Officers certainly received higher *stipendia* under Diocletian, but we have only one example, a *praepositus* receiving 18,000 *denarii* per annum, still a small sum when inflation is taken into account. They seem not to have received higher donatives.

The major portion of officer and non-commissioned officer pay came in increased ration and fodder allowances. We are fortunate to know the scales for non-commissioned officers. *Primicerii* received 5 *annonae* (and if in a cavalry regiment 2 *capitus*), *senatores* 4 (2?), *ducenarii* $3\frac{1}{2}$ ($1\frac{1}{2}$), *centenarii* $2\frac{1}{2}$ (1), *biarchi* and *circitores* 2 (1), and *semissales* $1\frac{1}{2}$ (1). The rewards of *vicarii* (regimental second-in-commands) are unknown, but were presumably higher than those of a *primicerius*. *Domestici* received 6 *annonae* and probably 6 *capitus*, while regimental actuaries received 6 of each. This suggests that regimental commanders received at least this much in allowances, if not more. The rank above regimental commanders, *duces*, received 50 *annonae* and 50 *capitus*, so presumably *comites* and *magistri militum* received still higher allowances.[15]

These figures allow us to produce some estimates of the annual cost of soldiers to the state. The basic formula for an infantry ranker is:

$\frac{1}{5}$ quinquennial donative + $\frac{1}{24}$ equipment + *annona* + $\frac{1}{24}$ discharge bounty

For cavalry, add: *capitus* + $\frac{1}{12}$ horse. Therefore the annual cost per soldier was as follows:

infantry $\qquad 1 + \frac{1}{4} + 4 + \frac{3}{4} = 6$
cavalry $\qquad 1 + \frac{1}{4} + 4 + \frac{3}{4} (+ 4 + \frac{1}{2}) = 10.5$ *solidi*

We do not know how these values changed over time. However, the general stability of gold prices meant there was little change,

---

[14] *LRE* 635–6; *CT* 7. 20. 3 (320), 8 (364); A. H. M. Jones, 'The Origin and Early History of the *Follis*', *JRS* 49 (1959), 34–8, calculating 1 *follis* as 1/1500 *solidus* in 363.
[15] *LRE* 643–4; on *domestici* see *CT* 6. 24. 1 (362), 2 (364); on *duces* see *NVal* 13.5 (445); Justinian, *Edicts*, 13. 18; on donatives see *LRE* 623 n. 31.

and in the major component of the payment, the *annonae* and *capitus*, change appears to have been limited. Approximate though they are, these figures show that fodder and ration allowances made up most of the annual cost of the army. They also show the cost of raising troops, though this is somewhat disguised by the above figures. The cost of equipping and paying an infantryman in his first year was 10 *solidi*, a cavalryman 21 *solidi*, but in their second year of service the costs were 4 and 8 *solidi* respectively, though these figures do not include donatives, replacement equipment, or discharge costs. The short-term expense in raising new troops made hiring allies an attractive option when resources were limited or when troops were needed for a short period only, as during usurpations. The costs of allies would probably be restricted to *annonae* and *capitus* (probably in kind rather than cash), and probably a cash bonus of some sort. Known payments to barbarian allies seem to have been lump sums, such as the 1,000 lb. of gold and 40,000 lb. of silver promised to Triarius and his 13,000 men in 478. There would be no need to provide horses for allied cavalry, a major element in reducing costs, though some remounts might be needed.[16]

How did income and expenditure relate? Using the above figures for individual costs, with a ratio of 1:4 cavalry to infantry and an increase in costs of 10 per cent for the higher ranks, the formula is as follows:

$$[(\text{men} \times 6) + \tfrac{1}{3} (\text{men} \times 4.5)] \times 1.1 = \text{annual cost in } solidi$$

If the army was 300,000 strong the annual cost in gold would have been 31,625 lb., if it was 450,000 strong, 47,438 lb., and 63,250 lb. if there were 600,000 in the army.

There were also other, non-quantifiable, military costs. Repair and upkeep of military fortifications was an imperial responsibility, and though maintenance of civil defences was theoretically the duty of the individual cities, in practice the government often had to use tax resources for the purpose, effectively increasing the military budget.[17] A similar outlay was the upkeep of equipment—boats, ships (expensive), artillery, wagons—and production of ammunition (spears, arrows, etc.). Military supplies also had to be

---

[16] Malchus fr. 15, 18. 3. 24–6, 20. 55–8.
[17] *CT* 15. 1. 32–3 (395).

paid for, wood for heating, paper, papyrus for records, etc. All this material also had to be transported to the armies from wherever it was produced.[18] A last extra cost was that of the army on campaign, when supplies had to be transported, in large volumes, to the army. Transporting supplies required large numbers of animals and handlers, all of whom had to be fed. Some emperors gave gifts to troops while on campaign.[19] Other 'defence-related' costs included the maintenance of the *cursus publicus* and taxation privileges, such as immunities for veterans and their families.[20]

C: FINANCIAL PROBLEMS

From the various estimates above we can outline the problems faced by the Roman state, even if we are unable to elaborate any of the details. Some problems were short-term. Thus in 475 the usurper Basiliscus 'was so greedy for money that he did not leave alone even those who pursued mean and mechanical occupations. There was universal lamentation because of the imposition of such taxes.' One reason for problems on accession was the immediate need to provide donatives for troops, while waiting for the *aurum coronarium* and other taxes to be collected.[21] Financial problems were not confined to the short term, and western Roman income fell dramatically after the early fifth century. According to a law of Valentinian III: 'from the revenue which is with difficulty collected from the exhausted taxpayer provision cannot be made for feeding and clothing even the old army, not to speak of newly levied troops'.[22] This is shown by Fig. 9, which plots calculated defence costs against theoretical imperial income. All costs include an arbitrary 50 per cent addition for support costs. These figures are estimates, but their relationship to imperial income is more

[18] *LRE* 834–6; *NTh* 6 (438).

[19] Hendy, *Byzantine Economy*, 221–4; on financial rewards see 363, 150 sp, Zos. 3. 13. 3; 100 sp, 3. 18. 6; R. MacMullen, 'The Emperor's Largesses', *Latomus*, 21 (1962), 159–66.

[20] On *cursus publicus* see *LRE* 830–34; on tax privileges see *CT* 7. 20. 2 (326), 4 (325), 13. 1. 2 (360), 13. 1. 7 (369), 14 (385).

[21] On taxes see *LRE* 430–2; on Basiliscus see Suda B. 164 (= Malchus fr. 9. 3); Hendy, *Byzantine Economy*, 175–8.

[22] *NVal* 15 (445).

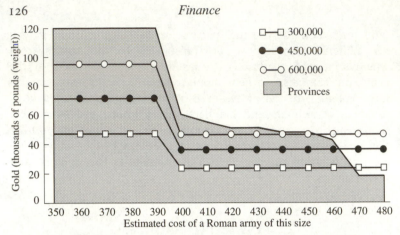

Fig. 9   Resources and military expenditure (West), 350–480

important than the figures themselves. Before the division of the
Empire, there was an appreciable surplus, but after 395, though
costs for each part were reduced, so was income. The margins were
now much smaller and income and cost curves came closer together.
During the 420s–440s reductions were probably forced on military
spending in the West. From the 450s, on all cost estimates,
insufficient income was being generated to support the Western
army at its original size.

   Although income was reduced, during the fifth century there is
no evidence of a decrease in the number of Western soldiers (though
there is little enough evidence for their numbers) and *limitanei* did
survive in Noricum and presumably elsewhere, still being paid for.
Not surprisingly, from Honorius' reign onwards, the West began
having problems paying for its troops, resulting in a search for
cheaper alternatives, found in the use of allied or barbarian contingents. In the economically stronger East, though allied contingents were used, they were not as common as in the West.
But complaints of shortages of money and difficulties in paying
troops were not confined to the West and also appeared in the
East.[23]

   These financial problems should not be overstressed. Many
emperors were able to accumulate large surpluses, while in 468

---

[23] *LRE* 1199 n. 128 suggests Western tax rates significantly higher than Eastern.

both east and west were able to launch a massive expedition against the Vandals, though its failure did not seem to affect imperial activity elsewhere in the ensuing years. If an army was needed for some purpose it could be provided. According to Whittaker, 'the costs of the army and bureaucracy were not the economic millstone which sank the Roman Empire'.[24]

[24] Whittaker, *Inflation and Economy*, 1–22, at 2; *LRE* 468–9; Hendy, *Byzantine Economy*, 224–7.

5

Recruiting

During the fourth and fifth centuries AD the Roman army recruited soldiers (a phrase including *foederati* but excluding allies) from both inside and outside the Empire. The Roman army in this period was at least 300,000 and may have been 600,000 strong. Recruits served for twenty years (or twenty-four years in the case of *limitanei* not in legions or vexillations). Given an even distribution of discharges, there was a *minimum* requirement of 15,000 men per year. This does not take losses in battle, to disease, or to desertion, into account. If the army was 600,000 strong then imperial requirements would be at least 30,000 men annually. Recruits were drawn from both inside and outside the Empire.[1]

A: RECRUITS FROM WITHIN THE EMPIRE

There were two main sources of recruits from within the Empire, volunteers and conscripts. It is difficult to know what proportion of recruits from within the Empire were volunteers because it is hard to compare the evidence for them with that for conscripts. Most evidence for volunteers is anecdotal, for example the story concerning the future Emperor Justin I and his friends joining the *excubitores* in the late fifth century. Conversely, evidence for conscripts is mostly found in law-codes. Furthermore, evidence for volunteers usually concerns individuals, that for conscripts groups. Volunteers are found throughout this period, but there is so little evidence that any changes in the pattern cannot be detected.[2]

Conscription took three forms. First, the sons of soldiers were required to enlist. Providing every soldier had at least one son (and

---

[1] On establishment see *LRE* 679–84; on service length see *CT* 7. 20. 4 (325).
[2] Evagrius, *HE* 2. 1; Procopius, *HA* 61. 2; *CT* 7. 2. 1 (383), 2 (385).

most married soldiers would have had at least one), this ought to have kept the manpower level roughly constant. However, some sons of veterans, the most famous being St Martin, tried to evade service, though the government continually tried to root out such defaulters. Most of the evidence for this defaulting comes from the *Codex Theodosianus*, which shows that the problem existed, but gives no idea of its extent.[3] We do not know whether sons of soldiers of extra-imperial origin were required to enlist, though since we know of no legal exceptions this seems likely for those living within the Empire. We know of a number of soldiers who were the sons of such men (e.g. Silvanus, Stilicho, and Aspar), though their fathers, where known, were officers. No serving sons of barbarian other ranks are known, though they probably existed.[4]

The second type of conscription was through annual levies of recruits. We have no idea of their numbers or of their proportions compared with sons of serving men. These levies of recruits were apparently taken annually, but could be commuted to a payment.[5] The third type of conscription was instituted in the early fifth century. This allowed for a supplementary levy to be raised from the *honorati* (the classes of *illustres* and *clarissimi*). This was often commuted to a simple levy of 30 *solidi* and used to provide extra funds for the government. Such levies seem to have been occasional rather than annual, and commutation is known to have occurred in 407, 410, 412, and 444, while recruits were recorded as being levied in 402, 412, 413, 423, and 428.[6]

Recruits were also levied from barbarian prisoners of war settled within the Empire. The sources use several words for these settlers, *laeti*, *gentiles*, *dediticii*, and *tributarii*.[7] The distinctions between

[3] For sons required to enlist see *CT* 7. 1. 5 (364), 8 (365), 11 (372), 18. 10 (400), 20. 12 (400), 22. 1 (319), 2 (326), 4 (332), 7–11 (372–80); *CJ* 12. 47. 2 (380); on son following father see *ILS* 2777, 2787, 2805; Evagrius *HE* 2. 1; AM 14. 10. 2; on attempts to avoid conscription see Sev. *V. Mart.* 2. 1–6; *CT* 7. 1. 8 (365), 22. 1 (319), 2 (326), 7–9 (372–80).

[4] *PLRE* i, Hormisdas 3, Silvanus, Stilicho; *PLRE* ii, Iordanes 3, Aspar.

[5] On conscription see *CT* 7. 13. 12 (397), 18 (407); *NVal* 6. 1 (440), 2 (443); Zos. 4. 12. 1; annually, see AM 31. 4. 4; on commutation see *CT* 7. 13. 2 (370), 13 (397), 14 (397); *NVal* 6. 3 (444); AM 19. 11. 7, 31. 4. 4.

[6] *LRE* 616; *CT* 6. 23. 2 (423), 26. 14 (412), 30. 20 (413), 7. 13. 15 (402), 18 (407), 20 (410), 22 (428), 11. 18. 1 (412); *NVal* 6. 3 (444); all these laws were issued in the West.

[7] C. R. Whittaker, 'Labour Supply in the Late Roman Empire', *Opus*, 1 (1982), 171–9; on collection of evidence see G. E. M. de Ste Croix, *The Class Struggle in the Ancient Greek World* (London, 1981), app. 3.

these terms are unclear. The only source which might allow any discussion of these words as technical terms is the *Codex Theodosianus*. A law of 409 concerning the settlement of some prisoners from the Sciri defines their position. The settlers should have the status of *coloni*, pay taxes, not be placed in border territory close to their homes, and should not be required to provide recruits for the army for twenty years. The restrictions were 'because of a shortage of farm produce', implying that agricultural production was of great importance and that in other circumstances the settlers would be required to do military service earlier. The settlers are not referred to as *dediticii* or *laeti*; instead, 'they shall have no title other than *coloni*'. The same situation is implied in the late third century, when a panegyric to Constantius I referred to 'the Frank, received into the laws' (*receptus in leges*), that is subject to the same laws as Roman citizens.

A historical record of this settlement of Sciri also exists. Sozomen recorded that the Sciri were settled as farmers, in certain areas, including Bithynia, and he himself had seen them farming. Sozomen's history was written between 409 and the 440s, so this shows that the settlements were distinctive enough to stand out up to a generation later. Sozomen does not use any technical terms, he simply says that the Sciri were farming. His vocabulary is the same as that of other authors recording other settlements, but it is only in this case that we have an imperial edict to compare with a historical account. The two sources reveal circumstances which may have been normal for other settlements.[8]

However, there is no reason to expect the terms of all settlements to be identical. Unless we are to suppose that there was a set of imperial regulations regarding settlements, the terms would have been decided by the men on the spot. Thus Julian's settlement of the Salii in 358 occurred during the campaigning season and there could have been little time for elaborate planning. Previous settlements could influence subsequent settlements, but not determine them.[9]

The edict of 409 suggests that any military service carried out by the Sciri would have been as normal recruits. This conflicts with orthodox (archaeological) opinion that these settlers formed their

---

[8] Sciri, *CT* 5. 6. 3 (409); Soz. *HE* 9. 5; Franks, *Pan. Lat.* 4(8). 21.
[9] AM 17. 8. 3–4; Lib. *Or.* 18. 75.

own units. The evidence for orthodoxy comes from the *Notitia Dignitatum* in the chapter of the western *magister peditum* (Occ. 42) where, after a list of units assigned to the command of the *magister* in various provinces, there is recorded a list of *praefecti laetorum* and *praefecti Sarmatarum gentilium*. These officers are assumed to have commanded military units, on the grounds that they appear under the command of the *magister peditum*. Most have stations noted, so if they were army units, they would be *limitanei*, rather than *comitatenses*. Most of these groups are found at a distance from the frontier and some are allocated to vague areas, 'between Rheims and Amiens' or 'Apulia and Calabria'. It thus seems likely that some at least did not have formal head-quarters, casting doubt on their being units. These locations, however, would suit farmers scattered through a region.[10]

The impression that these groups were not combat units may be confirmed by one of the few pieces of relevant legislation from the *Codex Theodosianus*. A law of 400 refers to Alamannic or Sarmatian *laeti*, along with other groups (including the sons of veterans) who ought to be enrolled in the army. There is no mention of any special laetic units for them, but they are treated as recruits in the same way as other Romans. In this case, what sort of organizations are recorded in the *Notitia* and in a law of 369 mentioning *praepositi laetis*? Roman officers (*praepositi*) were attached to these groups, though we do not know in what capacity. The laws of 369 and 409 were addressed to a praetorian prefect, not a *magister militum*, which may mean they were not just a military responsibility, though the law of 400 was addressed to the *magister militum*. Only the last directly concerned recruiting.[11]

There is also some evidence for a regular regiment named the *Laeti*. A unit called *Laeti* appears in Constantius II's 361 campaign against Julian. In sixth-century Italy there existed a regular regiment named *Felices L(a)etorum*. *Laeti* was also the name of an Alamannic canton and we know of other Roman regiments named

---

[10] On special units see e.g. S. James, 'Britain and the Late Roman Army', in T. F. C. Blagg and A. C. King, eds., *Military and Civilian in Roman Britain*, *BAR* 136 (Oxford, 1984), 161–86 at 171–2, deriving from T. Mommsen, *Gesammelte Schriften* (Berlin, 1910), 6. 256–60; on distribution see de Ste Croix, *Class Struggle*, 4. 17 and 19, app. 3; *ND* Occ. 42. 33–70, though there is no title for this section and an unknown quantity of text is missing between ll. 32 and 33.

[11] For *laeti* see *CT* 7. 20. 12 (400); to PPO, *CT* 5. 6. 3 (409), 7. 20. 10 (369); for *praepositi laetorum* see *CT* 7. 20. 10 (369); cf. Lib. *Or.* 59. 127.

after Alamannic cantons, e.g. the Brisigavi *iuniores* and *seniores* and the Bucinobantes. Another possible case of a regiment of *laeti* formed from settlers is Jordanes' mention of some Sarmatians among the Roman allies at the battle of the Catalaunian Plains in 451, since Sarmatian *laeti* are recorded as having been settled in Gaul. It is equally likely that Jordanes is referring to Alan *foederati*.[12]

Gentiles were grouped with *laeti* in the *Notitia*, suggesting they were similar in type, while laws in the *Codex Theodosianus* describe them in the same breath as *laeti*. In Africa, *gentiles* were barbarians assigned to defend sectors of the border, though the situation was probably different in Europe where the *gentiles* we know of were not deployed on the frontier.[13] Although they did not serve as units, *laeti* and *gentiles* certainly served as Roman soldiers. Evidence for this service comes from a panegyrical description of one of Constantius I's settlements: 'The barbarian farmer pays taxes. What is more, if he is called for military service, he hurries up, is improved by the discipline and is proud to serve under the name of soldier.' This sounds like normal conscription, not a short-term levy or militia service. It seems unlikely that individuals would be summoned to serve and then be allowed back to farming after a while. This accords with the evidence of the law concerning the Sciri and other laws discussing the liability of *coloni* for military service.[14]

If most settlements were made under similar conditions to that of the Sciri, they would probably have been quickly assimilated into Roman society. One example of the inability of these settlements to retain their identity is shown by some Taifali. They are recorded by the *Notitia* as *gentiles* settled in Poitou. By the sixth century, the area had become known as Taifalia and Taifali are recorded as

[12] On combat units see AM 21. 13. 16; cf. 20. 8. 13; for Italy see *CIL* 4. 7771; *P. Ital.* 24; on Sarmatians see Jordanes, *Getica*, 191; *ND* Occ. 42. 65–70; 'Liticiani' of *Getica*, 191, seem unlikely to be *laeti*; as Alamannic canton see AM 16. 11. 4 (presumably not those of 20. 8. 13); on Alamannic units see *ND* Occ. 7. 25, 128 (Brisigavi), Or. 6. 58 (Bucinobantes), Or. 28. 43, 33. 31 (Iuthungi); on Alamannic cantons, Bucinobantes, see AM 29. 4. 7; on Iuthungi see AM 17. 6. 1; Ambrose, *Ep.* 24. 8; *LV* 13. 22; *ND* Or. 28. 43, 33. 31.

[13] *CT* 7. 15. 1 (409), 11. 30. 62 (405).

[14] For militia see e.g. B. Cunliffe, *Greeks, Romans and Barbarians* (London, 1988), 192; *Pan. Lat.* 4(8). 9. 3–4, 7(6). 2; C. J. Simpson, 'Foederati and Laeti in Late Roman Frontier Defence', M.Phil. thesis (Nottingham, 1971); as *coloni* see *NSev* 2. 1 (465), but problems with text.

killing a Merovingian noble at Poitiers. Both of these facts are recorded by Gregory of Tours, but he calls these men Taifali only because that is what their *pagus* is called; the term for him has nothing to do with their ethnic origins and they act just as other Franks do. They seem to have lost all trace of their origins and if they had been recorded as Pictavi rather than as Taifali, we would not have noticed them.[15]

It has been thought that there are traces of these settlers in finds of 'Germanic' metalwork, burial styles, etc., principally in the Reihengräber of the (late) fifth century in north Gaul. Though these burials have generated an extensive archaeological literature, the association of these settlements with immigrants is still uncertain and it has recently been argued that these graves are in fact those of the indigenous Roman population and that the 'Germanic' metalwork is in fact derived from that of the Roman Empire and not vice versa.[16]

In conclusion, most of the (admittedly tenuous) evidence suggests that recruits drawn from settlements of prisoners within the Roman Empire were treated in the same way as other recruits from inside the Empire. Though it is difficult to form an assessment of the geographical origins of internal recruits for the army, contemporary impressions can be recorded. Gaul and Illyricum were famous for producing good soldiers and from the 460s in the Eastern Empire Isaurians supplied numbers of good troops. These vague impressions can be sup-

---

[15] *ND* Occ. 42. 65; GT *HF* 4. 18, *Vita Patrum* 15. 1; cf. Jordanes, *Getica*, 267; cf. Procopius, *BG* 5. 12. 9–19.

[16] For doubts see G. Halsall, 'The Origins of the Reihengräberzivilisation', in *Fifth-Century Gaul*, 196–207; E. James, 'Cemeteries and the Problem of Frankish Settlement in Gaul', in P. H. Sawyer, ed., *Names, Words, and Graves* (Leeds, 1979), 55–89; orthodoxy, summarized in R. Günther, 'Laeti, foederati und Gentilen in Nord- und Nordost Gallien im zussamenhang der sogennanten Laetizivilisation', *Zeitschrift für Archäologie*, 5 (1971), 39–59; for belt-fittings see R. S. O. Tomlin, 'Notitia Dignitatum omnium, quam civilium tam militarium', in R. Goodburn and P. Bartholomew, eds., *Aspects of the Notitia Dignitatum*, *BAR* S15 (Oxford, 1976), 189–209 at 191; distributions are mapped in Böhme, *Germanische Grabfunde*; S. C. Hawkes and G. C. Dunning, 'Soldiers and Settlers in Britain, Fourth to Fifth Centuries', *Medieval Archaeology*, 5 (1961), 1–70; S. C. Hawkes, 'Some Recent Finds of Late Roman Buckles', *Britannia*, 5 (1974), 386–93; C. J. Simpson, 'Belt Buckles and Strap Ends of the Late Roman Empire', *Britannia*, 7 (1976), 192–223, and D. Welsby, *The Roman Military Defence of the British Provinces in its Later Phases* (Oxford, 1982), 157–64, express some doubts as to their association with *laeti*, doubts very tentatively shown in Hawkes, 'Recent Finds', and Simpson, 'Foederati and Laeti', i. 130–1.

plemented by tabulations of known origins of field army troops from within the Empire, though the sample is too small to have much value (Table 2).[17]

Table 2: *Geographical origins of field army soldiers by prefecture and diocese,*
350–476

	GALLIA		ITALIA		ILLYRICUM		ORIENS	
	Gallia	7	Italia	2	Macedonia	0	Pontica	6
	Britannia	1	Illyricum	9	Dacia	7	Oriens	12
	Hispania	4	Africa	4			Asiana	1
							Thracia*	15
							Aegyptus	0
TOTAL		12		15		7		34

* Includes Constantinople.

B: RECRUITS FROM OUTSIDE THE EMPIRE

Men from outside the Empire could join the army in three ways. They could volunteer to join the army, be conscripted as a result of a treaty, or be recruited from prisoners of war. Recruits seem mostly to have come from beyond the Rhine and Danube, though occasionally Moors, Armenians, or Persians are found. Recruits from independent groups settled in the Empire are rare and, for example, we know of none from the Visigothic kingdom in Aquitaine. The regularity of recruiting from outside the Empire is unknown, but was clearly substantial.

Many barbarians crossed the borders of the Empire to volunteer for military service. Sarus, a Gothic noble, probably joined the army because he was forced to leave his people, but others may have enlisted for the prospect of regular pay and food or even to

[17] On Thrace, Illyricum, see *Expositio Totius Mundi*, 50; Claudian 30. 62; on Gaul see AM 15. 12. 3; Jul. *Or.* 1. 34CD, 2. 56AB; Claudian 30. 61–2.

see the world. Some joined with contracts limiting their area of service, in one case men from beyond the Rhine being limited to the area north of the Alps. The importance of these volunteers is uncertain. During the negotiations in the early stages of his usurpation, Julian promised to send barbarian volunteers (referred to as *dediticii*, though probably not in a technical sense) to Constantius II. This offer of them as a bargaining counter is often cited as evidence of their importance, though the simultaneous offer of Spanish horses for Constantius' triumphal chariots makes its value suspect.[18]

After defeating some tribes the Romans obtained conscripts (often called *tributarii* or *dediticii*) from them as part of the peace treaty. We do not know if they were used as groups or split up between regiments, but a passage of Ammianus suggests that they were split into small contingents and mixed with Romans. Evidence for this practice is confined to the fourth century.[19] Prisoners could be drafted wholesale into the army as happened after Stilicho's defeat of Radagaisus in 406, when he was said to have taken 12,000 barbarians into service. This may have been an emergency measure since Alaric was threatening Italy; on other known occasions smaller numbers were involved.[20] Individual prisoners could also be recruited, men such as the Alamannic King Vadomarius who was kidnapped in Gaul, but later served as a *dux* on the Eastern frontier. Defectors also joined the army, for example Pusaeus, a Persian officer who surrendered to Julian in 363 and who later achieved the rank of tribune.[21]

Although we know of numbers of barbarian soldiers in the army, we have few precise details as to their origin. The information we have is shown in Table 3. Trans-Rhenane barbarians were most common in the fourth century, trans-Danubians in the fifth.[22] A number of these barbarians were of royal status,

[18] For individual volunteers see AM 20. 4. 4, 8. 13; Zos. 4. 30. 1; Claudian, *De Cons. Stil.* 1. 233–4; for contracts see AM 20. 4. 4.

[19] On conscripted barbarians see Zos. 3. 8. 1, 4. 12. 1?, 5. 26. 5; AM 17. 13. 3, 21. 4. 8?, 28. 5. 4?, 30. 6. 1, 31. 10. 17; on mixing see AM 31. 10. 17, cf. 18. 9. 3, 19. 5. 2; for *dediticii* see AM 20. 8. 13; *CT* 7. 13. 16 (406); *ILS* 9184.

[20] Olymp. fr. 9; Zos. 4. 39. 5; AM 17. 2. 3; cf. Iustinianivandali, Procopius, *BV* 4. 14. 17.

[21] *PLRE* i, Pusaeus, Vadomarius.

[22] For origins see M. Waas, *Germanen im römischen Dienst* (Bonn, 1965), 14–15; on royalty see D. Hoffmann, 'Wadomar, Bacurius und Hariulf', *Museum Helveticum*, 35 (1981), 307–18.

Table 3. *Tribal origins of non-Roman soldiers, 350–476*

RHINE		DANUBE		EAST	
Alamanni	6 + 2	Alans	2	Armenians	2
Burgundians	0 + 4	'Goths'	7 + 1	Colchians	1
Franks	8 + 1	Tervingi	1	Iberians	1 + 1
		Visigoths	0 + 1	Persians	1 + 1
		Ostrogoths	0 + 2		
		Huns	1 + 1		
		Sarmatians	1		
		Suevi	1		
		Vandals	2		
TOTAL	14 + 7		15 + 5		5 + 2

though some of these (e.g. Attila) cannot really be counted as Roman soldiers.[23]

C: BARBARIZATION

The late Roman army contained large numbers of 'barbarians', here defined as men recruited from areas beyond the Empire's direct administrative control. These barbarian recruits are often said to have 'barbarized' the army. In a passage typical of modern historians, MacMullen states that 'the men credited with victory in one engagement after another from 312 on, came from outside the Empire; Celts, Germans, Huns, Saracens and Goths. No general wanted ... Romans. By the mid-fourth century the typical fight-

[23] In the following, (R) = Royalty maintaining office, (r) = royalty until Roman service. ALAMANNI, *PLRE* i, Agilo, Bitheridus, Fraomarius (r), Hortarius 2, Latinus, Scudilo, Vadomarius (r), Anon. (AM 31. 10. 3); ALANS, *PLRE* ii, Ardabur 3, Anon. (Pollentia); BURGUNDIANS, *PLRE* i, Hariulfus (R); *PLRE* ii, Chilpericus II (R), Gundioc (R), Gundobadus (R); FRANKS, *PLRE* i, Arbogastes, Bauto, Laniogaisus, Malarichus, Mallobaudes (R), Richomeres, Anon. (Jerome, *V. Hilarionis* 22), Anon. (*ILS* 2814); *PLRE* ii, Edobichus; HUNS, *PLRE* ii, Attila (R), Chelchal; SARMATIANS, *PLRE* i, Victor 4; SUEVI, *PLRE* ii, Ricimer 2; VANDALS, *PLRE* i, Anon. 209; *PLRE* ii, Ioannes 13; GOTHS, *PLRE* i, Gainas, Fravitta; *PLRE* ii, Alaric (R), Ariobindus 2, Blivila, Ostrys, Plinta, Tribigildus; TERVINGI, *PLRE* i, Munderichus; OSTROGOTHS, *PLRE* ii, Theoderic 5 (R), Theoderic 7 (R); VISIGOTHS, *PLRE* ii, Fredericus (R); PERSIANS, *PLRE* i, Hormisdas 2 (R), Pusaeus; ARMENIANS, *PLRE* ii, Vardan, Vasak; IBERIANS, *PLRE* i, Bacurius (R), Pharasmanes 2; COLCHIANS, *PLRE* i, Subarmachius.

ing force ... appears to have been half-imported. A generation later, imported soldiers formed the majority.' Modern historians appear convinced that this 'barbarization' was both widespread and deleterious in its effects. Despite MacMullen's confident assertions, there has been no systematic treatment. Indeed, according to Gerhart Ladner, 'this development [barbarization] is so well-known that references are superfluous'. But it is worth discussing the impact of the 'barbarization' (as well as the extent to which barbarians were permanently present in the field army) precisely because it is not a well-documented process.[24]

Barbarization is said to have occurred for three reasons. The first is the increasing use of barbarian allied contingents, though these were only a temporary part of the Roman army and have, therefore, nothing to do with the barbarization of the field army. Secondly, some contemporaries, such as Synesius, complained about the numbers of barbarians in the army. These men have two features in common. They were civilians for the most part and they were writing for political reasons, usually at the imperial court. Their statements must be taken into account, but it must also be remembered that no soldier, such as Ammianus or Procopius, nor any theoretical writer—Vegetius, Mauricius, or the anonymous author of the *De Rebus Bellicis*—suggests that barbarization affected the army's performance.[25] Thirdly, barbarian names stand out in descriptions of soldiers, much more so than Roman names, and give the impression of being preponderant.[26] None of this evidence for the orthodox position gives an idea of the extent of barbarization, suggesting that the problem is worth examining more closely, if only to see how strong the evidence is for the orthodox position.

[24] *LRE* 160, but see also 1037–8; R. MacMullen, *Corruption and the Decline of Rome* (London, 1988), 176; G. B. Ladner, 'On Roman Attitudes towards Barbarians in Late Antiquity', *Viator*, 7 (1976), 1–26 at 8.
[25] Synesius, *De Regno* 1089B–1093B mostly referring to *scholae*; *Ep.* 95, showing debate over need for barbarians; cf. AM 31. 16. 8, not passing judgement, only commenting on numbers; Jerome, *Comm. on Daniel*, 2. 40.
[26] Modern 'analyses' usually take the form of lists, e.g. MacMullen, *Corruption*, 176 and app. A; Waas, *Germanen*; *LRE* 135, 142, 160, 177, 181–2, 613–14; J. H. W. G. Liebeschuetz, *Barbarians and Bishops* (Oxford, 1991), 7–10.

Impact

Once barbarians joined the army, they seem to have been loyal to
the Empire. Instances of barbarian treachery were few and far
between. They do not appear to have been more treacherous
than Romans and, with the possible exception of Synesius, no
contemporaries suggested they were particularly dangerous.[27] E. A.
Thompson has stated that 'it is hard to believe that the Romans
would have recruited and promoted barbarians on such a scale as
they are known to have done if the danger of treachery had been
extreme'.[28]

The reasons for barbarians (or Romans) committing treachery
are obscure. Many barbarians joined up for an army career, which
may explain why so few of them betrayed the army. But not all
were volunteers. Some joined the army as a result of being conscripted, either as prisoners of war, or from levies imposed on
defeated barbarians by the Romans. These may not have been so
philo-Roman as the volunteers, though they would have received
the same benefits.

What would traitors gain from betraying the Empire? They
would lose all the benefits accrued from being in the Empire: pay,
regular meals, medical attention, etc. In some cases of betrayal,
information was passed by letter, suggesting the traitors wished to
maintain their Roman positions. When we do hear of treachery, it
was usually by officers, not by other ranks, when fighting against
a canton of their own people. Thus a conflict of interests might be
felt when men were opposed to friends and relatives from the same
village. These cases were rare and the Romans tried to avoid them
by employing such officers away from their own people, a practice
recommended in the sixth-century *Strategikon*.[29]

In this respect the Roman career of Vadomarius is interesting.

---

[27] On cases of treachery involving barbarians see AM 14. 10. 7–8 (suspected), 29.
4. 7; SA *Carm*. 2. 280–306; Jordanes, *Getica*, 194–5; for Romans see AM 31. 15. 4
and 8–9; for unspecified ones see AM 16. 4. 1, 16. 12. 2, 31. 15. 2; for suggestion
of treachery see Synesius, *De Regno*, 1091; I have not been able to take into account
A. Cameron and J. Long, *Barbarians and Politics at the Court of Arcadius* (Berkeley,
Calif., 1993).

[28] Thompson, *Romans and Barbarians*, 237; Tomlin, *Valentinian I*, 135.

[29] For writing see AM 29. 4. 7 (presumably in Latin); for own people see AM
14. 10. 7–8, 29. 4. 7; Mauricius, *Strat*. 7. 1. 15; cf. Sulpicius fr. 1; for transfers see
PLRE i, Bacurius, Fraomarius, Pusaeus, Vadomarius; Zos. 4. 30–1; *CT* 5. 6. 3
(409); but Moorish officers seem to have been employed in Africa and cf. *ILS* 2813.

He was king of the Brisigavi, an Alamannic canton from the area around Lake Constance and Freiburg, opposite Augst. They raided Gaul in 352/3, taking advantage of the disruption following the defeat of the usurper Magnentius. This raiding led to a Roman attack on their territory by the Emperor Constantius II in 354. After his victory, peace was imposed on Vadomarius. In 359, after further raiding, Vadomarius made peace again, using the treaty he had made with Constantius in 354 to convince the Romans of his worth and claiming his involvement in anti-Roman activities was because his subjects insisted, not through his own will. In 361 Vadomarius began raiding into Raetia, against the terms of this treaty, and defeated a Roman force in a small battle. Despite the raids, Vadomarius pretended it to be a time of peace. Julian took advantage of this and had him arrested when he was dining in the Empire with the commander of a local *limitanei* regiment. After Vadomarius' capture he was sent to Spain, to ensure that he could not disturb the peace when Julian marched east. Following the exile of Vadomarius, Julian crossed the Rhine and defeated his canton, a reprisal for previous raids as well as a disincentive to future action. After Vadomarius' exile, his son Vithicabius succeeded him as king of the Brisigavi. So far, Vadomarius' career was no different from that of many other barbarian kings.

At some point after this, Vadomarius became *dux Phoeniciae* on the Eastern frontier. We do not know why he was given this post (probably by Julian), though we might guess that he was known to be a competent soldier and was thus qualified for the job, as well as being dependent on Julian and thus loyal to him. Vadomarius is next mentioned in 365 as being sent by Valens to besiege Nicaea, which had been captured by the usurper, Procopius. Vadomarius is last heard of in 371, on the Eastern frontier again. Here, with the help of the general Trajan, he was able to repel an invasion by the Persian ruler Sapor II.

In these mentions of Vadomarius, though Ammianus referred to him as *ex-rege Alamannorum*, it seems to have meant little. Ammianus was more impressed by his deviousness than his origin and Eunapius also remarked on his 'strength and daring'. The only way in which he differed from other Roman officers was in being employed away from the Rhine and his own canton. Since his son now ruled the canton, this was probably a wise decision by the

Romans.[30] Similar caution is shown in the case of Fraomarius, former king of the Bucinobantes, another Alamannic canton. Forcibly expelled from his canton, Fraomarius had been taken under Valentinian I's protection and was transferred from the Rhine to Britain, being made tribune in command of a regiment (*numerus*) of Alamannic *foederati*. The dangers of deploying Alamannic officers on the Rhine frontier are shown by the case of Hortarius, an Alamannic noble (almost certainly from the Bucinobantes), who was executed for passing information to Macrianus, king of the Bucinobantes.

No Roman historian or poet mentions that barbarians were prone to desert and desertion often had an explanation that had nothing to do with nationality. Just before the battle of Strasbourg in 357, the Alamanni were informed of the size of Julian's force 'by a deserter from the *scutarii* [nationality unspecified] who, in fear of punishment for a crime he had committed, went over to them'.[31]

Infrequent treachery and desertion resulted from loyalty to the army, created, at least partly, by an efficient training programme. Once in the army and forced to conform to Roman military standards (as well as being removed from his homeland and often from his friends), a recruit would swiftly forget his barbarian past. His loyalty was now to his unit, his standard, and his Emperor. On joining the army the recruit swore an oath to the Emperor and repeated it annually. Frequent donatives increased the moral dependence and loyalty of the troops to the Emperor. A feeling of community was enhanced by orders being given in Latin and most of the soldiers in the West spoke Latin, through lack of any other *lingua franca*. By the end of the fourth century, most soldiers in the East spoke Greek, though still received their orders in Latin.[32]

But the isolating effect of this training should not be stressed too

[30] Vadomarius, *PLRE* i, Vadomarius; Hoffmann, 'Wadomar', 307–18.

[31] For desertion, unspecified, see AM 16. 4. 1, 16. 12. 2, 31. 7. 7; *CT* 7. 1. 10 (367), 16 (398), 17 (398), 13. 6. 1 (370), 14. 1 (398), 18. 1–17 (365–412), 20. 12 (400); *NVal* 6. 1. 1 (440); SA *Carm.* 2. 280–306; for Roman see AM 18. 6. 16, 31. 15. 4 and 8; for barbarian see Prosp. 1330.

[32] G. Reichenkron, 'Zur römischen Kommandosprache bei byzantinischen Schriftstellen', *BZ* 54 (1961), 18–27; Mauricius, *Strat.* 3. 2–5, 14, 15, 12. 8. 14, 16, 24; we do not know when the change took place and there probably remained a number of bilingual soldiers, especially among the officers, throughout the 5th cent.

strongly. We know of one Alamannic soldier who returned home on 'urgent business', and doubtless there were others. One Frank buried on the Danube described himself as '*Francus civis, Romanus miles*': a Frank, and a Roman soldier. The limited contracts some soldiers served under would make it easy for them to keep in touch with their homeland.[33] The impact of the army on barbarians is also shown by those barbarians who had retired from the army settling in the Empire. After twenty years or more in the army, few would have links with their homes. But this statement has to be qualified by admitting the impossibility of determining how many soldiers of barbarian origin returned home after completing their service. We do not know of any from this period, and it is hard to imagine what evidence one might find for this.[34]

The sons of these *émigrés* were legally bound to join the army, where they are usually referred to by modern historians as Germans or barbarians—'the Vandal Stilicho' being a favourite example. The barbarian nature of such men seems dubious. In Stilicho's case, the Vandal influences on his upbringing were minimal. His Vandal father had been an officer in a Roman cavalry unit and his mother was a Roman. Stilicho himself was brought up at court and camp, neither by any means a barbarian environment, employed his own Roman panegyrist, and married the niece of the Emperor Theodosius I. He seems to have been so Roman that any description of him as semi-barbarian or barbarian is absurd. Though he may have been unpopular, he was no different in this from other Roman politicians. Contemporaries treated him simply as a Roman general and few mention his non-Roman stock. The only judgemental writers are Jerome, who refers to him as a '*semibarbarus proditor*', and Orosius (partly on the grounds of his alleged anti-Christian policy). Even Rutilius Namatianus makes no mention of his origins

[33] For Alamann see AM 31. 10. 3; for Frank see *ILS* 2814; for contracts see AM 20. 4. 4.

[34] For loss of links see AM 15. 5. 16; the diplomas of the early Empire were no longer used (but see *CT* 7. 20. 1 (318), cf. 7. 20. 4 (325), 12 (400), 21. 4 (408), 8. 6. 1 (368); Veg. 2. 3), but even these are mostly found within, not outside, the Empire, M. Roxan, 'The Distribution of Roman Military Diplomas', *Epigraphische Studien*, 12 (Cologne, 1981), 265–86; retirement benefits were in the form of tax privileges, land grants, etc., only of use within the Empire and probably a disincentive for returning home; on return to *barbaricum* see Procopius, *BG* 8. 19. 7; *LRE* 621–2; against this, see Liebeschuetz, *Barbarians and Bishops*, 39 n. 75.

in a posthumous torrent of invective describing Stilicho as a traitor to the Empire by letting in barbarians.[35]

Other such 'barbarians' (e.g. Bauto or Richomeres) corresponded with Roman aristocrats like Libanius and Symmachus, and Bauto's daughter, Eudoxia, married the Emperor Arcadius. Zosimus describes Fravitta as 'by birth a barbarian, but otherwise a Greek, not only in habits, but also in character and religion'. Though some accused Fravitta of not pursuing Gainas after his defeat because they were both Goths, the Emperor Arcadius was sufficiently pleased with the result to make him consul for 401.[36] Though the mental attitudes of barbarians serving as soldiers had been changed, individuals are often picked out as barbarians by our sources, as in Zosimus' description of Fravitta. We know they are barbarians, but often only because we are told so or guess because of their names, not because of their behaviour. This suggests that they were recognizable to contemporaries as barbarians, probably through their accents and physical features. Thus blond hair was thought to show northern origins and beards often, but not invariably, belonged to barbarians. These features may have allowed Ambrose of Milan to distinguish the Gothic soldiers from other soldiers and Romans in his church in the 380s. Some caution needs to be used, since individuals from within the Roman Empire could also be described as 'barbarus' or 'semibarbarus'.[37]

Accusations of barbarization must be seen in their context, usually of political struggle. Thus in his *De Regno*, delivered in Constantinople in 399, Synesius attacked the Emperor Arcadius for employing barbarians in the army. This seems to be clear evidence for too many barbarians, so many that a bishop visiting from North Africa was driven to complain. The context suggests otherwise. At this date in Constantinople there was a struggle for political supremacy between Aurelianus, whose partisan Synesius

[35] For no mention of origin, but hostile, see Augustine, *Ep.* 97. 2–3; Rutilius Namatianus, *De Reditu Suo*, 2. 41–60; for mention of origin, friendly, see Claudian, *De Cons. Stil.* 1. 35–9; J. Ant. fr. 187 = Eunapius fr. 60. 1; for mention of origin, hostile, see Orosius 7. 38. 1; Jerome, *Ep.* 123. 16.

[36] Letters: Bauto, see Symmachus, *Ep.* 4. 15–16; Richomeres, Symmachus, *Ep.* 3. 54–69; Libanius, *Ep.* 886, 972, 1007, 1024; Modares, Gregory Nazianzus, *Ep.* 136–7; Ellebichus, Libanius, *Or.* 22, *Ep.* 2, 868, 884, 898; Stilicho, Symmachus, *Ep.* 4. 1–14; for Fravitta see Eunapius fr. 69. 4; Zos. 5. 20–1.

[37] For Fravitta see Zos. 5. 20. 3; for Ambrose see *Ep.* 20; for Romans as barbarians see *PLRE* i, ?Magnentius (Gaul), Maximinus 12 (Illyricum).

was, and Eutropius, who had recently granted generous peace terms to Alaric and his Goths to stop them ravaging Greece. Synesius was thus writing propaganda for Aurelianus against Eutropius. This argument is only one of many directed at Eutropius, and this speech skims lightly over the issue—had there been a serious problem, Synesius would surely have devoted more attention to it to embarrass Eutropius.[38]

Synesius himself was not consistent: on another occasion he was extravagant with praise for barbarian *foederati*, suggesting his stance in the *de Regno* reflected a political position, not a deeply held belief. However, the angry conversation between Anthemius and the '*pellitus Geta*' Ricimer suggests comments on foreign (rural?) ancestry could still be insults in times of tension.[39]

Against this point of view must be set the purges of barbarians which occurred in the late fourth and early fifth centuries. Yet, before it can be asserted that there was a programme hostile to barbarians or even a widespread dislike of them, the individual situations must be considered. In each case, there was a clear military or political reason for the purge. In 378 a newly recruited contingent of Gothic volunteers was massacred at Constantinople, for fear that they might revolt on hearing of the Gothic victory at Adrianople. The attack on Gainas' Gothic troops in Constantinople in 400 resulted from their participation in his rebellion. The Goths were attacked because they supported Gainas, not because they were Goths, an argument borne out by simultaneous attacks on Gainas' Roman troops and the fact that the army that fought against Gainas when he tried to cross the Hellespont from Asia Minor was led by another Goth, Fravitta. So barbarian groups seem not to have suffered particularly because they were barbarians, but because of their involvement in dubious activity. In similar situations Romans also suffered. During the confusion of the coup

---

[38] P. J. Heather, 'The Anti-Scythian Tirade of Synesius' *De Regno*', *Phoenix*, 42 (1988), 152–72.

[39] Synesius, against barbarians, see *Ep.* 95, in favour, see *Ep.* 78; against anti-barbarian policy, though arguing for strong anti-barbarian sentiment, W. N. Bayless, 'Anti-Germanism in the Age of Stilicho', *Byzantine Studies*, 32 (1976), 70–6; Anthemius, Ennodius, *V. Epiph.* p. 348; cf. Valens described as 'sabaiarius', *AM* 26. 8. 2; Liebeschuetz, *Barbarians and Bishops*, 105–6; on praise for using barbarians see Them. *Or.* 16. 211; Lib., *Or.* 59. 127; Claudian, *De 4 Cons. Hon.* 484–7, *In Eutropium*, 1. 382–3, *De 6 Cons. Hon.* 218–20; complaints, Jerome, *Comm. on Daniel*, 2. 40.

in 408, Stilicho (with a number of *foederati* leaders) planned an attack on other regular troops, to punish them for their involvement in anti-imperial activity.[40]

Contemporary reactions to barbarians, in fact, seem little different to Roman reactions to the strong pre-eminence at certain times of regional cliques. Under Valens and Valentinian, Pannonians were prominent, under Theodosius, Spaniards, under Gratian, Aquitanians, and under Zeno and Anastasius Isaurians stood out. Such groups rose and fell in prominence according to the fate of their patrons. Similarly, the temporary eminence of Gothic soldiers in the Eastern army of the late fourth century is a result of Theodosius' favouring this group, and their downfall the result of their involvement in politics, not of their ethnicity. When seen as different, they were expected to integrate, for example, Themistius hoped the Goths would become part of the Roman Empire as the Galatians in Asia Minor had.[41]

Barbarization is also suggested by modern writers to have had a detrimental impact on the army's conduct, equipment, clothing, etc. Contemporaries are silent as to specific problems, though there clearly was some debate on the need to use barbarians.[42] One example of barbarization is the Roman war cry, the *barritus*. According to Ammianus Marcellinus, 'in the heat of battle, this shout rises from a low murmur and grows little by little, like waves rolling against the cliffs'. This shout was of barbarian origin and has been attested as evidence of the Germanization or barbarization of the army. But it is difficult to understand the difference this made to the army's performance or how it reflected a change in ethnic composition.[43]

---

[40] On massacres see AM 31. 16. 8 (fear of revolt); Zos. 4. 30. 4–5 (badly disciplined recruits), 4. 40 (*foederati* threatening rebellion), 5. 19. 3–5 (Gainas), 5. 35. 5–6 (part of Olympius' coup against Stilicho); S. Elbern, 'Die Gotenmassaker in Kleinasien', *Hermes*, 115 (1987), 99–106; Romans, Zos. 5. 33–4. 1.

[41] On cliques, see A. D. E. Cameron, *Claudian* (Oxford, 1970), 81; for Pannonians see J. F. Matthews, *Western Aristocracies and Imperial Court AD 364–425* (Oxford, 1975), 35–9; for Aquitani see ibid. 69–77; for Spaniards see *PLRE* i, Cynegius 3, Matthews, ibid. 94–6; for Gauls under Avitus see R. W. Mathisen, 'Fifth-Century Visitors to Italy: Business or Pleasure?', *Fifth-Century Gaul*, 228–38; for Isaurians see *PLRE* ii, Illus 1, Leontius 17, Lilingis, Longinus 3, Longinus 4, Longinus 6; Themistius, *Or.* 16. 211CD.

[42] Synesius, *Ep.* 95; Jerome, *Comm. on Daniel*, 2. 40.

[43] On *barritus* see Hoffmann 135–7; AM 16. 12. 43, 26. 7. 17, 31. 7. 11; Veg. 3. 18; cf. Suda E. 2310; Tacitus, *Germania*, 3. 1; on Latin war cry see Veg. 3. 5; Mauricius, *Strat.* 2. 18. 1; AM 19. 2. 11.

Similarly uncertain in effect were the 'barbarian' fashions of long hair and trousers which became popular in the late fourth century, leading Honorius to legislate 'within the city of Rome no person shall wear either trousers or boots' and 'nobody shall be allowed to wear very long hair; no one, not even a slave, shall be allowed to wear garments made of skins'. This fashion for 'barbarian' clothing also affected the army and trousers had already become standard wear for the army by the third century. Some troops were probably encouraged to look 'barbarian', for example the members of the imperial bodyguard shown on the Column of Theodosius, the Missorium of Theodosius, and the Ravenna Mosaics of San Vitale, all with long hair and torcs.[44]

These developments were changes when compared to the army of the first century AD, but some differences in clothing and equipment since the principate should surely be expected. Indeed, the Romans are famous for taking on the ideas and equipment of other peoples, particularly in military matters. The Spanish gladius is one of their more famous adoptions, but they also made use of Eastern cavalry equipment and tactics and Greek engineering techniques. Looked at from the point of view of military effectiveness on the battlefield, these changes would have little impact. From a cultural point of view, confusion arises only if it is assumed that using cultural markers from another society necessarily means following the values of that society.[45]

Extent

Given the inconclusive nature of the evidence for barbarian impact on the army, can we suggest anything with regard to numbers? In a typical passage, A. H. M. Jones describes the extent of barbarization in the late fourth century.

Among the generals Germans came very much to the front in the west under Gratian and Valentinian; a leading role was played by two Franks, and most of the other generals have German names. In the east Theodosius kept a better balance. He employed a number of Romans, as well as

---

[44] *CT* 14. 10. 3 (399), 4 (416); cf. Procopius, *HA* 7. 8–14.

[45] e.g. Grosse 330, for *spatha* replacing *gladius* as sign of barbarization; on Roman military debts see J. C. Coulston, 'Roman, Parthian and Sassanid Tactical Developments', in P. W. Freeman and D. L. Kennedy, eds., *Defence of the Roman and Byzantine East* (Oxford, 1986), 59–75 at 68–70; E. L. Wheeler, 'The Occasion of Arrian's *Tactica*', *GRBS* 19 (1978), 351–65 at 357, 361–2.

Germans, two Goths and the Vandal Stilicho who became his right-hand
man at the end of his reign. He also promoted Orientals.

Here, the importance of names is clear, but this data has rarely
been systematically analysed. Five categories are defined on the
basis of individuals' names (supplemented, where possible, by other
evidence). These categories are 'Definitely Barbarian', 'Probably
Barbarian', 'Definitely Roman', 'Probably Roman', and 'Others'.
'Definitely Barbarian' covers those soldiers who are attested as
European barbarians by our sources: a historian says that so-and-
so is a Goth. The same definition applies to the 'Definitely Roman'
individuals. The last section, 'Others', includes Moors, Persians,
Iberians, and other easterners from outside the Empire. Men known
to have been born or brought up in the Empire, such as Stilicho
or Silvanus, are treated as Romans.

The other known members of the army can only be classified by
their names. If a name has a 'Germanic' ending, for example,
-gaisus, -marius, -ulfus, or -gildus, then it is counted as 'Probably
Barbarian', otherwise as 'Probably Roman'. These divisions into
'Probably Barbarian' and 'Probably Roman' are arbitrary, but this
is the only way of handling the problems of the evidence. Those
individuals classed as 'Probably Barbarian' are much more likely
to have been barbarians than those classed as 'Probably Roman'
were to be Romans, because names are known to have been changed
from barbarian to Roman forms, but not vice versa. A well-known
example of this is Victor the Sarmatian. However, the practice
seems not to have been common and out of 110 officers with
'Roman' names and stated racial or geographical origins, only eight
were of barbarian origin, about 7 per cent. Among other ranks we
know of no men with Roman names of barbarian origin, but the
sample is too small to support any meaningful conclusions. It is
important to remember that barbarian names were changed to
Roman names, but it should not greatly affect the results presented
here.[46]

The 'Probable' category is used since if only definitely attested
cases were used the samples would be too small to be of any
statistical value. The 'Definite' cases form only a small number of

---

[46] Officers with 'Roman' names and 'Barbarian' origins: *PLRE* i, Bonitus 1,
Latinus, Serapio 3, Silvanus 2, Victor 4; *PLRE* ii, Armatius, Ioannes 13, Iordanes
3.

the known members of the Roman army, some 19 per cent of officers, only 16 per cent of other ranks. More importantly, using only definite attributions would distort the picture by overlooking the silent majority here classified as 'Probably Roman', which in most groups is larger than the other four divisions put together. If 'Definite' cases alone are used, Romans still outnumber barbarians by 97 to 43, a ratio of approximately 2:1.

Table 4 divides Roman officers into six groups by rank and into three groups by date. The rank divisions are *magistri militum*, *comites rei militaris*, *duces*, guard officers (*comites domesticorum*, *comites stabuli*, *curae palatii*, and *comites scholarum*), *protectores* and *domestici*, and, lastly, regimental commanders, *tribuni*, *praepositi*, and *praefecti* (including *tribuni scholarum*). The date divisions are arbitrary fifty-year periods, the third ending with the fall of the western Empire. This divides the sample into eighteen distinct groups. Individuals are counted only once in each chronological group, but may appear in more than one rank group. Thus Silvanus is recorded in both the regimental commander and *magister militum* groups, but only once in the 'All Officers' group. A tabulation of all officers is provided at the bottom of Table 4 to allow each group to be compared to the sample as a whole (see Appendix 2 for further details).

This analysis suggests that fewer than a third of the army officers were of barbarian origin. Equally importantly, it suggests that the proportions of barbarians in the army did not increase in the period studied, a conclusion also suggested when officers are examined by decade (Figs. 10–12). The same conclusion is reached using either 'definite' cases only or 'definites' and 'probables' combined. The division of the sample into eighteen separate groups, all of which produce the same range of results, with no group made up of 70 per cent barbarians, together with the disparate nature of the evidence, suggests that the analysis is not wildly inaccurate.

Though the data are mathematically consistent, the statistical significance of the information is difficult to assess. We can determine the number of offices for a given period (using the *Notitia Dignitatum*) and for how many years they were filled. In the case of the best attested group, *magistri militum*, we have information on about two-thirds of the late fourth century and about half the fifth century. This suggests that we can be confident in our knowledge of *magistri militum*.

Recruiting

Table 4. *Roman army officers, 350–476*

Rank		350–399	400–449	449–476	undated	TOTAL	%
Magistri	Roman	40	48	24	1	113	71
Militum	Barbarian	18	15	12	0	45	28
	Other	2	0	0	0	2	1
		60	63	36	1	160	
Comites	Roman	43	26	14	1	84	76
	Barbarian	12	6	8	0	26	23
	Other	1	0	0	0	1	1
		56	32	22	1	111	
Duces	Roman	41	29	5	7	82	83
	Barbarian	10	1	2	0	13	13
	Other	2	1	1	0	4	4
		53	31	8	7	99	
Guard Officers	Roman	19	14	7	0	40	82
	Barbarian	6	1	0	0	7	14
	Other	2	0	0	0	2	4
		27	15	7	0	49	
Protectores,	Roman	25	16	0	29	70	85
Domestici	Barbarian	4	1	2	5	12	15
		29	17	2	34	82	
Regiment	Roman	79	37	8	58	182	83
Commanders	Barbarian	28	2	0	4	34	16
	Other	2	0	0	0	2	1
		109	39	8	62	218	
All Officers	Roman	215	156	50	96	517	80
	Barbarian	66	21	23	9	119	19
	Other	6	1	1	0	8	1
	TOTAL	287	178	74	105	644	

Given the reliability of one rank group of data and a similar pattern throughout all rank groups and time periods, it cannot be argued that there existed any long-term policy of deliberately

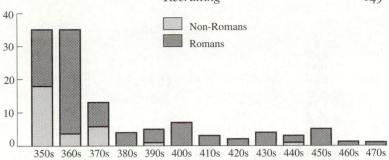

Fig. 10   Ethnicity of regimental commanders, by decade

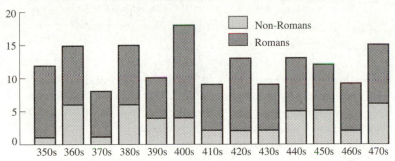

Fig. 11   Ethnicity of *magistri militum*, by decade

promoting barbarians simply because they were barbarians. The only logical conclusion (assuming no quota system to have been operating) to consistent numerical representation over time and space is that being 'barbarian' had no effect on promotion. Where we know of individual careers, barbarians followed the same path as Roman officers: *protector–tribunus–comes–magister militum*.[47]

Some other conclusions can be drawn from this analysis. First, the proportion of *magistri militum* who were apparently of barbarian origin seems higher than among other officer ranks. As suggested above, it is unlikely that this resulted from a policy of promoting barbarians through the ranks and is probably the result of better evidence for higher ranks, suggesting that barbarians may

---

[47] Normal progression: *PLRE* i, Dagalaifus, Malarichus, Richomeres; *PLRE* ii, Ariobindus 2, Arnegisclus, Ricimer 2, Sigisvultus; cf. *PLRE* i, Fravitta, Vadomarius; *PLRE* ii, Ioannes 13.

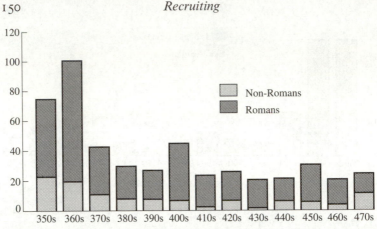

Fig. 12   Ethnicity of army officers, by decade

be slightly under-represented in figures for lower ranks. This is probably caused by more evidence for lower-ranking officers coming from tombstones, a source more likely to record 'Romans' than 'non-Romans', while that for higher-ranking officers includes more evidence from literary sources.[48]

A second conclusion is that there is no significant change in the balance of Romans and barbarians throughout the period as a whole. In the fifth century, there were no more Roman officers of barbarian origin than in the fourth. This can be illustrated by tabulating officers by decade (see Figs. 10–12). The small size of the sample means that any decade is easily subject to distortion by a few individual names. Similar results appear with regard to non-officers. Hoffmann has argued that *auxilia palatina* units were mostly barbarian. It is highly probable that a unit was formed from a single source of manpower at the moment of its foundation (though probably with officers and non-commissioned officers from other units), but such a character would be likely to be diluted almost immediately by new recruits. Records of individual soldiers do not suggest that the majority of *auxilia palatina* soldiers were barbarians. Thus Ammianus records that the first two soldiers of the *auxilia palatina* regiment of the Victores to make it through a tunnel in Persia in 363 were Exsuperius and Magnus, both Roman-

[48] R. MacMullen, 'The Epigraphic Habit', *AJP* 103 (1982), 233–46.

Table 5. Auxilia palatina *troops*

	Rankers	Officers	TOTAL	%
Definitely Roman	0	2	2	5
Probably Roman	19	2	21	54
Definitely Barbarian	1	1	2	5
Probably Barbarian	9	4	13	33
Other	0	1	1	3
TOTAL	29	10	39	100

sounding names. Of the twenty-nine soldiers and ten officers known from *auxilia palatina* regiments, over half are 'probably Roman' (Table 5). This does not suggest a pure barbarian force, but the evidence proves nothing because of the small size of the sample. All that can be said is that the pattern differs little from that of the army as a whole.[49]

Similarly, it has been suggested, particularly by Frank, that the *scholae* regiments were heavily or totally barbarian. This argument is based partly on Synesius' comment that those in the *scholae* had blond hair, that is were 'Scythians'. The *scholares* did have a barbarian appearance, and their long golden hair and torcs were prominently featured on the Missorium of Theodosius and the Column of Theodosius. Barbarian appearance does not prove barbarian origin, since it cannot be argued that only barbarians had long blond hair and wore torcs. The other part of this argument is an assumption based on the occurrence of barbarian names among *scholares*. According to Frank, 'during the fourth century, most of the *scholares* were Germans, and this was especially true of the enlisted men'. However, when the names of all known *scholares* are tabulated using the criteria discussed above, the barbarians in the *scholae* appear to have been few in number (Table 6), hardly more so than in *auxilia palatina* regiments.[50]

The analysis presented here contrasts with the orthodox view presented at the beginning of the chapter. The analysis of names suggests that the majority of regular Roman regiments continued

[49] Hoffmann, 137–41; for mixed see Zos. 4. 30. 1, 4. 31. 1, 45. 3; AM 31. 10. 17; for pure see AM 18. 9. 4.

[50] Frank, *Scholae Palatinae*, 59, 62–72; followed by MacMullen, *Corruption*, 201; Waas, *Germanen*, 11; Hoffmann 299–300; on barbarians in *scholae* see Synesius, *De Regno*, 1084A; AM 17. 2. 3?, 20. 8. 13; Procopius, *HA* 24. 16–17.

Table 6. Scholares

	Rankers	Officers	TOTAL	%
Definitely Roman	3	7	10	15
Probably Roman	25	16	41	60
Definitely Barbarian	2	3	5	8
Probably Barbarian	4	7	11	17
TOTAL	34	33	67	100

to be composed mostly of non-barbarians. Even so, a substantial proportion of the army, around one man in four, appears to have been of non-imperial origins, a proportion that remained constant throughout the period. This is what caused the social tensions outlined above, though they seem not to have affected the army's effectiveness.

D: MANPOWER SHORTAGE

It has been suggested by some authors, such as Boak and Crump, that the late Roman army suffered from a shortage of manpower and often had difficulty in recruiting men. There is no direct ancient evidence for this, but a number of arguments have been adduced to support the idea, although contemporaries tend to claim that soldiers were not doing their jobs, not that there were not enough of them.[51]

The first argument is the fact of recruitment of barbarians. It can be argued that they would not have been recruited if there were sufficient Roman recruits available. However, use of extra-imperial manpower was not new and barbarians had always served in the Roman army. Emperors did allow barbarians into the Empire to levy recruits from them and it is possible that this practice was more common in the fourth century than earlier. Constantius II hoped to allow in the Limigantes in 359, so that 'he would gain

---

[51] G. A. Crump, *Ammianus Marcellinus as a Military Historian* (Wiesbaden, 1975), 50–1; A. E. R. Boak, *Manpower Shortage and the Fall of the Roman Empire* (London, 1955), whose thesis receives severe criticism in a review by M. I. Finley, *JRS* 48 (1958), 157–64.

more people, and would be able to compel a very strong force of recruits', and a similar hope motivated Valens in 376 to allow some Goths into the Empire. But in both these cases, the reasoning recorded by Ammianus was not that there was a shortage of soldiers, but that more recruits allowed the commutation of more recruits for money. Emperors wanted taxpayers *and* recruits. Furthermore, during the fourth and fifth centuries, there appears to have been little change in the proportions of barbarians in the regular army according to the figures produced above.[52]

The second argument is that the *Codex Theodosianus* shows a severe shortage of men and demonstrates the Empire constantly trying to squeeze recruits out of reluctant landowners. The laws do show difficulties in exacting recruits, but do not allow us to estimate the scale of the problem. However, the frequent commutation of recruits for money suggests that there was not normally a desperate need for men. Although landlords may have preferred not to lose tenants, it seems unlikely that the government would have allowed landowners and imperial estates to commute their obligations (the earliest known law is from 370), if there had been a real shortage of troops. Nor does it seem likely that landowners could have continually resisted government demands, especially those of Valentinian and Valens. Finally and most importantly, commutation was occasional, not regular, and required special legislation so was more likely to be recorded in the *Codex Theodosianus*.[53]

Other evidence for a manpower shortage is adduced by the frequent practice of recruiting more troops before a campaign or in an emergency. This may show that the army was often understrength, but does not suggest that sufficient men could not be raised. Furthermore, the standards of the army were high and remained so throughout the period. Many categories of men were excluded from serving, for example *coloni*, *curiales*, slaves, and inhabitants of workhouses, all groups whom one would have expected to be called up if there was a shortage of men. Similarly, in 418 Honorius issued an edict expelling Jews from the army if they had joined illegally (a law repealed in the East in 438).

[52] For Constantius see AM 19. 11. 7, for Valens see AM 31. 4. 4; cf. Synesius, *Ep.* 95.
[53] On commutation see *CT* 7. 13. 2 (370) (but see 13. 12 (397), result of pressure), 13. 13 (397), 14 (397).

Non-Catholics were also banned under Honorius. Though laws prohibiting slaves, non-Catholics, freedmen, and Jews to serve imply that they did so, the fact that such laws could be issued suggests no desperate need for troops.[54]

If there was a real shortage of men these laws would probably have been relaxed. Thus a law of 406 issued during Radagaisus' invasion of Italy allowed slaves to serve, but this seems to have been a one-off measure, requiring special legislation; no other relaxations are known.[55] There were also restrictions on recruits drawn from other social groups. Imperial estates were even exempted from providing recruits in 370 and automatically paid money instead, a law countermanded in 397. This suggests no shortage of men. A law of 407 exempted tribunes and *praepositi* from the need to provide recruits from their estates while another of 423 exempted decurions and silentiaries. Some *palatini* and *agentes in rebus* were also exempt.[56] All three arguments for a shortage of manpower in the Late Roman army seem rather doubtful. Whatever deficiencies there may have been in providing men for the army do not seem to have been insuperable.

[54] On high standards see *CT* 7. 1. 5 (364), 13. 3 (367) (mininum height 1.63 m., cf. Veg. 1. 5), 22. 5 (333); on physical standards see Veg. 1. 5–6; on prohibition of *coloni* see *CJ* 12. 33. 3 (395/408); on guild members see *NVal* 5. 1. 2 (440); *Sirm.* 6 (425); on *curiales* see *CJ* 12. 33. 4 (Leo); on slaves see *CT* 7. 13. 8 (380), 11 (382); on Jews see *CT* 16. 8. 24 (418); *NTh* 3. 2 (438); on freedmen see *CT* 4. 10. 3 (426); on non-Catholics see *CT* 16. 5. 42 (408); Zos. 5. 46. 3–4.

[55] *CT* 7. 13. 16 (406); Symm. *Ep.* 6. 58, 62, 64 (397); cf. H A, *Marcus Aurelius* 21. 6.

[56] For decurial classes see *CT* 7. 2. 1 (383), 2 (385), 13. 1 (353), 7 (375), 12. 1. 1–192 (313–436); for imperial estates see *CT* 7. 13. 2 (370); for decurions see *CT* 6. 23. 2 (423); for *palatini* see *CT* 6. 30. 20 (413); for *agentes in rebus* see *CT* 6. 27. 13 (403); in general see *CT* 11. 18. 1 (412).

6

Fortifications

Permanent army bases and many urban areas in the late Empire were defended by fortifications. In addition, some fortified refuge sites existed. Though each site was important in its own right (especially military ones), it also had a place in a defensive network, dependent on its size and location. This chapter discusses the principles determining how individual sites were defended but does not analyse particular sites or how regional defensive systems operated.[1]

A: MILITARY FORTIFICATIONS

The Roman Empire was striking for the large number of fortifications on the frontier, giving an impression that it was an armed camp. An anonymous writer of the fourth century proposed that 'an unbroken chain of forts will best assure the protection of these frontiers, on the plan that they should be built at intervals of one mile, with a solid wall and very strong towers' and on many sectors of the frontier such a density was achieved.

This building or rebuilding of forts was a continual task for the army. A law of Valentinian I issued to the *Dux Daciae Ripensis* ordered that he construct towers (*turres*) annually along the frontier.[2] In the narrative of Ammianus, whenever Valentinian I, and

---

[1] For individual sites, see S. Johnson, *Late Roman Fortifications* (London, 1983); J. Lander, *Roman Stone Fortifications*, *BAR* S206 (Oxford, 1984); D. Welsby, *The Roman Military Defence of the British Provinces in its Later Phases* (Oxford, 1982); V. A. Maxfield, ed., *The Saxon Shore* (Exeter, 1989); M. Kandler and H. Vetters, *Der römische Limes in Österreich* (Vienna, 1986); C. Scorpan, *Limes Scythiae*, *BAR* S88 (Oxford, 1980).

[2] Anon. *DRB* 20; on Valentinianic law see *CT* 15. 1. 13 (364) (though the identification of the addressee, Tautomedes, with the *protector* Teutomeres, from *CT*, ed. Mommsen, followed by *PLRE* i, is doubtful).

to a lesser extent, Julian, were not campaigning, they built or repaired forts. New forts continued to be built in the West until at least the reign of Valentinian I, suggesting that the army continued to find them useful.[3] In the Eastern Empire, forts continued to be built along the middle and lower Danube throughout the fifth century.[4] We do not know why forts ceased to be constructed in the West, though continued Eastern construction suggests that they were not obsolete. The building of new structures suggests that, at least before the fourth century, there was not such a dense network of fortifications. It is possible that such constructions were filling gaps, not creating networks, a hypothesis supported by the small size of the newer forts and the fact that fifth-century Eastern construction concentrated on rebuilding rather than new work. The gradual loss of Roman control of the Rhine is also important, though this does not explain the lack of construction during the late fourth and early fifth centuries.

Late Roman forts can be divided into two constructional groups: totally new constructions and forts of an earlier date which continued to be used. At a first glance, the new forts seem to have had a great amount of variation, but these differences are more visual than functional. Newly constructed forts were designed with regard to defensibility, so the same principles always applied, though the design could be flexibly interpreted to take local conditions into account. Thus shape, size, and the number of towers and gates differed, but defensive advantages and the problems presented to an attacker did not. On many occasions forts were built to take advantage of the local geography. The use of high ground was favoured, since this enhanced visibility and increased the height advantage provided by the walls, as well as making drainage easier. In some cases forts were built alongside rivers, a practice which restricted easy access to the fort and eased supply. Forts on the

---

[3] For Western building, Julian, see AM 16. 11. 11, 17. 1. 11–12, 17. 9. 1, 18. 2. 5–7; Lib. *Or.* 18. 52; for Valentinian see AM 28. 2. 1–5, 3. 2, 29. 6. 2, 30. 3. 1, 7. 6; Symm. *Or.* 2. 20; *CIL* 13. 11537; *ILS* 762, 774–5, 8949; for Gratian see Ausonius, *Act. Grat.* 2; for Arbogastes see Sulpicius fr. 3, 4; for Honorius see Claudian, *De Cons. Stil.* 1. 200–2; for Constantine III see Zos. 6. 3. 3?; for undated inscriptions see *CIL* 7. 268 (= *RIB* 721), 13. 5190.

[4] Valens, Them. *Or.* 10. 135D; *ILS* 770; *CIG* 8621; Theodosius I, Lib. *Or.* 30. 14; SA *Carm.* 2. 199–201; *PLRE* i, Vitus; Procopius, *Buildings*, 5; A. M. Cameron, *Procopius* (London, 1985), esp. 84–112.

Rhine and Danube or the coasts could receive supplies by water.[5]

Fort Functions

The repeated, orderly, construction of forts suggests that the Romans had definite ideas for their use. According to an anonymous sixth-century Byzantine writer, 'Forts [φρούρια] are used for several purposes: first, to observe the approach of the enemy; second, to receive deserters from the enemy; third, to hold back any fugitives from our own side. The fourth is to facilitate assembly for raids against outlying enemy territories.'[6] These functions meant that forts tended to be built on movement avenues—river estuaries, fords, and mountain passes. Attempts were also made to control or hinder road movement by creating a deeper defensive zone in certain areas. Since off-road movement was slow, especially if the weather was bad, defences were concentrated on roads. A good example of fort placement is Julian's construction of a fort at Strasbourg, blocking the best pass through the Vosges and thus channelling Alamannic movements.[7]

This restriction of movement could also be achieved by linear barriers. Hadrian's Wall is the best known of these, but other similar barriers, though on a smaller scale, existed elsewhere in Europe. Their construction was similar to that of forts, with gateways, projecting towers, and ditches. These walls can be divided into three groups. The first is those blocking off peninsulas, i.e. Hadrian's Wall, the Long Wall at the Chersonese, and the Long Walls built at Constantinople in the late fifth century. A second group blocked various passes, for example the walls used to control the passes through the Julian Alps. Finally, access to some river valleys leading from the Danube was also blocked by walls.[8] Despite the occasional presence of fortifications beyond the border, there was no overall concept of 'defence-in-depth', and almost all fortified military sites lay close to the border. Defences within the Empire tended to be found only at choke points, not everywhere.

Forts varied in size according to their function, though they were

---

[5] Malchus fr. 20. 161–4; AM 28. 2. 2–4; Veg. 4. 1.

[6] Anon. *PS* 9; Jul. *Or.* 1. 7C.

[7] Anon. *PS* 7. 13–17; cf. Them. *Or.* 10. 137B; Strasbourg, AM 16. 11. 11.

[8] Literature collected by J. G. Crow, 'The Function of Hadrian's Wall and the Comparative Evidence of Late Roman Long Walls', in W. S. Hanson and L. J. F. Keppie, eds., *Roman Frontier Studies, 1979*, *BAR* S71 (Oxford, 1980), 724–9; N. Christie, 'The Alps as a Frontier', *JRA* 4 (1991), 410–30.

still composed of the same features—walls, towers, etc. Forts can be divided into four categories, garrison forts, detachment forts, watchtowers, and fortified landing places. These categories are modern definitions and are somewhat arbitrary.[9] These types of fortifications are illustrated in Fig. 13, showing the province of Valeria on the middle Danube.[10]

Garrison forts were large sites, usually upgraded earlier forts, which could hold a substantial garrison, generally a whole regiment, sometimes more. These sites tended to contain the headquarters and main body of units, though sub-units were often outposted to detachment forts or watchtowers. Most *limitanei* regiments in the *Notitia Dignitatum* have their headquarters at forts of this type. Examples from Valeria are Intercisa (headquarters of the Equites Dalmatae, Constantiniani, and Sagittarii), Brigetio (Legio I Adiutrix) and Cirpi (Equites Dalmatae, Auxilia Fortensia, and a part of Legio II Adiutrix).[11]

Detachment forts were usually newer constructions rather than refurbished older forts. They were generally small in size, less than 1 ha. These were usually sited on the border, but are also found behind the border, normally on roads. This category includes those forts defined by Von Petrikovits as 'road forts'. These forts are rarely recorded in the *Notitia*. They are termed 'detachment forts' since they were not big enough for whole units and contained only small detachments. Thus in Valeria one of the forts at Azaum, 7 km. east of Brigetio, was only 31.8 × 32.5 m. in size.[12]

Watchtowers (*burgi* or *turres*) were very small sites. They are defined by their size (and are equivalent to Von Petrikovits' 'fortlets'). These sites were single towers, sometimes with a wall, surrounded by a ditch. They generally had an area of less than 0.5 ha. and many were only 10 × 10 m. in size. Their height is unknown, though a Roman tower (not precisely datable) at Dover

[9] cf. H. Von Petrikovits, 'Fortifications in the Northwestern Roman Empire from the Third to the Fifth Centuries AD', *JRS* 61 (1971), 178–218, for other categories.

[10] Valeria *ND* Occ. 33; Johnson 181–8; S. Soproni, *Der spätrömische Limes zwischen Esztergom und Szetendre* (Budapest, 1978) and *Die letzten Jahrzehnten des Pannonischen Limes* (Munich, 1985); Z. Visy, *Der pannonische Limes in Ungarn* (Stuttgart, 1988).

[11] For Intercisa see *ND* Occ. 33. 25, 26, 38; for Brigetio see *ND* Occ. 33. 51; for Cirpi see *ND* Occ. 33. 33, 49, 56.

[12] Soproni, *Letzten Jahrzehnten*, 57.

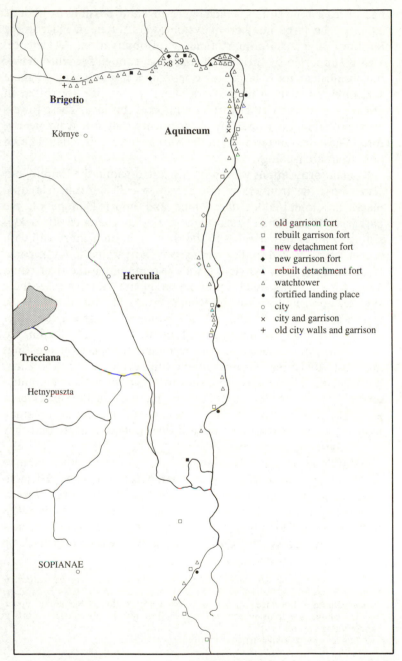

Fig. 13   Roman forts in Valeria

had at least four stories, reaching 13 m. (and possibly as high as 24 m.). The large number of watchtowers, often in inaccessible positions, suggests a primary function of observation, not defence. This is supported by their small size, large enough for self-defence, but insufficient for a large garrison. The siting of many of these structures on high ground overlooking the border and often in visual range of each other further reinforces this idea. These towers were probably garrisoned by detachments sent out from nearby forts. These are not recorded in the *Notitia* and are generally known only from archaeology.[13]

Roman fortifications were not only found within the Empire, but also across the frontier. A number of so-called fortified landing places are found along the Rhine and upper Danube on the barbarian bank. These sites all have similar characteristics, consisting of a gateway parallel to the river, built on a short wall with corner towers linked to the river by two short walls, 20–45 m. long. In at least one case, Whylen, a wall also ran along the river bank. These forts were all small, up to 0.3 ha. in size. In most cases these sites lay opposite forts on the Roman bank. The function of these forts was probably to allow a safe Roman landing on the other side of the river, without fear of interdiction while loading or unloading troops and supplies, the moment when river crossings are most vulnerable. There is little dating evidence for these forts, but what there is assigns most sites to Valentinian I's reign, and a few to that of Constantine I. The sparseness of the dating evidence available, together with the small size, would suggest only a small (and vulnerable) garrison, though it does not seem likely that they would not be garrisoned at all.[14]

As well as fortified landing places, numerous other Roman fortified sites existed across the frontier. Most of these were detachment forts, lying on or close to the river, such as the fort at Deutz, opposite Cologne. Others lay further inland, such as the nameless fort across the Rhine built by Julian in 358. Some sites which now appear to lie across the frontier, such as Breisach and Sponeck on

---

[13] For towers, siting, see Anon. *PS* 7. 13–19; Anon. *DRB* 20; AM 30. 7. 6; Malchus fr. 20. 161–4; for size see R. MacMullen, *Soldier and Civilian in the Later Roman Empire* (Cambridge, Mass., 1963), 38–9; for catalogue, Rhine and upper-middle Danube, see Johnson 270–9; for lower Danube and Britain see reports in various *LIMES* vols.

[14] Lander 248–9; Johnson 155.

the Rhine, were originally built on the Roman bank, but have been affected by the changing course of the river.[15]

Fort Construction

The first line of defence for any fort was usually the surrounding ditch, in many cases a considerable obstacle. Ditches were 2–4 m. deep and 5–15 m. wide, averaging 3 m. in depth, 10 m. in width, with sides of varying steepness. Thus the ditch at Qualburg was 2 m. deep and 16 m. wide, with shallow sides. The sheer size of this obstacle would make it difficult to bring rams, ladders, or other siege machinery to the walls without a great deal of preparatory work. Similarly, problems in exiting the ditch would make it difficult for attackers to co-ordinate an attack on the fort. While climbing from steep-sided ditches it would not be possible to use a shield, making the attackers more vulnerable to missile fire. Ditches usually lay 8–15 m. from the foot of the wall. There seems to have been no connection between wide ditches and the use of artillery in fort defences (Fig. 14).[16]

The problems presented by the ditch could be intensified in a number of ways. If the ditch were flooded it would form an effective moat. There is no literary evidence for this practice, though the Latin word for ditch, *fossa*, can also be used to mean 'moat'. Obstacles could be placed in the berm, for example the pit-traps at Piercebridge and Rough Castle. Such obvious obstacles are rare and other devices could have been used which would leave little archaeological trace, such as lines of stakes. Caltrops (*tribuli*) could be used in front of or in ditches, though attestations of their use are rare. It is possible that brambles or nettles were encouraged to grow on the berm or in the ditch, a practice unlikely to leave archaeological traces.[17]

Some forts, often the older ones, had multiple ditches (usually a pair, but on occasion three) that performed the same function as the single ditch. They were usually narrower, but retained the depth

[15] S. Soproni, 'Eine spätrömische Militärstation im sarmatischen Gebiet', *LIMES* 8, ed. E. Birley *et al.* (Cardiff, 1974), 197–203; AM 17. 1. 11; cf. *ND* Occ. 32. 41, 33. 44, 48, 55?

[16] Lander 261–2.

[17] For obstacles see Lander 262; A. Johnson, *Roman Forts* (London, 1983), 53–5; for caltrops see Anon. *DRB* 10; Anon. *PS* 6, 29; Veg. 3. 8, 24; Procopius, *BG* 7. 24. 16–18; E. A. Thompson, *A Roman Reformer and Inventor* (Oxford, 1952), 67–8; for stakes cf. Frontinus, *Stratagems*, 1. 5. 5; Agathias, *Hist.* 3. 21. 2.

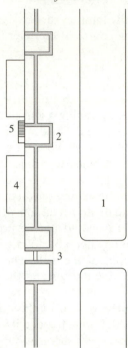

Fig. 14 Late Roman fort design. (1) large ditch; (2) projecting towers; (3) recessed gateway and portcullis; (4) interior buildings; (5) staircase

of the larger ditches. Double ditches of fourth-century date were found at Richborough and Breisach. Although ditches were a common feature, they were not universal. If the fort was built on a hilltop there might not be enough space to dig a ditch. If a fort was built on a spur, ditches could be used to cut it off from the rest of the plateau, as at Breisach or Isny.

Within any circuit of ditches lay the fort, whose main protection was its wall. No European fort is known to have had a defensive forewall (προτείχισμα). The fort wall was composed of a rubble core faced with stone, or occasionally, just stone. Brick seems not to have been used for fortifications except in bonding courses. Wall thickness varied, but averaged 3 m., and few examples are thinner than 1.5 m. The height of walls is difficult to judge because of the few surviving examples. The few known European cases (Pevensey and Zeiselmauer, both 9 m.) suggest that they were similar in height to city walls, that is 8–10 m. at rampart walk level. This was high enough to stop attackers from climbing them unaided, necessitating the use of scaling ladders. A crenellated parapet ran along the top of the wall, screening the walkway and allowing more effective return fire. These crenellations are illustrated in the *Notitia Dignitatum*, though none now survive.[18]

Most forts had three types of towers: corner towers, gate towers, and interval towers between corner and gate towers. Smaller forts often had no need for interval towers, and watchtowers could consist of a tower alone, sometimes surrounded by a wall circuit. There were a number of variations in the form of these towers (round, half-round, or square), but none of these affected their function, so they will not be discussed here. Square towers were rare, probably because they were more vulnerable to ram attacks.

Towers projected outside the wall circuit by 3–9 m.; sometimes the base of the tower projected inside. Fort towers, on the analogy of those surviving in cities, would have been 15–20 m. high, though none survive to this height in Europe. The towers at Pevensey extended above the walls, which stood at least 8 m. high, though their total height is unknown. Tower bases were often solid, as at Burgh Castle, probably to prevent collapse from subsidence or mining. Towers were usually 30 m. apart on the wall circuit, though distances varied, for example, at Bad Kreuznach and Alzey the interval was 40 m., at Jünkerath 20 m.[19]

By projecting from the wall, towers allowed enfilading fire on both sides of the tower while providing cover from missiles. Vegetius suggests that troops with distance weapons should be stationed on the walls and both bolt-shooters and hand-held weapons could be used from towers. The small intervals between the towers maximized the effect of such fire. The towers were linked by a rampart walkway. Access to this walkway could be through staircases contained in the towers if they did not have solid bases, otherwise by external stairs leading directly to the walls. Limited access made it easier for the defenders to seal off sections of the wall if they were captured. Towers had windows at rampart walk level, and judging by examples from city towers which survive above this

[18] *ND* Occ. 24, insignia of *Comes Italiae*.
[19] Lander 198–262, discusses types of towers and their use; for projection see Lander 217; for square tower vulnerability see Veg. 4. 6.

height, another floor above this. Roofs could be conical or flat, the latter providing another fighting platform.[20]

The number of entrances depended on the location and function of the fort. Most sites had two gates, though small sites such as watchtowers and detachment forts usually had only one. The gate itself was usually flanked by a tower on each side, creating a recessed entrance. This allowed the defenders to interdict the immediate approach to the gate. Occasionally, as at Pevensey or Sacidava, the gate was very deeply recessed. The gates themselves were made of wood, covered with iron plates to protect them against burning. Some forts had portcullises, as at Ulmetum and possibly Tropaeum Traiani.[21] Posterns were used for sorties and as covert entrances. They were usually placed at the foot of towers, as at Tokod, or built into the tower itself, as at Jünkerath. An alternative means of emergency entry or exit for individuals was by rope, though this would be uncomfortable.[22]

Within the fort were buildings for accommodation, administration, and storage. These were often, but not always, built directly against the fort wall. This was a characteristic of small sites and reduced the length of the perimeter to be defended (by removing the space between the buildings and the walls), as well as reducing the volume of building material needed. Although our knowledge of interior buildings is limited, they seem not to have been as specialized as some buildings of the early Empire. They were mostly built from timber and remains have rarely been found. *Valetudinaria* or *principia* built on the pattern of the early Empire are unknown, and granaries rare, though similar buildings (mostly without external buttresses) do exist, for example, at Tokod and Veldidena. This suggests that this design had gone out of use, and that different types of building used to store grain had come into service. It was normal practice to store provisions in forts, up to a year's supply in some cases.[23]

---

[20] On tower use see Lander 302–6; for enfilading fire see Veg. 4. 2.

[21] For recession see Lander 226; for Sacidava see Scorpan, *Limes Scythiae*, 52; for portcullis, Ulmetum, see Scorpan, *Limes Scythiae*, 43; for Tropaeum Traiani, ibid. 45.

[22] On posterns see Von Petrikovits, 'Fortifications', 178–218 at 201; Mauricius, *Strat.* 10. 3. 7; Procopius, *BP* I. 15. 33, *BG* 6. 11. 11–12; for rope see Procopius, *BG* 6. 12. 13; cf. Eutropius, *Breviarium*, 9. 23; AM 24. 2. 21, 28. 6. 14.

[23] On interior buildings see Lander 259–61; on stored supplies see AM 16. 11. 11, 17. 9. 2; Anon. *PS* 9; Veg. 4. 7–8; Them. *Or.* 10. 136.

Most forts probably had some artillery, though it seems unlikely that many had more than a few weapons. Artillery was not necessary for the defence of a fort, but was useful if it was there. A garrison, on the other hand, was indispensable. It has been suggested that artillery influenced fort design, though this seems unlikely, since none of the features described, such as wide ditches or projecting towers, were necessary for using artillery for defence and the Romans had had artillery available long before they started building forts in this pattern. Artillery alone could not defend a site and increased the effectiveness of the garrison rather than replacing it.[24] It has been suggested that some towers with solid bases and holes in their centres, as at Burgh Castle, were intended for rotating platforms for stone-throwers, but this seems extremely unlikely. Stone-throwers were cumbersome weapons with a long minimum range and slow rate of fire and were thus of limited use in defence against enemies without siege equipment.[25] It is probable that *ballistae* were preferred for fort defence unless the opposition were likely to use siege equipment.[26]

Where there were earlier Roman forts in important positions they could be upgraded (if this had not already been done in the third or early fourth century) to raise their defence capacity to the standard of later constructions. This was more common than replacing them with later types. Such rebuilding had been carried out since Diocletian's reign and continued until the early fifth century in the West, throughout the fifth century in the East (Fig. 15).

Upgrading could occur in several ways. If a site did not have projecting towers these would be added. They could be specially designed, as in the case of the fan-shaped towers peculiar to the Danube, added from Constantine's reign onwards to forts such as Zwentendorf and Intercisa. These were the most effective way of

[24] Salway, *Roman Britain*, 390–1; S. Johnson, *The Roman Forts of the Saxon Shore* (London, 1976), 117–20.

[25] P. Salway, *Roman Britain* (Oxford, 1981), 281; cf. AM 31. 15. 12.

[26] For artillery see Lander 258–9; the rate of fire was low and E. W. Marsden's books, *Greek and Roman Artillery: Historical Development* (Oxford, 1969) and *Greek and Roman Artillery: Technical Treatise* (Oxford, 1971) make no mention of rate of fire in the indices, and only one mention in the text itself (*Historical Development*, 94); finds are rare, D. Baatz, 'Recent Finds of Ancient Artillery', *Britannia*, 9 (1978), 1–17; for use on forts see AM 17. 1. 12; Anon. *DRB* 18. 1, 8; Them. *Or.* 10. 136A; for use in sieges see below, p. 261.

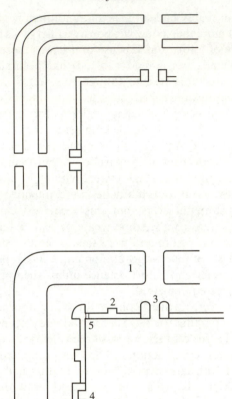

Fig. 15   Upgraded fort design. Top: old-style fort; Bottom: rebuilt fort
(1) ditch dug out; (2) projecting towers added; (3) gate rebuilt; (4) gate
blocked; (5) postern added

defending the walls of a rounded-cornered fort and were frequent
additions to Danubian defences. Elsewhere, fort walls were rebuilt
rather than modified. Walls could be thickened to bring them up
to a thickness of 3 m., as at Zeiselmauer, Contra Aquincum, and
Intercisa. This suggests that thinner walls were thought unsat-
isfactory, perhaps because they would be unable to stand up to
battering rams or undermining. On some occasions the multiple

ditches would be dug out to form a single larger obstacle, as at Eining where the old ditch was dug out, despite the fort having a reduced circuit within the original walls. In forts with multiple entrances, some of the gates were closed off and turned into bastions, as at Zwentendorf or Campona. These changes would make a fort equal in defensive terms to those that were newly constructed. They are found throughout Europe, though, as with fort construction itself, with local variations.[27]

Where these older forts remained different from the newer constructions was in their size. Most new forts were very small. According to Lander, 'a very large minority, and perhaps a majority, of new constructions in the late Roman period were less than 1.0 ha. in size'.[28] Valentinian I is not known to have built a fort larger than Tokod, approximately 1 ha. in size. The older forts were larger and could hold more men. Since they continued to be manned at the same time as smaller sites were being constructed, the Empire may have been putting more men onto the border, or at least, stationing men more widely along the border than previously. Most new sites are found between older large forts or towns, filling gaps on the frontier.

Upgrading was not always felt to be necessary. Britain seems to have had few older forts upgraded. The forts along Hadrian's Wall were never extensively modified, and when a new fort was built at Piercebridge in the third century, it had rounded corners and no projecting towers, making it no different from early second-century forts except in its characteristically late ditch, 8.7 m. wide.

Although durable, stone forts did require regular maintenance. It was another duty of frontier *duces* to ensure that these repairs were carried out, according to the already-mentioned law of Valentinian I from 364. If this did not happen, the silting of ditches, subsidence of walls and towers, and rotting of gates would weaken the defensive capacities of the forts.[29]

---

[27] On refurbishment see Them. *Or.* 10. 136; on fan-shaped towers see Lander 246–52; on bastions see Lander 252.
[28] Lander 261, cf. 283.
[29] *CT* 15. 1. 13 (364); *NTh* 24. 1. 1 (443); AM 16. 11. 11, 17. 9. 1, 20. 10. 3, 22. 7. 7, 28. 3. 7; SA *Carm.* 2. 199–201.

B: URBAN FORTIFICATIONS

By the second half of the fourth century many major cities in the Empire, whether in the frontier provinces or not, were walled. However, many sites remained unfortified until the fifth century, while others were never walled at all. In areas close to the frontiers, most towns were walled during the fourth and fifth centuries. But in more remote areas, for example, south Italy, walls were rare even in the sixth century, though a few towns, mostly coastal, such as Naples or Rimini, did have defences.[30]

Unlike earlier Roman walls which were important for reasons of prestige, later walls were functional, intended to protect the city in emergencies. To this end most circuits were smaller than the earlier walls, protecting only a limited area of the city. In Gaul, for example, the largest known late circuit is Metz, covering an area of 60 ha., but the average seems to be around 10 ha. The reduction in size from earlier walls is illustrated by Autun, whose Augustan walls enclosing 200 ha. were supplemented in the third century by an inner circuit covering 10 ha. The larger circuit continued to stand but its condition is uncertain and it may have had little defensive value.

Garrison towns and towns containing *fabricae* seem not to have had larger wall circuits, though the prefecture capitals (Trier and Sirmium) did have larger circuits, a result of their larger size. Ravenna had its wall circuit augmented under Valentinian III, though it had served as an imperial headquarters for at least twenty years previously.[31] The area enclosed by the walls did not contain all the buildings of the city. Large numbers were left outside the walls, occasionally suffering from barbarian attacks. This outside area was known as the *suburbanus*. Inside often lay government buildings, granaries, barracks, courts, factories, as well as private houses. But this placement was not universal and on many occasions such buildings lay outside the walls, for example the imperial palace at Poetovio. Provided most of these structures, and more

---

[30] For Italy see Procopius, *BG* 5. 8. 2; on lack of walls at Narbonne see SA *Carm.* 23. 48–68; Naples see *CIL* 10. 1485; N. Christie and A. Rushworth, 'Urban Fortifications and Defensive Strategy in Fifth- and Sixth-Century Italy: The Case of Terracina', *JRA* 1 (1988), 73–87 at 83–7.

[31] N. Christie and S. Gibson, 'The City Walls of Ravenna', *PBSR* 56 (1988), 156–97.

importantly, their personnel, were kept safe, the imperial administration would suffer little damage from any attacks. In most cases towns were walled as an emergency measure and the army was expected, by the civil population at least, to stop most threats before the town was reached.[32]

Emperors were concerned for the security of cities and took steps to make money available for building and maintaining city defences. It is possible that several groups of town walls in Gaul which display markedly similar characteristics, both in size and style, were built by the same team of workmen, perhaps following imperial orders.[33] Urban fortifications followed the same principles that guided the construction of forts and the description here can thus be more brief than in the preceding section. Urban defences can be divided into four groups: ditches, walls, towers, and gates.[34]

A ditch or moat, either single or multiple, surrounded many cities. At Trier there was a ditch 15 m. wide, 4–5 m. deep, a considerable obstacle in itself and at Constantinople the moat was 20 m. wide and *c.*7 m. deep with vertical sides. Some towns (e.g. Aldborough) had their earlier, narrow, double ditches close to the wall replaced by a single wide ditch, further away from the wall.[35]

The walls formed the core of the defences, and most city walls were 2–3 m. thick. One exception was Constantinople, whose inner Theodosian walls were almost 5 m. thick. At least one wall circuit, at Ravenna, was built of brick and the rubble cores of other walls were also brick-faced. Some walls contained galleries providing

[32] On distinction between wall and town see Eugippius, *V. Sev.* 4. 1, 22. 4; for outside areas suffering see Malchus fr. 2; AM 16. 11. 4; Zos. 4. 6. 4, 20. 1; for *suburbanus* see AM 18. 6. 14, 31. 15. 9; Lib. *Or.* 24. 15; on internal granaries see AM 18. 2. 3–4; for *fabricae* see S. James, 'The *Fabricae*' in J. C. Coulston, ed., *Military Equipment and the Identity of Roman Soldiers* (Oxford, 1988), 257–331 at 274; for Poetovio see AM 14. 11. 20.

[33] For imperial encouragement see *CT* 15. 1. 32–3 (395); *AE* 1968. 113. 7; for gangs see Johnson 113–15; on remit of money by Valentinian I for maintenance see *CT* 4. 13. 5 (358), 15. 1. 18 (374), 34 (396); AM 22. 7. 7, 29. 6. 11; cf. *Pan. Lat.* 5(8). 11.

[34] Christie and Gibson, 'Ravenna', 156–97; Christie and Rushworth, 'Urban Fortifications', 73–88; B. C. P. Tsangadas, *The Fortifications and Defence of Constantinople* (New York, 1980); R. Butler, 'Late Roman Town Walls in Gaul', *Archaeological Journal*, 66 (1959), 25–50; J. Hobley and B. Maloney, eds., *Roman Urban Defences in the West* (London, 1983), 78–124; A. Poulter, 'The Use and Abuse of Urbanism in the Danubian Provinces during the Late Roman Empire', J. Rich, ed., *The City in Late Antiquity* (London, 1992), 99–135.

[35] For ditches see Anon. *PS* 12. 37–46 (25 m. + wide); Priscus fr. 5; Veg. 4. 5; for moat, Phasis, see Agathias, *Hist.* 3. 21. 2.

additional firing positions for archers. The height of city walls is
uncertain, since only a few survive to their original height. A
height of around 8–10 m. appears average, judging from surviving
examples such as Périgueux with walls 10 m. high, or Barcelona,
9.19 m. at rampart walk level. A few walls were lower: for example,
Trier, 6.13 m. at rampart walk level, but even this height was too
high to climb unaided and would give the defenders a considerable
height advantage. These walls were crenellated.[36] On a few sites
defensive forewalls are known. The most famous example is that
of Constantinople, but an example probably dating to the fifth
century is known from Marseilles. In the fourth century Aquileia
appears to have had a forewall made of turf. There is also an
undated but possibly late Roman example at Thessalonica.[37]

Around the wall circuit were towers, almost always projecting
from the wall, about 15–20 m. high, at intervals averaging 30 m.,
designed for combat and observation. Towers were linked to each
other by a rampart walk and were entered either from ground level
by an internal or external staircase or from a staircase leading
directly on to the rampart walk. Roofs could be flat or conical.[38]

Gates were always the most vulnerable point in the city walls,
since they could be broken or burnt down. Gateways of large cities
in the first and second centuries often had double entrances. By the
third century, when defences had become more important than
easy access, gates were constructed with only a single entrance, as
they always had been in smaller cities. In other areas double gates
were blocked up, as at Rome in 402. The gateway was usually
flanked by two projecting towers covering the approaches to the
gate as well as enfilading the adjacent wall sections. The gate itself
lay at the rear of this passage, to allow the defenders to interdict
the immediate approaches. The gates themselves were of hard wood
and were iron-bound. Some gates at Rome had portcullises and

---

[36] On height see Procopius, *BP* 2. 13. 17; Anon. *PS* 12. 1–5 (a minimum of 3 m.
thick, 12.5 m. high); for galleries, Rome, see I. A. Richmond, *The City Walls of
Imperial Rome* (Oxford, 1930), 58, 65–75; for crenellations (*pinnae*) see Anon. *PS*
12; AM 16. 4. 2; *ND* insignia of most officials; Christie and Gibson, 'Ravenna',
156–97 at 163–7, 184–6.

[37] Forewalls: for Constantinople see Tsangadas, *Fortifications*; for Marseilles see
Gallia, 44 (1986), 418; for Aquileia see AM 21. 12. 13; for Adrianople? see AM 31.
15. 14; for Thessalonica see M. Vickers, 'The Late Roman Walls of Thessalonica',
LIMES 8, ed. E. Birley *et al.* (Cardiff, 1974), 249–55 at 251; Mauricius, *Strat.* 10.
3. 13 and Anon. *PS* 12. 31–6 envisage some fortifications having forewalls.

[38] Johnson 38–43; flat-roofed towers are shown on pl. 38, *Ilias Ambrosiana*.

they are also known from Nîmes, Die, Aosta, Trier, and Diocletian's palace at Split. They may have been more common than this since surviving unaltered gateways are rare.[39] Large gateways were supplemented by posterns for sorties. These were usually situated at the foot of towers as at Carcassonne, Silchester, and Aquileia.[40]

Artillery was used to defend towns, though it may be important that artillery seems mostly to have been used when there were troops present (although these are the sieges mostly likely to be recorded by historians). Both bolt-shooters and stone-throwers were used. At least one city, Amida on the Eastern frontier, had its own artillery park. As with military sites, artillery seems not to have affected the design of urban fortifications.[41] Many cities seem to have possessed permanent garrisons. Garrisons on the frontier (and occasionally within the Empire) are recorded in the *Notitia Dignitatum*. The presence of permanent garrisons is also mentioned in numerous other cities.

Periodic maintenance had to be carried out if the defences were to remain effective. Common problems were collapses or breaches in walls or towers, usually caused by subsidence or poor construction, occasionally by earthquakes. Rotting affected gates and ditches were susceptible to silting, downgrading their effectiveness as an obstacle. Repair could take place quickly if necessary. At Sirmium in 374 the praetorian prefect Probus 'cleared out the ditches which were choked with rubbish and being naturally inclined to building, since the walls through long-continued peace had in great part been neglected and had fallen, he raised them even to the completion of pinnacles of lofty towers'.[42]

---

[39] For blocked double gates see M. Todd, *The Walls of Rome* (London, 1978), 62–4; on construction see AM 24. 2. 14; on iron-clad gates see Zos. 2. 50. 1; AM 30. 5. 17; Procopius, *BG* 7. 24. 34; Claudian, *De Bello Gothico*, 215; for portcullises see Veg. 4. 4; Todd, *Walls*, 62–3; Richmond, *City Walls*, 110, 114, 136–7, 166–7, 177–8, 188, 204, 257; Aosta, each ·gate; Trier, Porta Nigra; Nîmes, Porta Augusta; AM 30. 5. 17.

[40] For posterns see AM 18. 6. 11, 21. 12. 13; on Carcassonne see Johnson pl. 9.

[41] On artillery in towns see Veg. 4. 8–9, 22, 29; on stone-throwers see AM 31. 15. 6 and 12; for *ballistae* see AM 19. 1. 7, 20. 7. 2, 21. 12. 10, 24. 5. 6; on Amida see AM 18. 9. 1.

[42] For maintenance see AM 16. 4. 2, 18. 2. 5, 22. 7. 7, 28. 3. 7, 29. 6. 9–13; Dexippus fr. 28 and discussion in F. G. B. Millar, 'P. Herennius Dexippus and the Third-Century Invasions', *JRS* 59 (1969), 12–29; on earthquakes see Todd, *Walls*, 66; *CT* 15. 1. 5 (338), 34 (396), 49 (412), 51 (413); *NVal* 5. 1. 3 (440); Marc. Com. sa 447; cf. *AE* 1952. 173; for Sirmium see AM 29. 6, cf. 31. 15. 6.

C: REFUGES

A third type of fortified site was the refuge, used in emergencies to harbour civilians and livestock. They were small in size and some-times only banked and ditched rather than walled. These sites were usually found away from roads on hilltops and were often simply reused hillforts dating from pre-Roman times. Their dating is often uncertain as their use in emergencies meant that there is little chance of datable material surviving. Such sites were most common in frontier areas, though they were still present deeper within the Empire. However, lack of evidence on many sites means they can be described only as potential refuges and could well have served other functions, if they were in fact Roman at all. They seem to have had no official role recorded and their military associations were probably minimal.[43]

Similar to hilltop refuges were 'fortified villas'. These domestic sites, built with defence in mind, appear during the fourth and fifth centuries. They are recorded in literature and epigraphy, as well as being known through the presence of towers on the site plan. It is possible that many other villas were built in a military style since anything that did not leave a trace at foundation level would go unrecorded, including arrowslits, crenellations, and bricked-up windows. Such sites are not common archaeologically and it is likely that the literary mentions have given them an artificially high profile.

We do not know against whom these sites were fortified. Their small size, generally prominent locations, lack of defensive features such as gateways, towers, or ditches and, most importantly, a small, amateur, and ill-armed garrison, would severely limit their defensibility. It seems likely that they were intended more to deter thieves or bandits than for defence against a military assault.[44]

---

[43] MacMullen, *Soldier and Civilian*, 149; Johnson 226–42, 280–90.
[44] Johnson 242–3; J. Percival, *The Roman Villa* (London, 1976), 131, 173, and 'The Fifth-Century Villa: New Life or Death Postponed?', *Fifth-Century Gaul*, 156–64; SA *Ep.* 4. 15, 5. 41, *Carm.* 22; *CIL* 12. 1524; E. Wightman, *Roman Trier and the Treviri* (London, 1970), 168–9; cf. AM 21. 13. 14.

D: EFFECTIVENESS OF FORTIFICATIONS

Some of our sources record large numbers of cities being sacked in barbarian attacks and this might be thought to show that some fortifications were ineffective. However, as suggested above, we know little about the dating of many city walls and it must be proved, not assumed, that a particular city was walled when it fell. Defence of an unwalled city could only be accomplished by an army. Secondly, it is important to distinguish between the city itself (*urbs, oppidum*) and its surrounding area (*civitas, suburbanus*). The area within the walls was small and beyond the walls lay many buildings and fields, still part of the city. These were vulnerable to attack, but it was much more rarely that the walled enclave itself fell. However, the sack of the extra-mural *suburbanus* could be recorded as the sack of the city, for example the treatment of Gothic attacks on Clermont by contemporaries. This was damaging to morale, but of no direct military consequence, providing the walled circuit remained intact.[45] Thirdly, according to Luttwak, 'Roman bases were rebuilt as fortified strongholds not because the barbarians had learned how to breach simple walls—which they must always have been capable of doing—but because the enemy had not acquired significant siege capabilities.'[46] Nevertheless, some explanation must be made of the apparently large numbers of towns which were sacked. Where there was any sort of military defence of a fortified structure it was rare for it to be captured quickly by barbarian attack. Aquileia, for example, took three months to fall to the Huns in 452 and fell only because it was not relieved. On the other hand, when we do know the reasons, cases of towns falling due to treachery or abandonment are common. This does not suggest that towns fell easily to the invaders, rather that they could do if they were not properly manned or supported. The Romans were aware of this; in 374 this knowledge motivated the defence of Sirmium by the praetorian prefect Probus, instead of a withdrawal of troops. This incident also shows the need to maintain the defences of a city and to keep a garrison there. The ease with which towns could be defended is shown by Eugippius' *Vita Severini*, a source illustrating the importance of morale. If the

---

[45] SA *Ep.* 3. 2–4, 5. 12; C. E. Stevens, *Sidonius Apollinaris and his Age* (Oxford, 1933), 130–60.
[46] E. N. Luttwak, *The Grand Strategy of the Roman Empire* (London, 1976), 165.

defenders knew that they would be relieved, or if they were well led, they could hold out. But if there was no one to encourage the citizens, cities rarely opposed the enemy. Dexippus' experiences at Athens in the third century show the problems faced in motivating the citizens to fight. This does not mean that fixed defences were useless, merely that walls alone would not keep out invaders.[47]

---

[47] AM 29. 6. 9–13; Eugippius, *V. Sev.* 25, 27; SA *Ep.* 3. 9; cf. Synesius, *Ep.* 104.

7

Foreign Policy

A: LIMITATIONS

The Roman Empire had an army to keep out or destroy its enemies by whatever means necessary. There was no need, or even thought, of compromise. Ammianus Marcellinus' account of a treacherous attack on a raiding band of Saxons in 370 concludes 'and though some fair judge of these things will condemn this act as treacherous and hateful, yet on having considered the affair, he will not think it improper that a destructive band of brigands was destroyed once the opportunity was given'. This brutality was not confined to the battlefield. Earlier in the fourth century, Constantine the Great threw two Frankish kings to the beasts in the amphitheatre. Usurpers were as brutally treated, executed in public and their heads put on display. Thus in 422 Honorius celebrated his *tricennalia* by executing a usurper and his general in the arena at Ravenna. Though it is easy to be shocked at such brutality, contemporaries probably took little notice.[1]

Given such a perspective, the Roman system of defence was bound to be savage, though probably viewed by the participants in more prosaic terms as 'efficient', 'comprehensive', or 'thorough'. Its object was clear, and Roman officers proceeded to attain their objectives ruthlessly. This section considers the choices open to the

---

[1] AM 28. 5. 7; cf. P. Bartholomew, 'Fourth-Century Saxons', *Britannia*, 15 (1984), 169–85 at 171–2, for possible ironic tone of AM passage; Franks, *Pan. Lat.* 7(6). 12. 3, 10(4). 16. 5–6; Honorius, *Annales Ravennae*, sa 422 (and MS illustrations); Zeno, Marc. Com. sa 497; Evagrius, *HE* 3. 35; cf. J. Ant. fr. 214. 5; A. Alföldi, 'The Moral Barrier on the Rhine and Danube', in E. Birley, ed., *LIMES: The Congress of Roman Frontier Studies* (Durham, 1952), 1–16; for triumphs see M. MacCormick, *Eternal Victory* (Cambridge, 1986), 35–63; for barbarians seen as animals see E. Frézouls, 'Les Deux Politiques de Rome fâce aux barbares d'après Ammien Marcellin', in E. Frézouls, ed., *Crise et redressement dans les provinces Européenes de l'empire* (Strasbourg, 1983), 175–91.

Roman state in achieving these objectives. But first it is necessary to consider who actually made these choices and whether there was any consistent policy.[2]

The Emperor (*Augustus*) was head of the Roman state and head of the army. This applied regardless of the number of *Augusti*, and *Caesares* were their subordinates. During the fourth century an *Augustus* made the decisions necessary to safeguard the state. He continued to do so during the fifth century, though his position as decision-maker was often supplemented or replaced by the actual head of the army, the dominant *magister militum*, men such as Stilicho or Aspar. The principle of centralization, however, remained intact. Throughout this section 'Emperor' is used to refer to the chief decision-maker, though it often encompasses a dominant *magister militum*. For the purposes of this section no distinction is necessary.

Emperors did not make their decisions alone. However, this does not mean that all decisions were discussed, only that they could be. Most decisions were made (or discussed) in the imperial council (*consistorium*), a small body that dealt with military and foreign affairs, as well as civil business. The composition was not fixed, but those making up the council worked together on official business, producing the personal contact necessary for efficient teamwork and decision-making. Members included *magistri militum*, praetorian prefects, *comites* and *tribuni scholarum*, and civilian officials, though the latter probably played a lesser part in some aspects of the discussions. The members were always in close proximity to the Emperor so meetings could be called quickly in response to a crisis. When news of Silvanus' usurpation arrived in 355, Constantius II called a meeting of the consistory at midnight. There were occasions, especially on campaign, when formal meetings of the consistory did not occur. Instead, important political and military decisions were made by the Emperor and an informal grouping of high-ranking military and civil officers. 'Those in the Emperor's presence' would probably be a better reflection of reality than 'council'.[3]

---

[2] AM 23. 1. 7; for a good introduction see F. Millar, 'Emperors, Frontiers and Foreign Relations, 31 BC–AD 378', *Britannia*, 13 (1982), 1–23, esp. 3 n. 12; see also discussion in B. Isaac, *The Limits of Empire* (Oxford, 1990), 372–418.

[3] For council see N. J. E. Austin, *Ammianus on Warfare* (Brussels, 1979), 113; *LRE* 329–41, 346–7; for timing see AM 15. 5. 18; on usurpation see AM 15. 5. 5–6, 12–14, 18–22, 21. 7. 1; on whether to send an expedition to Africa see Zos. 6. 7.

The Emperor was rarely at the troubled area in person when crises had to be resolved, so his decisions were constrained by the information available to him. Though emperors could be well-informed, decisions often had to be taken on a lamentably small amount of information. Thus Valentinian I heard of an Alamannic attack and the usurpation of Procopius on the same day in 365. He knew the Alamanni were attacking,

but as to dealing with the attempt of Procopius before it came to fruition, he was distracted by doubting anxiety and disturbed by this most powerful reason, that he did not know whether Valens was alive or whether his death had led Procopius to attempt the throne. For Equitius [*comes per Illyrici*] had received a report of the tribune Antonius, who was commanding troops in Dacia Mediterranea, and indicated nothing except a vague account which he himself had heard: and Equitius himself had not yet heard anything trustworthy, and reported the events to the emperor in simple words.

This sort of dilemma was common. Once one conflict started, another often followed elsewhere and a decision would have to be made as to which was to take priority. In 360 Julian had to decide whether to go to Britain himself or to send a subordinate, but he did not know if the situation required fighting or negotiation. Other similar situations were Valens' decision to cancel campaigning against the Goths for a campaign on the Eastern frontier in 370 and Honorius' recognition of the usurper Constantine III because of the closer presence of Alaric.[4]

Such dilemmas could be exacerbated, if not caused by, the supply of inadequate information. The major reason for this was the speed of communication. No means of communicating information (as opposed to a single, predetermined message) existed that was faster than a man on a horse. The imperial post (*cursus publicus*) was used as a means of delivering messages to the Emperor. Normal speed was around 80 km. per day, though in an emergency speeds

5–6; on appointing new emperor see AM 15. 8. 2–3, 25. 5. 1–4; on treatment of barbarians see AM 17. 12. 15; Eunapius fr. 42; Priscus fr. 45; below p. 245.

[4] For dilemmas see AM 26. 5. 9–10, cf. 20. 9. 3, 21. 7. 1; Symm. *Laud Val. I* 17; Zos. 5. 27; for available information see Eunapius fr. 66; cf. R. MacMullen, *Corruption and the Decline of Rome* (London, 1988), 146–8; J. F. Matthews, *The Roman Empire of Ammianus* (London, 1989), 40–1; Dio 53. 19. 5; 360, AM 20. 1. 1–2; on cancellation of one crisis for another see Eunapius fr. 42. 78–9; Zos. 5. 43.

of up to 320 k.p.d. were achieved.[5] Naval communication was
sometimes used to deliver information, though its use in Europe
seems to have been uncommon. It appears only to have been used
from Britain or Africa to Europe. Messages do not appear to have
been sent along rivers.[6]

From this it is clear that urgent information would often be
weeks old by the time it reached the Emperor, routine information
older still. Even the news of Procopius' usurpation, declared in
Constantinople on 28 September 365, did not reach Valentinian in
north Gaul until late October or the very beginning of November.
The situation could have changed since the dispatch of the message
and by the time the Emperor responded it had probably changed
again. Thus by the start of November Procopius had control of all
Thrace and was only kept out of Illyricum by the independent
action of Equitius. By early December, the soonest time at which
Valentinian's orders could have reached the area, Procopius also
controlled Bithynia.[7] A secondary problem was in contacting the
Emperor. All information had to go to the Emperor wherever he
was, not to a fixed point, and finding the Emperor's actual position
could further delay the message's arrival.[8]

There were ways of reducing the problems caused by slow
communications. The speed of communication could not be altered,
but problems with messages were minimized by sending the courier,
as well as the dispatch, the entire length of the journey, ensuring
that he was available for further questioning if necessary. Where
possible, responsible officers were sent to confirm information and
evaluate problems before taking action, for example the dispatch
of Severus and then Jovinus to Britain in 367, though this would
again slow further action.[9]

---

[5] On communication see A. M. Ramsay, 'The Speed of the Roman Imperial
Post', *JRS* 15 (1925), 60–74; Procopius, *HA* 30. 1–5; Malchus fr. 20. 121–2, 22; cf.
R. P. Duncan-Jones, *Structure and Scale in the Roman Economy* (Cambridge, 1990),
7–29; heliographs were theoretically possible but there is no evidence for their
military use; cf. Syrianus 7; on signal fires see Anon *PS* 8.

[6] Naval communication. Reddé, *Mare Nostrum*, 447–51; for Britain see AM 20.
9. 9; SA *Ep.* 1. 5. 3; for Africa see Zos. 5. 11. 3.

[7] AM 15. 8. 18–19; Procopius, AM 26. 8–11, 6–8; O. Seeck, *Regesten der Kaiser
und Päpste* (Stuttgart, 1919).

[8] F. G. B. Millar, 'Government and Diplomacy in the Roman Empire during
the First Three Centuries', *IHR* 10 (1988), 345–77 at 351; cf. AM 29. 5. 3.

[9] For couriers see Procopius, *HA* 30. 5; cf. Suetonius, *Augustus*, 49: Lib. *Or.* 18.
52; for evaluations see AM 15. 5. 18–22, 27. 8. 1–2, 30. 3. 2 (*notarius*).

A second means of easing difficulties was to give local commanders considerable autonomy to deal with problems. The regional field army would only be called in if the local *dux* or *comes* could not deal with a problem himself, and the praesental field army would only be needed if the regional commander could not

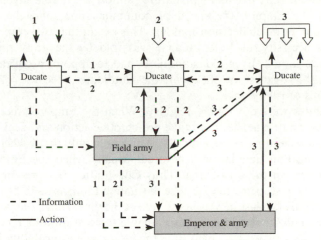

Fig. 16 Information and action: a model. (1) small raids; (2) large raid; (3) major attack

control the situation (Fig. 16). This is difficult to prove since attacks successfully repelled by *limitanei* were rarely recorded—evidence may only survive where the system broke down. Part of the process can be seen in 366, when Charietto, *comes per utramque Germaniam*, was defeated by raiding Alamanni (who had presumably already defeated the *limitanei*), a larger force under Jovinus *magister equitum* was sent against them from the praesental and regional armies. Crises in Britain in 360 and 367 and in Africa in 372 and 397 led to the dispatch of reaction forces from the praesental armies.[10]

In this confused situation of centralized information and decentralized local defensive action with a central intervention force, it is worth asking if there was any central policy. Any such concept is anachronistic to some extent. There was an overall necessity, to

[10] On autonomy see AM 26. 7. 11–12; on layered system see AM 26. 5. 9, 27. 1–2, 28. 5. 1–2; Lib. *Or.* 18. 71.

180   *Foreign Policy*

ensure the survival of the Empire, which entailed keeping barbarians
out and suppressing usurpers. Because of these requirements, much
of the Empire's action against its enemies was predetermined, at
least in form if not in timing. To this end the Emperor had to
decide only when or whether to act (or, in the case of Valentinian's
dilemma, whether or how to respond to both crises). Most operations were thus defensive in nature, almost inevitable given the
size of the Empire, the speed of communication, and the centralization of much decision-making. This meant that two emperors
were a necessity, as Valentinian I was told by the army on his
accession in 364. Even Constantius II had to appoint a colleague,
despite his distrust of the available candidates, because of the
pressures of ruling.[11]

Defences were not totally reactive. When the Emperor received
information in time, he could take pre-emptive action and deal with
a situation before it became a crisis. This could only occur when the
communication time-lag was reduced, usually when the Emperor
was present in the crisis area. Thus Constantius II's pre-emptive
diplomacy to stop an attack by the Sarmatian Limigantes in 359 was
possible only because he was in the area at the time. Had Constantius
been in Gaul, he would have been unable to react until he received
news of their plans, by which time the attack would probably have
already taken place. Speed of reaction would also be affected by the
delay in his orders reaching the crisis zone. Even when emperors had
advance information they did not always react. While preparing to
campaign in Persia in 363, Julian suspected that there would be
trouble from the Goths on the lower Danube, but was unable or
unwilling to act since he was committed to war with the Persians.[12]

Roman offensive actions were not always a response to information. The Alamannic wars of Valentinian I, involving cross-
border strikes in 368, 370, 372, and 374, show the Romans initiating
action, in this case in an attempt to destroy the Alamannic threat.
After the departure of Valentinian in 374 the initiative returned to
the Alamanni. Such strikes could also be carried out by *magistri
militum*, for example by Arbogastes against the Franks in 388–92,

---

[11] Need for multiple emperors. AM 15. 8. 1–2; Jul. *Or.* 1. 44D–45A; Lib. *Or.* 18.
16, 31; as perceived by troops see AM 26. 2. 3–4.
[12] For emperor on the spot in 359 see AM 17. 8. 3–4, 19. 11; for Danube see
Eunapius fr. 27. 1; AM 20. 8. 1, 22. 7. 8, 23. 2. 7; Jul. fr. 9; Lib. *Or.* 12. 78.

though they tended only to initiate these actions when the Emperor was not militarily active.[13]

There seems to have been no Grand Strategy to defend the Roman Empire, merely a reaction to crises as they occurred. On occasion the Romans might take the initiative against the barbarians. In the fourth century the borders of the Empire were fixed and there were no plans for contraction or expansion. The threat presented by the enemies of the Empire was constant so the Empire did not need to change its policies in response to events. With the growth of independent barbarian kingdoms during the fifth century, the pattern of the threat changed, but Roman policy remained reactive and few attempts were made to regain lost territory.

B: BARBARIAN ENEMIES

From the mid-first century AD until the late fourth century and the Gothic crossing of the Danube, the rivers Rhine and Danube and Hadrian's Wall were the northern limits of direct Roman administration in Europe. These were the areas where most of the army was stationed and borders which the army was expected to defend. This continuity in size from the Empire of the principate can be misleading. According to Mann, 'this gives the impression that there was a "standard size" Roman Empire, as if it was predetermined that it should achieve that size and shape'.[14]

From the late fourth century onwards, not all territory within this 'standard size' Empire was Roman-administered and much was permanently lost. But contemporaries noticed these losses only at the time. Within a few years they forgot or accepted them. Thus the Visigothic kingdom in Gaul was a fact of life to late fifth-century Romans and there seems to have been little pressure to eliminate it, though the region was recognized as once having been ruled by the Romans. Visigothia gradually came to be administered by a non-imperial Roman ruler, though the Romans would never have conceded their own right to intervene there. When this

---

[13] On Valentinian's objectives see AM 26. 5. 13, 27. 10. 5; E. N. Luttwak, *The Grand Strategy of the Roman Empire* (London, 1976); Millar, 'Emperors', 1–23.

[14] J. C. Mann, 'Power, Force and the Frontiers of the Empire', *JRS* 69 (1979), 175–83 at 176; for an example of this viewpoint, MacMullen, *Corruption*, 177–91.

intervention occurred, it was only after Visigothic hostility, never on Roman initiative.

The initial Visigothic settlement was negotiated by the Romans. However, not all territory was surrendered without a struggle and where territory was lost to conquest, attempts were made to regain those areas. Thus relations with the Suevi and Vandals in Spain, and later in Africa, swung between peace and Roman attempts at reconquest. Most losses of imperial territory occurred in the West. From the point of view of the Eastern Emperor there was no great change in the boundaries of his part of the Empire. Some parts of the Balkans drifted in and out of Roman control (or at least influence) before the Goths entered Italy, but the bulk of the peninsula remained under East Roman control throughout this period. Regardless of the size of the Empire, the Romans would fight to defend what they currently held.

For most of the fourth and fifth centuries the Romans had treaty relations with all barbarian kingdoms on their borders. According to their terms the barbarians would not attack the Romans. These treaties continued to be made with the Visigoths, Burgundians, and Vandals once their kingdoms had been established on imperial soil, suggesting that this territory was now no longer considered to be Roman. On the other hand, treaties were not made with bandits or rebels like the troublesome Isaurians, since Isauria was part of the Empire.

Embassies could be exchanged and negotiations take place between Romans and barbarians before any conflict. Peace treaties were made on these occasions. Treaties could also be made by barbarians after a defeat at the hands of the Romans. Roman diplomatic relations with barbarians were carried out by several different groups of officials, not necessarily military. Embassies were usually headed by an official of high status, frequently a patrician. Some barbarians even wished to receive high-ranking representatives. Lower-ranking representatives might be used to alter the terms of existing treaties or for secret missions.[15]

---

[15] For *tribuni* see *PLRE* i, Hariobaudes, Stilicho, AM 19. 11. 5 (with interpreters); *duces, PLRE* i, Urbicius; *comites rei militaris, PLRE* i, Arinthaeus, Prosper; *PLRE* ii, Censorius, Fronto, Mansuetus, Romanus 2, Romulus 2; *magistri militum, PLRE* i, Arinthaeus, Victor 4; *PLRE* ii, Anatolius 10, Aspar, Avitus 5, Dionysius 13 (= Dionysius 8), Iulianus 13 (if he = 15), Plinta, Sabinianus 4, Theodulus 2; civil officials, *PLRE* i, Sallustius 5 (PPO), Spectatus 1 (*tribunus et notarius*); *PLRE* ii, Adamantius 2 (*patricius*), Alexander 12, Avitus 5 (exPPO), Cassiodorus 2 (*tribunus*

As well as being made as a result of diplomatic approaches, treaties could come from Roman defeats of barbarians. Negotiations might also take place before battle, if the barbarians thought they might lose, perhaps to put themselves in a better bargaining position than if they were defeated.[16] Treaties with defeated barbarians involved delegations to the Roman commander in the field. Barbarian delegates were usually *regales* or *optimates*. They made a formal submission to the Romans by various methods: the Sarmatians, for example, threw down their arms then picked them up again.[17] If the Roman commander was the Emperor, he usually sat or stood on a raised dais, setting himself apart from the barbarians and from other Romans. Though other Roman commanders could make peace with barbarians, as did Theodosius the Younger in 374, in this case the Sarmatians appeared to have viewed the peace as only temporary and in the following year confirmed their treaty with Valentinian I in person. The Emperor was the highest authority in the Roman world and ultimately had to ratify any treaty. Because of this he usually received envoys in person. By the end of the fourth century it seems that if the Emperor was not present the *magister militum* on the spot could act as his representative. Thus Stilicho accepted the submission of the Franks on the Rhine in 395.[18]

et notarius), Dardanus (PPO), Epigenes (QSP), Euplutius (*agens in rebus*), Florentius 7, Hesychius 10 (*tribunus et notarius*), Iovius 3 (PPO), Nomus 1 (*patricius*), Olybrius 6 (exCOS), Promotus 1 (*praeses*), Rufinus 13 (PPO, exCOS), Senator 4 (exCOS), Severus 8 (*patricius*), Tatianus 1 (*patricius*), Telogius (*silentiarius*), Trygetius 1 (exCRP); bishops, Epiphanius of Pavia, Ennodius, *V. Epiph.* 79–91/85–94; Bleda, Priscus fr. 31; philosophers, *PLRE* i, Eustathius 1; SA *Ep.* 7. 6. 10; others, *PLRE* ii, Artemidorus 3, Carpilio 2, Fretimundus, Iustinianus 3, Olympiodorus 1, Opilio 2, Philoxenus 4, Phocas 2, Phylarchus, Priscus 1, Reginus 3, Tatulus; R. W. Mathisen, 'Patricians as Diplomats in Late Antiquity', *BZ* 79 (1986), 35–49; R. Helm, 'Untersuchungen über den auswärtigen diplomatischen Verkehr des römische Reiches im Zeitalter der Spätantike', *Archiv für Urkundenforschung*, 12 (1931–2), 375–436; on altering terms see Priscus fr. 7, 11. 1.

[16] AM 31. 12. 12–14; Procopius, *BV* 3. 6. 13–14.
[17] On rank of envoys see AM 28. 2. 6, 31. 12. 13 (where Gothic envoys were rejected by the Romans as being of insufficient rank); Priscus fr. 11. 1. 14–18, 11. 2. 1–20; *CT* 7. 1. 9 (369), 12. 12. 5 (364); on traditional practice see AM 14. 10. 16, 17. 1. 13, 17. 13. 7, 30. 5. 1; on submission see AM 17. 8. 3, 5, 12. 10, 13. 7; cf. Eunapius fr. 37; Them. *Or.* 16. 301.
[18] On submission to Theodosius see AM 29. 6. 16; to Valentinian see Zos. 4. 17. 2; for head of Roman world see Millar, 'Emperors, Frontiers and Foreign Relations', 1–23; for divinity? see Eunapius fr. 12; Zos. 3. 4. 7; Jordanes, *Getica*, 143; *LRE* 335–7; by emperor see AM 22. 7. 10; Eunapius fr. 42; AM 30. 6. 2–3, 31. 4. 4; for

The Romans could take the opportunity at this stage to display their military strength. Inspection at close quarters would confirm barbarian impressions of Roman power and the glory of the Empire.

On the day appointed for the conference, [Macrianus] stood majestically erect on the very bank of the Rhine, while his countrymen clashed their shields around him. From the other side, the emperor [Valentinian I], also attended by a host of officers of various ranks amid a display of gleaming standards ... When the frantic gesticulation and chatter of the barbarians at last died down, there was much exchange of talk from both sides, and a pact of friendship was concluded and confirmed by solemn oaths.[19]

These treaties of course were not guarantees of peace, merely a means of regulating relations between Romans and barbarians. The treaties were often broken, but since we usually hear of them only when they were made or broken, this may give a distorted picture of how they were regarded by barbarians. When we are informed that treaties were broken, there was almost always a reason, usually Roman military weakness or Roman provocation. In some cases the treaties could be seen, by the barbarians at least, to have been broken by the Romans before the barbarians took hostile action.

There seems to have been no standard format of treaty relations and each treaty was probably set up to take account of local conditions, although previous treaties would guide the new arrangements. Similar frontier conditions meant that the treatment of barbarians as described by Cassius Dio in the third century was similar to that shown by Menander in the sixth century, though they still do not allow us to do more than sketch the provisions used in various treaties. These provisions seem to have differed little in negotiations with defeated and undefeated barbarians.[20]

Some treaties were specified to last for a few months or years, but for most we do not know the duration. The frequent conflict

Stilicho, see Claudian, *De 4 Cons. Hon.* 439–59; cf. Priscus fr. 48. 1; Malchus fr. 2, 20. 222–5.

[19] On impression of Roman strength see AM 30. 3. 5, 16. 3. 2, 10. 6, 17. 12. 9–10, 19, 13. 3, 18. 2. 17 (though unconvincing, since Macrianus lived opposite Mainz), 27. 5. 3, 30. 6. 2, 31. 10. 9; Sulpicius fr. 7; Zos. 4. 34. 5; Them. *Or.* 10. 193; Jordanes, *Getica*, 143; Mauricius, *Strat.* 1. 2. 3; cf. J. B. Campbell, *The Emperor and the Roman Army* (Oxford, 1984), 135–6; for dais see Zos. 3. 4. 6; Lib. *Or.* 18. 108; for imperial tent see Zos. 2. 48. 5.

[20] Dio, e.g. 72. 11–12, 13, 15, 16, 18–21, 73. 2 and 3; Menander, e.g. fr. 5. 2, 4, 12. 5, 6.

following the death of a Roman Emperor suggests that in practice they were limited to the lifetime of the Emperor making the treaty and that once he had died they were considered void by the barbarians. Hun attacks are recorded in 395 on Theodosius' death and in 408 on Arcadius' death, while the Alamanni attacked in 364/5 after the deaths of Julian and Jovian.[21] This conflict may have reflected a formal ending of treaties, barbarians taking advantage of Roman administrative disruption, trying to improve their situation, or a new barbarian leader trying to confirm his position. Whatever the cause, trouble on the borders could be expected at the death of any ruler, Roman or barbarian.[22]

After any formal submission there followed a period of nego-tiations, culminating in a treaty. The negotiations seem always to have reached a peaceful conclusion. It should be remembered that negotiations following submission were different from the diplomatic agreements. Though the Romans were imposing peace, the terms could not be too harsh lest they produce further conflict. Standard terms were a cessation of hostilities and a return of Roman prisoners of war.[23] In addition to these conditions, the Romans could impose other terms on the vanquished. In some situations, usually only after a submission, provision of grain, or other resources, including recruits, could be required from the barbarians.[24] Access to Roman territory might be limited. If the Romans distrusted the king of a canton, he could be replaced.[25]

On some occasions, cantons were accepted as *clientes* by the Romans. Such agreements often involved the provision of troops by the barbarians for Roman use. The canton, or at least its king, became actively allied to the Romans, co-operating with them, as

---

[21] Romans and Sassanids informed each other of accessions, but not barbarians, though possible later exceptions were the Vandals, Priscus fr. 52; renewed on accession of new emperor, *Pan. Lat.* 11(3). 7. 3; ten months, AM 17. 1. 12; for lifetime limits see Menander, fr. 9. 1. 79–85; Theodosius, Philost. 11. 8; Arcadius, Soz. 9. 5; Jovian, Julian, AM 26. 5. 7.

[22] Lib. *Or.* 17. 30, 18. 290; Jordanes, *Getica*, 164.

[23] AM 17. 10. 4 and 7–8, 17. 12. 11, 16, 20, 18. 2. 19; Zos. 3. 4. 4–7; Eunapius fr. 19; Lib. *Or.* 18. 78, 89; cf. Malchus fr. 5.

[24] On supply of grain see AM 17. 1. 13, 10. 4, 9; Jul. *Ep. ad Ath.* 280c; for provision of other supplies see AM 17. 10. 9 (carts and timber), 18. 2. 6; Lib. *Or.* 18. 78 (timber and iron).

[25] On forbidding access to Roman territory see Zos. 4. 11. 4; cf. Dio 72. 15, 19, 73. 2, 3; on giving king to people see Priscus fr. 20. 3; Claudian, *In Eutropium*, 1. 381; Lib. *Or.* 59. 1332; cf. Procopius, *BV* 3. 25. 4–8; Aurelius Victor, *Caes.* 42. 21.

opposed to remaining passive. The term *cliens* was probably an expression of a closer relationship for a limited time, not a formal status.[26] Barbarian kings could be given Roman offices as part of a treaty. These all seem to have been honorary and there is no record of these men fulfilling the duties of Roman holders of the offices. But the offices could be exploited and Alaric used his authority (as a pretext?) to issue his men with arms from the *fabricae* of Illyricum in 398.[27]

After the negotiations had been completed, the barbarians swore to the terms according to their own customs. We do not know if the terms of the treaties were written down, though it seems probable that the Romans, at least, had copies. The Alamannic King Vadomarius had a scribe in 360, so agreements might have been recorded in writing by barbarians, but in a generally illiterate society oral agreements were probably considered binding.[28]

As a further guarantee of the treaties the Romans could take hostages, usually of royal or noble stock. In some cases a considerable amount of 'Roman' influence could rub off onto these hostages. One Alamannic king, Mederichus, even renamed his son after Serapis, an Egyptian mystery god, as a result of his time as an exile. The fate of hostages if the treaty was broken is unknown, though in one instance their execution can be inferred.[29] On rare occasions the Romans exchanged hostages with barbarians. This suggests that Roman military dominance was not absolute and that substantial concessions sometimes had to be made to obtain peace.

---

[26] D. Braund, *Rome and the Friendly King* (London, 1984), 23 and n., and 'Client Kings', in D. Braund, ed., *The Administration of the Roman Empire* (Exeter, 1988), 69–96; AM 30. 3. 6.

[27] *PLRE* i, Hariulfus? Mallobaudes; *PLRE* ii, Alaric 1, Attila, Gundobadus 1, Theoderic the Amal 7.

[28] For swearing of oaths see AM 17. 1. 13, 17. 10. 7 and 9, 17. 12. 21, 20. 1. 1, 30. 3. 5; Eunapius fr. 55; Zos. 4. 56. 2; for Roman records in 6th cent. see Menander fr. 6. 1. 408–23; for barbarian scribes see AM 21. 4. 6; Priscus fr. 11. 2. 320–1, 14. 3–8; for use of letters by barbarians see AM 21. 3. 5, 27. 5. 1, 28. 5. 10, 31. 12. 8–9, 31. 15. 5; for disagreements over terms see AM 21. 3. 5, 4. 6, 30. 6. 2; Lib. *Or.* 12. 78.

[29] For hostages see AM 17. 10. 8, 17. 12. 11, 13, 15, 16, and 21, 18. 6, 19, 27. 5. 10, 28. 2. 6–8; Zos. 2. 42. 1, 3. 7. 7; Eunapius fr. 12, 13; Jul. *Ep. ad Ath.* 280BC; Symm. *Or.* 2. 28; Paulinus of Pella, *Eucharisticus*, 379–80; SA *Carm.* 5. 571–3; Malchus fr. 18. 1, 18. 3. 14–15, 20. 137–57; *PLRE* i, Serapio; *PLRE* ii, Dagistheus, Huneric, Petrus 13, Soas, Theoderic 7; for conversion see AM 16. 12. 25; E. A. Thompson, 'Christianity and the Northern Barbarians', *Nottingham Medieval Studies*, 1 (1957), 3–21 at 2; for execution? see AM 28. 2. 6–8.

However, it was rarely high office-holders who were hostages. The examples we know of come from the early fifth century and were the sons of a *magister militum* and a Gallic noble. No member of the imperial household was ever involved and it seems unlikely that the presence of hostages would have affected imperial policy.[30]

These treaties were intended to stop attacks on the Empire, not to keep barbarians out of the Empire. Individuals could come and go freely and many did so. Trade, despite some legal restrictions, occurred on a large scale. Availability of goods had a direct correlation with distance from the frontier. In addition, the range of goods was always smaller and costs probably higher in the *barbaricum* than in the Empire.[31] Treaties regulated relations and reduced the likelihood of conflict. Furthermore, the army by its presence alone could often produce peace; force did not have to be used. Though there is no evidence that the Romans had a policy or concept of 'deterrence', the effect was produced while an army was present on the frontier. If the normal presence in a region was reduced, it could cause raids; barbarians were kept at bay only by fear of immediate retribution.[32] Once peace had been made the Romans usually left the barbarians alone. However, the Romans tried to keep themselves as well-informed as possible of events in the *barbaricum*. They did this by having spies beyond the borders, listening to rumours, and having regular contact with barbarian leaders.

Barbarian military action against the Empire consisted of raiding, attempts to gain territory, or self-defence. The same Roman countermeasures were applied to both raids and invasions. If the Romans were able to take direct military action against the raiding groups they would do this. However, a spate of raiding might provoke major Roman retaliation to deter any barbarians encouraged by

---

[30] *PLRE* ii, Aetius 7, Carpilio 2, Thela, Theodorus 12.

[31] On trade privileges held by barbarians see Petrus Patricius fr. 14; Them. *Or.* 10. 135CD; cf. Dio 72. 11. 3, 15, 19. 2; E. A. Thompson, *The Visigoths in the Time of Ulfila* (Oxford, 1966), 14–20; on trade restrictions see *Digest*, 39. 4. 11, 48. 4. 1–4; *CJ* 4. 41. 1 (370–5), 12. 44. 1 (420); *CT* 7. 16. 3 (420); on trade in general see J. C. Barrett *et al.*, eds., *Barbarians and Romans in North-West Europe* (Oxford, 1989) and review by P. W. Freeman, *Scottish Archaeological Review*, 8 (1991), 133–6; B. Cunliffe, *Greeks, Romans and Barbarians* (London, 1988) and review by J. Collins, *Antiquity*, 62 (1988), 805.

[32] For retaliation see T. S. Burns, 'The Germans and Roman Frontier Policy, *ca* AD 350–378', *Arheološki Vestnik*, 30 (1981), 390–404; for concept of deterrence see Lib. *Or.* 18. 81; Luttwak, *Grand Strategy*, 195–200.

the success of other raids. This retaliation would take the form of crossing the border and inflicting massive economic damage on those responsible.

Direct military action was the most frequently used defence against barbarian enemies. This action could be carried out directly by the Roman army or with the help of allies. Allies could act in support of a Roman field army, as with the Burgundians against the Alamanni in 370, the Taifali against the Sarmatians in 358, or the Visigoths against the Suevi in 422.[33] Allied groups could also act alone, as with the Alan attack on the Vandals in 406 or the Visigothic actions against the Vandals and Alans in 416–18.[34]

Using allies in place of or supplementary to Roman troops was an effective use of power by the Roman Empire, achieving results without expending their own resources. But this could lead to problems if the Roman state was not strong enough to control the barbarians. The extension of Visigothic influence, and then the Visigothic kingdom, into Spain in the mid-fifth century shows the dangers of this policy. The allied groups were hired for a single campaign and once it was over they would be dismissed. Until the mid-fifth century, large allied contingents were used irregularly in conjunction with Roman forces when fighting barbarians. It was only after this that barbarian forces became a large, permanent, proportion of the Western army, and they never seem to have done so in the East. The decision to use allied contingents was not always a free one. When there were (unsettled) barbarian groups within the Empire they *had* to be employed to stop them taking advantage of diversion of Roman military resources. Thus during the 422 campaign against the Suevi in Spain, Visigoths had to be used as allies, lest the diversion of the Gallic field army left them free to break their treaty.[35]

Diplomacy or force were used where it was possible to negotiate with a single leader or where a single enemy could be destroyed. But groups such as the Scotti, Franks, and Saxons had no overall

[33] For allies and Roman army, Burgundians, see AM 28. 5. 9–10; for Taifali see AM 17. 13. 19–20; for Visigoths 422 see Hyd. 77; 446; Hyd. 134; 451, Hyd. 150; for Franks see *Add. ad Prosp. Haun.* sa 451; for Ostrogoths see Malchus fr. 18. 2,3; for Alans see Paulinus of Pella, *Eucharisticus*, 377–95.

[34] For use alone, Alans, see RPF fr. 2; for Visigoths 416–18 see Philost. 12. 4; Hyd. 60, 63, 67, 68; 456, Hyd. 173–5; for Huns vs. Sciri see Soz. 9. 5.

[35] For organization and pay see above, p. 96; for use in usurpations see below, p. 228.

leader with whom to negotiate and were too far away (and insufficiently Romanized) to be easily conquered. Destroying such a threat militarily was almost impossible within reasonable constraints of money and manpower. Different approaches were therefore required against such enemies.

One such was subsidization, used for example by Julian on the Rhine to guarantee Frankish non-interference in shipments of grain from Britain. These subsidies or gifts seem usually to have been of money. In a treaty with the Huns of *c.*435, 'the treaty should be maintained and last as long as the Romans paid 700 lb. of gold each year to the Scythian kings; previously the payments had been 350 lb. of gold. On these terms the Romans and the Huns made a treaty.' Although it is often suggested that they were a weakness specific to the late Roman Empire, subsidies had existed in varying forms since the first century BC. Buying peace could be considerably cheaper in social and financial terms than paying the additional costs of an offensive campaign. It may also have allowed troops from the area to operate elsewhere.[36]

We do not know how regularly these subsidies were paid, though payments to the Huns in the 440s and the Goths in the 470s from the Eastern Empire were annual. They may have been handed over at the same time as the regular confirmations of the treaties, though one-off payments at the time of making the treaties might have been common. On occasion, payments might be made for specific reasons, as with Julian's payment to the Franks.[37] Nor do we know how big these payments were. We have figures for some of the payments in the fifth century, but few for the fourth. The only fourth-century payment known was of 2,000 lb. of silver (= 111 lb. of gold); the time period it covered is unknown. In the fifth century, at the apparent peak of subsidization in the 440s, the Eastern Empire paid 2,100 lb. of gold annually to the Huns from 441 to

[36] Priscus fr. 2; C. D. Gordon, 'Subsidies in Roman Imperial Defence', *Phoenix*, 3 (1949), 60–9; D. Braund, 'Ideology, Subsidies and Trade', in J. C. Barrett *et al.*, eds., *Barbarians and Romans*, 14–26; Thompson, *Early Germans*, 93–102; for gifts see AM 17. 8. 3, 10. 8; Jul. *Ep. ad Ath.* 280A; Zos. 4. 56. 1; Malchus fr. 1; Procopius, *BP* 2. 10. 23; M. F. Hendy, *Studies in the Byzantine Monetary Economy* (Cambridge, 1985), 257–64.

[37] Payments, annual: AM 26. 5. 7; Theoph. *AM* 5942; Priscus fr. 2, 9. 3, 37; Malchus fr. 2; Jordanes, *Getica*, 270; 6th cent. Menander fr. 2; occasional, see Malchus fr. 22.

449. Other known sums are less, suggesting that fourth-century payments were also smaller.[38]

The subsidies consisted of ingots, coins, and possibly plate. Silver ingots in small numbers have been found beyond the boundaries of the Empire, for example in Ireland and near Hanover, and were probably from subsidies. More common are coin hoards containing large numbers of die-linked coins. Gold collars are known to have been given to at least one group of Goths.[39] Payments were probably made to the barbarian king, making his position (to some extent) dependent on the continued supply of Roman money. This could allow the Romans to try to control barbarian hostility.

The effectiveness of subsidization is hard to assess and depends very much on the criteria used. At one extreme, any payment by the Romans can be viewed as a weakness, at the other, any means used to avoid war should be counted a success. Provided the payments were not extracted from the Romans and the Romans were strong enough to enforce their wishes by force, then subsidies would be successful, avoiding conflict. Only when barbarians could extort money, as Attila did in the 440s, could the policy be considered dangerous. Even here it seems to be the personal weakness of Theodosius and commitments in Africa, Sicily, and the East that brought about the high payments. On Marcian's accession the payments were stopped and Attila was unable to force their resumption.[40] This pragmatic viewpoint does differ from that of many contemporaries, but the context in which they wrote must be considered. Payments to barbarians, whatever the result or reason, made good propaganda.[41]

Pressure could also be brought to bear on barbarians by cutting them off from their food supplies. This occurred in 415–16 with Constantius' blockade of the Visigoths in Gaul. Similar economic pressure could be exerted by stopping trade with barbarians, as occurred during Valens' war of 367–9 against the Goths. However,

[38] On 4th-cent. payments see Jul. *Ep. ad Ath.* 280A; on silver–gold ratio 4 *solidi* per lb. silver (5 post 397) see *LRE* 439.

[39] For hack-silver see A. O. Curle, *The Treasure of Traprain* (Glasgow, 1923), 11–91; K. S. Painter, 'A Late Roman Silver Ingot from Kent', *Antiquaries Journal*, 52 (1972), 84–92, includes a catalogue of silver ingots; for collars see Zos. 4. 40. 8.

[40] R. L. Hohlfelder, 'Marcian's Gamble: A Reassessment of Eastern Imperial Policy towards Attila, AD 450–453', *American Journal of Ancient History*, 9/1 (1984), 54–69.

[41] Procopius, *HA* 11. 5–9, 19. 13–16; Priscus fr. 9. 3.

no barbarian society seems to have been dependent on trade with the Romans and in this case Roman military action, not the cessation of trade, seems to have had most effect. Economic pressure seems calculated to force barbarians to negotiate rather than to bring about peace since barbarians would probably fight or surrender rather than die of starvation.[42] As far as is known, the Roman Empire at this period made no attempt to use Christianity as a means of influencing or controlling barbarian groups, although many Goths were converted in the late fourth century. Though individual barbarians became Christians, there appears to have been no conflict or peace motivated by (as opposed to justified by) religion.[43]

On some occasions the Romans were able to exploit divisions within barbarian groups, to the extent that barbarians would actually fight each other. A spectacular example was the triumph of Paulinus of Pella in 414 when a Goth and Alan force was besieging Bazas. He managed to persuade the Alans to come over to the Romans so that they were besieging the town one day, garrisoning it the next. Unsurprisingly, the Goths lifted the siege. Such actions depended on the Romans being aware of the political situation within barbarian groups and reflect good intelligence work.[44]

A similar practice was the breaking up of confederations or alliances between barbarian groups. After the defeat of the Quadi and Sarmatians in 358 Constantius II destroyed the dependence of the Sarmatian Usafer on Araharius, a powerful Quadic leader, by insisting on making a separate peace with each of them: 'Usafer was admitted to plead, though Araharius strongly protested, claiming that the terms which he had obtained should extend also to Usafer, who was his partner, though of inferior rank and accustomed to obey his orders. But after a discussion it was decided that the Sarmatians should be freed from an alien yoke.' Arbogastes

---

[42] Blockades: for Visigoths see Marc. Com. sa 414; Olymp. fr. 29. 1; for ceasing trading see AM 27. 5. 7; Thompson, *Romans and Barbarians*, 13–15, probably over-estimates the importance of trade to the Goths.

[43] Thompson, 'Christianity and the Barbarians', 3–21, and *Romans and Barbarians*, 240–5; cf. D. M. Obolensky, *The Byzantine Commonwealth* (London, 1971), 99–140 and *passim*.

[44] Priscus fr. 49; Paulinus of Pella, *Eucharisticus*, 372–98; RPF fr. 2; Soz. 9. 5. 1–5; Mauricius, *Strat.* 11. 4. 30; Anon. *PS* 6. 16–17.

and Stilicho's campaigns against the Frankish confederation led by Marcomere and Sunno were similar in intent.[45]

A final type of Roman action was the removing of a hostile king. Troublesome kings could be murdered, as happened to Vithicabius in 368 and Gabinius in 373. On occasion this had repercussions: Gabinius' murder caused Quadic attacks on the Empire. These assassinations did not always succeed—the murder of Vithicabius in 369 was not the first Roman attempt on his life. The important point for the Romans was to remove the kings, so they could be driven out by Roman troops, as happened to Macrianus and a Frankish king in the late fourth century, or kidnapped, for example, Vadomarius. Their own people could be encouraged to turn against them, as happened to another Frankish king of the same period. Captured kings were exiled, as with Chnodomarius, or executed, as happened to Radagaisus, rather than being allowed to return home.[46] Regardless of the method used, the Roman objective was to remove the canton's leader. Where a replacement was imposed by the Romans he would be dependent on them and thus (they hoped) favourably inclined. Such plans were not always successful. Fraomarius, imposed by Valentinian I on the Alamannic canton of the Bucinobantes, was soon driven out by loyal supporters of the deposed King Macrianus.[47]

The Romans had a number of different means of dealing with barbarian threats. Diplomacy was often used to resolve crises and combined with destabilizing operations and subsidization kept barbarian threats to a minimum. However, not all threats could be deterred, negotiated away, or bought off, and recourse to force was often necessary.

---

[45] AM 17. 12. 12, 14–15; Claudian, *De Cons. Stil.* 1. 239–45; Priscus fr. 11. 2. 241–58.

[46] For kingship see above, p. 33; for murder see Claudian, *De Cons. Stil.* 1. 236–45; *PLRE* i, Gabinius, Vithicabius; *PLRE* ii, Attila; driven out, *PLRE* i, Macrianus 1; Claudian, *De Cons. Stil.* 1. 236–45; cf. GT *HF* 2. 12; on kidnap see *PLRE* i, Fritigern, Macrianus 1, Vadomarius; on exile see *PLRE* i, Chnodomarius, Vadomarius; on execution see *PLRE* ii, Radagaisus.

[47] For replacement king see *PLRE* i, Fraomarius, Zizais; cf. AM 29. 5. 35; on confirmation of new kings see Priscus fr. 20. 3; Claudian, *In Eutropium*, 1. 381; Lib. *Or.* 59. 1332; cf. Procopius, *BV* 3. 25. 4–8; Dio 72. 13. 3, 14. 1; Aurelius Victor, *Caes.* 42. 21; on adoption see Priscus fr. 20. 3; on asylum see Priscus fr. 2.

C: USURPERS

During the late Empire a number of Romans rebelled against the state and many declared themselves emperors. The reasons for their rebellions are often obscure and are here unimportant. Prevention was a political matter not a military one. But once a rebellion had taken place it was a problem which often had a military solution. A distinction has been made between rebels, who refused to accept imperial authority, and usurpers, who claimed it for themselves.[48]

No Roman Emperor could admit the right of anyone to call themselves 'Augustus' since this would render his own position liable to challenge. Consequently all usurpers had to be removed, by force if necessary. Family ties or imperial status were no protection. In 360 when the Caesar Julian, cousin of Constantius II, claimed the position of Augustus, Constantius could not tolerate this. He was prepared to forgive Julian only if he reverted to the rank of Caesar, otherwise war was inevitable. But Constantius' treatment of Gallus suggests that his clemency may not have lasted for too long and Julian, if he had any choice, may have been wise to reject the offer.[49]

Once a usurpation had taken place, embassies seeking recognition were almost invariably sent by the usurping power to the established Emperor. Embassies could be exchanged between rival courts more than once and sometimes a series of embassies would be exchanged before the two factions resorted to violence.[50] These negotiations were usually carried out by high-ranking civil officials (praetorian prefects, ex-consuls, or *patricii*), but sometimes by bishops, rarely by soldiers (perhaps because they were too concerned with military preparations). The praetorian prefect Philippus was sent by Constantius II to negotiate with Magnentius in 351 while Archbishop Ambrose was sent on an embassy to Magnus Maximus in 384/5. On at least

---

[48] Surprisingly little has been written on usurpations and rebellions; S. Elbern, *Usurpationen im spätrömischen Reich* (Bonn, 1984), provides a good guide to the sources and literature; A. E. Wardman, 'Usurpations and Internal Conflicts in the Fourth Century AD', *Historia*, 33 (1984), 220–37.

[49] For Constantius' offer see AM 20. 9. 4; for treatment of Gallus see AM 14. 11; cf. AM 21. 16. 10; Jul. *Or*. 2. 77C.

[50] Magnentius, Zos. 2. 46. 3–47; Petrus Patricius fr. 16; Julian, AM 20. 8. 2–18; Maximus, Zos. 4. 37; Eugenius, Zos. 4. 55; J. Ant. fr. 187; Constantine III, Zos. 5. 43; Olymp. fr. 13. 1.

two occasions eunuchs were used as ambassadors.[51] After talking with Constantius II, Vetranio was exiled to Bithynia without fighting taking place. This peaceful suppression of a usurpation is unusual and some sources suggest that he was put up by Constantius to buy time for himself and stop Magnentius capturing Illyricum. Though this is possible, it is hard to see Constantius taking such a risk since he could not guarantee that Vetranio would co-operate once he was Augustus. Why Vetranio retired is unknown.[52]

Rebels seem not to have had such a high priority for suppression and could survive unmolested for some time if they did not appear to be a threat. Their threat tended to be local or regional (such as Bonifatius in Africa until he supported Valentinian III in 425), unlike usurpations which tended to split the Empire into two or three parts. However, Gildo's transfer of allegiance to the east in 398 brought an immediate response from the West in the form of an expeditionary force led by Gildo's brother Mascezel.[53]

Once a rebellion or usurpation occurred there were several means of resolving it. A usurper could be recognized as a legitimate emperor. This recognition rarely came. When it did, for example in the agreements made by Theodosius I with Magnus Maximus or by Honorius with Constantine III, acceptance was repudiated as soon as it was safe to do so, or else the treaty was broken to gain an advantage. Maximus broke his treaty with Theodosius in 387 to launch a surprise attack on Valentinian II and Constantine III tried to attack Italy as soon as he could. Thus some chance was always felt to exist of a usurper being accepted, though the only usurper who became legitimate in this fashion was Julian, who succeeded as emperor only as a result of the death of Constantius II.[54]

---

[51] Ambassadors: bishops, Olymp. fr. 8. 1, 10. 1; Athanasius, *Apologia ad Constantium*, 9; *PLRE* i, Ambrose; civil officials, *PLRE* i, Domninus 3, Eutherius 1 (PSC), Nunechius (PPO), Orfitus 3?, Pentadius 2 (*Mag. Off.*), Philippus 7 (PPO), Rufinus 25 (PPO), Titianus 6 (PUR); *PLRE* ii, Iovius 3 (PPO), Iulianus 8 (*primicerius notariorum*), Potamius (QSP); soldiers, *PLRE* i, Marcellinus 9 (MUM), Ursicinus 2 (MUM); *PLRE* ii, Artemidorus 2 (*bucellarius*), Papimus (tribune?), Valens 1; 'Ambassadors', Zos. 2. 44. 2, 3. 9. 3–4; Eunapius fr. 58. 2; Olymp. fr. 13. 1; *PLRE* i, Clementius, Domninus 3, Maximus 12, Rufinus 6, Valens 4; Eunuchs, Zos. 4. 37. 1–2, 5. 43.

[52] Vetranio, *Chronicon Paschale*, sa 350; Philost. 3. 22.

[53] *PLRE* i, Gainas, Gildo; *PLRE* ii, Adaric, Anagastes, Bonifatius 3, Illus 1, Marcellinus 6, Marcianus 17, Tribigildus.

[54] Recognition for Maximus see Zos. 4. 37. 3; for Constantine III see Zos. 5. 43; for Julian see AM 22. 1–2; cf. Attalus, Soz. 9. 8.

Another way of winning a civil war was assassination, a technique rarely used. Possibly the only case (?) in the period under discussion is that of Silvanus, usurper in 355. He was murdered within a month of his usurping power by loyalist soldiers suborned by a negotiating team sent by Constantius II. Silvanus' seizure of power was forced upon him and it may be that his support was not as consolidated as it would have been if he had launched a usurpation on his own terms. The guard kept on most emperors was probably stronger and more loyal than that of Silvanus and distrusted ambassadors would be kept at a distance. In almost every case where the Emperor was murdered or attacked, the attack was carried out by bodyguards or court officials. No one else had sufficiently close access to the Emperor.[55] The difficulty in assassinating an emperor did not stop it being feared. Julian's troops feared his murder in 360 and Julian's own account of Constantius II addressing Vetranio's army in 350 stresses Constantius' lack of armour on this occasion, suggesting it would usually be worn.[56]

While military preparations were being made to deal with a rebel or usurper, other activity could be undertaken. The economic dependence of the city of Rome on African grain meant that it was vital for the Emperor controlling Rome also to control Africa. Where this was not the case, as in 360 and 410 (and probably in 413 and 425), the holders of Africa were able to put economic pressure on the Italian faction.[57] This importance of Africa meant that attempts were sometimes made to seize it during East–West civil wars. Expeditions were launched against Africa from the East in 352/3 and 388. When Africa was held by a rival emperor, expeditions were planned in 360 and launched from Italy to recapture it as in 410 and 426. This situation continued until after the death of Valentinian III, after which the loss of control of Africa by the Romans meant that this was no longer a feature of civil wars, but a strategic problem for the Roman Empire as a whole.[58]

---

[55] For Silvanus see AM 15. 30–1; Marcellinus, *Fast. Vind. Prior.* sa 468; Cass. *Chron.* sa 468; Marc. Com. *Chron.* sa 468; for close attention, see Frank, *Scholae Palatinae*, 99–102, 128; AM 24. 5. 6, 25. 3. 6, 27. 5. 9, 30. 3. 5, 31. 13. 14–16; Philost. 7. 15, 11. 1; Theoderet, *HE* 5. 19.

[56] On fear see AM 20. 4. 20–2; Jul. *Ep. ad Ath.* 285AB; cf. AM 25. 3. 3–6; for lack of escort being unusual see Jul. *Or.* 2. 77A.

[57] On economic pressure, 360, see AM 21. 7. 2–4; *Pan. Lat.* 11(3). 14; 410, Zos. 6. 11; on defensive measures vs. infiltration see *CT* 7. 16. 2 (410).

[58] Expeditions from East for 352/3 see Jul. *Or.* 1. 40C, 2. 74C; for 388 see *P. Lips.*

Those rebellions or usurpations that were attacked in their early stages generally collapsed quickly, as in the case of Nepotianus, Silvanus, and Marcellus. Prevention was better than cure, with the result that emperors treated severely anyone suspected of aiming for the purple. Though this was cruel and resulted in some unnecessary deaths, it stopped many attempts from coming to fruition and probably deterred others through the difficulty of organizing a coup in secret.[59]

Usurpations could finish in other ways. The civil war between Julian and Constantius II was stopped in its initial stages by the natural death of Constantius. After this the sole surviving claimant, Julian, was considered to have won. No other claimant tried to take advantage of Constantius' favourable military position. Similarly, in most other usurpations once the original claimant was killed his faction collapsed. Despite having troops and holding the rank of Caesar in 353, Decentius committed suicide when he heard of the death of his brother Magnentius. In 388 Maximus' supporters in Gaul, though they had custody of the child Caesar Victor and controlled Gaul, Spain, Africa, and Britain, did not use him to lead continued opposition. A few usurpations did produce a second emperor. In Britain in 406 Gratian replaced Marcus and Constantine replaced Gratian, though we know little about the reasons behind the replacements. Another was Procopius' usurpation of 365–6, when Marcellus declared himself emperor after the defeat of Procopius, but fell soon after. The usurpation of Jovinus in 411 followed immediately after the suppression of Constantine III (though the chronology is not secure) and was supported by the same group of Gallic nobles.[60]

If an emperor was captured after a military defeat it was necessary to remove him. The treatment of defeated rebels was no different. Most defeated emperors were executed. Even the youth of Magnus Maximus' son, the Caesar Victor, did not save him from execution on his capture in 388. Most rebels were also executed. Some were exiled, such as Vetranio in 350 (perhaps as a reward for his peaceful

1. 63; West for 360 see AM 21. 7. 5; for 410 see Soz. 9. 8; Zos. 6. 7. 5–6, 9. 1–3; for 426 see *C. Gall. 452*, 96; Prosp. 1294; either there were expeditions in 426 and 427 or one of the sources is misdated.

[59] AM 16. 8. 8–9, 26. 6. 3–4, 29. 5. 4; *PLRE* i, Africanus 2, Barbatio, Constantine 4 (= Gallus), Gainas, Procopius 4, Rufinus 18, Silvanus 2, Stilicho, Theodorus 13, Timasius, Valentinus 5, Ursicinus 2; *PLRE* ii, Aetius 7, Ardabur 1, Patricius 8.

[60] *PLRE* i, Marcellus 5; *PLRE* ii, Constantine 21, Gratian 3, Jovinus 2, Marcus.

submission). Attalus on his second deposition in 415 had the fingers of his right hand cut off and was exiled. During the later fifth century several emperors (e.g. Avitus and Glycerius) were consecrated as bishops.[61] The importance of killing the opposition's leader ensured that campaigns continued until one faction's leader was killed or his forces had been destroyed. The uncertain, but often fatal, prospects for the close supporters of the defeated faction also made for long wars, fought to the bitter end. Constantius II defeated Magnentius in three battles over a period of three years. After his third defeat Magnentius still had troops available and apparently willing to fight and the usurpation was ended only by his suicide and that of his Caesar Decentius.[62]

When a usurper was defeated, his high officers often died in battle—for example, Romulus, Magnentius' *magister militum*, who fell at Mursa. A number of prominent officers died in usurpation battles and it is possible that these battles were bloodier than those against barbarian enemies. Recorded casualties are certainly high (54,000 at Mursa, more than 10,000 at Frigidus), but the figures are unreliable and there are no comparable figures for fighting barbarians.[63] Some defeated generals committed suicide, such as Andragathius (after Maximus' defeat in 388) and Arbogastes (after Eugenius' defeat in 394). Other survivors could be dismissed, pardoned, exiled, or executed.[64]

But persecution of a rebelling or usurping faction was rarely

[61] Emperors: killed in battle see *PLRE* i, Nepotianus 5; *PLRE* ii, Anthemius 3, Constans 1, Maximus 22; for suicide see *PLRE* i, Decentius 3, Magnentius; for murder see *PLRE* i, Constans 1, Silvanus 2; *PLRE* ii, Gratianus 3, Heraclianus 3, Marcus 2, Nepos 2; for treatment of usurpers, execution, see *PLRE* i, Eugenius 6, Marcellus 5, Maximus 39, Procopius 4, Victor 14; *PLRE* ii, Basiliscus 2, Constantine 21, Ioannes 6, Jovinus 2, Leontius 17, Maximus 7, Sebastianus 2; for exile *PLRE* i, Vetranio 1; *PLRE* ii, Basiliscus 2, Maximus 4 (self-imposed), Nepos 3; for exile and mutilation see *PLRE* ii, Attalus 2; for consecration see *PLRE* ii, Avitus 5, Basiliscus 1, Glycerius; being spared see *PLRE* i, Anon. 223; for treatment of rebels, execution, see *PLRE* ii, Illus 1, Longinus 3, Longinus 4; for exile see *PLRE* ii, Marcianus 17; being consecrated, see *PLRE* ii, Longinus 6, Marcianus 17; being spared, see *PLRE* ii, Vitalianus 2.

[62] Zos. 2. 53–4; AM 14. 1. 1.

[63] Jul. *Or*. 1. 36BC but *Or*. 2. 59CD suggests this was exceptional; cf. AM 19. 7.

[64] Survivors: for suicide, see *PLRE* i, Andragathius 3, Arbogastes, ?Merobaudes 2; being dismissed see *PLRE* i, ?Gomoarius, Nannienus; being pardoned see *CT* 9. 38. 11 (410), 15. 14. 11 (395), 12 (395); Soz. 9. 8; *PLRE* i, Agilo, Hormisdas 3; *PLRE* ii, Aetius 7, Sigisvultus; being exiled see *PLRE* i, Gerontius 1; *PLRE* ii, Castinus 2; being executed see *CT* 9. 40. 21 (412); *PLRE* i, Asclepiodotus 1, Florentius 4, Lutto, Maudio, Nigrinus 1; *PLRE* ii, Allobichus, Jovinus 3.

carried out beyond its upper ranks, probably because it was counter-productive. Few soldiers below the rank of tribune are known to have been executed (though we would be unlikely to hear of them) and this suggests that the majority of troops and officers could have been excused as 'only following orders'. Defeated regiments might be transferred to another region, with two regiments, named after Decentius and Magnentius, being transferred from Gaul or Italy to Persia.[65] In John's usurpation of 423–5, treatment of the defeated faction was unusual. The usurper himself had been defeated, captured, and executed by the Eastern army, but the arrival of Aetius with an allied contingent of Huns put the defeated faction in a strong bargaining position. Despite losing their leader they still had an army. For Valentinian III's faction it was important to follow up the successes against John by ending the rebellion, otherwise further campaigning would be necessary. Pardoning the military supporters of John would have been the only way to do this.[66]

[65] For defeated regiments see AM 18. 9. 3, 21. 11. 2, 12. 19–20, 29. 5. 20–4; ?Malchus fr. 9. 4 (= Suda A. 3968); for nephew of usurper still serving in army see Procopius, *BG* 6. 5. 1; for persecution of suspected soldiers see AM 14. 5. 1–2; for amnesty see Jul. *Or.* 1. 38B, 2. 58B.

[66] John's usurpation is curiously understudied, Elbern, *Usurpationen*, 121–3, says little.

8

Strategy

A: DEFENCE AGAINST BARBARIANS

To preserve the Roman state it was necessary to keep barbarians
outside the Empire and to expel them if they did break in. The
ideal solution was a defensive system that could defeat all attacks
on (or beyond) the borders of the Empire. This resulted in the
stationing of large armies on the Rhine and Danube frontiers in
the early imperial period.

Overall, any Roman defensive system faced three major problems.
First, the enemies of the Empire could not be permanently eliminated. Secondly, wars were at least partly dependent on factors
that would not be affected by the Roman defensive system, for
example, the leadership abilities of the barbarian kings, disruption
following Roman civil wars, and famine causing food shortages in
the *barbaricum*. Thirdly, there was only a limited amount of money
and manpower available.[1] Allowing for these problems, what
were the weaknesses of the system followed in the early Empire?
It was inflexible, since most of the army was deployed on the
frontier, though not necessarily committed to border defence.
If serious trouble did occur in one area, it could often be dealt
with only by transferring troops from another area. This weakened the second area and rendered it liable to attack. The practice of transferring legionary detachments (*vexillationes*) rather
than whole units was a response to this, though not a very satisfactory one. The system of defence also made the Emperor
militarily weak, since he possessed military power only when
he was with the army. This could be acceptable only if the emperor

---

[1] E. N. Luttwak, *The Grand Strategy of the Roman Empire* (London, 1976), is a
convenient summary of the early Empire, but see the review by Mann, 'Power,
Force and the Frontiers of the Empire', *JRS* 69 (1979), 175–83.

was unchallenged, but the Emperor was never this secure.[2]

In the third century the same defensive system continued, but some troops were now permanently detached from the borders to become field armies operating with the Emperor. These were in addition to the (now weaker) border forces, not a replacement. The creation of these praesental armies gave the Emperor a force which moved with him and allowed operations to be undertaken in one area without weakening border defences elsewhere. Initially, there was only one field army, then one for each Emperor. By the fourth century regional armies had appeared to supplement the praesental forces. Thus in 350 there were three field armies, one each in the East, in Illyricum, and in Gaul. By the time of the drawing up of the *Notitia Dignitatum* (c.423 in the West) further small field armies had appeared in Spain, Africa, Britain, and western Illyricum, while a second Eastern field army had been created in Thrace to supplement that of Illyricum.[3]

During the late fourth century increasing numbers of troops were deployed behind the border, but the same principles of defence still applied. The civilian author of the *De Rebus Bellicis*, writing c.370, still wanted to keep all barbarians outside the Empire: 'A proper concern for the frontiers which surround the Empire on all sides is also to the advantage of the state: an unbroken chain of forts will best assure the protection of these frontiers ... so that the peace of the provinces, protected by a belt of vigilance, may rest unharmed in quiet.' Such views were probably common among civilians. Army officers probably had the same ideals, though they may have been more aware that not every incursion could be stopped on or beyond the border.[4]

Border Troops

The division of the army into two parts, border and field army troops, had first occurred in the third century and the army remained divided during the fourth and fifth centuries. Each part had its own role in defending against barbarians. One of the major problems in discussing the border troops (referred to throughout as *limitanei*) is the sparsity of evidence. Though *limitanei* are often recorded in inscriptions and papyri, they are rarely mentioned by contemporary his-

---

[2] J. B. Campbell, *The Emperor and the Roman Army* (Oxford, 1984).

[3] Mann, 'Power', 175–83 at 182.

[4] Anon. *DRB* 20; on dating see A. D. E. Cameron, 'The Date of the Anonymous', *De Rebus Bellicis* (Oxford, 1979), 1–10; for officers see AM 15. 8. 7.

torians. This was, in part, because Roman historians did not deal with the non-events which were frequently the major concerns of the *limitanei*. Ammianus admits that he has omitted many battles, 'because their results led to nothing worthwhile and because it is not fitting to spin out a history with insignificant details'. Outside detailed sources such as Ammianus' history or Hydatius' chronicle it is unlikely that many of the minor events would be reported. The fifth-century *Life of St Severinus* shows a confused and undefended frontier, but barbarians are present on such a small scale that a small force of *limitanei* would easily have been able to control the area. When Roman forces do occur in Eugippius' narrative, they have no problems in dealing with their enemies.[5]

The *limitanei* were deployed, for the most part, along the borders of the Empire. In continental Europe the Rhine formed the border from the North Sea as far as Lake Constance; from here the border ran across land to the River Iller at Kempten. The Danube formed the border from Kempten to the Black Sea. The Lake Constance–Kempten border had a line of watchtowers along it and the border was probably marked by a road or track between the watchtowers.

Units of *limitanei* were grouped together under *duces* or *comites* in military commands of one or more provinces. There were two commands in Britain and twelve along the length of the Rhine and Danube, mostly corresponding to provincial boundaries (Fig. 17). However, the Diocletianic separation of military and civil administrative structures meant that commands could cover more than one province, producing officers such as the *dux Pannoniae Primae et Norici Ripensis*. Most commands were held by a *dux*, though eight were held by *comites* at the time of drawing up the *Notitia*: the Saxon shore, Egypt, Isauria, Africa, Tingitania, Britain, Italy, and the *Tractus Argentoratensis*—the last three having no troops assigned in the *Notitia*. These commands consisted of a number of infantry and cavalry units, as well as some flotillas. The *duces* were responsible to the *magister militum* of their region, at least from the time of the *Notitia* and probably earlier.[6]

---

[5] AM 27 2. 11; Eugippius, *V. Sev.* 20. 1; cf. the reported effectiveness of 40 Unnigardae in Synesius, *Ep.* 78, cf. *Ep.* 104, 122; SA *Ep.* 3. 3. 3–4.

[6] J. C. Mann, '*Duces* and *comites* in the Fourth Century' in D. E. Johnston, ed., *The Saxon Shore* (London, 1977), 11–15; on hierarchy see *ND* Occ. 5. 125–43; *CT* 7. 17. 1 (412); *NTh* 4 (438), 24. 1–3 (443); *CJ* 12. 59.8 (Leo); *ILS* 762, 773–5; Augustine, *Ep.* 115.

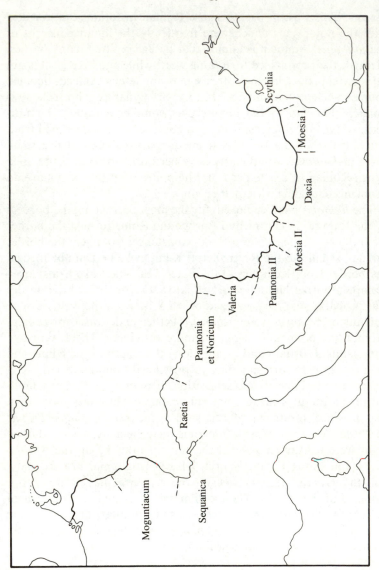

Fig. 17 *Limitanei* commands

Most *limitanei* units were stationed on the Roman side of the border, but in some cases units were stationed in the *barbaricum*, sometimes in forts.[7] Most, if not all, unit headquarters were sited in forts or towns, often by river crossing points (bridges or fords).[8] Some of the unit was stationed with its headquarters, the rest was often spread out along the border in various forts and watchtowers.[9] *Limitanei* could also be stationed in towns as garrisons, both on the frontier and within the Empire, though with outposts similar to forts.[10]

Limitanei were often based in forts, but these were not necessary for their duties. Thus lack of archaeological evidence for fort occupation cannot be taken to mean that *limitanei* were not deployed there, only that stone forts were no longer used. Units based in towns would be likely to leave archaeological traces only if they had a fortified headquarters. Positive literary evidence for the lack of *limitanei* is necessary to supplement the silence of archaeology regarding fort occupation.

Britain differed from the continental frontiers in that it had a wall, not a river, as a land border and because the garrison was deployed more deeply than those on the Rhine or Danube borders. There were two reasons for this unusual deployment. The exposed coastlines of the North Sea and Irish Sea made the extra depth necessary to guarantee communications with the rest of Britain, and the border was so short that units required to defend it had to

[7] For the *barbaricum* see *ND* Occ. 32. 41, 33. 44, 48, 55?; cf. *LV* 15; AM 17. 1. 11, 28. 2. 5, 29. 6. 2.

[8] Crossing points: for Rhine see Zos. 1. 30. 2; AM 28. 2. 1; for Danube see *ILS* 724, 8913; *CIL* 3. 3385; cf. Menander fr. 15. 1; Theophylact, *Hist.* 8. 2. 3–4; *CT* 15. 1. 13 (365).

[9] On outposting see J. C. Mann, 'The Historical Development of the Saxon Shore', Maxfield, ed., *The Saxon Shore*, 1–11 at 1; *ILS* 774; R. O. Fink, *Roman Military Records on Papyrus* (Cleveland, 1971), nos. 1, 2, 63; see also Vindolanda inv. 841, A. R. Birley, 'Vindolanda: New Writing Tablets, 1986–1989', in V. A. Maxfield and M. J. Dobson, eds., *Roman Frontier Studies 1989* (Exeter, 1991), 16–20; early 4th cent., *P. Beatty Panop.* 2. 169, ala II Herc. dromedariorum attested in two forts; many forts in the late 4th cent. have no garrison attested in the *Notitia*, so were presumably garrisoned by troops detached from nearby units; legions could be divided between several posts, *ND* index, *s.v.* II Adiutrix, II Herculia, II Italica, II Traiana, III Diocletiana, III Italica, V Iovia, V Macedonica, VI Herculia, VII Claudia, X Gemina, XI Claudia, XIII Gemina, XIV Gemina.

[10] *ND* Occ. 42. 6, 16, 17, 19, 26–30, 32; *NVal* 9 (440); AM 14. 2. 5, 8, 11. 13, 21. 11. 2, 31. 11. 2; Lib. *Or.* 18. 46, 46. 13–14, 47. 5; Malchus fr. 18. 2. 18–21, 20. 83–6; Candidus fr. 1. 3–4; Zos. 4. 3. 5, 20. 6, 40. 1; R. MacMullen, *Corruption and the Decline of Rome* (London, 1988), 145–6, 209–17.

be deployed in depth rather than laterally. This was not planned
as defence-in-depth and units would not fight from these stations,
but would deploy forward to meet the enemy. These special problems disappeared with the loss of Britain in the early fifth century.
Gaul also had long sea frontiers that were vulnerable to attack. A
third area vulnerable to marine attack was the Black Sea coast,
though there was no need to concentrate units in depth as in
Britain.[11]

Because of the length of these frontiers it was not possible to
garrison or even to watch every possible landing point. However,
by siting forts on river estuaries an attempt could be made to
prevent deep penetration inland by seaborne raiders. Thus in Britain
Burgh Castle was sited on the River Waveney and in Gaul the fort
at Boulogne lay on the Liane estuary. Like the garrisons of *limitanei*
on the land frontiers, the sites recorded in the *Notitia* represent
only the headquarters of these coastal defence units and units
were probably widely dispersed. These units also administered the
flotillas. Some men probably manned observation posts similar to
the chain of stone watchtowers along the Scarborough coast. Most
watchtowers were probably made of wood, left few traces, and are
lost to us. In Britain and Gaul special coastal commands, the Saxon
shore and *Tractus Armoricanus* respectively, were set up under
comites. As far as is known, the Black Sea coast had no special
command, perhaps because of the presence of the Eastern imperial
fleet at Constantinople.[12]

The border troops had three military functions: policing the
border, gathering intelligence, and stopping raids. We do not know
how contemporaries saw their role, though it was perceived as
being different from that of the *comitatenses*.[13] A sixth-century
description of the function of border fortifications gives us an
insight into contemporary views.

[Border] forts are used for several purposes: first, to observe the approach
of the enemy; second, to receive deserters from the enemy; third, to hold
back any fugitives from our own side. The fourth is to facilitate assembly
for raids against outlying enemy territories. These are undertaken not so

---

[11] Mann, 'Power', 175–83 at 180; British defences, *ND* Occ. 40; A. Dornier, 'Was
there a Coastal Limes of Western Britain in the Fourth Century?', in S. Applebaum,
ed., *Roman Frontier Studies* (Tel Aviv, 1971), 14–20.

[12] *ND* Occ. 27, 28, 37; Maxfield, ed., *Saxon Shore.*

[13] *P. Abinn.* 45; Synesius, *Ep.* 78; *CT* 7. 22. 8 (372).

much for plunder as for finding out what the enemy can do and what plans they are making against us.[14]

The policing function involved regulating movement of goods and people both in and out of the Empire. Export of military equipment and, from 374, of gold from the Empire was prohibited. There were also restrictions on allowing barbarians to trade freely within the Empire, presumably to control their movements and thus limiting opportunities for infiltration. This policing function would also extend to apprehending Roman deserters trying to leave the Empire and spies attempting to enter it. Movement into and out of the Empire appears generally to have been unrestricted, though markets seem often to have been limited to specific times and places. It was large groupings that were considered dangerous, not individual travellers. Policing was carried out by the *limitanei* since there was no government organization equivalent to a modern 'customs and excise' branch. In addition, troops were already employed on the frontier and it made good sense to use them rather than create a new body.[15]

A second function was intelligence gathering. Simply by being there the *limitanei* would have had an awareness of likely approach routes, military strength of nearby tribes, etc., and by maintaining contact with the barbarians across the border they would have an idea of changes occurring. Much of this information was retained at unit level, but some was sent to the local *dux* or *comes*. Intelligence could then be sent to the *magister militum* and Emperor if thought necessary. Thus rumours of the approach of the Huns in the 370s came first to frontier officers, then to local *duces*.[16] On marine frontiers, gaining information as to enemy intentions was difficult because of the lack of Roman contact with their homelands. It was hard to know when raiders would strike and their mobility and the length of the coastline made it hard to predict where they would land. These problems were mentioned by Sidonius Apollinaris in a letter to a friend serving in the Visigothic navy in

---

[14] Anon. *PS* 9. 3–8.
[15] On patrolling see Anon. *DRB* 20; on Roman deserters see Anon. *PS* 9; on barbarian spies see Anon. *PS* 9; cf. AM 18. 6. 16; on free movement cf. AM 28. 6. 3; on *limitanei* as officials see R. MacMullen, *Soldier and Civilian in the Later Roman Empire* (Cambridge, Mass., 1963), 57–9; for export of gold see *CJ* 4. 41. 2 (455/6), 63. 2 (374?); on weapons see *CJ* 4. 41. 2 (455/6) and above, p. 58.
[16] AM 31. 4. 2–4.

the 470s: '[The Saxon] attacks unforeseen and when foreseen he slips away; he dismisses those who bar his way, and he destroys those whom he catches unawares. . . . [Saxons] gladly endure dangers amid billows and jagged rocks, in the hope of achieving a surprise.'[17]

The third function of the *limitanei* was that of stopping raids, though their effectiveness is uncertain. MacMullen has recently remarked that 'they were the rural equivalent of the useless urban troops' (= *comitatenses*). However, evidence for *limitanei* in combat is minimal and there is insufficient to support the assertion that their fighting quality was low, though when they were incorporated into the field army they fought well. Besides, it was not their primary function to defeat invaders in open battle. To dismiss them as worthless because they did not stop all barbarian incursions is as valid as attacking modern customs officials on the grounds that smuggling still occurs.[18]

An idea of what the *limitanei* could do may be provided by the size of those groups that broke through the borders. In the winter of 357, a group of Franks occupied a deserted fort on the river Meuse. This band was estimated to be between 600 and 1,000 strong. In 457, Majorian defeated a band of 900 Alamanni who had crossed the Alps. These examples may suggest that the system prevented, either by deterrence or physical defeat, incursions by smaller numbers of raiders. Though an argument from silence, there are no raids smaller than 400 strong recorded in the fourth or fifth centuries.[19]

If this hypothesis is correct, then barbarians would have to assemble a raiding force of 400 or more, and the time taken to raise it might give the Romans a chance to learn of the raid. Furthermore, the low recorded frequency of such attacks in each region, at least when the system was operational, suggests its efficiency. Such a judgement is very much dependent on our

---

[17] For problems in predicting naval raids see SA *Ep.* 8. 6. 14; *NTh* 9 (440); Claudian, *De Cons Stil.* 2. 253–5; AM 28. 2. 12; for scouting boats see Veg. 4. 37.
[18] *LRE* 649–54; on small-scale fighting see AM 22. 7. 7, 27. 2. 11, 30. 7. 6; Lib. *Or.* 18. 71(?); cf. Procopius, *HA* 24. 12; on *limitanei* quality see *LRE* 649–54; Eugippius, *V. Sev.* 20. 1; AM 27. 2. 11; MacMullen, *Corruption*, 175–6; cf. D. Van Berchem, *L'Armée de Dioclétien et la réforme constantinienne* (Paris, 1952), 100.
[19] Raid sizes: for Meuse see Lib. *Or.* 18. 70; AM 17. 2. 1; for Majorian see SA *Carm.* 5. 373–80.

surviving source material and the evidence for the fifth century is very thin.

Defeating seaborne raiders was more difficult. The lack of warning of their approach meant they could often leave an area before *limitanei* reached it. A Roman pursuit at sea was less likely to catch raiders than pursuit on land, because of the greater area of sea and because there were no (or few) locals to question as to their route. Naval patrolling was carried out, though it was probably of little value in stopping marine raids. Roman naval patrols were carried out on rivers and at sea by small boats, so were presumably short-range. These patrols may have been provided by the units on the coast or river as suggested by the *Notitia*, rather than by special naval detachments. Using boats for patrolling would enable large areas of water to be covered quickly and effectively, as well as denying or restricting use of the river by potential enemies. Water transport also enabled the fast movement of troops and supplies over long distances, though usually only downstream.[20]

These three functions, of police work, intelligence, and stopping raids, were achieved by being stationed on the border and by patrolling regularly. Merely by being seen along (and across) the border, the *limitanei* contributed to the security of their frontier, though in a fashion liable to leave few historical traces. Assessing the value of the *limitanei* is difficult, especially as the scant evidence for them diminishes yet further during the fifth century. They continued to exist along the lower Danube at least, as well as in some parts of the West. Eugippius recorded two regiments of *limitanei* in Raetia and Noricum, at Batavi and Faviani, which were not withdrawn and continued to exist until at least the 450s. In Gaul some *limitanei* were incorporated into the Gallic *comitatenses* in the early fifth century according to the *Notitia Dignitatum*, but we do not know if this transfer was real or administrative, or whether the units changed functions and/or stations. In the East, units would have been withdrawn from the Danube after the treaty of 447 with Attila, but were re-established in the 450s. They were also re-established in Africa after its

[20] For scouting boats see Veg. 4. 37; for patrolling see AM 19. 11. 8 (unusual?), 31. 5. 3; for transport of troops see Zos. 2. 46. 2, 3. 10. 2–3, 4. 10. 4; for supplies see Zos. 4. 10. 4; also, for icebreaking on Meuse see AM 17. 2. 3.

reconquest by Justinian. This suggests that they were seen as valuable by the eastern government.[21]

Field Army Troops

In 350 the Roman *comitatenses* were divided into a number of field armies. Each Emperor (*Augustus* or *Caesar*) was accompanied by a number of units, both regular regiments and *scholae*, forming the praesental field army. This always moved with the Emperor. Thus the brigade of the Celtae and Petulantes was based in Gaul under Julian, campaigned in Illyricum in 361 and in Persia in 363, before returning to Gaul with Valentinian in 364, where they remained until 378. When allied contingents were used, they were attached to the praesental army. On campaign, the praesental army often joined the field army of the region where fighting occurred, accounting for the frequent mentions of *scholae* in descriptions of battle.[22]

When fewer emperors campaigned actively during the fifth century, the Western praesental army was usually based in Italy, often in the Po valley, and came under the command of the *magister peditum*. The Eastern praesental army was based around Constantinople under two *magistri militum*. The armies were still used on offensive operations, but the *scholae* remained with the Emperor and thus ceased to fight regularly.

There were also armies assigned to particular regions in 350. In the East the army on the Persian frontier was commanded by the *magister equitum* Ursicinus, though the Emperor Constantius II was also present. In the West there were two major armies, one in Illyricum (under the *magister militum* Vetranio) and one in Gaul (under the Emperor Constans). After the death of Constans, Magnentius presumably took the praesental army into Italy, but the army in Gaul remained a separate entity under Decentius and Silvanus later held the post of *magister militum* there in 354–5. The

---

[21] On Faviani see Eugippius, *V. Sev.* 4. 1–4; *ND* Occ. 34. 41; on Batavi see Eugippius, *V. Sev.* 20; *ND* Occ. 35. 24; for re-establishment, Danube, see S A *Carm.* 2. 199–201; *CJ* 12. 59. 8 (Leo); *PLRE* ii, Camundus?; for Africa see *LRE* 663; *CJ* 1. 27. 2 (534).

[22] On praesental army accompanying Emperor see *CT* 6. 36. 1 (326); since the Emperor and the army were always together the position of at least some of the army can be deduced from the places where laws were issued, O. Seeck, *Regesten der Kaiser und Päpste* (Stuttgart, 1919); *AM* 16. 4. 1 suggests that some *scholae* were always present with an emperor; cf. *P. Abinn.* 3 mentioning a unit in the *comitatus*; Celtae and Petulantes, *AM* 20. 4. 2, 21. 3. 2, 22. 12. 6, 31. 10. 4.

regional armies of the East, Illyricum, and Gaul continued to exist throughout the fourth century. Thus Julian, Valentinian I, and Magnus Maximus all left troops in Gaul while they campaigned in Illyricum. A further regional field army in Thrace was created during the 370s to supplement the Illyrian army on the Danube.[23]

Regional field armies seem not to have had a permanent base or fixed headquarters, instead being administered from wherever the army commander was; though the need to co-ordinate supply arrangements, whether campaigning or not, with the regional praetorian prefect meant that in Gaul and Illyricum the field armies often wintered in and around the prefecture capitals of Trier and Sirmium. After the transfer of the Gallic capital from Trier to Arles in the early fifth century the Gallic army was often based in south Gaul, though it still fought in the north. Prior to this it had been based at Rheims, Cologne, and Paris. The Thracian army was usually based at Marcianopolis, the Illyrian at Sirmium.[24]

Although the regional and praesental armies were distinct institutions, with commanders who had permanent staffs, the constituent units were not tied to them and were often transferred. It seems unlikely that there were regulations stating, for example, that there had to be an army in Gaul under a *magister equitum*. These 'armies' were probably never seen by the Romans as anything more than 'the troops currently in Gaul', which is how they were often described. The posts described in the *Notitia Dignitatum* are no more specific than *magister equitum per Gallias*—the officer commanding the troops in Gaul, not *magister equitum exercitui Gallicani*—though such distinctions may only be semantic. Titles may

---

[23] The date of the creation of regional field armies is disputed. Mann, '*Duces*', 11–15; G. A. Crump, 'Ammianus and the Late Roman Army', *Historia*, 22 (1973), 91–103; for Illyricum see Jul. *Or.* 1. 26C; for Gaul see AM 15. 5. 4 (no *magister militum* is known under Constans in Gaul); for army left in Gaul by Julian see AM 21. 11. 2; for Valentinian see AM 30. 10. 1; for Maximus see Sulphicius fr. 1. 2; cf. troops (including the Batavi) left in Illyricum by Julian in 363, Zos. 3. 35. 2; for creation of Thracian field army see AM 31. 4. 9; *PLRE* i, Saturninus 10, Sebastianus 2, Traianus 2 were *magistri militum* at the same time as Victor and Arinthaeus led the praesental army.

[24] GAUL: Arles, AM 14. 10. 1; Rheims, AM 16. 2. 8, 17. 2. 1; Paris, AM 17. 2. 4, 8. 1, 18. 1. 1, 20. 1. 1; Cologne, AM 15. 5. 15; Trier, AM 30. 3. 7, 10. 1; ITALY: Ticinum, Zos. 5. 26. 4, 30. 4, 31. 6, 32; Milan, AM 14. 10. 16, 15. 4. 13; Ravenna, Zos. 5. 30. 1; ILLYRICUM: Sirmium, AM 17. 12. 1, 19. 11. 1, 17, 21. 9. 5, 11. 2; Zos. 3. 35. 2; THRACE: Marcianopolis, Zos. 4. 10. 3; AM 27. 5. 5, 6, 31. 5. 5; Constantinople, AM 20. 8. 1; Malchus fr. 15.

not have greatly concerned contemporaries and Silvanus was described as *magister militum* and *magister equitum et peditum* in two laws issued in the same place on the same day.[25]

These armies could be adjusted to face new threats. During the fourth century small field armies were created in Africa, Spain, Britain, Western Illyricum, and Isauria. These armies were commanded by *comites rei militaris* and had functions similar to the expeditionary forces led by *comites* earlier in the century. Their creation seems to have been a response to particular crises, not merely an attempt to increase flexibility (though this did occur), since all the areas were troubled by barbarian attacks in the late fourth or early fifth centuries, but they were not disbanded once a crisis was over. The chronology is uncertain, though we know that they were formed before the drawing-up of the *Notitia Dignitatum*. The British and African commands were probably formed in response to the 367 attack and Firmus' revolt.[26]

A further (though also pre-*Notitia*) development in the West seems to have been the creation of subordinate army commanders for the two major armies of Gaul and Italy, in the form of the *comites Argentoratensis* and *Italiae*. At the time of the *Notitia* they had no directly assigned troops, though the structure of the army lists of the *magister peditum* and the *magister equitum per Gallias* suggests that their armies were divided into two groups, one of which could be commanded by these *comites*. But it is also possible that these officers were frontier *duces* of enhanced status whose troops had been absorbed into the *comitatenses*.[27]

We know little about the size of field armies. The largest force reliably recorded is Julian's expeditionary force against the Persians in 363, drawn from the entire Empire at a time when there were no other commitments, and mustering 83,000 men. This represents the Eastern field army, both praesental field armies (incorporating

---

[25] *CT* 7. 1. 2 (349), 8. 7. 2 (349); though see A. H. M. Jones, 'The Career of Flavius Philippus', *Historia*, 4 (1955) 229–33 at 232–3, for dating of these laws. Trying to establish the rules behind titles held at various times is difficult, if not impossible. A good starting-point is A. Demandt, 'Magister Militum', *RE* Suppl. 12 (1970), 553–788.

[26] On armies founded by 413? see *CT* 6. 14. 3 (413); for Illyricum by 382? see *CT* 11. 16. 15 (382), 18 (390).

[27] J. C. Mann, 'What was the *Notitia Dignitatum* for?', in R. Goodburn and P. Bartholomew, eds., *Aspects of the Notitia Dignitatum*, *BAR* S15 (Oxford, 1976), 1–9 at 7; Mann, 'Power', 175–83; *CT* 6. 14. 3 (413).

troops brought by Julian from Gaul and Constantius II's men), and some *limitanei*. This seems to have been an exceptional effort and other recorded armies were smaller. Thus in 478 Zeno promised to mobilize an army of 30,000 infantry and 8,000 cavalry from the Thracian and Eastern praesental armies. This is similar to the armies opposing the Alamanni in 357 when Julian had 13,000 men in Gaul and Barbatio led 25–30,000 men in Raetia. Even these forces were large, and armies could be smaller, perhaps 10–15,000. This is probably the correct order of magnitude for the thirty units Stilicho led against Radagaisus in 406. The army sent by Stilicho to Africa under Mascezel numbered only 5,000. The range of sizes recorded is similar in the fourth and fifth centuries.[28]

The size of these expeditions is often compared with the theoretical size of the whole army calculated from the *Notitia*. For example, Jones's calculations suggest a total of 113,000 *comitatenses* in the West, 104,000 in the east. No field army was ever this big. But once these figures are divided into regional armies, using Jones's figures, only the Gallic army mustered over 30,000 men. Armies bigger than this could be gathered only by reinforcing from the praesental field army. These totals are of the same order of magnitude as the figures recorded above for expeditions and suggest the reliability of the *Notitia*.[29]

Field army regiments were not tied to their armies and could be transferred. Thus Constantius II demanded four regiments by name from Julian in 360 (the brigades of Heruli-Batavi and Celtae-Petulantes) and in 409 six regiments were transferred from Dalmatia to Italy. The men themselves could be loath to leave their homelands, as shown by the Gallic troops' response to Constantius II's

[28] For 363 see Zos. 3. 12. 5–13. 1; for Zeno see Malchus fr. 18. 2. 12–23; for Julian, 357 see AM 16. 11. 2, 12. 2; for Radagaisus see Zos. 5. 26. 4; for Anastasius see Marc. Com. sa 499; for Mascezel see Orosius 7. 36. 6; cf. Marc. Com. sa 514 (60,000 from Thrace) and Victor Tonnensis sa 511 (65,000), presumably praesental, Thracian, and Illyrian armies combined; on 6,000 men in Italy in 470 see J. Ant. fr. 207; cf. Mauricius, *Strat.* 12. 8. 8 envisaging armies over 25,000 strong.

[29] On field army size see R. MacMullen, 'How Big was the Roman Imperial Army?', *Klio*, 62 (1980), 451–60; *LRE* 682–6; there were limits on the size of an army that could be led or supplied effectively, M. Van Creveld, *Command in War* (London, 1985), 104–5; for confusion see J. H. W. G. Liebeschuetz, *Barbarians and Bishops* (Oxford, 1991), 40–2; sizes according to Jones, *LRE* 1434, 1449, are West, praesental: 28,500, Gaul: 34,000, Illyricum: 13,500, East, praesental I + II: 21,000 each, Thrace: 24,500, Illyricum: 17,500.

summons in 360, though they did not need much encouragement to move east in 361. Sometimes the transfers consisted of drafts of men rather than units, though this was probably an unpopular practice. On some occasions, as with Constantius II in 360, the senior *Augustus* took advantage of these transfers to appropriate better quality units.[30] Transfers took place between the forces of Eastern and Western Emperors in the fourth century and even after 395 East–West transfers took place. Thus in 410 six regiments were sent from the East to the West by Theodosius II. Western units were probably transferred to the Eastern army in 431, perhaps only temporarily, when the Eastern general Aspar took control of the African army from Bonifatius.[31]

Lastly, regiments could be transferred from the *limitanei* into the field armies. The fact that this took place suggests that they were worth having in the *comitatenses* (though the limited evidence says nothing of the fifth-century transferred units in combat). These transferred regiments ceased to be *limitanei* and instead became *pseudocomitatenses*, ranked below *comitatenses* in precedence. They probably continued to be paid as *limitanei* but received the rations of *comitatenses*. Most of the known transfers occurred in the late fourth and early fifth centuries, but we would be unlikely to know of others after this owing to the paucity of source material. There are no recorded difficulties in combining the two types of troops in the same army. The *limitanei* may not have been as well-trained or proficient as the *comitatenses*, but they were not markedly inferior to them. An interesting illustration of different capabilities of units is the inability of some Gallic *comitatenses*, transferred in 359 from Gaul to Amida on the Eastern frontier, to cope with defensive siege

[30] For 4th-cent. unit transfers see *CT* 1. 7. 1 (359); AM 20. 4. 2, 26. 6. 12, 27. 10. 6, 29. 6. 16; for 5th cent. see Malchus fr. 18. 1; Zos. 5. 45. 1; for men see AM 20. 4. 2, 31. 11. 2; on appropriations see Zos. 5. 4. 2; cf. AM 20. 4. 2; Jul. *Ep. ad Ath.* 282D; Constantius wanted particular units, possibly some Eastern *cataphracti*, most of whom were stationed originally in the West, but by the date of the *Notitia* were stationed in the East, *ND* Or. 5. 34, 6. 36, 8. 29.

[31] Post-395 East–West transfers: for 410 see Zos. 6. 8. 2; for 467 see Hyd. 234, 247; Cass. *Chron.* sa 467; Jordanes, *Romana* 336; Marc. Com. sa 467; West–East: for 431, arrival of Aspar, see Procopius, *BV* 3. 3. 35; Evagrius, *HE* 2. 1; for Bonifatius' departure (with troops?) see Prosp. 1310 and *PLRE*; it is unlikely that Marcian sent troops to help Valentinian III in 452, Hyd. 177; R. W. Burgess, 'A New Reading for Hydatius Chronicle 177 and the Defeat of the Huns in Italy', *Phoenix*, 42 (1988), 357–63; R. L. Hohlfelder, 'Marcian's Gamble', *American Journal of Ancient History*, 9/1 (1984), 54–69.

warfare. This was presumably a result of their lack of training for this role, rarely required in the West.[32]

As well as units, senior officers were transferred between Eastern and Western sections of the Empire. Thus Frigeridus was *dux Valeriae* in the 370s before serving as *comes rei militaris* against the Goths in Thrace in 377 and Promotus was *comes Africae* at some point before 386, by which time he was *magister equitum* in Thrace. A Chariobaudes is attested as *dux Mesopotamiae* at a date between 383 and 392 and as *magister militum per Gallias* in 408. While there is nothing to link the two names, it was probably the same man. If they were not the same we would have to assume that there was another officer called Chariobaudes in the higher echelons of the army at the same time—not impossible, but unlikely. A tribune Hariobaudes is recorded for 359, but would probably be too old to be *magister militum* in 408. Another transferred individual was Sebastianus, who served as *comes et dux Aegypti* in the 350s. He became attached to the *comitatus* as *comes rei militaris* for the Persian campaign of 363, then moved with Valentinian I and fought in Gaul in 368. He was still in the West in 378 when he seems to have lost his post as *comes* in a court intrigue. He was then requested to return to the East by Valens where he became *magister peditum* commanding against the Goths, but was killed at the battle of Adrianople in 378.

Officer transfers between East and West were less common in the fifth century though they still occurred. The units transferred in 410, 431, and 467 would have taken their commanding officers with them. The general Varanes also had a career spanning both East and West. In 393 he was serving at court in Constantinople, and he probably accompanied Theodosius in his expedition to Italy against Eugenius. He is next heard of in the West in 408 when he was promoted to *magister peditum* in the aftermath of Olympius' coup against Stilicho. Soon after this he was replaced and reappeared in Constantinople in 409, again in an official capacity, and

---

[32] For *limitanei* in field army, see Lib. *Or.* 24. 38; Zos. 4. 30–31; (*pseudocomitatenses*, *LRE* 651, 1435–6, Hoffmann 405–24); Crump, 'Ammianus', 91–103; for Gauls see AM 19. 5. 2, 6; cf. Synesius on the Unnigardae, seeing the *limitanei* as a distinct grade below the *comitatenses*, Synesius, *Ep.* 78; *LRE* 653, 665; R. S. O. Tomlin, 'Meanwhile in North Italy and Cyrenaica', in P. J. Casey, ed., *The End of Roman Britain*, *BAR* 71 (Oxford, 1979), 253–70; a number of units in the *Notitia* appear in both field and border commands and were probably transferred from the latter to the former; see Hoffmann under unit names.

was appointed as consul, probably in the East, in 410.[33]

On some occasions, field armies sent out expeditionary forces, to recapture an area or as reinforcements for attacked areas. These were usually commanded by *comites* and were the forerunners of the small local armies. A number of these were sent to Africa, being drawn from areas with currently unused troops, for example in 372, 398, 410, 413, and 426/7. Africa always contained a small force of *comitatenses* but seems not to have justified basing a large field army there. The two expeditions sent to Britain in 360 and 367 were drawn from the Gallic army and sent by an emperor. Such expeditions were always initiated by an emperor (or dominant *magister militum*). In some cases these expeditions could be commanded by *magistri militum*, such as the forces sent against Procopius from Illyricum and Oriens in 365 or those led by Aspar against the Vandals in 431. This may be a result of the seriousness of the situation, the size of the force, or a combination of these (and other) factors.[34]

Defensive Measures

The *comitatenses* were the striking forces of the Roman army and conducted most of the fighting against barbarians. Though most of the threats faced were from raiding parties, there were frequent occasions when the Romans faced armies of barbarians, either peoples on the march or armies trying to conquer an area. The military problems in dealing with barbarian armies attacking from beyond the borders of the Empire, on the march, or settled within the Empire, were similar and can be dealt with together. In military terms, these problems differed significantly from those posed by raiders only in scale.

Since not all attacks could be stopped on or beyond the border, measures were necessary to safeguard the population and the resources of an area until the attackers could be dealt with. To this end as many of the population as could sheltered in refuges, cities, towns (and perhaps forts) when barbarians were in the area. These

[33] *PLRE* i, Cariobaudes (= *PLRE* ii, Chariobaudes), Frigeridus, Sebastianus 2; *PLRE* ii, Onoulphus, Varanes 1.

[34] Expeditionary forces to Africa, from Gaul see AM 29. 4 (373); Illyricum see Zos. 4. 16. 3; Italy see Claudian, *De Bello Gildonico*, 1. 415–23 = *ND* Occ. 5. 145, 146, 170/211, 179/180/208/217, 183, 171/172; 410, Zos. 6. 7. 6, 9. 2; to Britain see AM 20. 1. 3 (360), 27. 8. 7 (367); for Procopius see AM 26. 8. 4, 10. 4; for Aspar see Procopius, *BV* 3. 3. 35–6; Theoph. AM 5931; Evagrius, *HE* 2. 1.

refugees often took their portable valuables, food, and especially livestock, with them. In an ideal situation, the attackers would be faced with a deserted countryside containing little in the way of easy pickings.[35] If most of the food supplies were stripped from the countryside, raiders would suffer from food shortages, though this in itself would not force them to withdraw. Sebastianus, *magister peditum* in Thrace in 378, hoped to delay any Gothic activity until they retreated or starved. But forcing barbarians to withdraw was not a satisfactory means of defence, rather a hastening of an inevitable process. It also had no or little long-term impact on the ability of the barbarians to attack again.[36]

Barbarians could not be attacked until the regional field army had arrived, something that might take some time. No estimates of the delay can be made, but it was probably weeks or months. The sixth-century *Strategikon* even suggested that the army should delay its arrival to maximize the effect of the food shortage.[37] While the population were sheltering in their refuges, the nearest field army should have been marching to relieve them. Without this guarantee of relief walled sites were vulnerable to blockade and, despite the minimal level of barbarian siege technique, would eventually fall. In the fourth century the city of Cologne was lost to the Franks in 355 because it was not relieved by a Roman army. If an army arrived while the blockade was in progress the besiegers would usually withdraw to avoid being caught between two enemies, as for example in 351 Magnentius was forced to retreat from Mursa because of Constantius II's advance. Besiegers caught between two forces, perhaps as happened to Radagaisus in 406, could suffer badly.[38]

---

[35] For withdrawal of people see Olymp. fr. 29. 2; Anon. *PS* 6. 6–10; Eunapius fr. 42; Zos. 1. 43. 2, 1. 48. 1, 4. 16. 4, 5. 19. 7; AM 18. 7. 3, 28. 6. 13–14, 31. 6. 6, 31. 8. 1; for food see AM 31. 6. 6, 8. 1; Zos. 1. 48. 1, 5. 19. 7; Veg. 4. 7; Eugippius, *V. Sev.* 30. 2; Malchus fr. 20. 110, 115–20; Procopius, *BG* 5. 14. 17; Mauricius, *Strat.* 10. 2. 8; for livestock see AM 18. 7. 3; Zos. 1. 48. 1, 5. 19. 7; Veg. 4. 7; Mauricius, *Strat.* 10. 2. 8; Procopius, *BP* 2. 13. 18; on burning to deny enemy fodder see AM 18. 7. 3–4.

[36] On barbarians forced to withdraw see Zos. 4. 23. 6; cf. AM 14. 2. 13; on starving barbarians see AM 14. 2. 13, 16. 5. 17, 31. 11. 5; Eugippius, *V. Sev.* 30. 4; Zos. 1. 48. 1, 4. 23. 6, 5. 7. 2, 21. 2.

[37] Mauricius, *Strat.* 10. 2. 1–5, 11. 3. 15–17; Luttwak, *Grand Strategy*, 137–44.

[38] For Ravenna see *Anon. Val.* 53; for Cologne see AM 15. 8. 19; for Mursa see Zos. 2. 49. 3–50. 4; for others see Malchus fr. 2; AM 16. 2. 1, 4. 2–3; Mauricius, *Strat.* 10. 1. 1.

Once a field army arrived, it was usually faced with a number of dispersed barbarian groups.[39] The Romans had three strategic choices which were to some extent dependent on barbarian actions. They could conduct harassing warfare, ambushing the barbarians and engaging in running fights; they could fight a field battle, though this was only possible if the barbarians united; or they could blockade the enemy. On occasion no action was necessary as the arrival of the army might induce the barbarians to withdraw. Where possible, the Romans confined barbarians to certain areas by blocking strategic mountain passes. This limited the area vulnerable to attack and restricted food supplies available to the barbarians. An example of this is the occupation of Succi pass in 378 by Frigeridus, confining the Goths to Thracia.[40]

The preferred strategy for engaging barbarians was harassing warfare. The sixth-century *Strategikon* recommended that 'above all, therefore, in warring against them [Franks, Lombards, and Western barbarians], one must avoid engaging in pitched battles, especially in the early stages. Instead, make use of well-placed ambushes, sneak attacks, and stratagems. Delay things and ruin their operations.' Such a strategy could best be implemented by the Romans dividing into small groups themselves. Although large Roman forces could defeat in detail any enemy groups they met, the larger size of such groups would reduce mobility, thus making it more difficult to catch any particular group of raiders and limiting the number of groups which could be engaged. For the troops themselves the difficulties of engaging the enemy could be frustrating. Despite their tiredness, Julian's men wished to engage the Alamanni at Strasbourg, on the grounds that they could now see the enemy in front of them. Assuming Roman operational superiority over the barbarians existed, dividing themselves into small groups was the most effective use of Roman resources.[41]

However, dividing one's forces in this fashion required a good deal of initiative from officers below the level of *magister militum*. The commanders of these small forces had to be able to work on

---

[39] AM 16. 2. 2, 7, 11. 3, 12. 4, 17. 12. 1, 19. 11. 1, 21. 3. 1, 27. 1. 1, 2. 1–2, 8. 7, 9, 31. 5. 8, 10. 21, 11. 5; Zos. 3. 7. 4.
[40] AM 31. 10. 21, 12. 2; above, p. 157, and below, p. 231.
[41] Mauricius, *Strat.* 8. 2. 4, 48; AM 16. 2. 2, 27. 8. 9, 31. 7. 2; Anon. *PS* 33.

their own, to fight with minimum support services, and have an efficient tactical intelligence network. Such efficient commanders were hard to find, but their spectacular successes confirm the efficiency of this means of fighting.[42]

The greatest Roman problem was finding the enemy, since they could not be destroyed if they could not be located. When threatened, barbarians often hid in forests, marshes, or other difficult terrain where they could evade Roman notice. At times the barbarians seem to have overestimated the value of their concealment and were caught by surprise, for example the Goths caught by Sebastianus in 378, who were attacked while 'some were drinking, others bathing in the river'.[43]

An example of this type of warfare occurred when Alamannic raiders in 365–6 were engaged by small Roman parties. The frontier *comes*, Charietto, engaged the attackers with some *comitatenses* legions but was defeated and he himself died in battle. The Alamanni dispersed to plunder. The *magister peditum* Dagalaifus was sent in 366 to deal with them, but had little success in pinning down the dispersed barbarians. He was replaced by the *magister equitum* Jovinus, who destroyed the attackers in a number of actions. One victory resulted when Jovinus

learnt from a faithful scouting party that a group of plunderers, having laid waste the nearby villas, was resting by a river. Coming closer and hidden in a valley made obscure by the thick growth of trees, he saw some bathing, others colouring their hair red, as was their custom, and others drinking. And taking advantage of a most favourable time he immediately gave the signal by horn and attacked the bandits' camp.

Other running battles followed, many on a small scale, and the Alamanni were defeated before the end of the year without a major battle occurring.[44]

The second Roman option was to fight a field battle. This

---

[42] On dispersed Roman troops see AM 27. 8. 7, 31. 11. 2–5; Zos. 3. 7. 1–3, 4. 23. 4–6; on Strasbourg see AM 16. 12. 13–14; cf. SA *Ep.* 3. 3. 7; on unsuccessful commander see AM 27. 2. 1; on value of experienced generals see AM 22. 7. 7, 28. 5. 1.

[43] For difficulty in locating scattered enemy see Zos. 3. 7. 4, 4. 48. 1–2; AM 16. 12. 13–14, 27. 2. 1, 29. 5. 7; Anon. *DRB* 6. 3; for barbarians hiding see AM 27. 2. 2–3; Zos. 3. 7. 4, 4. 48. 1–2; for surprised barbarians see Merobaudes, *Pan.* 1, fr. 2B, 18–19; AM 27. 2. 1–3, 31. 11. 4; Zos. 3. 7. 2, 4. 23. 4, 25. 2.

[44] AM 27. 1–2; Charietto's position may have been the forerunner of the *Tractus Argentoratensis.*

was only possible against concentrated barbarians, though smaller clashes would occur as part of the harassing warfare outlined above. In 378 Gratian met an allied group of Alamanni at Argentaria and defeated them, following up his success with a campaign in Alamannia. Field battles always involved some element of risk, dramatically illustrated by the Roman defeat at Adrianople, and the sixth-century *Strategikon* recorded 'it is well to hurt the enemy by deceit, by raids or by hunger, and never be enticed into a pitched battle'.[45]

Such disasters were rare, however, and the Romans won most field battles in this period. Occasional Roman defeats in major battles did occur. In 352/3 the Alamanni defeated Decentius and in 357 they defeated Barbatio. At Adrianople Valens was beaten by a Gothic army in 378. It is unfortunate that we have few details of these battles, though the small number of Roman defeats over such a long period is noteworthy.[46] There were also a few battles such as Salices in 377, Pollentia in 402, and the Catalaunian Plains in 451, when the Romans were unable decisively to defeat a barbarian force. The usual Roman response after such a failure was to continue harassing or blockading actions rather than to attempt to fight another field battle.[47]

The third Roman option, blockade, required that the enemy be forced into a position where they could be isolated from supplies. On a small scale this is illustrated by the blockade of a Frankish raiding party in a captured Roman fort in 357–8.

Julian ... halted his army and made his plans to surround the strongholds, which the river Meuse flows past, and for fifty-four days (namely in the months of December and January) the delays of the siege were dragged out, while the barbarians with stout hearts and incredible resolution withstood him. Then Caesar, being very shrewd and fearing that the barbarians might take advantage of some moonless night and cross the

---

[45] Veg. 3. 26, no. 3; Mauricius, *Strat.* 8. 2. 4, 10. 2. 1; Zos. 4. 23. 6; AM 31. 7. 2.

[46] Field army victories for Strasbourg see AM 16. 12; 366, AM 27, 1, 2; for Solicinium see AM 27. 10; for Argentaria see AM 31. 10; for Florence see below n. 49; for Constantine III see Zos. 6. 3. 2; defeats: for 352/3 see AM 16. 12. 5; for 357 see AM 16. 11. 14; for 378 see AM 31. 12–13; for 442 see Marc. Com. sa 441. 3, 442; for 447 see Marc. Com. sa 447. 5; for 471 see *C. Gall. 511*, 49; possibly also AM 27. 1, though scale uncertain.

[47] Indecisive battles: on Salices see AM 31. 7; on Pollentia see Claudian, *De Bello Gothico*, 558–647; on 451 see Prosp. 1364.

frozen river, gave orders that every day from near sunset to the break of dawn, soldiers should row up and down streams in scouting vessels, so as to break up the cakes of ice and let no one get an opportunity of easy escape. And because of this device, since they were worn out by hunger, sleeplessness, and extreme desperation, they surrendered of their own accord.

Unless it was necessary to achieve a quick decision there was no need for the Romans to attack a blockaded enemy. Without relief the barbarians would be compelled to surrender. The strategy of blockade could also be carried out by penning barbarians in mountainous country where there would be little forage and the difficulties of movement meant that escape was easy to block. This occurred in the Haemus mountains in 377, when the Romans were able to blockade large numbers of hostile Goths successfully for several months. Similarly, in 402 Stilicho was able to blockade Alaric in the Po valley. If barbarians were on the coast, naval blockade could also be used to limit their access to supplies, as happened in 414 when Goths on the south Gallic coast were blockaded.[48]

Roman operations against Radagaisus in 405–6 illustrate field battles and blockades. Radagaisus, with a large force of Goths, crossed the Alps and entered Italy, plundering as he went. In central Italy he divided his forces into three groups, probably for ease of supply. Some of these troops besieged Florence, almost forcing it to surrender before Stilicho arrived with the praesental field army. Stilicho won a battle outside the town, then drove Radagaisus into the hills and blockaded him. After some time the Goths began to starve. Radagaisus tried to break out, was captured, and executed. Leaderless, his men surrendered. It was a great triumph for the Romans and Stilicho justifiably made much of it.[49]

There was nothing fundamentally wrong with the system, provided that the military strength was present. The need was for an effective field army together with a system of fortified bases. Though

---

[48] Blockades: for Franks see AM 17. 2. 2–3; for Haemus see AM 31. 7. 3, 8. 1–9; for others see Priscus fr. 49; Claudian, *De 4 Cons. Hon.* 478–83; AM 31. 10. 15; Eugippius, *V. Sev.* 30. 4; Zos. 4. 23. 6, 5. 7. 2; Claudian, *De 6 Cons. Hon.* 238–48; Hyd. 77; J. Ant. fr. 190; on naval blockade, see Orosius 7. 43. 1; on deliberate strategy see Eunapius fr. 44. 1; Mauricius, *Strat.* 8. 2. 4.

[49] For Radagaisus see Prosp. 1228; *Add. ad Prosp. Haun.* sa 405; *C. Gall. 452,* 50, 52; Zos. 5. 26. 3–5; Orosius 7. 37. 4–16; Aug. *De Civitate Dei,* 5. 23; *ILS* 798–9.

the border troops were useful, they were not necessary for the system and their gradual decline did not compromise the system's effectiveness. Once territory was lost and barbarian kingdoms established in Europe, defence lay in the hands of the field army alone. It seems that the *limitanei* were not re-established on the new boundaries of Roman authority, the borders with the Visigoths or the Burgundians. This is an argument from silence, but there are no epigraphic attestations of 'internal' *limitanei* and almost no mention of any new borders in either the laws or literary sources. The lack of forts is not a conclusive argument that there were no *limitanei* in a particular area.[50]

Since the Romans maintained complete control of the Mediterranean coast during this period, there was little need for any naval strategy. Fleets were confined to supporting land operations, transporting men and supplies to threatened regions, for example convoying troops to Africa in 372 and 397 and to Britain in 360 and 367. They could also be used for blockades, as when Constantius blockaded the Goths in Gaul in 414.[51]

The overall effectiveness of the system can be judged by its (apparent) lack of development between 350 and 425 (and beyond). If the system had been defective it would presumably have changed somewhat, but it does not seem to have done so. The system described here continuously placed Roman strengths in intelligence and logistics against barbarian weaknesses in these areas. It also avoided, as far as possible, the risks inherent in direct confrontation, in battle. Its major weakness was that it was a slow system and did not result in the defeat of attacks in a short time. However, such considerations only had military (as opposed to social or political) importance if the defenders were prevented from engaging a second threat by their being involved with a first, a situation that appears rarely to have arisen.

---

[50] In Spain a number of *limitanei* units recorded in the *Notitia* have the same name as their stations, suggesting that they had been there for some time, *ND* Occ. 42. 25–32; the arguments of J. M. Blazquez, 'The Rejection and Assimilation of Roman Culture in Hispania during the Fourth and Fifth Centuries', *Classical Folia*, 32 (1978), 217–42, that these constituted a *limes* to defend parts of Spain against the Bagaudae or Suevi can be dismissed.

[51] Transport for Europe–Africa see AM 29. 5. 5–7; Zos. 5. 11. 3–4; for Gaul–Britain see AM 20. 1. 3, 27. 8. 6–7; for Italy–Greece see Zos. 5. 7. 1; on blockade see Orosius, 7. 43. 1.

B: ATTACK AGAINST BARBARIANS

The Roman army was not confined to defensive activity and, in the fourth century especially, launched campaigns against barbarians beyond the Empire. These offensive operations were led by the emperor or a *magister militum*. Offensive operations could also occur while following up a defeat of raiders inside the Empire. However, the distinction between attack and defence is a narrow one, and pursuits across the border could easily be defined as part of defensive operations. We do not know how the Romans conceived these situations and it may be that they saw defence as a phase preparatory to counter-attack or as a phase in its own right. It would be equally possible to divide Roman operations into planned and unplanned or active and reactive. Here the distinction is made between operations inside and outside the areas currently directly administered by the Empire, reflecting differences in the Roman treatment of barbarians in these areas.[52]

The Roman political objective when attacking barbarians was to force them to stop hostilities in the future. This was best achieved by negotiating a treaty. Application of force, whether defeating the barbarians in battle or by destroying their crops or villages, was a means of bringing this about. The threat of victory or destruction could be as effective as the action itself and was sometimes sufficient to force the barbarians to surrender. If defeat or destruction was not sufficient to persuade the king to make peace, he could be removed. The same criteria applied whether the attack was initiated by the Romans or was the follow-up to a defeated barbarian raid. Once the enemy had been repulsed they were forced into treaty relations, to reduce the chance of further hostilities.

When offensives started, Roman troops entered the *barbaricum*. If sufficient troops were available, a pincer movement could be launched. This would involve two armies jumping off from separate points and marching through the *barbaricum* to a common objective. This plan was successfully carried out by Valentinian I in 375 against the Quadi, but a similar operation in 357 was ruined by the Alamanni who defeated the southern arm of the pincer under Barbatio.[53] It was rare for barbarians to try to resist the Romans

---

[52] The definitions used here are those of Anon. *PS* 5.

[53] AM 16. 11. 1–3, cf. 28. 5. 8–15; Mauricius, *Strat.* 11. 4. 41–5; cf. Malchus fr. 20. 226–48; below, p. 250; Van Creveld, *Command in War*, 24–5.

by fighting them in a field battle. The only known occasion is Solicinium, when Valentinian defeated a force of Alamanni in 368. At other times the Romans were engaged in running warfare against small groups of barbarians. Valens' attack on the Greuthungi in 369 appears typical: 'Having forced his way onto barbarian territory, after continuous marches, he attacked the warlike people of the Greuthungi who lived far away, and after some slight contacts, Athanaric, at that time the most powerful ruler (*iudex*) who has dared to resist with a force he believed to be sufficient, was forced to flee for his life.' In either case Roman strategy was similar to fighting barbarians in the Roman Empire.[54]

On rare occasions the mere presence of a Roman force in tribal territory could bring peace. Thus in 358, the Limigantes 'at the first sight of our army, as if struck by a bolt of lightning and expecting the worst, having pleaded for life, promised annual tribute, the pick of their young men, and slavery'.[55] In these cross-border offensives it was profitable to use as large a force as possible, as in Valens' campaign against the Tervingi in 367–9. This minimized the risk, however small, of a defeat in a field battle, as well as reducing Roman casualties. It also reinforced barbarian impressions of Roman power. The Romans made sure that the barbarians knew that the Roman army was an efficient machine. This was an effective use of Roman power, having an effect on both the current campaign and on future actions of the barbarians, though whether assembling large numbers of troops was policy or merely prudence is unknown.[56]

At other times barbarians refused to engage the Romans in battle and took refuge in the highlands or forests. The Romans would then begin to ravage barbarian territory. Thus some of Julian's men crossed the Rhine into Alamannia in 357 after the battle of Strasbourg.

At the very break of day, the barbarians were seen drawn up along the

---

[54] For Solicinium see AM 27. 10; for Athanaric see AM 27. 5. 6; on running battles see AM 16. 11. 9, 17. 1. 4–9, 12. 4–5, 13. 17–19, 20. 10. 2, 27. 5. 4, 6, 31. 10. 15–17; Sulpicius fr. 1. 6.

[55] On submitting to threat of force see AM 14. 10. 9, 17, 13. 4, 31. 10. 17; for lack of food see AM 27. 5. 7; Burns, 'Germans and Roman Frontier Policy', 390–404.

[56] For overkill see AM 17. 12. 4, 27. 5. 3; overawing, cf. AM 17. 13. 5–8 on dangers of provoking trouble.

hill tops, and the soldiers, in high spirits were led up to the higher ground; but they found no one there (since the enemy, suspecting this, had hastily decamped) and then great spirals of smoke were seen at a distance, revealing that our men had burst in and were devastating the enemy's territory. This action broke the Germans' spirit. . . . Upon their departure our soldiers marched on undisturbed and plundered farms rich in cattle and crops, sparing none; and having taken prisoners, they set fire to and burned down all the houses, which had been carefully built in Roman style.

Ravaging also occurred after a Roman military victory and continued until the barbarians made peace. The Romans systematically burnt crops and villages and killed or enslaved any inhabitants they could find. This process was deliberately brutal and demonstrated to the entire people the hopelessness of resistance. Such action inevitably had more impact on farmers than on societies with numerous herd animals. At the same time, denial of food could force the enemy to submit.[57]

The brutal Roman methods ensured that serious short-term damage was caused to barbarian agriculture. However, it was virtually impossible to do long-term damage to an agrarian agricultural system in the ancient world. Although crops and seeds could be destroyed, the only means of preventing agriculture in succeeding years was physical occupation of the ground. Furthermore, denial of agricultural cultivation did not mean that other forms of subsistence (grazing animals and hunting and gathering) could not continue or that food could not be obtained from elsewhere. The result of such devastation was hardship, not genocide. Without long-term occupation, the Romans could not destroy an enemy's economy.

The systematic nature of Roman devastation can also be overestimated. The frequent mention of buildings in Roman accounts of destruction suggest that devastation was concentrated on the settlements and the areas around them. It probably also concentrated on easily accessible areas. Given the difficult terrain

[57] On destroying crops see AM 17. 1. 7, 10. 6, 18. 2. 19, 27. 10. 7; *Or.* 18. 89; Suda I. 437 (= Eunapius fr. 27. 7); for livestock see AM 17. 1. 7, 10. 6; for houses see Lib. *Or.* 18. 69: AM 17. 1. 7, 10. 7, 13. 3, 18. 2. 15, 27. 10. 7, 30. 5. 13; Mauricius, *Strat.* 11. 4. 41; for inhabitants see AM 16. 11. 9, 17. 10. 6. 17. 13. 12, 18. 2. 15, 30. 5. 14; Mauricius, *Strat.* 11. 4. 45; on 'ravaging' see Lib. *Or.* 18. 76. 89; AM 17. 1. 4, 12. 6, 29. 4. 6, 30. 5. 13; cf. AM 27. 5. 4 and 6, where there seem to have been no villages to burn.

inhabited by some barbarians, some upland farms, for example in the Carpathians or the Black Forest, probably never saw a Roman soldier. To the practical problems in finding and reaching crops must be added the difficulty of destruction, since not all crops can be burnt all year round (wheat can only be burnt in the month before harvesting, before this it is still green), and the danger of dividing one's forces in the face of an undefeated enemy. Other methods of destruction, such as trampling or cutting down crops, required large resources of time and manpower, not always available.[58]

This devastation by itself did not always bring the barbarians to defeat. Sometimes barbarians were determined to resist and avoided contact by moving the whole canton into forests, mountains, or marshes. Such determination was unusual and seems to have occurred only when the barbarians were well-led. In such cases barbarians were often forced to submit through an inability to obtain sufficient food, not a destruction of all available food-stuffs.[59]

For the Romans an effective peace could be secured only by making treaties with the barbarians, so campaigns were almost always continued until a treaty was made. It seems that, unless there was a formal concession of defeat by their leaders, barbarians did not consider the war over. Thus Gratian's 383 campaign against the Alamanni in Raetia was aborted by Magnus Maximus' usurpation, but was completed in 384 by the *magister militum* Bauto. If the campaign had not been completed, it seems probable that raiding would have continued.[60] When cantons on the frontier had been defeated, those deeper within the *barbaricum* often submitted to the Romans rather than risk being attacked. Thus a number of Quadic cantons came to Constantius II's camp in 358 to submit to avoid fighting the Romans. This was a bonus for the Romans, avoiding the long supply lines and further risks that would be necessary to suppress these peoples.[61]

The whole process of a Roman offensive is well illustrated by

---

[58] cf. V. D. Hanson, *Warfare and Agriculture in Classical Greece* (Pisa, 1983), 146, 148, and *passim*; on grain destruction see ibid. 42–6; houses see D. H. Gordon, 'Fire and Sword', *Antiquity*, 27 (1953), 144–52.

[59] On withdrawing to wilderness see AM 16. 11. 10, 27. 5. 3–4, 30. 5. 13, 31. 10. 12, 16; Lib. *Or.* 18. 69; Mauricius, *Strat.* 11. 4. 38; on submission because of starvation see AM 18. 2. 18, 27. 5. 7.

[60] For 383 see Soz. 7. 13. 1; Aurelius Victor, *Epit.* 47. 6; for 384 see Ambrose, *Ep.* 24. 8; for others see AM 31. 10. 16–17; on finishing wars see Herodian 1. 6. 5.

[61] AM 17. 12. 12, 16, 18. 2. 19.

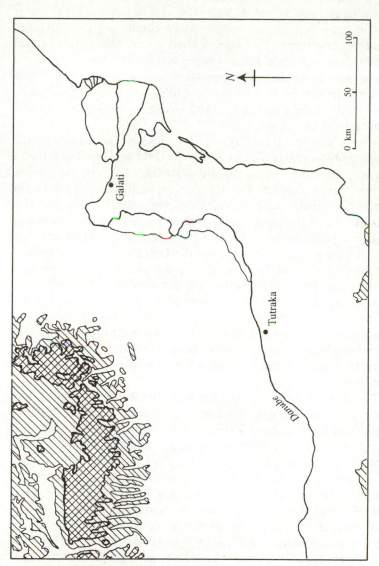

Fig. 18 Valens' Gothic campaigns, 367–9, contours at 500 and 1000 m.

Valens' 367–9 campaigns against the Goths (Fig. 18). The ostensible cause of the war was the assistance given to the usurper Procopius by the Greuthungi in 365–6. Valens sent his *magister militum* Victor to find out why they had supported Procopius and then attacked them as punishment. However, a crisis on the lower Danube had been threatening since Julian's reign and before Procopius' revolt Valens had been making preparations for a Gothic war. From Victor's mission he had probably gained some intelligence as to the Goths' leaders, intentions, and strengths, as well as valuable geographical knowledge.[62]

After assembling the army, a base camp was created at Tutraka and a pontoon bridge thrown across the Danube. Once the Romans crossed, the Goths began to withdraw into the Serri mountains, trying to avoid contact. The Romans captured some of the Goths before they could reach the hills, but the majority escaped. This was the end of the campaign and Valens recrossed the Danube to winter in Marcianopolis. The campaign had not been completed so in 368 Valens again tried to cross the Danube, but was prevented by flooding. In 369 he returned to the offensive and this time crossed the Danube at Galati by pontoon bridge. After some skirmishing, the Goths fled in fear of defeat. Then the Romans again retired to Marcianopolis for the winter. The Goths, unable to defeat the Romans and short of food, sent envoys to the Romans for peace. Valens met the Gothic King Athanaric in a boat on the Danube. Peace was made, though the terms are unknown, and the Goths gave hostages.

The Roman objective, to force the Greuthungi to submit, had been achieved. Though Athanaric may have increased his own status slightly by meeting Valens in the middle of the Danube, such a concession cost the Romans nothing. Valens left for the Eastern front in 370 to campaign against the Persians, but there seems to have been no pressing need for this and he could have continued campaigning against the Goths again if he had felt it necessary. The Romans were only involved in skirmishes since the Goths thought that they would be unable to defeat the Romans in the field. When Athanaric did try to fight he was forced to flee, 'for fear of his life'. The Goths moved to the high ground to evade

---

[62] For crisis see AM 22. 7. 7–8, 26. 6. 11, 7. 9; Jul. fr. 9; Eunapius fr. 27. 1; for preparations see AM 26. 6. 11–12.

attack, taking their herds with them. There was presumably little or nothing left for the Romans to plunder or destroy. Though direct Roman action did not bring the Goths to terms, the threat of starvation by being kept away from fields and pastures, combined with the knowledge that the Romans would not go away, forced the Goths to make peace.[63]

It is hard to assess the effectiveness of Roman strategy in this period but several observations can be made. First, strategy seems not to have changed much over the period covered, suggesting it was felt to be adequate for the demands placed on it. Secondly, it was practical and the demands it placed on the army could be achieved. The system did not demand permanent elimination of barbarians threatening the Empire—this was impossible and would have been a waste of resources if attempted, bad strategy. Thirdly, attempts were made to avoid direct confrontation if possible, since it was expensive in lives and risky. Nevertheless, the army was well-prepared to carry out this role and was successful in it. The evidence presented here suggests that Roman strategy was adequate to defend the Empire from barbarian threats.

C: CIVIL WARS

Roman strategy for fighting civil wars was very different from that for fighting barbarians, in that it was the same for both sides. Political victory was attainable only by removing the enemy leader, usually by victory in battle, though other means were possible. When a civil war started therefore, campaigns revolved around fighting a field battle in the most favourable circumstances possible.

Three factors made fighting in civil wars different from fighting barbarians. First, as the effectiveness of the Roman army was roughly uniform, the larger army was more likely to win. This accounts for the massive recruitment that took place before campaigning started. Secondly, all the fighting took place within the Empire, which gave fleets a role they rarely had when fighting barbarians, at least until the Vandal conquest of Africa. It also meant that sieges were common. Thirdly, since usurpations usually

---

[63] AM 27. 5; Zos. 4. 10–11; Eunapius fr. 37; Them. *Or.* 8, 10; Seeck, *Regesten*, sa 367–9; P. J. Heather, *Goths and Romans* (Oxford, 1991), 115–20; Wolfram, *History of the Goths* (London, 1988), 67–8.

ended only with the death of one of the emperors involved, struggles tended to be long and bloody; rebellions were not always so bloody.

As civil wars occurred between parts of the Roman army, the two sides were equal in combat potential: no side had a necessary advantage over the other. This differed from the situation when fighting barbarians, when a force of Romans would expect to defeat equal numbers of barbarians. Thus, in the unlikely event that all other factors, including numbers and leadership, were equal, both sides in a civil war battle would have the same chance of victory. Because of this, large armies were important and all factions in civil wars therefore engaged in recruiting before embarking on campaign.

Regiments were brought up to strength as much as possible, with recruits being mostly drawn from within the Empire. New units could also be raised, such as the regiments named Magnentiaci and Decentiaci raised by Magnentius to fight Constantius II.[64] In almost all usurpations both the legitimate emperor and his rival also recruited large contingents of allied barbarians. These were hired 'for the duration' and then dismissed. As experienced warriors they would be more effective than hasty levies of citizens. Magnentius hired Franks and Saxons, Constantius II and Procopius hired forces of Goths. Ambrose recorded Magnus Maximus' boast that 'so many thousands of barbarians fight for me and receive rations (*annonae*) from me'. In 394 Eugenius' army contained Frankish and Alamannic contingents, while Theodosius again mobilized the Goths he had used against Maximus. Franks and Alamanni were also used by Constantine III and Huns by John in 425.[65] With the appearance of independent barbarian groups within the Empire after the Gothic settlement of 382 in Thrace, the need to employ these allied groups became twofold. Their manpower was still

[64] On recruiting regulars see AM 18. 9. 3 (unless these are renamed units), 21. 6. 6; Jul. *Or.* 1. 34CD, 2. 56B; Lib. *Or.* 18. 104; possibly *ND* Or. 6. 62–7, following J. F. Matthews' suggestion that 6. 24–5 are blank as they had not yet been allocated shield patterns.
[65] Recruiting allies: for Magnentius see Jul. *Or.* 1. 34CD, 2. 56BD; for Silvanus? see Jul. *Or.* 2. 98D; for Constantius II see Lib. *Or.* 12. 62; AM 20. 8. 1; for Procopius see AM 26. 10. 3; Eunapius fr. 37; for Magnus Maximus see Ambrose, *Ep.* 24. 4; for Theodosius, 388, see *Pan. Lat.* 12(2) 32, 33; Zos. 4. 39. 5; 394, see Zos. 4. 57–8; Soc. 5 25; Soz. 7. 24; J. Ant. fr. 187; Them. *Or.* 15. 189D, 16. 207, 18. 219B; for Eugenius see Sulpicius fr. 2; Orosius 7. 35. 11–12; Constantine III, Soz. 9. 13–14; Maximus, Olymp. fr. 17; for John see Philost. 12. 14; Jovinus, Olymp. fr. 18; Avitus, *Auct. Prosp. Haun.* sa 456; Olybrius, J. Ant. fr. 209.1.

needed, and it was necessary to stop these barbarians from taking advantage of Roman activity elsewhere and the enemy from hiring the settled barbarians for themselves. Something of the danger is shown when Theodosius I was about to set out against Maximus in 388. 'Word was brought to the emperor that the barbarians mixed up in the Roman units were contemplating treason under promise of great rewards from Maximus.' Some were killed in 388, but some escaped and 'plundered Macedonia and Thessaly without resistance while Theodosius was busy with the civil war'.[66]

Several civil wars developed into a confrontation between the Eastern and Western parts of the Empire, with one emperor holding Italy (and sometimes Illyricum) and the land to the west, while another held territory from this region east. The usurpations of Magnentius, Julian, Maximus, Eugenius, and John all belong to this category. When this East–West division occurred, the Mediterranean Sea became important as a means of outflanking the enemy. If one faction had control of the sea it could land troops in its enemies' rear areas, capturing weakly defended regions. Thus Constantius II carried out landings in Spain when fighting Magnentius, and Italy was assaulted from the sea by Theodosius' troops in 388 and by Ardabur in 425.[67] Even when the conflict did not develop into an East–West confrontation sea power was of great importance. Since the Empire was centred on the Mediterranean, most areas had long coastlines vulnerable to attack. Procopius stormed Cyzicus from the sea in 365, Gainas attempted to fight his way across the Hellespont in 400, and Heraclianus made a crossing from Africa to Italy in 413 after his usurpation. Lastly, both Magnus Maximus and Constantine III crossed by sea from Britain to Gaul after seizing the purple.[68] Civil wars produced an upsurge in shipbuilding, or at least the utilization of existing resources. At the start of a usurpation there were few ships available,

[66] Zos. 4. 45. 3, 48. 1; cf. rumours of Constantius II encouraging the Alamanni against Magnentius and Julian for Roman fears of barbarian intervention in civil wars, J. Szidat, *Historische Kommentar zu Ammianus Marcellinus Buch 20–21*, *Historia Einzelschriften*, 38 (Wiesbaden, 1981), ii. 88–91.

[67] On Constantius II see Zos. 2. 53. 3; Jul. *Or.* 1. 40C, 2. 74C; on Magnus Maximus see Zos. 4. 45. 4, 46. 1; Orosius 7. 35. 3–4; Ambrose, *Ep.* 40. 23; on Ardabur see Philost. 12. 13–14.

[68] For Procopius see AM 26. 8. 7–11; for Gainas see Zos. 5. 21. 1–4; for Heraclianus see Orosius 7. 42. 12–14; Hyd. 56; Maximus and Constantine III, not directly attested, but no other means of crossing; for Marcian see J. Ant. fr. 211. 3; Illus, J. Ant. fr. 214.

so coups like those of Maximus, Constantine III, and Heraclianus could not be obstructed. But after mobilization large fleets would be used, for example by Magnus Maximus in the Adriatic in 388.

In the initial stages of a civil war control of information was vital. In 361 Julian was careful to restrict information going to Britain since he did not trust the leader of an expeditionary force currently there and feared he might declare for Constantius II, thus threatening Julian with a war on two fronts. Information could also be restricted to reduce the risk of usurpation, as when Merobaudes was summoned to the *comitatus* in 375 in the name of the already deceased Valentinian I.[69] The lack of information could allow deceptions or misunderstandings to occur. In 361 Julian's men were let into Sirmium because it was believed that their shouts of 'Augustus' referred to the arrival of Constantius II rather than of his cousin. In 387 Maximus seems to have broken through the Alps by deceiving an ambassador of Valentinian II, though Zosimus' account is unclear. More certain is the capture by treachery of Actus in 350, allowing Magnentius through the Julian Alps.[70]

When two armies came face to face, attempts could also be made to suborn troops of the other faction. This occurred outside Paris in 383 when Maximus' army stood opposite that of Gratian for several days, eventually leading to the abandonment of Gratian by most of his troops. Most desertions in usurpations occurred as a result of these negotiations. Other defections were smaller in scale, such as that of Silvanus and the *schola armaturarum* at Mursa in 351.[71]

Campaigning within the Empire frequently involved cities and made siege warfare important. Hostile or garrisoned cities had to be captured before armies could advance, so both before and after field battles sieges were often necessary. The battle of Mursa in 351 was preceded by Magnentius' siege of the city and Constantius' pursuit afterwards was halted by the need to besiege Aquileia. Theodosius faced the same problem with Aquileia in 388. Cities were also important as bases and had prestige value. News that a

---

[69] On limiting information see AM 20. 9. 9; on Merobaudes see AM 30. 10. 2; cf. Zos. 5. 27.

[70] On deception see AM 21. 9. 5–7; Zos. 4. 42. 3–7; for Actus see AM 31. 11. 3 (reading of name is unclear but unimportant).

[71] Zos. 2. 46. 3, 4. 35. 5; Soc. 2. 32; AM 15. 5. 33, 26. 6. 12, 7. 14–17, 9. 4–7; Philost. 12. 13–14; Soz. 7. 24. 4–5; Jul. *Or.* 1. 48BC; Orosius 7. 35. 16.

city had fallen could encourage one faction and unsettle another, making relief of a besieged city more important.[72] Urban defences also meant that cities could protect themselves if they were opposed to a usurper. Thus Aquileia revolted against Julian in 361 and Rome in 351 produced its own usurper, Nepotianus. When faced by invading armies, cities still had the same role. The walls of Mursa were invaluable for Constantius II in slowing down the advance of Magnentius, and Salona was an important outpost for John in 424, forcing Aspar's troops to besiege it before they could advance on Italy.[73]

The geography of the Empire often determined the location of battles in civil (and foreign) wars. There were three major strategic bottlenecks provided by mountain passes. These were the western (Cottian) Alps (353, 387, 409), the passes through the Julian Alps (352, 388, 394, 425, 493), and Succi, between Serdica and Philippopolis in the Haemus mountains (361, 366). At times, Acontisma (near modern Kavalla) in Macedonia (365), Thermopylae (447), the passes through the Haemus from Dacia Ripensis (365), and through the Pyrenees (409) acquired importance.[74]

The war between Constantius II and Magnentius in 350–3 illustrates most of the points discussed above (Fig. 19). The usurper Magnentius had recruited troops from within Gaul, as well as hiring Franks and Saxons from beyond the Rhine before marching east. Constantius II collected supplies in Pannonia in late 350 at Naissus. Magnentius in spring 351 crossed the Julian Alps from Italy into Illyricum, capturing by treachery Constantius' general Actus who was defending the passes. Magnentius started moving into Pannonia down the Savus valley. Constantius' army advanced from Sirmium up the Savus, but his advance guard was defeated in an ambush by Magnentius at Atrans and he retreated to Poetovio on the Dravus. Magnentius followed up his success and captured

---

[72] For Mursa see Zos. 2. 49. 3–4, 50; for Aquileia see Jul. *Or.* 1. 38D–39A; *Pan. Lat.* 12(2). 38–9; for Rome see J. Ant. fr. 209.

[73] For Aquileia see AM 21. 11–12; for Rome see Zos. 2. 43. 2–4; for Salona see Philost. 12. 13; for others see AM 15. 6. 4.

[74] Passes: for W. Alps see Zos. 4. 42. 6–7, 6. 2. 5–6; for Julian Alps see Zos. 4. 46. 2, 5. 29. 4; AM 21. 12. 21; for Succi see AM 21. 10. 2–4, 13. 16, 26. 7. 12, 27. 4. 5–7, 31. 10. 21; Malchus fr. 18. 2. 14, 26 (accepting Valesius' reading of Σουκιν for Σονδιν); for Acontisma see AM 26. 7. 12, 27. 4. 8; for Thermopylae see Zos. 5. 5. 3–7; Marc. Com. sa 447. 4; for Dacia see AM 26. 7. 12; for Pyrenees see Soz. 9. 12; Orosius 7. 40. 6.

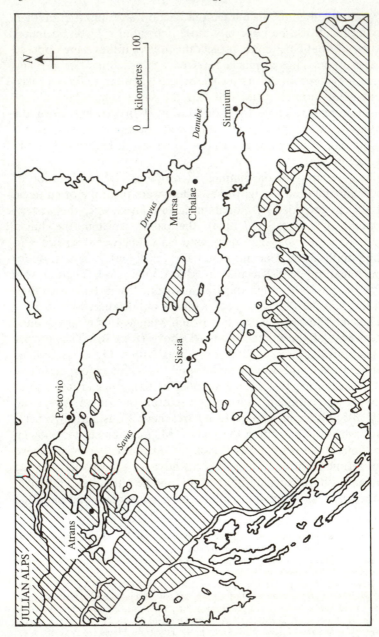

Fig. 19 Mursa campaign, 351. Contours at 400 m.

Poetovio, then pursued Constantius south to the Savus and fought his way back across the river. So far the fighting had been inconclusive and only small skirmishes had taken place. A period of negotiations followed, though without result, and Magnentius then stormed Siscia. Avoiding further contact with Constantius, he continued to advance down the Savus valley to Sirmium which he attacked but failed to capture. By this point Constantius II's main force had taken up strong positions in field defences at Cibalae, threatening Magnentius' communications down the Savus. Magnentius' failure at Sirmium forced him to retreat, bypassing Constantius at Cibalae, to Mursa which he needed to capture to secure his communications along the Dravus or Savus valley. The city's failure to surrender forced him to besiege it. This finally gave Constantius II an opportunity to attack Magnentius on his terms.

Magnentius could either continue besieging Mursa, thereby dividing his forces between two enemies, or he could give up the siege (thereby losing the strategic initiative) and face Constantius with his whole force. He chose to face Constantius on the broad plains of Mursa, terrain advantageous to Constantius because of his large force of cavalry. A further advantage was brought to Constantius by the defection of the *schola armaturarum* of Magnentius with its commanding officer Silvanus. The battle was fought and Magnentius defeated, but he was able to retreat to Italy. Constantius was forced to storm the passes across the Julian Alps in 352. In 352 Constantius also began assembling naval forces which were used to land troops in Spain and Africa. Magnentius retreated down the Po valley and took up a position in the Isère valley at Mons Seleucus. He was defeated in battle here and retreated to Gaul where he committed suicide on learning of the loss of Africa and Spain to Constantius' landings.[75]

The strategy involved in Roman civil wars seems to have been simpler than that involved in fighting barbarians. Once hostilities started, the objective was to fight a decisive battle as soon as possible, on the most advantageous terms possible.

---

[75] The main source, Zosimus, is extremely confusing; *Zosime*, ed. F. Paschoud, vol. i (Paris, 1971), has a good commentary on the campaign; N. H. Baynes, 'A Note of Interrogation', *Byzantion*, 2 (1925), 149–51, seems rather negative; Zos. 2. 45–54; Jul. *Or.* 1, 2.

9

Operations

A: OPERATIONS

Boundaries between strategic and operational, and between operational and tactical decisions are very flexible and the selection of material that belongs here, rather than in Chapter 8, is difficult. Some of the topics discussed, such as strategic intelligence, belong equally well there. Since most field operations were conducted by the *comitatenses* this section refers mostly to them, not to *limitanei*. However, the two parts of the army appear to have been similar in capability.

Operational aspects of the fourth-century army are well-known thanks to the detailed narrative of Ammianus Marcellinus, but the fifth-century army is much less well documented. In this section, therefore, evidence from outside Europe and from the third and sixth centuries is especially widely used to provide analogies and to illustrate what the army could do. Here it is assumed that the regular elements of the army were little different in both parts of the Empire, an assumption from silence, but one that the sparse evidence does not contradict. Since the type of external problems faced by the Eastern and Western Roman armies in Europe did not change, there were no external reasons for the army to develop. Thus any changes that did take place probably reflected the political or economic situation or changes in strategy. These developments appear to have been limited. By the sixth century, though more emphasis was placed on cavalry, the rest of the army differed little from that of the fourth century. Therefore, historians from the sixth century, such as Procopius, Menander, or Agathias, provide useful comparative material, as do the military writings of Mauricius, Urbicius, and the anonymous author of the *Peri Strategikes*.[1]

---

[1] R. S. O. Tomlin, 'The Army of the Late Empire', in J. Wacher, ed., *The Roman*

Training was an important part of army routine, not just for new recruits. Theoretically, all units carried out some form of daily training, including route marches and archery practice, while we also hear of larger exercises taking place before major operations, for example, Sebastianus in 378 preparing to fight against the Goths. Some generals are mentioned as being particularly efficient at carrying out training, but this does not mean that their troops were of low quality.[2]

When not campaigning, that is for most of the time and particularly in winter, field army troops were billeted in cities and dispersed over a wide area to ease supply. This meant that before starting a campaign an army had to be assembled.[3] At the same time, recruiting took place to bring units up to as near full strength as possible and equipment and horses were obtained where necessary.[4] These preparations could take some time and planning started ahead of offensive operations. Valens began planning his campaign against the Goths in 364 and troops were still arriving in Thrace in 365 with campaigning intended to start in 366. This was over eighteen months of preparation in advance of the campaign.

Preparations for defensive campaigns could take less time since troops were often present in the attacked area and the luxury of

---

World (London, 1987), 107–33; R. Grosse, *Römische Militärgeschichte* (Berlin, 1920), is particularly useful since it deals with the 5th and 6th cents.; see App. 1 for military writers.

[2] On training recruits see Zos. 4. 12. 1; Veg. 1. 9–18; for regular training see *NTh* 24. 1. 1 (443); AM 14. 11. 3; Zos. 5. 20. 2; Claudian, *De Bello Getico*, 250–1, *De 4 Cons. Hon.* 320–3; Lib. *Or.* 12. 44; on archery practice see J. Ant. fr. 201. 4; Anon. *PS* 45–7; Mauricius, *Strat.* 12. 8. 3; Veg. 1. 15; for other weapons see Mauricius, *Strat.* 12. 8. 2; for route marches see Veg. 1. 9; for parade grounds see Claudian, *De Bello Getico*, 250–4; J. Ant. fr. 201. 4; on exercises see Zos. 4. 23. 1–4; on famous generals see *PLRE* i, Sebastianus; *PLRE* ii, Generidus, Fravitta; for poor quality see Lib. *Or.* 24. 3. 5; for naval training see Veg. 4. 32; on battle drills see Mauricius, *Strat.* 3. 5, 6, 12. 8. 24.

[3] On billeting see Symm. *Ep.* 6. 72, 9. 48; *CT* 7. 8 (361–435), 9 (340–416), 13. 3. 3 (333), 16. 2. 8 (343); *CJ* 12. 40 (393–530); *NTh* 25 (444); Zos. 2. 34. 2; for billets marked on doorposts see *CT* 7. 8. 4 (393); for lodging rosters, see Procopius, *BV* 3. 21. 10; on troops dispersed see AM 14. 11. 15, 16. 4. 1, 17. 10. 10, 19. 11. 2, 20. 4. 9; Malchus fr. 18. 3. 49–56, 20. 132–4; Lib. *Or.* 12. 44; on assembling troops see AM 14. 10. 3, 17. 12. 4, 18. 2. 4, 19. 11. 2, 23. 2. 3, 26. 9. 1, 27. 8. 3, 10. 6; Lib. *Or.* 12. 44; Zos. 3. 4. 1, 5. 50. 1; *Pan. Lat.* 12(2). 32. 4; Malchus fr. 18. 1. 16–21, 20. 135–6; *Auct. Haun. Ordo Prior.* sa 487.

[4] AM 18. 9. 3, 20. 8. 1, 21. 6. 6; Jul., *Or.* 1. 34CD, 2. 56B; Zos. 3. 3. 2, 4. 12. 1; *CT* 7. 13. 16–17 (406); Eunapius fr. 44. 1; cf. Theophylact, *Hist.* 3. 12. 4; Herodian 6. 3. 1–2; cf. M. Van Creveld, *Command in War* (London, 1985), 79–80.

choosing a time of year to fight was not open to the Romans. Adopting a strategy of harassment allowed more time to prepare a large force. Fewer troops tended to be involved, which reduced the time taken to collect supplies. On the other hand, troops sometimes had to be brought into the area from another region, which could take some time.[5]

The collection of supplies and their transport to the army was the concern of civilian officials under their regional praetorian prefect. In peacetime supplies were either delivered directly to units or requisitioned by the units themselves. When the army was marching through friendly territory stockpiles were sometimes set up in advance along the line of march. Otherwise material was delivered directly to the army.[6]

The use of stored supplies allowed the army to fight at any time of the year, though most offensive operations took place in summer. The campaigning season usually started only when the spring wheat had been collected and once the roads had had a chance to dry out from the spring rains and grass to grow for fodder. In Gaul and on the Danube this was July, in Italy, May.[7] Sometimes strategic considerations outweighed those of supply. The best time for attacking heavily forested areas was winter, since 'all the retreats of Francia could be penetrated and burnt out now that the leaves were off the trees and that the bare and sapless forests could offer no concealment for ambushers'. The same practice was recommended in Mauricius' *Strategikon* and is illustrated by Arbogastes' attack on the Franks in winter 389. Winter warfare could also be forced by barbarian attacks, for example, Julian's counterattack on raiding Franks in winter 358.[8] When attacking nomads, the inhabitants of the steppes around the lower Danube,

---

[5] For Valens see AM 26. 6. 11–12, 7. 9; for defensive campaigns see *NVal* 9 (440).

[6] On responsibility of PPO see AM 14. 10. 4, 18. 2. 4, 19. 11. 2, 20. 4. 6; Zos. 4. 10. 4; *CT* 7. 4. 1–36 (325–424); on civilian contractors see AM 17. 10. 4; on stockpiles see Zos. 4. 10. 4; Ambrose, *Expositio in Psalmum 118, Sermo* 5. 2, *PL* 15. 1250–1; Jul. *Ep. ad Ath.* 286B; AM 23. 2. 5, 8; Veg. 3. 3.

[7] Natural constraints: for wheat see AM 14. 10. 2, 17. 8. 1; cf. *France*, Admiralty Naval Intelligence Division, i. 203, fig. 19; for fodder see AM 30. 3. 3; Hyland, *Equus*, 92; for spring see AM 27. 10. 6.

[8] Winter campaigning: defensive, see AM 17. 2, 8, 27. 1. 1–2; Claudian, *De 6 Cons. Hon.* 440–69; *Fast. Vind. Prior.* sa 464; offensive, see Sulpicius fr. 6, cf. fr. 1 for consequences of attacking while the leaves were still on the trees; SA *Carm.* 5. 510–52; AM 17. 1. 3–13; Mauricius, *Strat.* 7 prologue, 11. 4. 19.

there were two preferred times. One was February or March, when the lack of grazing over the winter had reduced nomadic mobility. The other was July to September, when dry grass burnt easily and fodder was scarce and easily destroyed.[9] Troops could also be transferred from one area to another in winter, by land or sea.[10]

The accumulation of supplies for any offensive expedition required forward planning. In 360 when Constantius II was still in Constantinople he ordered supplies to be set up on the borders of Gaul before he marched against Julian. Similar preparations were taken when marching against barbarians, as in 409 when Honorius was organizing troops against Alaric. 'Wishing for food to be ready for those who were present, he ordered those in Dalmatia to bring in corn, sheep and cattle.' The collection of food supplies and other equipment could take a long time. Having reached Carnuntum from Gaul, Valentinian I spent three months in 375 preparing for an expedition against the Quadi.[11]

Organization on such a scale was necessary since armies took a lot of feeding. Even Julian's small army at Strasbourg, 13,000 men, of whom perhaps 3,000 were cavalry, would require a minimum of 30 tons of grain, 13 tons of fodder, and 30,000 gallons of water *every day*. These estimates consider only fighting men and horses. The baggage train that accompanied all ancient armies with its grooms and pack mules would also need food and fodder. The movement of supplies also consumed supplies and the larger the baggage train the more food it required. Though some of this could be collected on the march, the greater part of it would have to be delivered to the army. The effectiveness of the supply system is shown by the fact that Roman forces are rarely attested as running out of supplies. Shortages were suffered, for example by Julian in Persia, but were unusual. The efficiency is also shown by the volume of supplies that could be handled. Constantius II's measures in 360 included stockpiling three million bushels of wheat.[12]

---

[9] Mauricius, *Strat.* 7. 1. 12, 10. 4. 8.

[10] Transfers: for land see Lib. *Or.* 12. 44, 18. 40; for sea see AM 20. 1. 3.

[11] On collecting supplies before campaigning see Jul., *Ep. ad Ath.* 286B, *Ep.* 58/402B; Malchus fr. 18. 1; Zos. 4. 10. 4, 5. 50. 1; Marc. Com. sa 499; AM 16. 2. 8, 17. 8. 2, 19. 11. 2, 21. 6. 6, 23. 2. 8, 23. 3. 6 (as diversion), 27. 10. 6, 30. 5. 11; *CT* 7. 4. 15 (369); Philost. 11. 2; on quantity cf. *PLRE* ii, Calliopius 5; Olymp. fr. 30.

[12] On required amounts see D. W. Engels, *Alexander the Great and the Logistics of the Macedonian Army* (London, 1977), 123–30; M. Van Creveld, *Supplying War*

Once supplies had reached the army they were usually transported by wagon or pack animal until consumed. In emergencies cavalry could be used to transport supplies, as in 439 when Litorius' cavalry brought corn into Narbonne. Supplies could also be transported by sea or river if the army was in the right place. Thus in 367, the praetorian prefect Auxorius 'conveyed the soldiers' provisions on a large fleet of transports through the Black Sea to the mouths of the Danube and thence by means of river boats stored them in towns along the river to facilitate the supply of the army'.[13] Troops usually carried twenty days to a month's rations with them, in addition to other personal equipment. This kept the baggage train small and thus speeded movement. These supplies also enabled a force to survive without a baggage train for a short time.[14] If there was a shortage of supplies, the Romans could forage as effectively as the barbarians. Some foraging seems to have taken place anyway, even when marching through friendly territory, though officers probably tried to control this. Once in enemy territory anything was fair game. Some summer and autumn campaigns were planned so that the Romans could forage from enemy harvests, though this was probably seen as a bonus, not something that could be relied on.[15]

As well as food supplies, the army transported spare weapons and equipment. Artillery and other bulky gear that could not be moved easily was carried in kit form and assembled if needed. The tools necessary for building equipment were also transported. Thus in 438 Aetius built a siege tower to capture a town from the Visigoths. As well as the pack animals and wagons, the baggage train also contained the baggage and impedimenta of senior officers. The *comi-*

(Cambridge, 1977); on shortages see AM 17. 9. 3, 25. 2. 1–2 (both involving Julian whose strategic acumen is somewhat dubious); SA *Carm.* 2. 278; *Pan. Lat.* 12(2). 32. 5; Ambrose *Ep.* 40. 22; on supply volumes see Jul. *Ep. ad Ath.* 286B; cf. Marc. Com. sa 499.

[13] For wagons see Veg. 3. 6; Malchus fr. 18. 1; Marc. Com. sa 499; Mauricius, *Strat.* 12. 8. 6; for pack animals see AM 16. 11. 14, 29. 4. 5; Ausonius, *Grat. Act.* 17; Malchus fr. 2; Veg. 3. 6; *CT* 7. 1. 9 (367); Procopius, *HA* 30. 15. 1; Mauricius, *Strat.* 1. 2. 11, 12. 8. 6; for emergencies see Prosp. 1324; for naval supply see Zos. 4. 10. 4; for river supply see Zos. 3. 13. 3, 4. 10. 4; AM 23. 5. 6 ?; *CT* 7. 17. 1 (412), 13. 9. 2 (372/5); Lib. *Or.* 54. 47.

[14] On carried rations see *CT* 7. 4. 5 (360); AM 16. 2. 8, 17. 8. 2, 9. 2; Procopius, *BV* 3. 13. 15; for composition see *CT* 7. 4. 6 (360); Mauricius, *Strat.* 7. 11; for quality see Paulinus of Nola, *Ep.* 23. 6.

[15] On foraging in friendly territory, Zos. 5. 7. 2–3, 13. 3; AM 21. 12. 15, 29. 4. 5; for enemy territory see AM 17. 1. 11; Zos. 3. 14. 2, 23. 1–2, 27. 3; on harvesting from enemy see AM 16. 11. 11–12, 14, 17. 9. 2–3, 27. 10. 7; Lib. *Or.* 18. 52.

tatus would accompany the Emperor if he was present, massively increasing the tail of the army and providing a further logistical burden. At times the baggage would be separated from the army to increase mobility and avoid its loss if defeated in battle.[16]

In the fourth century offensive operations were usually led by the Emperor, but could also be initiated by *magistri militum* and *comites rei militaris*. We do not know how much initiative local commanders had, but *duces* seem rarely to have played an active role in field army operations. During the fourth century attacks across the border seem to have been initiated only by emperors, for example, Valentinian I's strikes against the Quadi in 374–5. But *magistri militum* and Emperors conducted operations to pursue barbarian raiders back across the border, for example, Nannienus and Quintinus against Franks in 388 and Gratian against Alamanni in 378. Defensive operations were commanded by the senior officer present.[17]

After the 390s there were fewer offensive operations and emperors took less part in field campaigning. Constantine III and Attalus (and later Marcian, Majorian, Anthemius, and Zeno) did lead troops in the field, but most offensive operations were led by *magistri militum*, often with subordinate *comites*. As in the fourth century, defensive operations and any consequential actions were led by the senior officer present. *Comites* could also lead expeditions in their own right.[18]

---

[16] On artillery see Zos. 3. 13. 3; Veg. 2. 25; Aetius, Merobaudes, *Pan.* 2. 165–72; for boats see Anon. *PS* 19. 56–65; Veg. 2. 25; for spare equipment, see Column of Arcadius, above, p. 113; Marc. Com. sa 499; on tools see Veg. 2. 25; Procopius, *BG* 6. 12. 6; Anon. *PS* 18. 42–6; Mauricius, *Strat.* 1. 2. 10, 12. 8. 6; on officers' mules see AM 25. 2. 1; Zos. 5. 34. 1; *CT* 8. 5. 3 (326); on civil officials see AM 31. 12. 10; *LRE* 366–8; F. G. B. Millar, *The Emperor in the Roman World* (London, 1977), 28–40; on *agentes in rebus* see *CT* 6. 27. 7 (395), 36. 1 (326); for baggage handlers see Zos. 3. 14. 1, 24. 1, 30. 3, 4. 11. 2–3; Mauricius, *Strat.* 1. 2. 11; on separating from baggage see AM 31. 11. 6, 12. 10; Mauricius, *Strat.* 5. 3. 1, 12. 8. 22.

[17] For 4th-cent. cross-border attacks initiated by emperors see AM 17. 10. 1, 17. 12. 4, 18. 2. 7 and 9, 20. 10. 2, 21. 4. 8, 27. 5. 2, 5, and 6, 27. 10. 6, 29. 4. 2; for *magister militum* see Sulpicius fr. 6; AM 28. 5. 15; on role of *duces* see Eunapius fr. 42. 20–44; cf. Zos. 4. 20. 6; for other offensives, *magistri militum*, see AM 26. 8. 4, 10. 4; for pursuits, emperors, see AM 17. 1. 1–2, 31. 10. 11; for *magistri militum* see Sulpicius fr. 1; for *duces* see AM 29. 6. 15 ?; Millar, 'Emperors, Frontiers and Foreign Relations', *Britannia*, 13 (1982), 1–23; on *comites* sent by emperor see *CT* 6. 14. 3 (413).

[18] On 5th-cent. offensives led by emperors see Malchus fr. 18. 3; Olymp. fr. 14, 33; Soz. 9. 12. 4, 13. 1–2; for *magistri* see RPF fr. 6; Philost. 12. 13–14; Theoph. AM 5942; Priscus fr. 42; Malchus fr. 18. 2, 20; for *comites* see Soz. 9. 8; Hyd. 74, 176; Procopius, *BV* 3. 6. 8.

Comites domesticorum are often found leading troops and, despite their position as commanders of the *domestici*, appear to have acted like other *comites*. Thus the Western *comes domesticorum* Richomeres commanded the Roman army at Ad Salices in 377 and in 420 Castinus was involved in campaigning against Franks in north Gaul. The change in character of the *domestici* at the end of the fourth century may have restricted their opportunities to fight, but Bonifatius defended Africa as *comes domesticorum et Africae* in the 420s.[19] The *magister officiorum*, despite his responsibility for the *fabricae* and *scholae* seems to have been primarily a civil official, though he is occasionally found leading troops (but never *scholae*). In 350 Magnentius' *magister officiorum*, Marcellinus, defeated Nepotianus in Italy. *Magistri officiorum* could also lead troops against barbarians and in 409 Olympius attacked a force of Goths in Italy.[20] Although the functions of military and civil branches of the government were divided, both were still part of the government. In emergencies, civil officials had the authority to lead troops. In 359 the praetorian prefect Florentius led reinforcements to an army in the field and Petrus, *magister epistularum*, relieved the siege of Lyons in 458. Lastly, command against bandits could be the responsibility of civil officials if they were the senior government official in the area.[21]

Roman expeditions across the border could range deep into enemy territory, as in Gratian's follow-up to the battle of Argentaria. These operations were usually carefully planned and their objectives obtained. In the fifth century the number of campaigns launched by Aetius in successive years in different regions also suggests good planning and strategic intelligence. Unfortunately we

[19] For *comites domesticorum* see *PLRE* i, Dagalaifus, Latinus, Richomeres, Serenianus 2, Severus 10, Valerianus 6?; *PLRE* ii, Bonifatius 3, Castinus 2, Pierius 5.

[20] For *magister officiorum* see *PLRE* i, Marcellinus 8; *PLRE* ii, Celer 2, Hilarianus 2, Illus 1, Longinus 3, Olympius 2; M. Clauss, *Der Magister Officiorum in der Spätantike* (Munich, 1980); cf. *PLRE* ii, Hermianus.

[21] For civil officials see Tomlin, 'Notitia Dignitatum', 189–209 at 195–202; R. MacMullen, *Soldier and Civilian in the Later Roman Empire* (Cambridge, Mass., 1963), 152–77; AM 21. 16. 1–3 suggests civilian command occurred, but was not approved of in some (military?) quarters; *PLRE* i, Anicetus 1 (PPO), Florentius 10 (PPO), Hormisdas 3 (proconsul), Iovianus 1 (*notarius*), Iovius 2 (QSP), Nebridius 1 (*comes Orientis*), Probus 5 (PPO), Syagrius 3 (*notarius*), Ulpianus 3 (*praeses Arabiae*); *PLRE* ii, Eutropius 1 (PSC), Maurocellus? (*vicarius*), Petrus 10 (*magister epistularum*).

have few details of the process and have to reconstruct it from events.[22]

Strategic intelligence can be divided into two types, active and passive. Active intelligence is defined as that actively sought by the Romans, usually only before or during hostilities, passive as that received continuously without their taking specific action to gather information.[23] Passive intelligence covered general knowledge of the local barbarians—their strength, location of villages, and character of their leaders. This was combined to form an idea of their capabilities. It would also provide the Romans with an understanding of likely targets and attack routes. This was very much a question of local knowledge, much of which would be passed on informally through unit personnel and most changes in the situation would occur gradually. Some of this information may have been written down.[24]

This local knowledge could be enhanced by the *dux* or *comes* in charge of a frontier sector (or his subordinates) keeping in touch with local *regales* and *optimates*, for example by dining with them. In 360, 'Vadomarius crossed the river [Rhine]. . . . He visited the commander of the local troops and had a brief formal conversation with him; then, in order that no suspicion should be aroused at his departure, he actually accepted an invitation to a banquet.' Regular meetings for the confirmation of treaties or donation of subsidies also provided opportunities for gathering intelligence. Maintenance of such relations would also make it easier to avoid conflict, giving an opening for grievances to be discussed, instead of forcing immediate action.[25] Passive strategic intelligence could also be

[22] For planning councils see N. J. E. Austin, *Ammianus on Warfare* (Brussels, 1979), 22–116; AM 16. 2. 3–4 (discussing a route), 9, 10. 21, 26. 5. 8–13, 30. 3. 3–4, 31. 12. 5–7, 14–15; Sulpicius fr. 1; Eunapius fr. 42. 11–19; Aug. *Ep.* 220. 7; above, p. 176.

[23] A. D. Lee, *Information and Frontiers* (Cambridge, 1993); Millar, 'Emperors, Frontiers and Foreign Relations', 1–23, and 'Government and Diplomacy in the Roman Empire', *IHR* 10 (1988), 345–77.

[24] On local knowledge see *P.S.Sabae*, 8. 1; on monitoring mood see AM 21. 3. 4–5, 28. 3. 8, cf. 29. 5. 35; cf. Dio 73. 2. 4; on knowledge of enemy objectives see Menander fr. 33; Zos. 1. 30. 2.

[25] For dining see AM 21. 4. 3, 29. 6. 5 (= Zos. 4. 16. 4), 31. 5. 5; Eunapius fr. 59; Lib. *Or.* 18. 107; Zos. 4. 56. 1; Jordanes, *Getica*, 135–6, 289; A. L. F. Rivet and C. Smith, *The Place Names of Roman Britain* (London, 1983), 212, reject the view that the *loca* of the *Ravenna Cosmography* (5. 31) are meeting places, as argued by I. A. Richmond, *Roman and Native in Northern Britain* (London, 1958), 148–9; cf. Dio 72. 15, 19, 73. 2.

received from deserters from the enemy, though there was a danger of planted information. This intelligence was useful in predicting enemy actions. Once hostilities had started it could be difficult to predict enemy movements or even to locate the enemy.[26]

Active strategic intelligence could be provided by Roman spies, the *arcani* who operated in the *barbaricum*. These are only explicitly attested for Britain, but equivalents existed elsewhere. At least one of Valentinian I's operations used such agents. In 370 he was communicating with the kings of the Burgundians by means of 'certain quiet, loyal men'. Such men could have been involved in the assassination of Vithicabius. These men apparently reported directly to the Emperor. By their very nature, organizations such as this are secretive and leave little evidence. They may have been controlled by the *magister officiorum*. His control of *interpretes omnium gentium* would allow adequate training to take place and the various *agentes in rebus* and *curiosi provinciarum* could provide manpower for these operations. *Protectores* and *domestici* would also have provided a pool of suitable officers, as demonstrated by Ammianus' reconnaissance mission on the Eastern frontier in 359. It may be significant that, unlike most soldiers he mentions, Ammianus never mentions these men by name or unit.[27] Other information was obtained by officers being sent to areas for information. Sometimes this was on a deliberate military mission, as in the case of Hariobaudes, at other times it was a by-product of a diplomatic mission, such as that of Victor to the Goths in 367.[28]

Once information had been obtained it was either reported directly to the Emperor or to the local field army commander who

---

[26] On intelligence from deserters see AM 29. 4. 2; cf. interrogation of deserters, AM 31. 15. 9; Mauricius, *Strat.* 8. 1. 35, 9. 3. 6–9; Anon. *PS* 41.

[27] For active strategic intelligence see Austin, *Ammianus on Warfare*, 22–41; for spies see AM 26. 5. 5–6, 28. 3. 8, 29. 5. 33; Anon. *PS* 42; Priscus fr. 14. 1. 58–65; Procopius, *BP* 1. 21. 11–12, *HA* 30. 12–13; *arcani*, AM 28. 3. 8; the MSS read *areani*, a unique word in Latin, *arcani* makes sense instinctively; C. E. Stevens, 'Hadrian and Hadrian's Wall', *Latomus*, 14 (1955), 384–403 at 394–5, and I. A. Richmond, *Roman and Native in Northern Britain* (London, 1958), 114–15, both struggle to find plausible meanings for *areani*; possible *arcani*, AM 27. 10. 4, 28. 5. 10, 29. 5. 33; Zos. 4. 38. 2–4.

[28] For *protectores* see AM 18. 6. 21; for tribunes see AM 18. 2. 2; for *magistri militum* see AM 27. 8. 2; for legates, tribunes, see AM 19. 11. 5 (with interpreters), 18. 2. 2; for *magistri militum* see AM 27. 5. 1, 9; on escorts for ambassadors see *P. Abinn.* 1; cf. Frontinus, *Stratagems*, 1. 2. 4.

Operations   243

could then forward it to his superiors. From 443 and probably earlier, *magistri militum* had to report annually to the Emperor on the state of their commands and these reports probably updated the general situation. Such reports depended on information from their subordinate *duces*. We know that reports had been made previously and annual reporting seems likely. Special reports were presumably sent out in the case of crises. Thus in 365, a tribune in Dacia Mediterranea heard rumours of Procopius' usurpation, which he passed on to the *comes rei militaris* Equitius, who in turn sent the news to Valentinian I.[29]

Within the Empire the army marched by road, following pre-arranged itineraries from town to town until it reached the vicinity of the enemy. From here it could be guided by friendly locals or by men captured from the enemy, but if these were unavailable, by scouts from the army. Local knowledge was at a premium and men with prior acquaintance of an area were much sought after.[30] No use seems to have been made of maps as we know them, though Vegetius recommends that, as well as annotations, distances and geographical details (hills, rivers, etc.) be added to itineraries. It is difficult to see what advantages contemporary maps would have had over itineraries, since movement was usually confined to roads where they were available and it was rare for Roman forces to be split unless in the vicinity of the enemy. Even when close to the enemy, cross-country movement was unusual, though not unknown. In 479,

Sabinianus himself took command of the cavalry and sent a considerable body of infantry on a roundabout route through the mountains, telling them where and when to put in their appearance. Then he dined, assembled his army and set out at nightfall. He attacked the Goths at daybreak when

[29] On reports see AM 15. 8. 1, 16. 10. 20, 17. 12. 1, 19. 11. 1, 26. 5. 10, 6. 11, 7. 5, 27. 8. 1, 30. 3. 1; Lib. *Or.* 18. 52; *NTh* 24. 5 (443) (annually); Zos. 4. 20. 6; Eunapius fr. 42. 10–11; cf. A. K. Bowman and J. D. Thomas, 'Vindolanda 1985: The New Writing Tablets', *JRS* 76 (1986), 120–3 at 122 for a possible (2nd-cent.) intelligence report, but cf. A. R. Birley, 'Vindolanda', in V. A. Maxfield and M. J. Dawson, eds., *Roman Frontier Studies* (Exeter, 1991), 16–20 at 18; on passing up chain of command see AM 16. 11. 7, 26. 5. 10; Lib. *Or.* 18. 52; Jul., *Ep.* 45/432B.

[30] On itineraries, Dura Shield, see F. Cumont, 'Fragment de bouclier portant une liste d'étapes', *Syria*, 6 (1925), 1–15; Ambrose, *Expositio in Psalmum 118, Sermo* 5. 2, *PL* 15. 1250–51; HA *Sev. Alex.* 45. 2; on campsites picked in advance see Veg. 2. 7; Anon. *PS* 26; Mauricius, *Strat.* 2. 12; for guides see AM 14. 10. 7, 17. 10. 7, 27. 10. 5, 29. 4. 5.

they were already on the move. . . . When the infantry appeared over their heads according to plan, the [Goths] were routed.[31]

The Roman army marched in a large column, referred to as an *agmen quadratum*. It was led by scouts, followed by cavalry, and then the main body of infantry. After them (Fig. 20.1), or sometimes within the infantry columns (Fig. 20.2), came the baggage train,

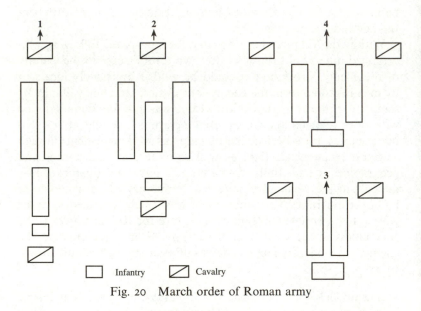

Fig. 20   March order of Roman army

and then a rearguard of infantry and cavalry. When in the vicinity of the enemy, cavalry were sent out to the flanks to protect the infantry and to enable the army to deploy into line faster (Fig. 20.3). Alternatively, the army could split into a number of columns producing the same effect. This could also be forced by difficult terrain (Fig. 20.4). The army marched in this formation at Solicinium in 368, when Valentinian I led the centre, the generals Jovinus and Severus the wings. The whole army could cover a large area. Ammianus records that Julian's army in Persia in 363 (65,000

[31]   Veg. 3. 6; for cross-country movement see Malchus fr. 20. 226–48.

at its peak) extended for four miles on the march.[32]

A day's march obviously varied in length, but seems to have averaged 20 km. In emergencies it could be increased, but only by detaching wagons or pack animals was there any probability of exceeding 30 km. per day. According to a sermon of Ambrose, the army marched for three days and rested on the fourth, but we have no other confirmation of this practice.[33] Troops could also be transported by river. This movement tended to be confined to the Rhine and Danube because of the easy availability of boats. Movement downstream could be much faster than land movement, but the constraints of moving upstream, especially on the Upper Rhine, meant that it was not often used for moving troops. Where it was used it could have spectacular results, for example Julian's swift move down the Danube in 361 which took Constantius II's *magister equitum* Lucillianus by surprise.[34]

The army frequently had to cross rivers while on the march. Inside the Empire fords and bridges were often available, but were not always present on the Rhine and Danube. In winter rivers could be crossed while frozen.[35] If none of these means were available, the Rhine and Danube were usually crossed by pontoon bridge. This would require advance planning to find a suitable site and assemble the bridging materials. There were some established

[32] On march order see Veg. 3. 6; AM 24. 1. 2, 25. 3. 2, 27. 10. 6, 29. 5. 39, 31. 9. 3, 12. 4; cf. Herodian 8. 1. 2–3; Anon. *PS* 20; Mauricius, *Strat.* 12. 8. 19; for scouts (*procursatores*) see AM 16. 12. 8, 24. 1. 2, 3. 1, 27. 2. 2, 4, 10. 8; Zos. 3. 19. 1; for advance guard see Zos. 3. 14. 1 (with 70 stades (14.95 km.) between advance guard and main body), 23. 3, 24. 1; AM 29. 4. 5; for baggage see AM 24. 1. 4; for flanking cavalry see AM 16. 12. 7, 24. 1. 2; for flanking infantry see AM 27. 10. 6; for rearguard see AM 16. 12. 10, 24. 1. 2, 25. 3. 2; on length see AM 25. 5. 6, cf. 24. 1. 3, 10 Roman miles (= 16 km.) at full extent; cf. Zos. 3. 14. 1.

[33] Rate of march: see Procopius, *BV* 4. 13. 32–3, 50 stades (9.25 km.)/day for 7 days; AM 24. 2. 3, 200 stades (37 km.) in 2 days, 24. 3. 10, 23 km. in one day, marches longer because of river supply (i.e. less baggage)?; cf. SA *Ep.* 4. 8. 2, 29 km. in one day for mounted noble and servants; Sirmium to Strasbourg, 1,238 Roman miles via Milan and Aquileia according to the Antonine Itinerary, 40 days' march (= *mansiones*), AM 16. 12. 70 (rhetorical?); for rest days see Ambrose, *Expositio in Psalmum 118, Sermo* 5. 2, *PL* 15. 1250–1; cf. Theophylact, *Hist.* 2. 2. 6–7 showing Sunday as a rest day; for training marches see Veg. 1. 9, 20 Roman miles in 5 hours (= 30 km.), 24 Roman miles at the quick step; 1 stade = 185 m.; see also Engels, *Alexander the Great*, 153–6.

[34] For river transport see Zos. 2. 46. 2, 3. 10. 2–3 (Raetia–Sirmium in 11 days), 4. 10. 4; AM 21. 9. 2, 31. 11. 6; Lib. *Or.* 18. 111.

[35] For fords see AM 14. 10. 7, 16. 11. 9; for frozen rivers see above, p. 78; Mauricius, *Strat.* 11. 4. 19; AM 27. 6. 12.

crossing places, and it is likely that *limitanei* officers had a knowledge of these in their area of command. It is also possible that the fortified landing places were developed to allow safe bridgeheads. The Rhine and Danube were both large rivers (200+ m. wide in places) and would require large pontoon bridges to be crossable. These pontoon bridges were constructed from boats, probably provided by local flotillas on the Rhine and Danube, though at least one river crossing (in Persia) was achieved by using inflated wine-skins. No specialist engineers are known to us, which may indicate a high level of basic engineering ability among the troops. Most of our knowledge of these crossings comes from the fourth century but there is no reason to suppose that the fifth-century army was incapable of crossing such obstacles and the sixth-century army certainly could.[36]

Another means of crossing rivers was by boats. These crossings could be carried out at night, as shown by two of Julian's operations against the Alamanni in 357 and 359.[37] Some units were able to swim across rivers if no boats could be found. Swimming a military unit (complete with weapons and armour) across a major water obstacle was difficult and could only be carried out if unopposed.[38] The dangers inherent in river crossing are shown by the ability of the barbarians to deny a crossing to the Romans. Though they were rarely able to hold other positions against the Romans, they could stop the Romans from forcing river crossings or at least make them difficult.[39]

Movement of troops from Africa to Europe and from Britain to Europe took place by sea. Otherwise troop transfers were usually by land. Thus the Western praesental army marched overland from

[36] River crossing: see Veg. 3. 2; for pontoon bridges, 3rd cent., see Herodian 6. 7. 6; for 4th cent. see AM 14. 10. 6, 16. 11. 8, 17. 1. 2, 10. 1, 12. 4, 18. 2. 7–14, 27. 5. 2 and 6, 29. 4. 2, 30. 5. 13; Lib. *Or.* 18. 50; Jul. *Or.* 3. 129C; for 6th cent. see Anon. *PS* 19; Mauricius, *Strat.* 11. 4. 17, 12. 8. 21; for inside empire see AM 27. 1. 3; Zos. 2. 48. 4, 3. 13. 2; for wine-skins see Zos. 3. 30. 5; AM 24. 3. 11, 25. 6. 15, 8. 2; cf. Anon. *dRB* 16; Zos. 2. 48. 4.

[37] Boats: see AM 17. 1. 4, 13. 17, 18. 2. 12, 25. 8. 3; Lib. *Or.* 18. 88; Veg. 3. 7; (improvised) AM 24. 3. 11, 25. 8. 2.

[38] For swimming see Lib. *Or.* 18. 76; *Pan. Lat.* 12(2). 34. 1; Zos. 3. 19. 4; AM 16. 11. 9, 24. 2. 8 (including pack animals), 6. 7, 25. 6. 12–14, 8. 1–2; for soldiers trained to swim see Veg. 1. 10, 2. 23, 3. 4.

[39] On barbarians blocking crossings see AM 14. 10. 6–7, 18. 2. 8–14; on problems in forcing crossing see Lib. *Or.* 18. 50, 87–9; Mauricius, *Strat.* 11. 4. 33, 12. 8. 21; Anon. *PS* 19.

Gaul to Persia in 360 and back in 364. Naval transportation could take place in winter in emergencies, such as Lupicinus' crossing to Britain in 360, but usually occurred in safer sailing seasons, between March/April and November in the Mediterranean.[40] More use was made of naval transport during civil wars and in the fifth century against the Vandals. The Romans also made a number of marine landings in hostile territory. The length of coastlines and the small numbers of men meant that most of these were unopposed and thus were primarily logistical operations rather than beach assaults. However, this must not be allowed to minimize the organization necessary to transport large numbers of men and horses by sea, even though this left no traces. These troop movements continued throughout the period, from Constantius II's landings in Spain and Africa in 352/3 to Ardabur's failed landing in Italy against John in 425.[41]

At the conclusion of the day's march a fortified camp was constructed. This consisted of a ditch and palisade inside which tents were pitched. Caltrops could be laid outside the ditch, probably for warning purposes and not as a barrier. The anonymous *Peri Strategikes* suggested that bells could be placed around the camp which would serve in the same way. Camps could be constructed quickly and easily (in perhaps one to two hours), and once built would increase the security of the army and allow the majority of the men a good night's sleep. It is probable that a single camp was dug for the army, no matter how big it was, since we never hear of multiple camps.[42] While digging camps, units had to take care to avoid being surprised. As well as providing night security these camps also provided a secure base to fall back on if the army met

---

[40] On naval transport see AM 20. 1. 3; Zos. 3. 10. 2–3; Soz. 9. 8. 6; for winter see Veg. 4. 39; *CT* 13. 9. 3 (380); AM 30. 3. 3, 6. 2.

[41] For 352/3 see Jul. *Or.* 1. 40C; for 388 see Zos. 4. 45. 4, 46. 1; Ambrose, *Ep.* 40. 23; 413, Orosius 7. 42. 13; for 425 see Philost. 12. 13–14; for 508 see Marc. Com. sa 508; cf. Procopius, *BV* 3. 11. 1–20.

[42] For camps see Grosse 304–5; Procopius, *BV* 4. 11. 15; *Pan. Lat.* 12(2). 10. 3; AM 15. 4. 9–12, 16. 12. 12, 18. 2. 11, 25. 4. 11, 6. 1, 5–7, 27. 2. 5, 5. 2, 31. 8. 9, 12. 4; *Anon. Val.* 50; Veg. 1. 21–5 (ditch 9 feet wide, 7 feet deep, 1. 24); Anon. *PS* 26–9, (ditch 5 × 5 feet, 29. 4–7); Mauricius, *Strat.* 5. 4. 3, 12. 8. 22 (ditch 5–6 feet wide, 7–8 feet deep); on lack of archaeological evidence see Johnson, *Late Roman Fortifications*, 32; Crump, *Ammianus Marcellinus*, 75–7; Grosse 225–9; tents, AM 17. 13. 33, 18. 2. 10, 20. 11. 6, 29. 4. 5, 5. 55; Anon. *PS* 27; *Pan. Lat.* 12(2) 10. 2; for camps built daily see AM 25. 3. 1; Procopius, *BV* 4. 11. 15; for stakes normally carried by army see AM 18. 2. 11; for caltrops see Veg. 3. 8, 24; Anon. *PS* 29. 25–6; Mauricius, *Strat.* 12. 8. 22. 1, 10; for bells see Anon. *PS* 29. 26–32.

a reverse. Thus in 355 a Roman force that had been ambushed by the Alamanni retreated to the camp and in a battle the following day were able to defeat them.[43]

Tactical intelligence was only required during hostilities. The requirements were simple: how strong were the enemy, what were their intentions (where were they going and what were they going to do?), and, most importantly, what was their position? With this information a decision to engage in battle could be made. Without it, forces risked being caught by surprise, overwhelmed, or made to fight in disadvantageous circumstances.[44]

Knowledge of enemy strengths and location could be acquired by observation alone, though capturing prisoners and receiving deserters would allow an assessment of intentions and help to fill out the picture. Knowledge of local terrain and conditions in the *barbaricum* could be provided by capturing enemy soldiers, within the Empire by locals or soldiers detached from local *limitanei*. Such knowledge was especially important because of the limitations of contemporary maps. The system appears to have been effective enough. There are few accounts of the Romans losing track of the enemy and the ignorance of the location of some Gothic cavalry at Adrianople appears to be an unusual event, not a common one.[45]

This information was not collected by formed bodies of scouts, which seem not to have existed, but by men assigned to scouting duties as necessary. These duties were general intelligence gathering and confirmation (*exploratores*), strategic reconnaissance and information gathering (*speculatores*), and tactical reconnaissance (*procursatores*). These missions were not mutually exclusive. Although some units had the title *exploratores*, their small number, uneven distribution, and original assignment to the border troops suggest that they were not specialist reconnaissance units at this date.[46]

---

[43] On surprised Romans see AM 25. 3. 1, 31. 8. 9; cf. Veg. 3. 8; Mauricius, *Strat.* 12. 8. 20; on night security see AM 27. 2. 5, 8; for camp useful against reverse see AM 15. 4. 8–12.

[44] Austin, *Ammianus on Warfare*, 117–40.

[45] For deserters see AM 17. 1. 8, 21. 7. 7, 13. 4; for prisoners see AM 16. 11. 9, 12. 19–21, 17. 10. 5; on losing track of enemy see Suda E. 396, II. 380.

[46] For distinctions see Austin, *Ammianus on Warfare*, 127–9; for *exploratores* see AM 21. 7. 7, 29. 5. 40, 31. 9. 2, 12. 11, 16. 2; for *speculatores* see AM 18. 8. 1, 21. 13. 4, 27. 2. 2, 4; Veg. 3. 22; for *procursatores* see AM 16. 12. 8, 24. 1. 2?, 3. 1, 5.

At times generals felt it necessary to make personal reconnaissances, thus speeding up the interpretation of information or clarifying uncertain points. This is presumably the reason for Valentinian's risky personal reconnaissance at Solicinium, in which he lost his helmet and almost his life. With this information available, a general could decide how best to engage the enemy. The concern for autopsy may also have been an attempt to avoid receiving inadequate information.[47]

As well as making efforts to collect intelligence, the Romans attempted to ensure that their enemies had difficulties in gathering information. They tried wherever possible to capture scouts, in order to stop information getting back to the enemy. Measures were sometimes taken to stop the casual transfer of information. Valentinian I had some slave dealers killed in 374 when he was leading a flying column in Alamannia, lest they reveal his presence to the Alamanni. Other counter-intelligence measures included advancing too swiftly to allow the enemy to assimilate information, seemingly a speciality of Julian, though practised by other generals. Forces could advance on a broad front or in extended formation to confuse the enemy as to numbers and objectives. This was practised on both strategic and operational levels. Thus in 361, moving from Gaul into Italy, Julian

divided his army and sent one part with Jovinus and Jovius to march rapidly along the familiar roads of Italy: the others were assigned to Nevitta, *magister equitum* to advance through the middle of Raetia, so that, being spread over various parts of the country, they might give the impression of a huge force and fill everywhere with alarm.[48]

3, 5, 25. 8. 4, 27. 10. 8, 31. 12. 3; for κατάσκοποι see Zos. 2. 48. 1, 3. 3. 3, 14. 1, 3, 15. 4, 16. 2, 19. 1, 20. 5, 4. 25. 2, 5. 50. 1; Agathias, *Hist.* 2. 20. 2, 5. 16. 4; Anon. *PS* 20 recommends mounted scouts; Mauricius, *Strat.* 9. 5; there are seven units of *exploratores* recorded in the *Notitia*, all *pseudocomitatenses* or *limitanei*, *ND* Occ. 7. 10, 28. 21, 40. 25; Or. 41. 34, 35, 37, 42. 29, but no *speculatores* or *procursatores*; naval scouts, Syrianus 6–7.

[47] For Valentinian at Solicinium see AM 27. 10. 10; Zos. 4. 48 (Theodosius); AM 23. 5. 7, 24. 1. 13, 4. 3–4; Zos. 3. 20. 2–3, (Julian); for autopsy see Austin, *Ammianus on Warfare*, 130–2; on inadequate information see possibly AM 31. 12. 3, but note Austin 77–80.
[48] On capturing scouts see AM 16. 11. 9, 12. 19–21, 24. 1. 10; on slave dealers see AM 29. 4. 4; for speedy advance see AM 17. 8. 2–3, 12. 4, 18. 2. 1, 20. 10. 2, 21. 4. 8, 9. 5–7, 23. 2. 2; Philost. 12. 13; J. Ant. fr. 187; for broad front see AM 21. 8. 3, 24. 1. 3; on restricting spies see Jul., *Ep.* 58/402A; Mauricius, *Strat.* 9. 5. 20–3; for diversion see AM 23. 3. 6; for extended battle front see AM 27. 2. 5; Mauricius, *Strat.* 7. 8a.

At its best this was an effective intelligence system and Roman commanders often knew of events occurring at some distance from the field army. Thus in 357 while besieging a group of Franks in a fortress on the Meuse the Romans received warning of an approaching Frankish relief force. However, we do not know if the Romans knew of the Frankish advance from *limitanei*, field army scouts, casual reports from locals or merchants, or even from Frankish deserters.[49]

The efficiency of their tactical intelligence is also shown by the rarity with which the Romans, as opposed to the barbarians, were surprised. This should not be stressed too strongly. The Romans could be surprised, and the results could be catastrophic. Thus the unexpected return of the Gothic cavalry led to defeat at Adrianople. Although most Roman defeats were attributable to surprise, this was because it was much harder to defeat them in any other way, though it has to be admitted that details are lacking of many of the Roman defeats in battle. It is difficult to judge whether more might be expected from the system and the (apparent) lack of change might suggest that contemporaries did not find any major shortcomings in the system.[50]

B: BATTLES

This section is an attempt to describe events on the battlefield. Like any attempt, whatever the period, it forces past events into modern categories into which they will not fit. So if contemporary descriptions occasionally lack clarity, we should remember the remark of the Duke of Wellington:

The history of a battle is not unlike the history of a ball. Some individuals may recall all the little events of which the great result is the battle won or lost; but no individual can recall the order in which, or the exact moment at which they occurred, which makes all the difference to their value or importance.[51]

There are few precise accounts of battles in this period and the only field battles understood to any extent are Strasbourg (357)

---

[49] AM 17. 2. 4; cf. Malchus fr. 20. 232–48.
[50] For ineffectiveness, Adrianople, see AM 31. 12. 3; on surprised Romans see AM 15. 4. 8, 16. 2. 10, 27. 10. 1; Sulpicius fr. 1; Zos. 4. 49. 1–2.
[51] Quoted in J. Keegan, *The Mask of Command* (London, 1987), 158.

and Adrianople (378), thanks to the accounts of Ammianus. We thus have little hope of tracing any changes in tactics that occurred. But the situation is not hopeless and a reasonable picture can be drawn from various historians supplemented by military writers, though the latter need to be used with care. The accounts of Procopius and Agathias suggest that little had changed in the way field battles were fought by the sixth century.[52]

The standard march formation when near the enemy could be simply transferred into a battle line, the only action necessary being

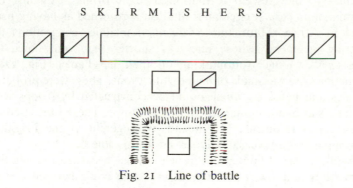

Fig. 21   Line of battle

to draw the columns up into lines (Fig. 21). Cavalry units deployed on the flanks, infantry units in the centre, sometimes in more than one line. Heavy cavalry deployed near the infantry, light cavalry further away. Light armed troops sometimes deployed in front of the main line. The baggage was left in the camp (usually fortified) some way behind the army, preferably with a guard unit. A reserve force of infantry and cavalry was kept behind the main line, to guard against enemy breakthroughs or to exploit success.[53] Units

[52] N. Bitter, *Kampfschilderungen bei Ammianus Marcellinus* (Bonn, 1976); C. P. T. Naudé, 'Battles and Sieges in Ammianus Marcellinus', *Acta Classica*, 1 (1958), 92–106, discuss some of the problems; for tactics see Grosse 254–7, 313–15; cf. J. B. Campbell, 'Teach Yourself how to be a General', *JRS* 77 (1987), 13–29, with 28–9 discussing early imperial tactics.

[53] For marching column into battlefield line see AM 31. 12. 12; Mauricius, *Strat.* 12. 8. 19; on flanking cavalry see AM 16. 12. 21 (only right flank as left flank wooded), 31. 12. 11, 13. 2; Anon. *PS* 35. 6–23; Jul. *Or.* 2. 57B–C; Veg. 2. 15, 3. 16; Lib. *Or.* 18. 54; Mauricius, *Strat.* 12. 8. 13; *Pan. Lat.* 12(2) 35. 3; on multiple lines see AM 24. 6. 9; Mauricius, *Strat.* 2. 1; for light armed troops see Veg. 3. 20 (no. 5); AM 31. 12. 16; for baggage guards see Lib. *Or.* 18. 59; AM 31. 12. 10; Mauricius, *Strat.* 5. 3. 1, 7. 9a; for reserves see Veg. 3. 17; AM 14. 6. 17, 31. 7. 12, 13. 9.

generally fought in linear formations, though wedges were sometimes used to break through enemy lines. These formations were several ranks deep—Vegetius recommended six ranks for infantry; Mauricius recommended four to sixteen ranks for infantry, five to ten ranks for cavalry. These depths obviously varied according to the numbers available, quality of troops, and the tactical situation.[54]

In most circumstances troops were drawn up in a straight line. Vegetius suggested a number of variations on a straight line deployment, with refused left or right flanks or a refused centre (similar to the crescent formation used at Brumath against the Alamanni in 356). A circular formation is recorded as having been used in Africa. Mauricius' *Strategikon* includes suggestions for fighting an enemy whose line was shorter than one's own (= crescent) or longer (outflanking on their left flank) (Fig. 22).[55] Sometimes use was made of field fortifications. These were probably ditches and palisades which could be constructed by troops with materials at hand, similar to overnight camps. These were used by Constantius II outside Mursa and by Eugenius at the Frigidus. Overnight camps occasionally served in this role.[56]

Artillery was of limited use in field battles because of its relative immobility and low rate of fire. However, it could be used if sited to fire over friendly troops, for example from a fort or city wall or high hill, but such positions were rare. It could also be used to cover river crossings. But as far as is known, artillery was not used in a field battle in this period and was confined to static positions. Two theoretical writers suggested mounting *ballistae* on wagons, a practice which occurred in the early Empire and which may have survived. This would give the *ballistae* greater mobility.[57]

After deployment, battles usually started with a brief exchange

[54] On wedges see AM 16. 12. 20, 17. 13. 9, 24. 2. 14, 31. 9. 3; Veg. 1. 26, 3. 17–19; on other formations see Veg. 3. 19; on depths see Veg. 3. 14; on infantry see Mauricius, *Strat.* 12. 7. 5–6, 8. 8; on cavalry see Mauricius, *Strat.* 2. 6.

[55] On deployment variations see Veg. 3. 20; Anon. *PS* 31–2, 34; for crescent see AM 16. 2. 13, 25. 1. 16, 31. 12. 11; Mauricius, *Strat.* 3. 10, 14; Procopius, *BG* 8. 32. 5; for circle see AM 29. 5. 41; for dismounted cavalry see Procopius, *BG* 6. 1. 6, 8. 31. 5.

[56] On fortifications see Zos. 2. 48. 4; Claudian, *De 3 Cons. Hon.* 89–92; cf. *Pan. Lat.* 12(2) 34. 3; AM 18. 7. 6; on camps see AM 15. 4. 9–12; on caltrops see Herodian 4. 15. 2–3.

[57] Artillery: for river crossing see Anon. *DRB* 16. 5; Anon. *PS* 19. 15–18; for static position see AM 18. 7. 6; on wagons see Anon. *DRB* 7; Urbicius, *Epitedeuma*, 8; Mauricius, *Strat.* 12. 8. 18; Veg. 2. 25, 3. 24.

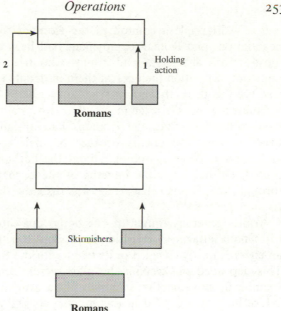

Fig. 22   Line of battle variations. Top: flanking attack; bottom: refused centre

of missiles, followed by a shout and a charge. When fighting barbarians it was in the Roman interest to prolong these exchanges since they usually had more missile troops than their enemies. If the enemy did have missile superiority, the Romans might use the *testudo* in their advance. When the Romans had a great superiority in missile troops, they could stand off and engage the enemy at a distance. This probably happened in a skirmish between some Goths and a *foederati* regiment of 300 Huns in 409, when the losses were supposedly 1,100 Goths and 17 Romans.[58]

Sometimes this skirmishing could not be controlled and escalated into battle. This was not necessarily dangerous, though it could be,

[58] On pre-battle skirmishing see Veg. 2. 17; AM 16. 12. 36, 26. 7. 15, 27. 1. 3, 31. 7. 11–12; on missile exchanges see *Pan. Lat.* 12(2). 35. 4; cf. Jordanes, *Getica*, 213 where the Romans seem to have had missile superiority over the Huns; for 409 skirmish see Zos. 5. 45. 6 (Zosimus is here following Olympiodorus whose figures are generally considered reliable); on 3rd-cent. missile supremacy see Herodian 6. 7. 8, 7. 2. 2; cf. fighting Persians who were usually engaged as soon as possible, AM 24. 2. 5, 6. 11, 25. 1. 17–18; Lib. *Or.* 18. 266; cf. Frontinus, *Stratagems* 2. 2. 5; on *testudo* see AM 29. 5. 48; Mauricius, *Strat.* 12. 8. 16.

and at Adrianople it committed the Romans to attacking before
negotiations and Roman deployment had been completed. It was
most serious against nomad armies who tried to tempt Roman
units out of position then defeat them in detail. The Romans could
also use this tactic themselves.[59]

Following missile exchanges, the two main bodies met. In
hand-to-hand combat, the Romans had a significant advantage
over barbarian opponents because of their training, discipline,
and armour. After a prolonged fight the barbarians were usually
routed. On occasions the impetus of the barbarian attack broke
through the Roman line, but was usually dealt with by the
Roman reserves.[60]

Armies generally fought in one body, but could detach a force
for a flank attack. One battle plan involved a flanking attack on
an enemy already engaged to its front with the Roman main body.
This depended on keeping the plan secret from the enemy, for
example by screening the main body of the army from enemy scouts.
Edobichus was defeated in this manner in 411 while marching to
relieve the siege of Arles. Valentinian I's plan at Solicinium was
similar to this, when, before the battle, he sent an outflanking force
to catch the Alamanni as they retreated.[61] Ambushes could be set,
for example Magnentius' attempt to surprise Constantius II by
hiding men in a disused amphitheatre at Mursa or the surprise
attack on a Saxon column in 370. They do not appear to have been
used often, though in the sixth century Mauricius devoted a whole
chapter of his *Strategikon* to them.[62]

Most fighting took place in daylight, but night marches or attacks
could be used to gain surprise. Thus in 361 Julian 'crossed the
Rhine in the deep silence of night with groups of particularly
lightly-armed troops, and surrounded [the Alamanni] while they
feared nothing of the kind. And when they were awakened by the

---

[59] For escalation see AM 27. 10. 10, 28. 5. 5–6, 31. 12. 16; cf. 14. 2. 17; for
nomad tactics see Mauricius, *Strat.* 11. 2. 27; on Romans tempting see Mauricius,
Strat. 12. 8. 16; Agathias, *Hist.* 1. 22.

[60] On hand-to-hand fighting see AM 16. 12. 37 and 43–54, 27. 1. 4; for barbarian
breakthroughs see AM 16. 12. 49, 27. 1. 4, 31. 13. 7; cf. Agathias, *Hist.* 2. 9. 1; on
Roman advantages see AM 16. 12. 47, 27. 10. 13; for pursuit see Jul. *Or.* 2. 60C.

[61] Flank marches: see AM 17. 1. 4–5; Zos. 3. 16. 2–17. 2 (as diversion); Edobichus,
Soz. 9. 14; Solicinium, AM 27. 10. 9–15; cf. Malchus fr. 20. 226–48; Mauricius,
Strat. 11. 4. 35; Frigidus, Orosius 7. 35. 16.

[62] Zos. 2. 50. 2–4; AM 28. 5. 5–6; Orosius 7. 35. 16; Anon. *PS* 40; Mauricius,
Strat. 4.

clash of hostile arms, he flew upon them swiftly.'[63] The accounts of battles in civil wars seem to be similar to battles with barbarians. The main difference seems to have been the prolonged nature of the fighting, with some civil-war battles continuing to nightfall, for example at the Frigidus. This was a rare occurrence when fighting barbarians, though it did occur during the Adrianople campaign.[64]

The battle of Strasbourg in 357 between Julian's army of 13,000 and an Alamannic force of 30–35,000 is one of the few battles in this period for which we have an adequate description (Fig. 23). Before the battle both sides knew little about the opposition. The Alamanni had no idea of the size of Julian's army until a deserter told them, though they were well aware of its location. Julian himself was uncertain of the size of the enemy force until he captured a barbarian scout before the start of the battle.

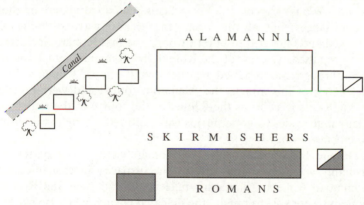

Fig. 23   The battle of Strasbourg, 357

The Alamannic right wing rested on a canal, where they concealed troops in the reeds and in ditches. On their left they placed some of their better troops, with much of their cavalry. The centre was

[63] For night attacks see AM 21. 4. 8, 24. 6. 4–6, 31. 11. 4; Jul. *Or.* 1. 39C; J. Ant. fr. 187; Marc. Com sa 493?; Anon. *PS* 39; Zos. 3. 7. 2, 5; Mauricius, *Strat.* 9. 2, 11. 2. 21, 31. 14; for night march and dawn attack see Malchus fr. 20. 235–40; Zos. 4. 58. 4.

[64] On civil war battles to nightfall, Mursa, see Zos. 2. 51. 2–3; 388, *Pan. Lat.* 12(2) 36. 2; for Frigidus see Zos. 4. 58. 4; for barbarians see AM 27. 2. 8, 29. 5. 48?, 31. 7. 15, 10. 13, 13. 7.

composed of multiple lines of infantry with a group of *optimates* and their followers behind, probably intended as a second wave rather than as a reserve. The Romans deployed their infantry in multiple lines, with cavalry only on the right flank, their élite troops on the right. Their left flank was refused to avoid being ambushed from the Alamanni by the canal, a cautious move even though there was no confirmation of Alamannic troops in the reeds. When the Romans spotted the ambushers, they were able to engage them without difficulty and drive them back. Such an ambush was only dangerous if it was not spotted.

The battle began with missile exchanges and skirmishing, then the Alamanni charged the Roman line. The initial shock of their attack swept away some of the right-flank Roman cavalry, but these were able to rally behind the Roman infantry. In the centre, the impetus of the Alamannic charge was unable to break the Roman line and steady hand-to-hand fighting followed. The Romans would expect quickly to gain the upper hand in these circumstances, but at this point the second wave of *optimates* attacked and managed to burst through the first Roman line before being repulsed. The rest of the Roman line remained intact and the breakthrough was repulsed by the second line of Romans. With the failure of this attack, the Alamanni routed and were pursued by the Romans as far as the Rhine. In the course of the retreat the Alamannic leader Chnodomarius was captured, though at least five other kings escaped.

Despite the apparent ease of Roman victory, the battle was probably a closely fought affair. The disparity in casualties, 247 Roman to 6–8,000 Alamanni, reflects the fact that the Romans won and were able to pursue the defeated enemy, who also suffered by having to cross the Rhine to escape. Since the Romans held the battlefield, they were able to save many of their wounded and could kill any wounded Alamanni that they found. The exactitude of Ammianus' account suggests that he had official reports to work from, being able to name three of the four dead tribunes and give a precise number of Roman deaths.[65]

---

[65] AM 16. 12; Lib. *Or.* 18. 53–68; Zos. 3. 3. 3–5; N. Bitter, *Kampfschilderungen bei Ammianus Marcellinus* (Bonn, 1976), 56–101; N. J. E. Austin, 'In Support of Ammianus' Veracity', *Historia*, 22 (1973), 331–5; Crump, *Ammianus Marcellinus*, 85–9.

Naval battles

The Romans seem to have regarded naval warfare as an extension of land warfare, not as a branch of service in its own right. This, together with the lack of a permanently established large fleet, meant that most naval actions were land actions on water, consisting of an exchange of missile fire in the approach, followed by ramming and boarding actions. Most of our knowledge is derived from later or theoretical writers.

Fleets usually deployed in linear formations, sometimes more than one line deep. Variations on this included concave formations, with the best ships on the wings to encircle the enemy, or a convex formation with the best ships in the centre, to break through the enemy line.[66] Battle was fought under oars, since sails would not give the required mobility. As ships approached, there would be an exchange of missile fire, from individuals and artillery pieces mounted on towers. This fire included incendiary weapons.[67] At closer quarters ships would start ramming. At the same time, boarding actions would take place, either from bridges or by grappling hooks. In these actions, troops fought in full armour.[68] As well as boarding, attempts were made to cripple ships by cutting ropes and sails using axes and halberds, sometimes using small boats to get closer to enemy vessels.[69]

C: SIEGE WARFARE

Most sieges took place in civil wars or when defending against barbarians. Attacks against barbarians in fortified positions were rare. Sieges tended to be more structured than battles and this

---

[66] For linear formations see Syrianus 9. 30; for multiple lines see Syrianus 9. 32–3; for concave see Syrianus 9. 30–1; Veg. 4. 45; for convex see Syrianus 9. 35.

[67] For oars see Veg. 4. 43; on missile fire see Veg. 4. 44; Procopius, *BG* 8. 23. 30, 34; Zos. 5. 21. 3; on artillery see Mauricius, *Strat.* 12. 8. 21; Veg. 4. 44; Agathias, *Hist.* 3. 21. 4; for towers see Veg. 4. 44; for incendiaries see Veg. 4. 44.

[68] On ramming see Veg. 4. 46; AM 26. 8. 8; Procopius, *BV* 3. 6. 21, *BG* 8. 23. 34; Zos. 5. 21. 3; on boarding see Veg. 4. 44; Procopius, *BG* 8. 23. 30; for armour see Veg. 4. 44; AM 26. 8. 9–10; Procopius, *BG* 3. 6. 23; Agathias, *Hist.* 5. 22. 4.

[69] On cutting sails and ropes see Veg. 4. 46; for *falces* (= δορυδρέπανα) see Veg. 4. 46; Agathias, *Hist.* 5. 22. 4, 9; on *bipenni* see Veg. 4. 46; AM 26. 8. 10 (though Austin, *Ammianus on Warfare*, 147 n. 16 argues that this is a sledgehammer); for small boats see Veg. 4. 46; for fireships, cf. Procopius, *BV* 3. 6. 17–20.

allows a clear division into phases. This discussion can be subdivided into attack and defence. Though we understand the mechanisms, there is only one detailed account of a siege in Europe in this period, that by Ammianus describing the siege of Aquileia in 361, and there are few examples to quote here. Therefore many of the references are to operations conducted in Persia, though techniques in Europe seem similar.[70]

Attack

When a fortified site was to be attacked, the first Roman action was to surround the site. They then had the choice of blockade or assault in order to capture the fortified site. Assaults would be chosen only if there was a need to capture the site quickly (usually only if there was an enemy army able to relieve it), otherwise blockades were preferred (perhaps because they resulted in fewer friendly casualties). Attacks on barbarians in fortified sites were usually blockades, for example the siege of a group of Franks in two Roman forts on the Meuse in 358. Conversely, in civil wars, most attacks on fortified sites were assaults, for example, Procopius' seizure of Cyzicus in 365. The decision to assault was usually based on strategic, not tactical, criteria. Thus Ricimer besieged Rome for eight months in 472 since he had no immediate need to storm the city.[71]

When blockading a site units were deployed around its circumference to stop entry and exit of troops, supplies, etc. Earthworks or palisades might also be constructed. As the blockade continued the defenders would run short of food and eventually be forced to surrender. The time this took depended on the amount of food stored in the city. Theoderic the Great's siege of Ravenna lasted from 490 to 493, though it took so long because there was no naval blockade until 492/3, allowing the defenders to be supplied by sea. Long sieges were common and the defenders were often reduced to eating horses and occasional rumours of cannibalism surfaced. Once the city was surrounded, an appeal might be made to the enemy to

---

[70] Veg. 4. 1–30; Mauricius, *Strat.* 10; Anon. *PS* 11–13.
[71] On strategic choice see Zos. 2. 49. 2–4; cf. AM 19. 2. 1, 7. 1, 21. 12. 3; for Meuse see AM 17. 2; Lib. *Or.* 18. 70; for Cyzicus see AM 26. 8. 7–11; for Rome see J. Ant. fr. 209. 1; for others see Priscus fr. 5.

surrender, though such appeals were rarely successful.[72]

When assaulting a site the major decision for the attackers was how to get across the walls. There were three methods of doing this, over (using siege towers, mounds, or ladders), through (rams), or under (mining). Before any assault took place attempts were made to dominate the wall area by missile fire. Unless the attackers were able to deny the continued safe use of the wall to the defenders an assault would be unlikely to succeed. This domination was accomplished by killing or demoralizing defenders and destroying their artillery.[73] It was in this phase of the battle that artillery was of most use. The main aim was to destroy enemy artillery, to stop the latter being used against the attacker's siege equipment. The available artillery equipment can be divided into two types by their area of effect, on individuals or on groups. Bolt-throwers (*ballistae*) were usually used for sniping purposes, to pick off prominent individuals. Stone-throwers (*scorpiones*, *onagri*) were used to fire stones at large groups of enemy. In both cases, the morale effect could be as great as, or greater than, the physical damage caused. Stone-throwers could also cause structural damage, but were generally confined to firing at towers, gates, or siege machinery.[74] Artillery might use incendiary ammunition when firing at gates or equipment. Individual archers could also use fire arrows with an incendiary effect. Starting fires within the city would divert defenders' attention and resources from the walls.[75]

Once domination of the wall area had been gained, an assault could begin. To get close to the walls it would be necessary to fill the ditch surrounding the site, so that equipment could be brought into position next to the walls. Once the ditch was filled a siege

---

[72] For Ravenna see Anon. Val. 53–5; J. Ant. fr. 209. 1; for circumvallation see Austin, *Ammianus on Warfare*, 144 n. 9; AM 19. 2. 2, 5. 1, 6. 6, 21. 12. 4, 24. 2. 9, 4. 10, 12; Veg. 4. 28; Mauricius, *Strat.* 10. 1. 2; for appeals see AM 19. 1. 3–6, 20. 7. 3–4, 11. 7, 24. 1. 8, 2. 1, 9, 4. 11; Mauricius, *Strat.* 10. 1. 6–7; on food shortages see Malchus fr. 2; Olymp. fr. 29. 2; Zos. 5. 39; Soz. 9, 8; Theoph AM 5964; on blockade see AM 16. 4. 1–2 (1 month), 17. 2. 3 (54 days); J. Ant. fr. 209. 1 (5 or 8 months).

[73] AM 19. 1. 8, 2. 8, 20. 7. 6, 24. 2. 9; Zos. 3. 21. 3; Priscus fr. 5; Veg. 4. 21.

[74] On *ballistae* for sniping see Zos. 1. 70; AM 20. 11. 20, cf. 19. 5. 6; on stone-throwers vs. personnel see AM 19. 2. 8, 7. 5, 21. 12. 10; vs. structures see AM 21. 12. 14; vs. siege equipment see AM 19. 7. 6–7.

[75] AM 23. 4. 14–15; Veg. 4 18; Mauricius, *Strat.* 10. 1. 13; M. F. A. Brok, 'Ein spätrömischer Brandpfeil nach Ammianus', *Saalburg Jahrbuch*, 35 (1978), 57–60; cf. AM 31. 15. 8.

tower or ram could be brought into the selected position. At the same time missile exchanges continued.[76] Rams were used to attack gates, towers, or vulnerable points (areas weakened by subsidence or recent repair) in the wall. A similar tactic was to try to collapse a wall section, tower, or vulnerable point by attacking it with crowbars, picks, etc. The rams, or men with crowbars, could be protected by mobile penthouses.[77] Siege towers were brought up to the wall and used to launch an attack onto the walkway, aided by missile fire (sometimes including *ballistae*) from the higher levels of the tower. At the same time, or on their own, attacks with scaling ladders took place.[78] A siege mound consisted of an earth ramp to the height of the walls, to allow a storming party to enter. These mounds sometimes had artillery placed on them.[79]

At the same time as any of these methods, mining could take place. To hinder countermining concealed entrances might be used. Thus, even if the defenders realized a mine was being dug, they would not know which part of the wall was being attacked. From the minehead a tunnel was dug until it was inside the walls, then a storming party attacked the town. Alternatively, the tunnel could be fired to collapse a wall section or tower, then the breach would be assaulted on the surface. Mines are not known to have been used in sieges in Europe in this period.[80]

Once a breach was made a storming party would enter the city. These storming parties usually used a *testudo* as the attack formation for protection against missiles. The fighting here was usually very fierce with heavy casualties on both sides. After its fall the city could be sacked.[81]

[76] Zos. 3. 21. 3; AM 24. 2. 11, 4. 12; Veg. 4. 16.

[77] On rams see AM 20. 6. 5–6, 7. 12–13, 11. 11–15, 21, 21. 12. 8, 23. 4. 8–9, 24. 2. 12, 4. 19; Zos. 3. 21–2; Veg. 4. 14; Mauricius, *Strat.* 10. 1. 14; for vulnerable areas see AM 20. 6. 5–6, 7. 9–13, 11. 6; for crowbars, etc. see AM 20. 6. 3, 11. 8, 21, 21. 12. 6; Veg. 4. 14; for penthouses, Veg. 4. 14–15.

[78] For towers see Zos. 3. 18. 3; AM 19. 5. 1, 7. 5, 21. 9 (on boats), 23. 4. 10–13, 24. 2. 18–19; Veg. 4. 17, 21; Merobaudes, *Pan.* 2. 168–9; for ladders see AM 19. 5. 6, 20. 6. 3, 7. 6, 11. 21, 21. 12. 6 and 13, 24. 4. 24; Veg. 4. 12, 21, 26; Procopius, *BG* 6. 19. 19–20; Mauricius, *Strat.* 10. 1. 14.

[79] Zos. 3. 21. 3; AM 19. 6. 6, 8. 1–2; Veg. 4. 15; Mauricius, *Strat.* 10. 1. 14.

[80] On mining see Zos. 3. 21. 4, 22. 2–5; AM 20. 11. 8, 21. 12. 8, 24. 4. 12, 21–3; Veg. 4. 24; Anon. *PS* 13. 1–21; Procopius, *BG* 5. 23. 17–18; cf. Agathias, *Hist.* 1. 10. 3–8; Rostovtzeff, *Dura Europos, Sixth Season*, 188–203; on assault see AM 24. 4. 22–4; Zos. 3. 24.

[81] For storming parties, AM 20. 7. 14–15; *testudo*, AM 20. 11. 8, 24. 2. 14, 4. 15, 26. 8. 9; sacks, AM 20. 6. 7, 24. 4. 25; Zos. 3. 24. 5–7.

Defence

Defence against barbarians attacking fortified sites was simple for the Romans. Provided that the walls were in good condition and there was plenty of stored food, all the Romans had to do was wait to be relieved. While waiting, walls and gateways had to be guarded and care had to be taken that morale was kept high to avoid the possibility of treachery or infiltration.[82] When being attacked by Roman armies (and on those rare occasions when barbarians had obtained siege machinery) a more active defence was needed. No attack could take place unless the attackers reached the walls, so the defenders tried to keep them as far away as possible. The main method of doing this was by missile fire from hand-held weapons and artillery. The major function of artillery was to destroy enemy siege equipment (often using incendiaries), but it also had an anti-personnel function and *ballistae* could be used for sniping.[83] Passive measures included keeping attackers and their equipment away from the walls by the ditch. Other defensive measures included hides or padding which could be hung away from and in front of the walls to provide a screen to reduce the impact of enemy artillery missiles. Cloth screens could also be set up overhanging the wall to reduce the effectiveness of arrow fire.[84]

As the attack proceeded the defenders might identify the sector to be assaulted. If so, a second wall might be constructed inside the original circuit. Though this would not be as strong as the original wall, it would still have to be breached and this time the process of attack would take place in close proximity to the defenders, exposing the attackers to more casualties.[85] If rams were used, the wall could be padded to absorb the impact and nooses, chains, or hooks used to snare their heads. Against siege towers and mounds the wall could be heightened, forcing the attackers to

---

[82] Veg. 4. 26–27; Mauricius, *Strat.* 10. 3. 10.

[83] For missile fire see AM 19. 1. 8, 2. 7, 7. 4, 20. 6. 4, 7. 2, 11. 8, 12, 21. 12. 6, 9, 24. 2. 9, 26. 8. 8, 31. 6. 3, 15. 10–11; artillery, sniping, see AM 19. 1. 7, 20. 7. 2, 21. 12. 10, 24. 5. 6; Veg. 4. 23 (suggesting the use of monumental architecture), 29; vs. personnel, see AM 19. 2. 7, 5. 6, 6. 6, 7. 4, 20. 6. 4, 11. 22, 21. 12. 9–10, 24. 2. 13, 15, 4. 16, 31. 15. 12; Veg. 4. 22; vs. siege equipment, see AM 19. 7. 6–7, 20. 6. 4–6, 7. 10, 12, 11. 15; Veg. 4. 22; Mauricius, *Strat.* 10. 3. 5; for incendiaries see AM 19. 7. 7, 20. 6. 6, 7. 10, 12, 11. 15–16, 18, 22–3, 21. 12. 10, 13, 24. 4. 16; Zos. 3. 21. 1; Veg. 4. 8, 18; Anon. *PS* 13. 102–14; Mauricius, *Strat.* 10. 3. 5.

[84] On padding see AM 24. 2. 10; Mauricius, *Strat.* 10. 3. 2–3; Theophylact, *Hist.* 2. 18. 3; Anon. *PS* 13. 115–20; on screens see AM 21. 11. 9; Veg. 4. 6.

[85] Jul. *Or.* 2. 66b; AM 19. 6. 6?, 8. 1–2; Anon. *PS* 13. 49–60.

increase their efforts, thus lengthening the siege. Caltrops could be scattered outside attack points such as gates.[86] Mines were more difficult to defend against. If it was known that the enemy were mining then a countermine could be constructed and used to collapse the attackers' mine. They could also be used to undermine siege towers. Mines could be detected by careful observation or by methods such as placing stones in metal bowls around the wall circuit as these would vibrate if there was underground movement.[87] Another option open to the defenders throughout the siege was to sortie, often at night, generally in a bid to kill the opposing general or to destroy siege equipment. Julian wished to sortie against the Alamanni besieging him in Sens in 356–7 but was prevented by lack of men; Odovacer was able to sortie from Ravenna in 491, disrupting the Ostrogothic besiegers in a night attack.[88]

Many of these techniques were employed in Julian's siege of Aquileia in 361. Although the city had accepted him as *Augustus*, it rebelled following the arrival of troops who had theoretically submitted but were still loyal to Constantius II. The rebels consisted of two legions, a regiment of archers, and a regiment of cavalry, probably numbering no more than 4,000. The artillery used in the defence of the town was probably integral to these units rather than part of the urban defences.

When Julian learnt of the revolt he detached the *magister equitum* Jovinus to deal with it. When he was advised that the siege would be long but not difficult Jovinus was replaced by Immo, a *comes rei militaris*. Immo's first action was to encircle the city with defence works, after which an unsuccessful attempt was made to induce the defenders to surrender in a session of negotiations. Then a first wave of attackers approached the walls under screens in an attempt to undermine the walls with picks and crowbars, while others used scaling ladders. Both these attacks were driven off.

After the failure of this assault engineering operations began. Nowhere suitable could be found to employ rams, to conduct an effective artillery bombardment, or to dig a mine under the walls.

---

[86] For padding see Mauricius, *Strat.* 10. 3. 3–4; Anon. *PS* 13. 72–91; for nooses, etc. see Veg. 4. 23; AM 20. 11. 15, 19; Mauricius, *Strat.* 10. 3. 4; for caltrops see Procopius, *BG* 7. 24. 15–18.

[87] Anon. *PS* 13. 22–48; Veg. 4. 20; cf. Rostovtzeff, *Dura Europos, Sixth Season*, 188–99.

[88] AM 19. 6. 4–11, 21. 12. 13, 26. 8. 3; Cass. *Chron.* 1326; *Anon. Val.* 54; Lib. *Or.* 18. 44; Veg. 4. 18; Mauricius, *Strat.* 10. 3. 7.

One reason for the difficulties was the river Natesio which ran along the eastern edge of the city. But the river did provide the means of the next attempt on the city. Towers of a height able to overlook the wall (i.e. higher than 10 m.) were built on rafts of three boats lashed together. The plan was to lower ramps from the towers to allow an assault on the wall. The attempt failed because of accurate artillery and incendiary fire from the defenders (the towers were large targets and presumably easy to hit), as well as being more vulnerable by being placed on rafts. The third attack consisted of an assault on the gates, combined with scaling ladders. This attack on the gates was unsuccessful and the defenders began to act more aggressively, sortieing from the posterns and repulsing some of the scaling parties.

Continued reconnaissance by the attackers in the suburbs (the city walls were obviously well within the urban section of the city) was unable to find any weak points and after this a blockade of the city was undertaken. To make this more effective the aqueducts were cut and the river diverted, though the existence of wells within the city meant that this had little immediate impact. Not long after, the garrison of the city surrendered once reliable news of Constantius' death had been received. Negotiations took some time since the garrison was wary of this being a ruse to induce them to surrender. The length of the siege is impossible to calculate. We know it began before Constantius' death, that is, before 3 November, and the city was still under siege when Julian reached Constantinople on 11 December. The siege must therefore have lasted at least five weeks, but could have taken a few weeks longer.[89]

At the start of this chapter it was suggested that little change occurred in operational aspects of the Roman army between 350 and 425. This is a simplification, though in view of the shortage of evidence perhaps a justifiable one. At least we can say that there is little recorded change. Other chapters have suggested that there was little change in the military abilities of the barbarians at this period. Claims of growing tactical sophistication, increasing numbers of cavalry, or use of horse archers appear unjustified.

[89] For Aquileia see AM 21. 11–12; cf. 3rd-cent. siege, Herodian 8. 2. 1–5. 9; for 452 siege see Jordanes, *Getica*, 219–22; Procopius, *BV* 3. 4. 30–5; on defences see M. Boura, 'Le Mura Medievale di Aquileia', *Antichita Altoadriatico*, 32 (1988), 323–63.

Thus there were no external factors which might have forced change. On the Roman side there were no technological or tactical developments to bring about changes. The suggestion that infantry ceased to use armour appears unfounded. The increasing use of allied contingents of barbarians may have had some impact, but this is hard to assess. It seems unlikely that those barbarians employed affected operational matters greatly in the period.

❖

Conclusion

This book has covered the period 350–425, a period in which no one could imagine that the Roman Empire was in any danger of failing. Yet, only fifty years later, the Western Empire was tottering on the verge of collapse, and the last Western Emperor, Romulus Augustulus, was deposed in 476. This book has said much about how the Roman army worked before this, but does not attempt to explain the collapse. Here I attempt to justify this, since the end of the Western Empire is often seen as the result of failure within the army. The conventional argument runs as follows: there was increasing barbarian pressure from the third century, while from the time of Constantine on the army was barbarized, leading to ineffectiveness. In turn, this led to barbarian settlements and thus the collapse in the West.

I believe this explanation to be wrong. As we have seen, barbarization is doubtful in both extent and impact. The effectiveness of armies is hard to measure, and the simplest means, that of battlefield performance, is not always the best. Victory is often the product of numbers, as Leonidas was doubtless aware at Thermopylae, though few would argue that the quality of his troops was lower than that of the Persians. Even winning battles does not mean winning wars, and Hannibal's successes at Cannae and Lake Trasimene did not result in Carthaginian victory in the Second Punic War.

Here I have argued that there was little perceptible decline in the effectiveness of the army during the period 350–425. If this is accepted, then either the cause of collapse must be looked for in the army after 425, or else it may not lie in the structure of the army at all. Did the Western Empire fall because there was something wrong with the late Roman army?

Structurally, the army after 425 was no different from the army before. All elements of 'decline', such as barbarian troops and

Conclusion

officers, were already in place. Even if we were to imagine the problems as having been solved—if all the 'barbarians' in the army had been replaced by men born in the city of Rome, if there were no deserters, no corrupt or cowardly officers, if troops were not garrisoned in towns—then would the Western Empire have continued? I doubt it. Looking at events, rather than processes, is more important. Much can be traced back to the battle of Adrianople, though (with the important exception of Ammianus) contemporaries do not treat it as the end of an era. The errors which led to defeat here were not structural failures—it was not a case of too few cavalry, too few armoured infantry, too many barbarians, or poor training. Disappointingly for those looking for simple answers, the failure at Adrianople lay in the impatience of Valens, in his desire to win a victory before the arrival of Gratian, then, as a result of his impatience, a faulty interpretation of an intelligence report, and finally, commitment to battle before the army had come out of line of march, the result of some over-eager tribunes. It was a military disaster, but one no different to that of Varus in Germany in AD 9, a defeat blamed on Varus, not on his army.

The loss at Adrianople eventually led to the settlement of Goths in the Balkans, neither a new nor a dangerous practice. But the use of Goths as Roman allies, twice in the next twenty years, against the Western usurpers Magnus Maximus and Eugenius, was new. This allowed the Goths to create a group identity never previously possible for settled barbarians. But to explain the usurpation of Magnus Maximus and Eugenius by the defeat at Adrianople would be wrong.

On the other hand, why did the Roman army not destroy the Goths in the battles after 378, or during the campaigns of Stilicho? This is a much more difficult question to answer, and Stilicho's failures have produced groundless accusations of collusion with Alaric. Theodosius should probably be congratulated for making a negotiated peace with the Goths in 382 after the destruction of much of the Roman field army—surely better to make peace as fast as possible, then absorb the Goths, as other barbarians had been absorbed before, rather than spend more time fighting? The Romans seem hardly to have suffered from the initial settlement of the Goths in 382. Alaric's survival has more to do with his military abilities: he could hold Stilicho to a draw, but was able to defeat Stilicho's successors. With his death in 410, the Romans were able to force compliance from the Goths, moving them out of Italy and into Gaul, and then Spain.

By this time the Goths had become an established part of the military and political landscape, a power to be negotiated with inside the borders of the Empire, while foreign threats were no less diminished. Again the response was to settle the barbarians, this time in Aquitaine in 418, and hope they would be absorbed over time. Now they had a king, which gave them strong leadership, but even this was not critical to the Western Empire. It was not until the 450s that the Goths in Gaul began to be dangerous, and by that point other problems were more important.

It is in such political and military events that I believe we should look for explanations of the collapse of the Western Roman Empire. They do not seem to me to be the result of barbarization or inefficiency. None the less, these events had military and financial consequences.

It was only in the decades after 450 that the fall of the West became inevitable, something which I would connect with the loss of control of Africa, important as a reservoir of manpower and money, and similar to Egypt or Anatolia in the East. This in itself was not enough to bring down such an immense organization as the Roman Empire, and even at this date the Roman army was not a force to be trifled with. The effectiveness of armies directed from Constantinople was never in doubt, and in 468 a serious operation to reconquer Africa was launched. Western power was also still strong in the 450s. In 456 Ricimer won a naval victory against the Vandals at Agrigentum. From 457, Majorian had campaigned on the Danube, made alliances in Gaul, and fought in Spain. He began preparations for an amphibious assault on Africa in 460, worrying Geiseric so much that he ordered the wells in Mauretania to be poisoned to hinder the assault.

In 461 Ricimer murdered Majorian and placed his protégé Libius Severus on the throne. Severus was faced with hostile Goths and Vandals. He was also faced with political instability, being unable to conciliate the army commanders (and Majorian's friends), Aegidius in Gaul and Marcellinus in Dalmatia. The fall of the West could not be delayed for long. Their hostility made it impossible for any Western Roman leader, themselves included, to deal with the existing frontiers on the Rhine and Danube, with the Goths in

Gaul, and with the Vandals in Spain, to mention only military problems.

Military failure may have been a major cause of the West's collapse, but this failure was not caused by structural weaknesses in the army itself. Too much pressure on the frontiers, defeat at Adrianople, too many civil wars, not enough soldiers—these all contributed to the fall of the West. We do not need to add structural failure of the army to the list.

APPENDIX I

Notes on Sources

A number of theoretical writings on military affairs have been used in this book and some notes on them may be useful. They are, in chronological order, the anonymous *De Rebus Bellicis*, Vegetius, Urbicius, Syrianus, the anonymous *Peri Strategikes*, and Mauricius.

The anonymous author of the *De Rebus Bellicis* wrote in the mid-fourth century, probably under Valentinian and Valens. His work is a series of suggestions for improving the defence of the Empire. There are two types of suggestions: ideas already in use and 'inventions', the latter varying between implausible and useless. The author seems not to have had any military experience and is probably best used as a guide to what could be done, not what was done. A text, translation, and conference papers are presented by M. W. Hassall and R. I. Ireland, eds., *De Rebus Bellicis*, *BAR* S63 (Oxford, 1979), and a Teubner text is available, ed. R. I. Ireland (Leipzig, 1982).

Like the *De Rebus Bellicis*, Vegetius' *De Re Militari* is a confusing work. Its date is uncertain, the parameters being 383–450. Scholarly opinion is divided between Theodosius and Valentinian III as dedicatees of the work. The former is preferred here, though the date has little effect on the arguments presented. A second set of problems lie in determining the period Vegetius is discussing, since he deals with both contemporary events and an *antiqua legio*, a composite of early imperial practice. Much of the material, especially in books three and four is very practical and the work was popular with medieval and Renaissance soldiers. The text of Vegetius is edited by C. Lang, *De Re Militari* (Leipzig, 1885) and translated by N. Milner, *Vegetius* (Liverpool, 1993). On dating, W. Goffart, 'The Date and Purpose of Vegetius' De Re Militari', *Traditio* 33 (1977), 65–100, argues convincingly for a fifth-century date, but see also T. D. Barnes, 'The Date of Vegetius', *Phoenix*, 33 (1979), 254–7, who argues for composition under Theodosius I.

Urbicius' *Epitedeuma* was written in the reign of Anastasius. It is in some senses similar to the *De Rebus Bellicis*, though most of its suggestions are more practical and confined to military affairs. It is a short work, only

preserved in three manuscripts of Mauricius' *Strategikon*, and it is not
well-known. The most easily accessible text is H. Mihaescu, ed., *Arta
Militară* (Bucharest, 1970), 368–73, with a Romanian translation. The
manuscript illustrations are now unfortunately lost. There are some comments in A. Dain, 'Les Stratégistes byzantins', *Travaux et Mémoires*, 2
(1967), 317–92 at 341–2. Urbicius also wrote a *Tactica* which is an epitome
of Arrian's *Tactica*, not an original work. Text and translation are presented
by R. Förster, 'Studien zu den griechischen Taktikern: II. Kaiser Hadrien
und der Taktika des Urbicius', *Hermes*, 12 (1877), 449–71. Urbicius is
named as the author of Mauricius' *Strategikon* in some manuscripts. This
is almost certainly in error for Mauricius; as far as is known Urbicius did
not write a *Strategikon*.

Syrianus wrote on naval warfare in the late fifth or early sixth century.
The work (whose beginning is lost) is a practical consideration of naval
warfare, discussing ship types, tactics, and strategy. A text is published in
A. Dain, *Naumachica* (Paris, 1943), 43–55 and there is a brief discussion
in A. Dain, 'Les Stratégistes byzantins', *Travaux et Mémoires*, 2 (1967),
317–92 at 342. See also F. Lammert, 'Die älteste erhaltene Schrift über
Seetaktik und ihre Beziehung zum Anonymus Byzantinus des sexte
Jahrhunderts, zu Vegetius und zu Aineas' *Strategika*', *Klio*, 33 (1940), 271–
88. M. Reddé, *Mare Nostrum* (Rome, 1986), 680–4, translates 9. 1–7 and
9–41.

The anonymous *Peri Strategikes* has also lost its beginning. It has to be
dated from internal evidence and may belong to Justinian's reign. There is
a treatise on archery appended to the work. The text is written simply and
clearly by a soldier, though probably not by a commander of combat
troops. It has recently been edited and translated by G. T. Dennis, *Three
Byzantine Military Treatises* (Washington, DC, 1985), 1–136. Doubts on
the Justinianic date have recently been raised by B. Baldwin, 'On the Date
of the Anonymous *Peri Strategikes*', *Byzantinische Zeitschrift*, 81 (1988),
290–3, and A. D. Lee and J. Shepard, 'A Double Life: Placing the *Peri
Presbeon*', *Byzantinoslavica*, 52 (1991), 15–39, while C. Zuckermann, 'The
Military Compendium of Syrianus Magister', *Jahrbuch der Österreichische
Byzantinistik*, 40 (1990), 209–24 argues that Syrianus' naval work and the
anonymous *Peri Strategikes* are both part of the same sixth-century work.

The last military writer used is Mauricius, who wrote a *Strategikon* in
the late sixth century. Most of the work is concerned with organization,
equipment, tactics, and operations. There is some duplication, but most of
the advice is clear and practical. A following section (chapter 11) consists
of four short essays giving strategic and operational recommendations for
fighting the Persians, Slavs and Antes, Huns and other Scythians, and
Western barbarians. These theoretical recommendations are similar to the
practices followed by generals in the histories of Ammianus, Procopius,

and Agathias. The last chapter (12) was appended after the main text was written. It incorporates a (probably) Justinianic treatise on infantry equipment, organization, and tactics (here cited as 12. 8), a *Cynegetica* (probably written by Urbicius), a diagram of a fortified camp, and, in three manuscripts, Urbicius' *Epitedeuma*. A text and German translation has been published by G. T. Dennis, *Das Strategikon des Maurikios* (Vienna, 1981) and an English translation, *Maurice's Strategikon* (Philadelphia, 1984). The former was not available to me, so text references (almost identical except in chapter 12) are from the text and translation of H. Mihaescu, ed., *Arta Militară* (Bucharest, 1970). Dennis' editions do not include Urbicius' *Epitedeuma*.

A few other sources require some comment. The *Notitia Dignitatum* is frequently cited. Its dating is contentious, and here I will state the assumptions I have made without trying to defend them. The Western part dates from 395, but has been completely revised to *c.*408, then partially thereafter to *c.*423, with these later revisions being concentrated on military matters, particularly those concerning the office of the *magister peditum*. The Eastern part dates from 395. The *Notitia* has generated a considerable body of secondary literature: R. Goodburn and P. Bartholomew, eds., *Aspects of the Notitia Dignitatum*, *BAR* S15 (Oxford, 1976). A new edition is badly needed, with colour plates of the major manuscripts.

The fragments of Eunapius, Olympiodorus, Priscus, Malchus, Candidus, and Menander are quoted from Blockley's editions, which contain a concordance for cross-reference with earlier numbering systems. Renatus Profuturus Frigeridus (RPF) and Sulpicius are extracted from Gregory of Tours, *History of the Franks*, 2. 8–9, as follows. RPF fr. 1 [GT *HF* 2. 8]: *Dum haec ... celebrandus*; fr. 2 [GT *HF* 2. 9]: *Interea Respendial ... subvenisset*; fr. 3: *Accito Constantinus ... redituri*; fr. 4: *Vix dum quartus ... truncatus est*; fr. 5: *Hisdem diebus ... inruptione*; fr. 6: *Eodem tempore Castinus ... mittitur*. Sulpicius fr. 1 [GT *HF* 2. 9]: *Eo tempore Genobaude ... praestituerunt*; fr. 2: *Eo tempore Carietto ... diversabantur*; fr. 3: *Nihil Arbogastis ... poneretur*; fr. 4: *Post dies ... concessit*; fr. 5: *Dum diversa ... apparuere*; fr. 6: *Dehinc Eugenius ... ostentaret*. The appropriate passages are italicized in Arndt and Krusch's edition of Gregory of Tours.

APPENDIX 2

Barbarization and the Late Roman Army

The data used in Chapter 5 are drawn from *The Prosopography of the Later Roman Empire*, i and ii, supplemented by the author's collection of inscriptions, primarily of other ranks. Though there are undoubtedly inaccuracies and omissions in the material collected, these are too few seriously to affect the overall results presented here. Table 7 is a fuller version of Table 4, with the barbarian and Roman categories separated into 'Definite' and 'Probable'.

The evidence for other ranks, here defined as soldiers below the rank of *tribunus* or *praefectus* and excluding *protectores* and *domestici*, is more diverse than for officers. The results presented here represent a large proportion of the literary sources, but less of the epigraphic material (Tables 7–9). Work is presently being carried out to produce a catalogue of these men using a computer database. I am grateful to Ralph Mathisen and the Biographical Database for Late Antiquity for assistance. This survey has not been exhaustive by any means, and Romans and non-commissioned officers are probably over-represented, as are literary sources in general. Though the total sample is much smaller than that for officers, the results are similar.

Only field army soldiers have been used for this analysis, since the *limitanei* were usually recruited locally and would thus not contribute towards an analysis of barbarization. All thirty-one soldiers named in Abinnaeus' papers have non-Germanic names, as would be expected of men recruited in Egypt in the 340s. The small numbers involved, together with the arbitrary chronological divisions, makes drawing any meaningful conclusions from the data impossible. Between AD 350 and 500, assuming a field army of 450,000 and (unrealistically) that every soldier served a full twenty-year term, there were over three million serving Roman soldiers! We know of so few soldiers that any conclusions drawn from such limited data are not statistically significant.

These figures treat the army as a whole, but tell us nothing about how these barbarians were incorporated into the army. All of these men are from regular regiments (*bucellarii*, *domestici*, and οἰκέται have been excluded from all figures). We do not know whether units were mixed or whether

Table 7. *Roman army officers, 350–476 (expanded)*

Rank		350–399	400–449	450–476	undated	Total	%
Magistri	DR	14	11	14	0	39	24
militum	PR	26	37	10	1	74	46
	DB	8	6	7	0	21	13
	PB	10	9	5	0	24	16
	O	2	0	0	0	2	1
		60	63	36	1	160	
Comites	DR	7	2	9	0	18	16
	PR	36	24	5	1	66	60
	DB	4	2	3	0	9	8
	PB	8	4	5	0	17	15
	O	1	0	0	0	1	1
		56	32	22	1	111	
Duces	DR	4	5	0	1	10	10
	PR	37	24	5	6	72	73
	DB	3	1	1	0	5	5
	PB	7	0	1	0	8	8
	O	2	1	1	0	4	4
		53	31	8	7	99	
Guard Officers	DR	7	4	3	0	14	29
	PR	12	10	4	0	26	53
	DB	3	0	0	0	3	6
	PB	3	1	0	0	4	8
	O	2	0	0	0	2	4
		27	15	7	0	49	
Protectores,	DR	6	1	0	6	13	16
Domestici	PR	19	15	0	23	57	69
	DB	0	0	2	1	3	4
	PB	4	1	0	4	9	11
		29	17	2	34	82	
Regiment	DR	10	3	1	2	16	7
Commanders	PR	69	34	7	56	166	77
	DB	7	0	0	0	7	3
	PB	21	2	0	4	27	12
	O	2	0	0	0	2	1
		109	39	8	62	218	
All Officers	DR	36	20	20	9	85	13
	PR	179	136	30	87	432	67
	DB	19	6	13	1	39	6
	PB	47	15	10	8	80	13
	O	6	1	1	0	8	1
	TOTAL	287	178	74	105	644	

DR = Definitely Roman, PR = Probably Roman, DB = Definitely Barbarian, PB = Probably Barbarian, O = Other.

there were separate regiments of Romans and barbarians. In cases where we have names of more than one man from the same regiment, about a third seem to have been of mixed nationality, but the samples are so small that this cannot be relied on and all it really shows is that regiments could be mixed.

Table 8. *Other ranks, field army, 350–500*

	350–399	400–449	450–500	undated	TOTAL
DR	5	2	5	4	16
PR	17	7	5	65	94
DB	3	1	0	2	6
PB	1	0	0	20	21
O	0	0	0	1	1
					138

Table 9. *Other ranks, field army, 350–500 (expanded)*

Name	Nationality	Regiment	Reference
Abruna	PB	Batavi Seniores	*ILCV* 544
Adabrandus	PB	Scutarii	*ILS* 9213
Aemilianus	DR	Cornuti Seniores	*HSCP* 81 (1977), 257–84
Agustus	PR	Mattiaci Seniores	*CIL* 5. 8737
Alagildus	PB	Equites Bracchiati Seniores	*ILS* 2804
Albinus	PR		*CIL* 5. 1796
Ampio	PR	Mattiaci Seniores	*ILS* 2800
Andia	PB	Bracchiati	*ILS* 2798
Antiochus	PR	Candidati	*CIL* 6. 32953
Antoninus	PR	Dalmatae	*CIL* 13. 3457
Aristophanes	PR	Candidati	Nilus, *Ep.* 2. 220
Augustus	PR		Evagrius, *HE* 2. 1
Avitianus	PR		Eugippius, *V. Sev.* 44. 2
Bantio	PB		*ILS* 2807
Batemodus	PB	Heruli Seniores	*ILCV* 500
Buraido	O	Numerus Hippo Regium	*ILS* 2811
Carterius	PR		Libanius, *Ep.* 656
Cascinivus	PR	Schola Armaturarum	*ILCV* 497
Charietto	PR		AM 17. 10. 5
Claudius	PR	Ioviani	AM 29. 3. 7
Constantinus	PR		Orosius 7. 40. 4
Danielus	PR	Scutarii Clibanarii	*SEG* 20. 332
Dassiolus	PR	Mattiaci Iuniores	*CIL* 5. 8744
Derdio	PB	Ioviani Seniores	*ILS* 2789

Name	Nationality	Regiment	Reference
Diocles	PR	Hiberi	*CIL* 5. 8745
Ditubistus	DR	Excubitores	Procopius, *HA* 6. 3
Domninus	PR	Excubitores	*MAMA* 8. 323
Dorus	PR	Scutarii	AM 16. 6. 2
Emeterius	PR	Gentiles	*CIL* 13. 8331
Eucarius	PR	ɔutarii Secundi	*CIL* 6. 32949
Eusebius	PR	Schola Palatina Gallica	Symm. *Ep.* 9. 55
Eutocius	DR		Suda E. 3770
Eutychianus	DR	Primoarmeniaci	Malalas 332
Evingus	PB	Equites Bracchiati Seniores	*ILS* 2804
Exsuperius	PR	Victores	AM 24. 4. 23
Fasta	PB	Equites Batavi Seniores	*ILCV* 498
Firminus	PR		Basil, *Ep.* 116
Flainus	PB	Mattiaci Seniores	*ILS* 9215
Fortunatus	PR	Ioviani	*ILCV* 551
Frontinus	PR		*ILS* 2783
Gainas	DB		Soz. 8. 4. 1
Gaudentius	PR	Scutarii	AM 26. 5. 14
Gennadius	PR		*CIL* 5. 8749
Hariso	PB	Heruli Seniores	*ILS* 2801
Higgo	PB	Scutarii Tertii	*ILS* 2790
Ianuarinus	PR	Mattiaci Iuniores	*CIL* 5. 8751
Ilateuta	PB	Bracchiati	*ILS* 2798
Ingenuus	PR	Equites Catafracti Seniores	*CIL* 13. 1848
Ioannes	DR	Schola Prima	*V. Sabae* 38
Ioannes	PR	Schola	*CIG* 8869
Ioannes	PR		*AE* 1891. 157
Ioannes	DR	Numerus Isaurorum	*V. Sabae* 1
Iovianus	PR		AM 23. 5. 12
Iovinianus	PR	Equites Octavodalmatae	*ILS* 2805
Isidorus	PR	Excubitores?	Nilus, *Ep.* 2. 322
Iustinianus	DR	Candidatus	Vict. Tonn. 518
Iustinus	DR	Excubitores	Procopius, *HA* 6. 3
Iuventinus	PR	Pezetairoi	Theod. *HE* 3. 15. 4
Launius	PR	Batavi Seniores	*ILS* 2802
Lupicinus	PR	Schola Gentilium	AM 27. 10. 12
Lycianus	DR	Scutarii	*AE* 1961. 197
Macameus	PR		Zos. 3. 26. 5
Manio	PB	Bructeri	*CIL* 5. 8768
Mansuetus	PR	Leones Seniores	*CIL* 5. 8755
Marcianus	DR		Evagrius, *HE* 2. 1
Marcianus	PR	Felices Leones Seniores	AE 1937. 254
Marcus	DR	Vexillatio Fesianesa	*ILS* 2783
Marinus	PR		*CIL* 12. 149
Marinus	PR		AM 15. 3. 10
Maritus	PR		*CIL* 6. 32973

Name	Nationality	Regiment	Reference
Martinus	PR	Prima Minerva	*ILS* 2782
Martinus	DR	Schola	Sev. *V. Mart.* 2
Maurus	PR	Petulantes	*AM* 20. 4. 18
Maurus	PR		Zos. 3. 26. 5
Maxentius	PR		*ILS* 2783
Maximianus	PR	Martii	*ILCV* 473
Maximinus	PR		*ILCV* 822
Maximinus	PR	Pezetairoi	Theod. *HE* 3. 15. 4
Memorius	PR	Ioviani	*ILS* 2788
Menas	PR	Mattiaci Seniores	*ILS* 9481a
Mundilo	PB	Schola Gentilium	*CIL* 11. 1708
Natuspardo	PB	Scutarii	*AM* 27. 10. 16
Odiscus	PB	Equites Bracchiati Seniores	*ILCV* 514
Olympius	PR		*MAMA* 7. 129
Paulus	PR	Milites Histricorum?	*ILS* 2787
Paulus	PR	Schola Secunda	*CIL* 6. 31971
Perula	PB		*ILS* 2783
Plaianus	PR	Quintodalmatae	*CIL* 13. 3458
Provincalius	PR	Schola	Palladius, *Dialogus*, 20
Reginus	PR	Candidati	Nilus, *Ep.* 2. 329
Roveos	PR	Comites Sagittarii Seniores	*CIL* 5. 8758
Sabinianus	PR		*ILS* 2780
Sallustius	PR	Scutarii	*AM* 29. 1. 16
Sallustius	PR	Ioviani	*AM* 29. 3. 7
Salvius	PR	Scutarii	*AM* 27. 10. 12
Sanbatis	PB	Lanciarii Iuniores	*AE* 1927. 169
Sanctus	PR	Iovii/Ioviani	*ILS* 9205
Sauma	PB	Equites Bracchiati Seniores	*ILS* 2804
Savinus	PR	Batavi Seniores	*ILS* 2797
Segetius	PR	Schola Gentium	*CIL* 11. 1711
Servilius	DB	Bracchiati	*ILS* 2798
Severianus	DR	Equites Catafractarii	*ILCV* 504
Silvestrius	PR	Chattuarii	*CIL* 13. 7298
Silvimarus	PB	Heruli	*ILCV* 548
Sindila	PB	Heruli Seniores	*ILS* 2796
Sophianus	PR	Schola	Nilus, *Ep.* 1. 236
Sporacius	PR	Schola	Malalas 387
Stephanus	PR	Schola Armaturarum	*ILS* 8883
Superianus	PR		*ILS* 2783
Taulas	PR	Iovii/Ioviani	*AE* 1940. 214
Theodorus	PR	Schola	*MAMA* 7 p. 40 n. 225
Totila	PB		*CIL* 6. 32967
Valentinus	PR		*ILS* 9206
Valerius	PR	Sagitarii	*Bull. arch. e storia Dalmata*, 33 (1910), 59 n 4122

Name	Nationality	Regiment	Reference
Vassio	PR	Batavi Seniores	*ILS* 2803
Victorinus	PR	Batavi Seniores	*CIL* 5. 8761
Victurus	PR	Sagittarii Nervii	*CIL* 5. 8762
Vitalianus	PR	Iovii/Victores	AM 26. 7. 15
Vitalianus	PR	Vexillatio Hip. Catafracti	*BGU* 316
Vitalianus	PR	Eruli	AM 25. 10. 9
Vitalianus	PR	Felices Theodosiaci	*CIL* 6. 32978
Vitalis	PR	Martii	*ILCV* 473
Ursacius	PR	Batavi Seniores	*CIL* 5. 8776
Ursacius	PR	Leones Seniores	*ILCV* 501
Ursinus	PR		*ILS* 2783
Ursus	PR		Jord. *Getica*, 235
Zemarchus	DR	Excubitores	Procopius, *HA* 6. 3
Ziper	PR	Martii	*ILCV* 473
...ercus	PR	Equites Octavodalmatae	*CIL* 5. 8777
...olus	PR	Fortenses	*ILCV* 547
...runa	PR	Scutarius	*CIL* 6. 32951
...talis	PR	Ioviani Seniores	*CIL* 13. 3687
...tinus	PR	Schola Scutarii Primi	*CIL* 6. 32948
Anon.	DB		*ILS* 2814
Anon.	DB	Scutarii	AM 31. 10. 3
Anon.	DR	Equites	AM 18. 6. 16
Anon.	DR		Evagrius, *HE* 2. 1
Anon.	DB	Candidati	Jerome, *V. Hil.* 22

DB = Definitely Barbarian, DR = Definitely Roman, O = Other, PB = Probably Barbarian, PR = Probably Roman.

APPENDIX 3

Danubian Archaeology in Late Antiquity

Given the problems with the literary sources, an understanding of the dramatic political changes that took place in the Danube basin in the fourth and fifth centuries is obviously strengthened by use of the archaeological material. Its use involves several serious problems. Nationalistic sentiment can influence interpretation of material.[1] Much of the documentation is difficult to obtain, and often written in Russian or Romanian. Most importantly, the problems are complex and insufficient work has been done in many cases to allow meaningful conclusions to be drawn. This appendix attempts to summarize some material, but should not be considered conclusive.

Most settlements were not permanent, many sites were short-lived, and no period seems marked by exceptional discontinuity. The inhabitants used a mixture of subsistence strategies.[2] Where found, many bone assemblages seem to be dominated by sheep, others by cattle. However, most excavated sites are cemeteries, unlikely to produce much bone, especially in cremations, while few of the bone assemblages from settlements have been adequately analysed. As with all aspects of Danubian archaeology of this period, more work needs to be done to produce a clear picture.[3]

Settlements of the Carpic culture are known from the second and third centuries from Moldavia and the Prut–Dneister region. Settlements are dominated by surface dwellings with wattle-and-daub walls and clay-coated, often sunken, floors. The only weapons found are knives. Artefacts included bronze and iron simple crossbow brooches. Mirrors, decorated with ribbed backs, are frequent. No bone combs have been found. The pottery was predominantly wheel-made grey wares, the forms mostly large,

[1] R. Batty, 'The Peoples of the Lower Danube and Rome', D.Phil. thesis (Oxford, 1990), 201–4, 454–61.

[2] Batty, 'Peoples', presents an outline of the dominant conditions, especially 404–15; J. H. W. G. Liebeschuetz, *Barbarians and Bishops* (Oxford, 1991), 83–5; hunting, A. Häusler, 'Zu den sozialökonomischen Verhältnissen in der Černjakhov-Kultur', *Zeitschrift für Archeologie*, 13 (1979), 28.

[3] I. Ionita, 'Contributii', *Arheologia Moldovei*, 4 (1966), 256; C. Bloşiu, 'Necropola', *Arheologia Moldovei*, 8 (1975), 223; Häusler, 'Sozialökonomischen Verhältnissen', 27–9 at 27, cattle predominate.

open jars, though different from Sîntana-de-Mures/Chernjakhov (SdM) forms. The sites of this culture also produced heavy, faceted, glass beakers, similar to those from SdM sites. Most burials were cremations.[4]

Assemblages of C material in the lower Danube and Dneister regions are mostly from the Sîntana-de-Mures/Chernjakhov, and has been suggested to represent the Goths.[5] Its introduction was not even. CI material (late second to early third century) appears only in the region of the Dneister. Later phases spread into Wallachia, Moldavia, the steppe region, and the Carpathians. The Carpathians, Moldavia, and Muntenia were occupied later than the plains, and show more C3 sites, dating to the first half of the fourth century, while such sites only appear in Transylvania from the mid-fourth century. The area of the Hungarian plain was an interface between southern elements of the Prezeworsk culture and eastern elements of the SdM culture. The dominant features of the culture were simple crossbow brooches (supplemented from C3 by monstrous knob brooches), wheel-thrown grey wares, bone combs, faceted glass beakers, and cremation in small cemeteries. Weapon burials were rare. During these early phases much of the pottery shows strong similarities to the Carpic material.[6]

At a later stage, cremations began to be replaced by inhumations, though many cemeteries contained graves of both types, and cremation never totally disappeared. Some sites show continuity from the late third to the late fourth/early fifth century—for example, Mihalaşeni, Tirgşor (with a bronze coin of Honorius in grave fill), and Mogoşani, though the problems with establishing a terminal date for the culture have not yet been resolved. Kazanski has recently suggested a terminal date in the first half of the fifth century.[7]

The C cultures began to be supplemented, then replaced, by D cultures in the late fourth and early fifth centuries. Period DI (*c.*380–430) is characterized by confusion, D2 (*c.*430–50) shows strong nomad influence, and D3 (450–500) nomad domination.[8] There was continuity of occupation

---

[4] G. Bichir, *Archaeology and History of the Carpi* (Oxford, 1976); G. Marinescu and N. Miritoiu, 'Die karpische Nekropole von Şopteriu', *Dacia*, 31 (1987), 107–18; M. B. Shchukin, *Rome and the Barbarians in Central and Eastern Europe, 1st Century BC–1st Century AD* (Oxford, 1989); Batty, 'Peoples', 193–212; A. Kaltofen, *Studien zur der Völkerwanderungszeit im südöstlichen Mitteleuropa* (Oxford, 1984).

[5] M. Kazanski, *Les Goths* (Paris, 1991); P. J. Heather and J. F. Matthews, eds., *The Goths in the Fourth Century* (Liverpool, 1991), provide an introduction; see also J. Werner, 'Dančeny und Brangstrup', *BJ* 188 (1988), 241–86.

[6] I. Ionita, 'The Social-Economic Structure of Society during the Goths' Migration in the Carpatho-Danubian Area', in M. Constantinescu *et al.*, eds., *Relations between the Autochthonous Populations and the Migratory Populations on the Territory of Romania* (Bucharest, 1975), 77–89 at 79.

[7] Kazanski, *Les Goths*, 66.

[8] I. Bona, *Das Hunnenreich* (Stuttgart, 1991); *Germanen, Hunnen, Awaren* (Nuremberg, 1989) provides a selection of material, though chaotically organized;

on some sites, and where sites go out of use, cessation of occupation seems as likely an explanation as movement because of political change. There are no widespread signs of violent destruction.[9]

The D cultures differed principally in having more elaborate brooches, particularly the monstrous knob brooches, also found in later stages of SdM sites, and by the presence of more military equipment in graves. From this period also begins to be found material defined as Hunnic— bow and arrow assemblages, mirrors, and kettles. This material is generally confined to élite burials, some of which were inhumations.[10] In the Danube basin, this material is primarily associated with assemblages of D2 and D3 material, so it seems more likely to be a reflection of changes in burial customs than to reflect the arrival of the Huns in the mid- to late fourth century, the period represented by D1 and D2 material. Though new elements are introduced, other characteristic elements (pottery, brooches, building structures) of the earlier periods continue to be found. These new elements are only found on some sites, for example, Conçesti, which are then defined as Hunnic.

Other sites, contemporary with SdM and 'Hunnic' sites, but without such 'nomadic' artefacts, are classified as Bratei culture sites. The dominant burial rite was cremation culture, dating from the second half of the fourth century and lasting until the early sixth century. On early sites there is considerable continuity with sites of the SdM culture, particularly in the pottery. Settlements were of a rural character, unfortified, based on a mixed economy of agriculture, pastoralism, and artisans. Sites in Moldavia include Botoşana and Costişa-Manoaia, in Oltenia, Dodeşti (Vaçlui) and Cazaneşti. There was some overlap in the late fourth to early fifth century in Moldavia and Wallachia with sites of the SdM culture. Building types were sunken-floored huts and surface dwellings, with clay-coated floors and wattle-and-daub walls.[11]

The impression from this sketchy examination of the material is the lack

R. Harhoiu, 'Chronologischen Fragen der Völkerwanderungszeit in Rumanien', *Dacia*, 34 (1990), 169–208; J. Tejral, 'Zur chronologie der frühen Völkerwanderungszeit im mittleren Donauraum', *Archaeologia Austriaca*, 72 (1988), 223–304.

[9] 'continuous discontinuity', Batty, 'Peoples', p. viii; continuity, V. Bierbrauer, 'Zur chronologischen', *Die Volker an der mittleren und unteren Donau im fünften und sechsten Jahrhunderts* (1980), 131–42; G. Teodor, *The East Carpathian Area of Romania* (Oxford, 1980), 5; R. Harhoiu, 'Aspects of the Socio-Political Situation in Transylvania during the Fifth Century', in Constantinescu, ed., *Relations*, but with no sources mentioned; Kazanski, *Les Goths*, 73.

[10] Kettles are rare in Europe, especially from cemeteries of settlements; Bona, *Das Hunnenreich*, 140–6; O. Maenchen-Helfen, *The World of the Huns* (Berkeley, Calif., 1973), 337–54, rejects mirrors as solely Hunnic.

[11] Teodor, *East Carpathian Area*; E. Zaharia, 'Données sur l'archéologie des IVᵉ– XIᵉ siècles sur le territoire de la Roumanie', *Dacia*, NS 15 (1971), 269–88.

of change in way of life during the fourth and fifth centuries. Though dramatic political changes took place, they left little impact on the economic archaeology of the region. There is change in the material, but any arguments for precise identification of political units seem unfounded. The prevalent identification of particular cultures seems unhelpful and more useful would be an expansion of Godlowski's C/D/E sequences. If the arguments about the structure of these societies as presented in Chapter 1 are accepted, this is not surprising—environmental conditions meant that few significant variations in subsistence strategies were possible, while political changes occurred principally at élite levels, not transforming the lives of most of the population.

BIBLIOGRAPHY

PRIMARY SOURCES

Further details of sources marked with an asterisk are found in Appendix 1.

Acta Maximiliani, ed. H. A. Musurillo, *The Acts of the Christian Martyrs* (Oxford, 1972).

Additamenta ad Chronica Prosperi Hauniensis, ed. T. Mommsen, *MGH AA* 9 (Berlin, 1892).

Agathias, *Histories*, ed. R. Keydell (Berlin, 1967).

Ambrose, *Epistulae*, ed. J. P. Migne, *PL* 16.

—— *Expositio in Psalmum 118*, ed. J. P. Migne, *PL* 15.

Ammianus Marcellinus, *Res Gestae*, ed. J. C. Rolfe (London, 1935–9).

Anglo-Saxon Chronicle, ed. D. Whitelock, *English Historical Documents²*, i (London, 1977).

Annales Ravennae, ed. B. Bischoff, *Medieval Studies in Memory of A. Kingsley Porter* (Cambridge, Mass., 1939).

Anonymous, *De Rebus Bellicis*, ed. R. I. Ireland (Leipzig, 1982)*.

Anonymous, *Peri Strategikes*, ed. G. T. Dennis, *Three Byzantine Military Treatises* (Washington, DC, 1985)*.

Anonymus Valesianus, ed. J. C. Rolfe, *Ammianus Marcellinus*, iii (London, 1939).

Athanasius, *Apologia ad Constantium*, ed. J. P. Migne, *PG* 25.

Auctarium Prosperi Hauniensis, ed. T. Mommsen, *MGH AA* 9 (Berlin, 1892).

Augustine, *Contra Epistulam Parmeniani*, *CSEL* 51.

—— *De Civitate Dei*, ed. B. Dombart (Leipzig, 1887).

—— *Epistulae*, *PL* 33.

Aurelius Victor, *De Caesaribus*, ed. F. Pichlmayer and R. Gründel (Leipzig, 1966).

Ausonius, *Opera*, ed. H. G. Evelyn White (London, 1919–21).

Bede, *Historia Ecclesiae*, eds. B. Colgrave and R. A. B. Mynors (Oxford, 1969).

Beowulf, tr. M. Alexander (Harmondsworth, 1973).

Candidus, *History*, ed. R. C. Blockley, *Fragmentary Classicising Historians of the Later Roman Empire*, ii (Liverpool, 1983).

Cassiodorus, *Chronica*, ed. T. Mommsen, *MGH AA* 11 (Berlin, 1894).

—— *Variae*, ed. T. Mommsen, *MGH AA* 12 (Berlin, 1894).
Chronica Galliae ad 452, ed. T. Mommsen, *MGH AA* 9 (Berlin, 1892).
Chronica Galliae ad 511, ed. T. Mommsen, *MGH AA* 9 (Berlin, 1892).
Chronicon Paschale, ed. T. Mommsen, *MGH AA* 9 (Berlin, 1892).
Claudian, *Opera*, ed. M. Platnauer (London, 1922).
Codex Justinianus, ed. P. Krüger (Berlin, 1877).
Codex Theodosianus, ed. T. Mommsen (Berlin, 1905).
Constantine Porphyrogenitus, *de Caeremoniis*, ed. A. Vogt (Paris, 1935–40).
—— *De Administrando Imperii*, ed. G. Moravcsik (Budapest, 1949).
Constantius, *V. Germani*, ed. R. Borius (Paris, 1965).
Corpus Papyrorum Raineri, ed. C. Wessely (Vienna, 1895).
Cyril of Scythopolis, *V. Sabae*, ed. E. Schwartz, *Texte und Untersuchungen*, 49/2.
Dexippus, *History*, ed. C. Müller, *FHG* 3 (Paris, 1849).
Digest, ed. T. Mommsen (Berlin, 1870).
Dio (Cassius Dio Cocceianus), *History*, ed. E. Cary (London, 1914–27).
Ennodius, *V. Epiphanii*, ed. F. Vogel, *MGH AA* 7 (Berlin, 1885).
Eugippius, *V. Severini*, ed. H. Sauppe, *MGH AA* 1/2 (Berlin, 1877).
Eunapius, *History*, ed. R. C. Blockley, *Fragmentary Classicising Historians of the Later Roman Empire*, ii (Liverpool, 1983).
Eusebius, fr., ed. C. Müller, *FHG* 5 (Paris, 1883).
Eusebius, *Ecclesiastical History*, ed. G. Bardy (Paris, 1952–60).
Eutropius, *Breviarium*, ed. F. Rühl (Leipzig, 1887).
Evagrius, *Historia Ecclesiastica*, ed. J. Bidez and L. Parmentier (London, 1898).
Expositio Totius Mundi et Gentium, ed. J. Rougé (Paris, 1966).
Fasti Vindobonenses Priores, ed. T. Mommsen, *MGH AA* 9 (Berlin, 1892).
Gregory Nazianzus, *Orationes*, ed. J. P. Migne, *PG 35*.
—— *Epistulae*, ed. J. P. Migne, *PG 37*.
Gregory of Tours, *Vita Patrum*, ed. W. Arndt and B. Krusch, *MGH SRM* 1 (Berlin, 1885).
—— *Historia Francorum*, ed. W. Arndt and B. Krusch, *MGH SRM* 1/1 (Hanover, 1884).
Herodian, *History*, ed. C. R. Whittaker (London, 1969–70).
Historia Augusta, ed. D. Magie (London, 1921–32).
Hydatius, *Chronicle*, ed. T. Mommsen, *MGH AA* 11 (Berlin, 1894).
Ine, *Laws*, ed. D. Whitelock, *English Historical Documents*[2], i (London, 1977).
Jerome, *Adversus Iovinianum*, ed. J. P. Migne, *PL 23*.
—— *Chronicon*, *PL 27*.
—— *Commentaria in Danielem*, *PL 25*.

Jerome, *Epistulae, CSEL* 54–6.

—— *V. Hilarionis*, ed. J. P. Migne, *PL* 23.

John Chrysostom, *Ad Stagyrum*, ed. J. P. Migne, *PG* 47.

John of Antioch, *Chronicle*, ed. C. Müller, *FHG* 4–5 (Paris, 1851).

Jordanes, *Opera*, ed. T. Mommsen, *MGH AA* 5 (Berlin, 1882).

Julian, *Opera*, ed. W. C. Wright (London, 1913–23).

Julianus, *Historia Wambae*, eds. B. Krusch and W. Levison, *MGH SRM* 5 (Hanover, 1910).

Laterculus Veronensis, ed. O. Seeck, *Notitia Dignitatum* (Frankfurt, 1876).

Lex Ribuariae, ed. F. Beyerle and R. Buchner, *MGH, Leges* 3/2 (Hanover, 1954).

Libanius, *Opera*, ed. R. Förster (Leipzig, 1903–23).

Lydus, *De Magistratibus*, ed. A. C. Bandy (Philadelphia, 1983).

Malalas, *Chronicle*, ed. L. Dindorf (Bonn, 1831).

Malchus, *History*, ed. R. C. Blockley, *Fragmentary Classicising Historians of the Later Roman Empire*, ii (Liverpool, 1983).

Marcellinus Comes, *Chronicon*, ed. T. Mommsen, *MGH AA* 11 (Berlin, 1894).

Mauricius, *Strategikon*, ed. G. T. Dennis, *Das Strategikon des Maurikios* (Vienna, 1981)*.

Maximus of Turin, *Opera*, ed. J. P. Migne, *PL* 57.

Menander, ed. R. C. Blockley, *The History of Menander the Guardsman* (Liverpool, 1985).

Merobaudes, *Opera*, ed. F. M. Clover, *Transactions of the American Philosophical Society*, 61/1 (1971).

Muirchu, *V. Patriciae*, ed. A. B. E. Hood, *St. Patrick* (London, 1978).

Notitia Dignitatum, ed. O. Seeck (Frankfurt, 1876)*.

Novellae, ed. P. M. Meyer (Berlin, 1905).

Olympiodorus, *History*, ed. R. C. Blockley, *Fragmentary Classicising Historians of the Later Roman Empire*, ii (Liverpool, 1983).

Orientius, ed. J. P. Migne, *PL* 61.

Orosius, *Historiarum Adversus Paganos Libri Septem*, ed. C. Zangemeister (Vienna, 1882).

P. Abinn., ed. H. I. Bell *et al.*, *The Abinnaeus Archive* (Oxford, 1962).

P. Beatty Panop., ed. T. C. Skeatt, *Papyri from Panopolis* (Dublin, 1964).

P. Cairo, ed. J. Maspero, *Catalogue générale du Musée du Cairo* (Cairo, 1911–16).

P. Ital., ed. J. O. Tjäder, *Die nichtliterarischen lateinischen Papyri Italiens aus der Zeit 445–700* (Lund, 1955).

P. Lips., ed. L. Mitteis, *Griechische Urkunden der Papyrussammlung zu Leipzig* (Leipzig, 1906).

P. Monac, ed. A. Heisenberg and L. Wenger, *Byzantinische Papyri* (Leipzig and Berlin, 1914).

P. Nessana, ed. C. J. Kraemer, *Excavations at Nessana*, iii (Princeton, NJ, 1958).

Pactus Legis Salicae, ed. K. Eckhardt, *MGH Leges*, 4/1 (Hanover, 1962).

Palladius, *Dialogus*, ed. P. R. Coleman-Norton (Cambridge, 1928).

Panegyrici Latini, ed. E. Galletier (Paris, 1949–55).

Passio Sanctae Sabae, ed. H. Delehaye, *Analecta Bollandiana*, 31 (1912).

Patrick, *Confessio*, ed. A. B. E. Hood, *St. Patrick* (London, 1978).

Paul the Deacon, *Historia Langobardorum*, eds. L. Bethmann and G. Waitz, *MGH Scriptores Rerum Langobardorum* (Hanover, 1878).

Paulinus, *V. Ambrosii*, *PL* 14.

Paulinus of Nola, *Epistulae*, *CSEL* 29.

Paulinus of Pella, *Eucharisticus*, ed. H. G. Evelyn White, *Ausonius*, ii (London, 1921).

Petrus Patricius, fr., ed. C. Müller, *FHG* 4 (Paris, 1851).

Philostorgius, *Historia Ecclesiastica*, ed. J. Bidez (Leipzig, 1913).

Possidius, ed. M. Pellegrino (Rome, 1956).

Priscus, *History*, ed. R. C. Blockley, *Fragmentary Classicising Historians of the Later Roman Empire*, ii (Liverpool, 1983).

Procopius, *Opera*, ed. H. B. Dewing (London, 1914–40).

Prosper, *Epitoma Chronicon*, ed. T. Mommsen, *MGH AA* 9 (Berlin, 1892).

Pseudo-Augustine, *Epistulae*, ed. J. P. Migne, *PL* 33.

Renatus Profuturus Frigeridus, in Gregory of Tours, *Historia Francorum**.

Rutilius Namatianus, *de Reditu Suo*, ed. J. Vessereau and F. Préchae (Paris, 1961).

Salvian, *de Gubernatione Dei*, ed. C. Helm, *MGH AA* 1 (Berlin, 1877).

Severus, *V. Martini*, ed. J. Fontaine (Paris, 1967–9).

Sidonius Apollinaris, *Opera*, ed. W. B. Anderson (London, 1936).

Sirmondian Constitutions = Codex Theodosianus.

Socrates, *PG* 67.

Sozomen, *Historia Ecclesiastica*, eds. J. Bidez and G. C. Hansen, *Griechische Schriften*, 50 (1960).

Suda, ed. A. Adler (Leipzig, 1928–35).

Sulpicius Alexander, in Gregory of Tours, *Historia Francorum**.

Symmachus, *Opera*, ed. O. Seeck, *MGH AA* 6 (Berlin, 1883).

Synesius, ed. J. P. Migne, *PG* 66.

Syrianus, ed. A. Dain, *Naumachica* (Paris, 1943)*.

Themistius, *Orations*, ed. G. Downey and A. F. Norman (Leipzig, 1965–74).

Theoderet, *Ecclesiastical History*, ed. L. Parmentier, *Greichische Schriften*, 84 (Berlin, 1911).

——*Epistulae*, ed. Y. Azema (Paris, 1955).

Theophanes, *Chronographia*, ed. C. de Boor (Hildesheim, 1883).
Theophylact, *History*, ed. C. de Boor (Leipzig, 1887).
Urbicius, *Epitedeuma*, ed. H. Mihaescu, *Arta Militară* (Bucharest, 1970)*.
V. Remigii, ed. B. Krusch, *MGH SRM* 3 (Hanover, 1890).
Vegetius, *De Re Militari*, ed. C. Lang (Leipzig, 1885)*.
Victor Tonnensis, *Chronicle*, ed. T. Mommsen, *MGH AA* 11 (Berlin, 1894).
Victor Vitensis, *Historia Persecutionis Africanae Provinciae*, ed. M. Pet-schenig (Bonn, 1881).
Vita Danielis Stylitae, ed. H. Delehaye, *Analecta Bollandiana* 32 (1913).
Zosimus, *New History*, ed. L. Mendelssohn (Leipzig, 1887).

SECONDARY SOURCES

Admiralty Handbook, Naval Intelligence Division, *France* (London, 1942).
—— *Yugoslavia* (London, 1945).
Alcock, L., *Arthur's Britain* (London, 1971).
—— 'A Survey of Pictish Settlement and Archaeology', in J. G. P. Friell and W. G. Watson, eds., *Pictish Studies*, *BAR* 125 (Oxford, 1984), 7–41.
Alföldi, A., 'The Moral Barrier on the Rhine and Danube', in E. Birley, ed., *The Congress of Roman Frontier Studies* (Durham, 1952), 1–16.
Altheim, F., *Geschichte der Hunnen* (Berlin, 1959–62).
Anderson, P., *Passages from Antiquity to Feudalism* (London, 1974).
Anton, H. H., 'Trier im Übergang von der Römische zur frankischen Herrschaft', *Francia*, 10 (1982), 1–52.
Austin, N. J. E., 'In Support of Ammianus' Veracity', *Historia*, 22 (1973), 331–5.
—— *Ammianus on Warfare* (Brussels, 1979).
Baatz, D., 'Recent Finds of Ancient Artillery', *Britannia*, 9 (1978), 1–17.
Baldwin, B., 'On the Date of the Anonymous *Peri Strategikes*', *Byzantinische Zeitschrift*, 81 (1988), 290–3.
Balthy, J. C., 'Apamea in the Second and Third Centuries AD', *JRS* 78 (1988), 91–104.
Banchich, T. M., 'Eunapius and Jerome', *GRBS* 27 (1981), 319–24.
Barker, P. A., 'The Plumbatae from Wroxeter', in M. W. Hassall and R. I. Ireland, eds., *De Rebus Bellicis*, *BAR* S63 (Oxford, 1979), 97–100.
Barnes, T. D., 'The Date of Vegetius', *Phoenix*, 33 (1979), 254–7.
Barnish, S. J. B., 'Taxation, Land and Barbarian Settlement in the Western Empire', *PBSR* 54 (1986), 170–95.
Barrett, J. C., Fitzpatrick, A. P., and Macinnes, L., eds., *Barbarians and Romans in North-West Europe*, *BAR* S471 (Oxford, 1989).

Bartholomew, P., 'Fourth-Century Saxons', *Britannia*, 15 (1984), 169–85.

Batty, R., 'The Peoples of the Lower Danube and Rome', D. Phil. thesis (Oxford, 1990).

Bayard, D., and Piton, D., 'Un bâtiment public du bas-Empire à Amiens', *Cahiers Archéologiques du Picardie*, 6 (1979), 153–68.

Bayless, W. N., 'Anti-Germanism in the Age of Stilicho', *Byzantine Studies*, 32 (1976), 70–6.

Baynes, N. H., 'A Note of Interrogation', *Byzantion*, 2 (1925), 149–51.

Becatti, G., *La Colonna Coclide Istoriata* (Rome, 1960).

Beckhoff, K., 'Die eigenzeitlichen Kriegsbogen von Nydam', *Offa*, 20 (1963), 39–48.

Beisel, F., *Studien zu den fränkischen-römischen Beziehungen* (Idstein, 1987).

Bell, H. I., Martin, V., Turner, E. G., and Van Berchem, D., eds., *The Abinnaeus Archive* (Oxford, 1962).

Bennett, J., 'Plumbatae from Pistunda (Pitsyus), Georgia', *Journal of Roman Military Equipment Studies*, 2 (1991), 59–63.

Bianchi Bandinelli, R., *Hellenistic-Byzantine Miniatures of the Iliad* (Olten, 1955).

Bichir, G., *Archaeology and History of the Carpi*, *BAR* S16 (Oxford, 1976).

Bierbrauer, V., 'Zur chronologischen, sozialischen und regionalen Glie-derung des ostgermanischen Fundstoffs des 5. Jahrhunderts in Südosteuropa', *Die Volker an der mittleren und unteren Donau im fünften und sechsten Jahrhunderts* (*Österreichische Akademie der Wissenschafte, Phil. Hist. Kl. Denkschriften 145*) (1980), 131–42.

Birley, A. R., 'Vindolanda: New Writing Tablets 1986–1989', in V. A. Maxfield and M. J. Dawson, eds., *Roman Frontier Studies 1989* (Exeter, 1991), 16–20.

Birley, E., 'Local Militias in the Roman Empire', *The Roman Army*, *MAVORS* 4 (Amsterdam, 1988), 387–94.

Bitter, N., *Kampfschilderungen bei Ammianus Marcellinus* (Bonn, 1976).

Blazquez, J. M., 'The Rejection and Assimilation of Roman Culture in Hispania during the Fourth and Fifth Centuries', *Classical Folia*, 32 (1978), 217–42.

Blockley, R. C., 'Dexippus, Priscus and the Thucydidean Account of the Siege of Plataea', *Phoenix*, 26 (1972), 18–27.

Bloşiu, C., 'Necropola dia secolul al 4-lea e. n. de la Letçani (jud. Iaşi)', *Arheologia Moldovei*, 8 (1975), 203–80.

Boak, A. E. R., *Manpower Shortage and the Fall of the Roman Empire* (London, 1955).

Böhme, H., *Germanische Grabfunde des 4 bis 5 Jahrhunderts zwischen unterer Elbe und Loire* (Munich, 1974).

Bona, I., *Das Hunnenreich* (Stuttgart, 1991).

Boura, M., 'Le mura medievale di Aquileia', *Antichita Altoadriatico*, 32 (1988), 323–63.

Bowman, A. K., and Thomas, J. D., 'Vindolanda 1985: The New Writing Tablets', *JRS* 76 (1986), 120–3.

Braund, D., *Rome and the Friendly King* (London, 1984).

—— 'Client Kings', D. Braund, ed., *The Administration of the Roman Empire*, (Exeter, 1988), 69–96.

—— 'Ideology, Subsidies and Trade: The King on the Northern Frontier Revisited', in J. C. Barrett *et al.*, eds., *Barbarians and Romans in North-West Europe*, *BAR* S471 (Oxford, 1989), 14–26.

Brennan, P., 'Combined Legionary Detachments as Artillery Units in Late Roman Danubian Bridgehead Dispositions', *Chiron*, 10 (1980), 553–67.

Brok, M. F. A., 'Ein spätrömischer Brandpfeil nach Ammianus', *Saalburg Jahrbuch* 35 (1978), 57–60.

Brown, P., *The World of Late Antiquity* (London, 1971).

Burgess, R. W., 'A New Reading for Hydatius Chronicle 177 and the Defeat of the Huns in Italy', *Phoenix*, 42 (1988), 357–63.

Burns, T. S., 'The Germans and Roman Frontier Policy, *ca* AD 350–378', *Arheološki Vestnik*, 30 (1981), 390–404.

—— *A History of the Ostrogoths* (Bloomington, Ind., 1984).

—— 'The Settlement of 418', in J. F. Drinkwater and H. W. Elton, eds., *Fifth-Century Gaul: A Crisis of Identity?* (Cambridge, 1992), 64–74.

Butler, R. M., 'Late Roman Town Walls in Gaul', *Archaeological Journal*, 66 (1959), 25–50.

Cameron, A. D. E., *Claudian* (Oxford, 1970).

—— review of Syme, *Ammianus and the Historia Augusta*, *JRS* 61 (1971), 255–67.

—— 'The Date of the Anonymous', in M. W. Hassall and R. I. Ireland, eds., *De Rebus Bellicis*, *BAR* S63 (Oxford, 1979), 1–11.

—— and Cameron, A. M., 'Christianity and Tradition in the Historiography of the Late Empire', *CQ* NS 14 (1964), 316–28.

Cameron, A. M., *Procopius* (London, 1985).

Campbell, D. B., 'Auxiliary Artillery Revisited', *BJ* 186 (1986), 117–32.

Campbell, J. B., *The Emperor and the Roman Army* (Oxford, 1984).

—— 'Teach Yourself how to be a General', *JRS* 77 (1987), 13–29.

Casson, L., *Ships and Seamanship in the Ancient World* (Princeton, NJ, 1971).

Cecchelli, C., *I mosaici della basilica di S. Maria Maggiore* (Turin, 1956).

Christie, N., 'The Alps as a Frontier', *JRA* 4 (1991), 410–30.

—— and Gibson, S., 'The City Walls of Ravenna', *PBSR* 56 (1988), 156–97.

—— and Rushworth, A., 'Urban Fortification and Defensive Strategy in

Fifth and Sixth Century Italy: The Case of Terracina', *JRA* 1 (1988), 73–88.

Clauss, M., *Der Magister Officiorum in der Spätantike* (Munich, 1980).

Clover, F. M., 'Geiseric and Attila', *Historia*, 22 (1973), 104–17.

Collis, J., review of Cunliffe, *Greeks, Romans and Barbarians*, *Antiquity* 62 (1988), 805.

Constantinescu, M., Pascu, S., and Diaconu, P., eds., *Relations between the Autochthonous Populations and the Migratory Populations on the Territory of Romania* (Bucharest, 1975).

Cooper, P. W., 'The Third-Century Origins of the "New" Roman Army', D. Phil. thesis (Oxford, 1968).

Couissin, P., *Les Armes romaines* (Paris, 1926).

Coulston, J. C., 'Roman Archery Equipment', in M. C. Bishop, ed., *The Production and Distribution of Roman Military Equipment*, *BAR* S275, (Oxford, 1985), 220–366.

—— 'Roman, Parthian and Sassanid Tactical Developments', in P. W. Freeman and D. L. Kennedy, eds., *Defence of the Roman and Byzantine East*, *BAR* S297 (Oxford, 1986), 59–75.

—— 'Roman Military Equipment on Third-Century Tombstones', in M. Dawson, ed., *The Accoutrements of War*, *BAR* S336 (Oxford, 1987), 141–56.

—— 'The Value of Trajan's Column as a Source for Military Equipment', in C. van Driel-Murray, ed., *Roman Military Equipment: The Sources of Evidence*, *BAR* S476 (Oxford, 1989), 31–44.

—— 'Later Roman Armour, 3rd–6th Centuries AD', *Journal of Roman Military Equipment Studies*, 1 (1990), 139–60.

Courtois, C., *Les Vandales et l'Afrique* (Paris, 1955).

Cribb, R., *Nomads in Archaeology* (Cambridge, 1991).

Croke, B., 'Mundo the Gepid: From Freebooter to Roman General', *Chiron*, 12 (1982), 125–35.

Crow, J. G., 'The Function of Hadrian's Wall and the Comparative Evidence of Late Roman Long Walls', in W. S. Hanson and L. J. F. Keppie, eds., *Roman Frontier Studies, 1979*, *BAR* S71 (Oxford, 1980), 724–9.

Crumlin-Pedersen, O., 'The Boats and Ships of the Angles and Saxons', in S. McGrail, ed., *Maritime Celts, Frisians and Saxons*, *CBA Research Report* 71 (London, 1990), 98–116.

Crump, G. A., 'Ammianus and the Late Roman Army', *Historia*, 22 (1973), 91–103.

—— *Ammianus Marcellinus as a Military Historian*, *Historia Einzelschriften*, 27 (Wiesbaden, 1975).

Cumont, F., 'Fragment de bouclier portant une liste d'étapes', *Syria*, 6 (1925), 1–15.

Cunliffe, B., *Greeks, Romans and Barbarians* (London, 1988).

Curle, A. O., *The Treasure of Traprain* (Glasgow, 1923).

Dahl, G., and Hjort, A., *Having Herds* (Stockholm, 1976).

Dain, A., 'Les Stratégistes Byzantins', *Travaux et Mémoires*, 2 (1967), 317–92.

Deichmann, F. W., *Frühchristliche Bauten und Mosaike von Ravenna* (Baden-Baden, 1958).

Delbrück, R., *Spätantike Kaiserporträts* (Berlin, 1933).

Demandt, A., 'Magister Militum', *RE* Suppl. 12 (1970), 553–788.

Demougeot, E., *La Formation de l'Europe et les invasions barbares* (Paris, 1979).

Dennis, G. T., 'Flies, Mice and the Byzantine Crossbow', *Byzantine and Modern Greek Studies*, 7 (1981), 1–5.

de Ste Croix, G. E. M., *The Class Struggle in the Ancient Greek World* (London, 1981).

De Wit, J., *Die Miniaturen des Vergilius Vaticanus* (Amsterdam, 1959).

Diaconu, G., 'On the Socio-Economic Relations between Natives and Goths in Dacia', in M. Constantinescu *et al.*, eds., *Relations between the Autochthonous Populations and the Migratory Populations on the Territory of Romania* (Bucharest, 1975), 67–75.

Diesener, H.-J., 'Das Buccelariertum von Stilicho und Sarus bis auf Aetius', *Klio*, 54 (1972), 321–50.

Dirlmaier, C., and Gottlieb, G., eds., *Quellen zur Geschichte der Alamannen* (Heidelberg, 1976).

Dittrich, U.-B., *Die Beziehungen Roms zu den Sarmaten und Quaden im vierten Jahrhundert n. Chr.* (Bonn, 1984).

Dixon, K. R., and Southern, P., *The Roman Cavalry* (London, 1992).

Dorigo, W., *Late Roman Painting* (New York, 1971).

Dornier, A., 'Was there a Coastal Limes of Western Britain in the Fourth Century?', in S. Applebaum, ed., *Roman Frontier Studies*, 7 (Tel Aviv, 1971), 14–20.

Drew-Bear, T., 'A Late-Fourth Century Latin Soldier's Epitaph at Nakolea', *HSCP* 81 (1977), 257–74.

Drinkwater, J. F., and Elton, H. W., eds., *Fifth-Century Gaul: A Crisis of Identity?* (Cambridge, 1992).

Dumville, D., 'Sub-Roman Britain: History and Legend', *History*, 62 (1977), 173–92.

Dunbabin, K. M. D., *The Mosaics of Roman North Africa* (Oxford, 1978).

Duncan-Jones, R. P., *Structure and Scale in the Roman Economy* (Cambridge, 1990).

Eadie, J. W., 'The Development of Roman Mailed Cavalry', *JRS* 57 (1967), 161–73.

Elbern, S., *Usurpationen im spätrömischen Reich* (Bonn, 1984).
—— 'Die Gotenmassaker in Kleinasien', *Hermes* 115 (1987), 99–106.
Elton, H. W., 'The Defence of Gaul', in J. F. Drinkwater and H. W. Elton, eds., *Fifth-Century Gaul: A Crisis of Identity?* (Cambridge, 1992), 167–76.
Engels, D. W., *Alexander the Great and the Logistics of the Macedonian Army* (London, 1977).
Evans, J., 'Settlement and Society in North-East England in the Fourth Century', in P. R. Wilson *et al.*, eds., *Settlement and Society in the Roman North* (Bradford, 1984), 43–8.
Feffer, L. C., and Perin, P., *Les Francs* (Paris, 1987).
Ferrua, A., *Le pittura della nuova Catacomba di Via Latina* (Vatican, 1960).
Fink, R. O., *Roman Military Records on Papyrus* (Cleveland, 1971).
Finley, M. I., review of A. E. R. Boak, *Manpower Shortage*, *JRS* 48 (1958), 157–64.
Förster, R., 'Studien zu den griechischen Taktikern: II. Kaiser Hadrien und der Taktika des Urbicius', *Hermes*, 12 (1877), 449–71.
Fragmenta Virgiliana (Cod. Vat. Lat. 3225) (Vatican, n.d.).
Frank, R. I., *Scholae Palatinae* (Rome, 1969).
Freeman, P. W., review of J. C. Barrett *et al.*, eds., *Barbarians and Romans*, *Scottish Archaeological Review* 8 (1991), 133–6.
Freshfield, G. H., 'Notes on a Vellum Album', *Archaeologia*, 62 (1921–2), 87–104.
Frézouls, E., 'Les Deux Politiques de Rome fâce aux barbares d'après Ammien Marcellin', in E. Frézouls, ed., *Crise et redressement dans les provinces Européenes de l'empire* (Strasbourg, 1983), 175–91.
Friell, J. G. P., and Watson, W. G., eds., *Pictish Studies*, *BAR* 125 (Oxford, 1984).
Gale, D. A., 'The Seax', in S. C. Hawkes, ed., *Weapons and Warfare in Anglo-Saxon England* (Oxford, 1989), 71–83.
Gauld, W. W., 'Vegetius on Roman Scout-Boats', *Antiquity*, 64 (1990), 402–6.
Germanen, Hunnen, Awaren (Nuremberg, 1987).
Giglioli, G. O., *La colonna di Arcadio a Constantinopoli* (Naples, 1952).
Goffart, W., 'The Date and Purpose of Vegetius' *De Re Militari*', *Traditio*, 33 (1977), 65–100.
—— *Barbarians and Romans* (Princeton, NJ, 1980).
—— 'Rome, Constantinople and the Barbarians', *AHR* 86 (1981), 275–306.
Goodburn, R., and Bartholomew, P., eds., *Aspects of the Notitia Dignitatum*, *BAR* S15 (Oxford, 1976).
Gordon, C. D., 'Subsidies in Roman Imperial Defence', *Phoenix*, 3 (1949), 60–9.

Gordon, D. H., 'Fire and Sword', *Antiquity*, 27 (1953), 144–52.

Griffiths, W. B., 'The Sling and its Place in the Roman Imperial Army', in C. van Driel-Murray, ed., *Roman Military Equipment: The Sources of Evidence*, *BAR* S476 (Oxford, 1989), 255–79.

Grigg, R., 'Inconsistency and Lassitude: The Shield Emblems of the *Notitia Dignitatum*', *JRS* 73 (1983), 132–42.

Grosse, R., *Römische Militärgeschichte* (Berlin, 1920).

Gundel, H. G., *Untersuchungen zur Taktik und Strategie der Germanen nach den antiken Quellen* (Marburg, 1937).

—— 'Die Bedeutung des Geländes in der Kriegkunst der Germanen', *Neue Jahrbücher für Antike und Deutsche Bildung*, 3 (1940), 188–96.

Günther, R., 'Laeti, foederati und Gentilen in Nord- und Nordost Gallien im zussamenhang der sogennanten Laetizivilisation', *Zeitschrift für Archäologie*, 5 (1971), 39–59.

Haarnagel, W., *Die Grabungen Feddersen Wierde²* (Wiesbaden, 1979).

Hagberg, U. E., *The Marsh of Skedemosse* (Stockholm, 1967).

Haldon, J. F., 'Some Aspects of Byzantine Military Technology from the Sixth to the Tenth Centuries', *Byzantine and Modern Greek Studies*, 1 (1975), 11–47.

Halsall, G., 'The Origins of the Reihengräberzivilisation: Forty Years on', in J. F. Drinkwater and H. W. Elton, eds., *Fifth-Century Gaul: A Crisis of Identity?* (Cambridge, 1992), 196–207.

Hanson, V. D., *Warfare and Agriculture in Classical Greece* (Pisa, 1983).

Hardy, R., *Longbow* (Cambridge, 1976).

Harhoiu, R., 'Aspects of the Socio-Political Situation in Transylvania during the Fifth Century', in M. Constantinescu *et al.*, eds., *Relations between the Autochthonous Population and the Migratory Populations on the Territory of Romania* (Bucharest, 1975), 99–109.

—— 'Chronologischen Fragen der Völkerwanderungszeit in Rumanien', *Dacia*, 34 (1990), 169–208.

Hassall, M. W., and Ireland, R. I., eds., *De Rebus Bellicis*, *BAR* S63 (Oxford, 1979).

Haüsler, A., 'Zu den sozialökonomischen Verhältnissen in der Černjakhov-Kultur', *Zeitschrift für Archäologie*, 13 (1979), 23–65.

Hawkes, S. C., 'Some Recent Finds of Late Roman Buckles', *Britannia*, 5 (1974), 386–93.

—— and Dunning, G. C., 'Soldiers and Settlers in Britain, Fourth to Fifth Centuries', *Medieval Archaeology*, 5 (1961), 1–70.

Haywood, J., *Dark Age Naval Power* (London, 1991).

Heather, P. J., 'The Anti-Scythian Tirade of Synesius' *De Regno*', *Phoenix*, 42 (1988), 152–72.

—— 'Cassiodorus and the Rise of the Amals: Genealogy and the Goths under Hun Domination', *JRS* 79 (1989), 103–28.

—— *Goths and Romans, 332–489* (Oxford, 1991).

—— 'The Emergence of the Visigothic Kingdom', in J. F. Drinkwater and H. W. Elton, eds., *Fifth-Century Gaul: A Crisis of Identity?* (Cambridge, 1992), 84–94.

—— and Matthews, J. F., eds., *The Goths in the Fourth Century* (Liverpool, 1991).

Heege, A., *Grabfunde der Merowingerzeit aus Heidenheim-Grosskuchen* (Stuttgart, 1987).

Helm, R., 'Untersuchungen über den auswärtigen diplomatischen Verkehr des römische Reiches im Zeitalter der Spätantike', *Archiv für Urkundenforschung*, 12 (1931–2), 375–436.

Hendy, M. F., *Studies in the Byzantine Monetary Economy, c300–1450* (Cambridge, 1985).

Hines, J., 'The Military Context of the *adventus saxonum*: Some Continental Evidence', in S. C. Hawkes, ed., *Weapons and Warfare in Anglo-Saxon England* (Oxford, 1989), 25–48.

HMSO, *Manual of Horsemanship* (London, 1937).

Hobley, J., and Maloney, B., eds., *Roman Urban Defences in the West* (London, 1983).

Höckmann, O., 'Rheinschiffe aus der Zeit Ammianus: neue Funde in Mainz', *Antike Welt*, 13/3 (1982), 40–7.

Hodges, R., *Dark Age Economics* (London, 1982).

Hoffmann, D., *Das spätrömische Bewegungsheer und die Notitia Dignitatum* (Düsseldorf, 1969).

—— 'Wadomar, Bacurius und Hariulf', *Museum Helveticum*, 35 (1981), 307–18.

Hohlfelder, R. L., 'Marcian's Gamble: A Reassessment of Eastern Imperial Policy towards Attila, AD 450–453', *American Journal of Ancient History*, 9/1 (1984), 54–69.

Hole, F., 'Pastoral Nomadism in Western Iran', in R. A. Gould, ed., *Explorations in Ethnoarchaeology* (Albuquerque, 1978), 127–67.

Hyland, A., *Equus* (London, 1990), 71–86.

Ilias Ambrosiana (Berne, 1953).

Ionita, I., 'Contributii cu privire la cultura Sîntana de Mureş-Černeahov pe teritoriul Republicii Socialistii România', *Arheologia Moldovei*, 4 (1966), 189–259.

—— 'The Social-Economic Structure of Society during the Goths' Migration in the Carpatho-Danubian Area', in M. Constantinescu *et al.*, eds., *Relations between the Autochthonous Populations and the Migratory Populations on the Territory of Romania* (Bucharest, 1975), 77–89.

Isaac, B., 'The Meaning of the Terms *Limes* and *Limitanei*', *JRS* 78 (1988), 125–47.

—— *The Limits of Empire* (Oxford, 1990).

James, E., 'Cemeteries and the Problem of Frankish Settlement in Gaul', in P. H. Sawyer, ed., *Names, Words, and Graves* (Leeds, 1979), 55–89.

—— *The Franks* (Oxford, 1988).

James, S., 'Britain and the Late Roman Army', in T. F. C. Blagg and A. C. King, eds., *Military and Civilian in Roman Britain*, *BAR* 136 (Oxford, 1984), 161–86.

—— 'Evidence from Dura-Europos for the Origins of Late Roman Helmets', *Syria*, 63 (1986), 107–34.

—— 'The *Fabricae*', in J. C. Coulston, ed., *Military Equipment and the Identity of Roman Soldiers*, *BAR* S394 (Oxford, 1988), 257–331.

Johnson, A., *Roman Forts* (London, 1983).

Johnson, S., *The Roman Forts of the Saxon Shore* (London, 1976).

—— 'A Late Roman Helmet from Burgh Castle', *Britannia*, 11 (1980), 303–12.

—— *Late Roman Fortifications* (London, 1983).

Jones, A. H. M., 'Military Chaplains in the Roman Army', *Harvard Theological Review*, 46 (1953), 249–50.

—— 'The Career of Flavius Philippus', *Historia*, 4 (1955), 229–33.

—— 'The Origin and Early History of the *Follis*', *JRS* 49 (1959), 34–8.

—— *The Later Roman Empire* (Oxford, 1964).

—— review of R. I. Frank, *Scholae Palatinae*, *JRS* 60 (1970), 227–9.

Jones, C. P., '*Stigma*: Tattooing and Branding in Graeco-Roman Antiquity', *JRS* 77 (1987), 139–55.

Kaltofen, A., *Studien zur der Völkerwanderungszeit im südöstlichen Mitteleuropa* (Oxford, 1984).

Kandler, M., and Vetters, H., *Der römische Limes in Österreich* (Vienna, 1986).

Kazanski, M., 'À propos des armes et des éléments de harnachement "orientaux" en Occident à l'époque des Grandes Migrations (4e–5e siècles)', *JRA* 4 (1991), 123–39.

—— *Les Goths* (Paris, 1991).

Keegan, J., *The Mask of Command* (London, 1987).

Kent, J. P. C., and Painter, K. S., eds., *Wealth of the Roman World* (London, 1977).

Kienast, D., *Untersuchungen zu den Kriegsflotten der römischen Kaiserzeit* (Bonn, 1966).

Klumbach, H., *Spätrömische Gardehelme* (Munich, 1973).

Kneissl, P., *Die Siegestitular der römischen Kaiser* (Göttingen, 1969).

Kolias, T., *Byzantinische Waffen* (Vienna, 1988).

Kollwitz, J., *Oströmische Plastik der theodosianisch Zeit* (Berlin, 1941).

Köppel, G. M., 'Die historischen Reliefs der römischen Kaiserzeit, IV', *BJ* 186 (1986), 1–90.

Kraeling, C. H., *The Synagogue* (New Haven, Conn., 1956).

Kropotkin, A. V., 'On the Centres of the Černjakhov Tribes', *Sovietskaya Archeologiskaya* 1984. 3, 35–47.

Kunow, J., 'Bemerkungen zum Export römischer Waffen in das Barbaricum', *LIMES Studien zu den Militärgrenzen Roms 3* (Stuttgart, 1986), 740–46.

Ladner, G. B., 'On Roman Attitudes towards Barbarians in Late Antiquity', *Viator*, 7 (1976), 1–26.

Lammert, F., 'Die älteste erhaltene Schrift über Seetaktik und ihre Beziehung zum Anonymus Byzantinus des sexte Jahrhunderts, zu Vegetius und zu Aineas' *Strategika*', *Klio*, 33 (1940), 271–88.

Lander, J., *Roman Stone Fortifications from the First Century AD to the Fourth*, BAR S206 (Oxford, 1984).

Le Bohec, Y., review of M. Reddé, *Mare Nostrum*, *JRA* 2 (1989), 326–31.

Lee, A. D., *Information and Frontiers* (Cambridge, 1993).

—— and Shepard, J., 'A Double Life: Placing the *Peri Presbeon*', *Byzantinoslavica*, 52 (1991), 15–39.

Leube, A., 'Archäologische Formengruppen im nördlichen Elb-Oder-Gebiet während des 1. bis 4. Jhrhndrt', *Prace Archeologiczne*, 22 (1976), 355–70.

Leyser, C., 'The Battle at the Lech, 955', *History*, 50 (1965), 1–25.

Liebeschuetz, J. H. W. G., 'Generals, Federates and Buccelarii in Roman Armies around AD 400', in P. W. Freeman and D. L. Kennedy, eds., *The Defence of the Roman and Byzantine East*, BAR S297 (Oxford, 1986), 463–74.

—— *Barbarians and Bishops* (Oxford, 1991).

—— 'Alaric's Goths: Nation or Army?', in J. F. Drinkwater and H. W. Elton, eds., *Fifth-Century Gaul: A Crisis of Identity?* (Cambridge, 1992), 75–83.

Lindner, R. P., 'Nomadism, Horses and Huns', *Past and Present*, 92 (1981), 1–19.

Lønstup, J., 'Das zweischneidige Schwert aus der jüngeren römischen Kasierzeit im freien Germanien und im römischen Imperium', *LIMES Studien zu den Militärgrenzen Roms 3* (Stuttgart, 1986), 747–9.

L'Orange, H. P. and Von Gerken, A., *Der spätantike Bildschungen des Konstantinsbogens* (Berlin, 1939).

Luff, R.-M., *A Zooarchaeological Study of the Roman North-Western Provinces*, BAR S137 (Oxford, 1982).

Luttwak, E. N., *The Grand Strategy of the Roman Empire* (London, 1976).

MacBain, B., 'Odovacer the Hun?', *CP* 78 (1983), 323–7.

MacCormick, M., *Eternal Victory* (Cambridge, 1986).

Mackay, J., and Barker, P., 'Three Plumbatae from Wroxeter', *Antiquaries Journal*, 54 (1974), 275–7.

MacMullen, R., 'The Emperor's Largesses', *Latomus*, 21 (1962), 159–66.

—— *Soldier and Civilian in the Later Roman Empire* (Cambridge, Mass., 1963).

—— 'How Big was the Roman Imperial Army?', *Klio*, 62 (1980), 451–60.

—— 'The Roman Emperor's Army Costs', *Latomus*, 43 (1984), 571–80.

—— *Corruption and the Decline of Rome* (London, 1988).

MacNeill, W. H., *Europe's Steppe Frontier* (Chicago, 1964).

Maenchen-Helfen, O., 'The Date of Ammianus Marcellinus' Last Books', *AJP* 76 (1955), 384–99.

—— *The World of the Huns* (Berkeley, Calif., 1973).

Mann, J. C., 'What was the *Notitia Dignitatum* for?', in R. Goodburn and P. Bartholomew, eds., *Aspects of the Notitia Dignitatum*, *BAR* S15 (Oxford, 1976), 1–9.

—— '*Duces* and *comites* in the Fourth Century', in D. E. Johnston, ed., *The Saxon Shore* (London, 1977), 11–15.

—— review of E. N. Luttwak, *Grand Strategy*, 'Power, Force and the Frontiers of the Empire', *JRS* 69 (1979), 175–83.

—— 'The Historical Development of the Saxon Shore', in V. A. Maxfield, ed., *The Saxon Shore* (Exeter, 1989), 1–11.

Marinescu, G. and Miritoiu, N., 'Die karpische Nekropole von Şopteriu', *Dacia*, 31 (1987), 107–18.

Marsden, E. W., *Greek and Roman Artillery: Historical Development* (Oxford, 1969).

—— *Greek and Roman Artillery: Technical Treatise* (Oxford, 1971).

Mathisen, R. W., 'Patricians as Diplomats in Late Antiquity', *BZ* 79 (1986), 35–49.

—— 'Fifth-Century Visitors to Gaul, Business or Pleasure', in J. F. Drinkwater and H. W. Elton, eds., *Fifth-Century Gaul: A Crisis of Identity?* (Cambridge, 1992), 228–38.

Matthews, J. F., *Western Aristocracies and Imperial Court AD 364–425* (Oxford, 1975).

—— *The Roman Empire of Ammianus* (London, 1989).

Maxfield, V. A., ed., *The Saxon Shore* (Exeter, 1989).

Menghin, W., *Das Schwert in frühen Mittelalter* (Stuttgart, 1983).

Mildenburger, G., *Germanische Burgen* (Münster, 1978).

Millar, F. G. B., 'P. Herennius Dexippus and the Third-Century Invasions', *JRS* 59 (1969), 12–29.

—— *The Emperor in the Roman World* (London, 1977).

—— 'Emperors, Frontiers and Foreign Relations, 31 BC–AD 378', *Britannia*, 13 (1982), 1–23.

—— 'Government and Diplomacy in the Roman Empire during the First Three Centuries', *International History Review*, 10 (1988), 345–77.

Millett, A. R., and Murray, W., eds., *Military Effectiveness* (London, 1988).

Mommsen, T., *Gesammelte Schriften*, 6 (Berlin, 1910).

Moss, J. R., 'The Effects of the Policies of Aetius on the History of Western Europe', *Historia*, 22 (1973), 711–31.

Müller, H. F., *Die alamannische Gräberfeld von Hemmingen* (Stuttgart, 1976).

Müller, W., ed., *Zur Geschichte der Alamannen* (Darmstadt, 1975).

Murray, A. C., *Germanic Kinship Structure* (Toronto, 1983).

Myers, H. A., and Wolfram, H., *Medieval Kingship* (Chicago, 1982).

Myres, J. N. L., *The English Settlements* (Oxford, 1986).

Naudé, C. P. T., 'Battles and Sieges in Ammianus Marcellinus', *Acta Classica*, 1 (1958), 92–106.

Nixon, C. E. V., 'Relations between Visigothic and Roman Gaul', in J. F. Drinkwater and H. W. Elton, eds., *Fifth-Century Gaul: A Crisis of Identity?* (Cambridge, 1992), 64–74.

Obolensky, D. M., *The Byzantine Commonwealth* (London, 1971).

Okamura, L., *Alamannia Devicta* (Ann Arbor, Mich. 1984).

Painter, K. S., 'A Late Roman Silver Ingot from Kent', *Antiquaries Journal*, 52 (1972), 84–92.

Percival, J., *The Roman Villa* (London, 1976).

—— 'The Fifth-Century Villa: New Life or Death Postponed', in J. F. Drinkwater and H. W. Elton, eds., *Fifth-Century Gaul: A Crisis of Identity?* (Cambridge, 1992), 156–64.

Perrin, O., *Les Burgondes* (Neuchâtel, 1968).

Pfister, R., and Bellinger, L., *Excavations at Dura-Europos, Final Report 4.2: Textiles* (New Haven, Conn., 1945) .

Pirling, R., 'Ein fränkischer Fürstengrab aus Krefeld-Gellep', *Germania*, 42 (1964), 188–216.

Pitts, L., 'Roman Style Buildings in Barbaricum (Moravia and SW Slovakia)', *Oxford Journal of Archaeology*, 6 (1987), 219–36.

Poulter, A., 'Nicopolis Interim Report 1989' (unpublished).

—— 'The Use and Abuse of Urbanism in the Danubian Provinces during the Late Roman Empire', in J. Rich, ed., *The City in Late Antiquity* (London, 1992), 99–136.

Raddatz, K., 'Die Bewaffnung der Germanen vom letzten Jahrhundert vor Chr. Geb. bis zur Völkerwanderungszeit', *ANRW* 2/12/3 (Berlin, 1985), 281–361.

—— 'Pfeilspitzen aus den Moorfund von Nydam', *Offa*, 20 (1963), 49–56.

—— *Der Thorsberger Moorfund* (Neumünster, 1987).

Ramsay, A. M., 'The Speed of the Roman Imperial Post', *JRS* 15 (1925), 60–74.

Reddé, M., *Mare Nostrum* (Rome, 1986).

Reichenkron, G., 'Zur römischen Kommandosprache bei byzantinischen Schriftstellen', *BZ* 54 (1961), 18–27.

Reynolds, R. L. and Lopez, R. S., 'Odovacer: German or Hun?', *AHR* 52 (1947), 36–53.

Richmond, I. A., *The City Walls of Imperial Rome* (Oxford, 1930).

—— *Roman and Native in Northern Britain* (London, 1958).

Richter, W., 'Die Darstellung der Hunnen bei Ammianus Marcellinus (31. 2. 1–11)', *Historia*, 23 (1974), 343–77.

Rivet, A. L. F., and Smith, C., *The Place Names of Roman Britain* (London, 1983).

Robinson, H. R., *The Armour of Imperial Rome* (London, 1975).

Rösch, G., Ὄνομα βασιλεύς: *Studien zum offiziellen Gebrauch der Kaisertitel im spätantike und frühbyzantinische Zeit* (Vienna, 1978).

Rosenthal, E., *The Illustrations of the Virgilius Romanus* (Zürich, 1972).

Rostovtzeff, M. I., Baur, P. V. C., and Bellinger, A. R., eds., *Excavations at Dura Europos, Fourth Season* (London, 1933).

Rostovtzeff, M. I., Bellinger, A. R., Hopkins, C., and Welles, C. B., eds., *Excavations at Dura Europos, Sixth Season* (London, 1936).

Roxan, M., 'The Distribution of Roman Military Diplomas', *Epigraphische Studien*, 12 (Cologne, 1981), 265–86.

Rupprecht, G., ed., *Die Mainzer Römerschiffe* (Mainz, 1986).

Salway, P., *Roman Britain* (Oxford, 1981).

Sawyer, P. H., and Wood, I. N., eds., *Early Medieval Kingship* (Leeds, 1977).

Schleiermacher, M., *Römische Reitergrabsteine* (Bonn, 1984).

Schmidt, L., *Geschichte der Wandalen*² (Munich, 1942).

Schnurbein, S. von, 'Zum Ango', in G. Kossack and G. Ulbert, eds., *Festschrift für Joachim Werner zum 65 Geburtstag* (Munich, 1974), 411–33.

Schuldt, E., *Perdöhl* (Berlin, 1976).

Scorpan, C., *Limes Scythiae, BAR* S88 (Oxford, 1988).

Scott, I. R., 'Spearheads of the British *Limes*', in W. S. Hanson and L. J. F. Keppie, eds., *Roman Frontier Studies, 1979* (Oxford, 1980), 333–43.

Seeck, O., *Regesten der Kaiser und Päpste* (Stuttgart, 1919).

Shaw, B. D., ' "Eaters of Flesh, Drinkers of Milk": The Ancient Mediterranean Ideology of the Pastoral Nomad', *Ancient Society*, 13/14 (1982/3), 5–31.

Shchukin, M. B., *Rome and the Barbarians in Central and Eastern Europe, 1st Century BC–1st Century AD* (Oxford, 1989).

Shennan, S. J., ed., *Archaeological Approaches to Cultural Identity* (London, 1989).

Sherlock, B., 'Plumbatae, a note on the method of manufacture', in M. W. Hassall and R. I. Ireland, eds. *De Rebus Bellicis, BAR* S63 (Oxford, 1979), 101–2.

Shettig, H., 'Das Nydamschiff', *Acta Archaeologia Copenhagen*, 1 (1930), 1–30.

Simpson, C. J., 'Foederati and Laeti in Late Roman Frontier Defence', M. Phil. thesis (Nottingham, 1971).

—— 'Belt Buckles and Strap Ends of the Late Roman Empire', *Britannia*, 7 (1976), 192–223.

Sivan, H., 'On *Foederati, Hospitalitas* and the Settlement of the Goths in AD 418', *AJP* 108 (1987), 759–72.

Smith, C. A., 'Exchange Systems and the Spatial Distribution of Elites', in C. A. Smith, ed., *Regional Analysis 2* (New York, 1976), 309–74.

Soproni, S., 'Eine spätrömische Militärstation im sarmatischen Gebiet', *LIMES* 8, ed. E. Birley *et al.* (Cardiff, 1974), 197–203.

—— *Der spätrömische Limes zwischen Esztergom und Szetendre* (Budapest, 1978).

—— *Die letzten Jahrzehnten des Pannonischen Limes* (Munich, 1985).

Speidel, M., 'Stablesiani: The Raising of New Cavalry Units during the Crisis of the Roman Empire', *Chiron*, 4 (1974), 541–6 [= *MAVORS* I (Amsterdam, 1984), 391–6].

—— 'Cataphractii Clibanarii and the Rise of the Later Roman Mailed Cavalry', *Epigrafica Anatolica*, 4 (1984), 151–6.

Stevens, C. E., *Sidonius Apollinaris and his Age* (Oxford, 1933).

—— 'Hadrian and Hadrian's Wall', *Latomus*, 14 (1955), 384–403.

Swanton, J., *The Spearheads of the Anglo-Saxon Settlements* (London, 1983).

Szidat, J., *Historische Kommentar zu Ammianus Marcellinus Buch 20–21*, ii, *Historia Einzelschriften* 38 (Wiesbaden, 1981).

Tausend, K., 'Hunnische Poliorketik', *Gräzer Beiträge*, 12–13 (1985–6), 265–81.

Teall, J., 'The Barbarians in Justinian's Armies', *Speculum*, 40 (1965), 294–322.

Tejral, J., 'Zur chronologie der frühen Völkerwanderungszeit im mittleren Donauraum', *Archaeologia Austriaca*, 72 (1988), 223–304.

Teodor, G., *The East Carpathian Area of Romania, 5th–11th Centuries AD*, *BAR* S81 (Oxford, 1980).

Thompson, E. A., 'Priscus of Panium, fr. 1b', *CQ* 39 (1945), 92–4.

—— *A History of Attila and the Huns* (Oxford, 1948).

—— *A Roman Reformer and Inventor* (Oxford, 1952).

—— 'Christianity and the Northern Barbarians', *Nottingham Medieval Studies*, I (1957), 3–21.

—— *The Early Germans* (Oxford, 1965).

—— *The Visigoths in the Time of Ulfila* (Oxford, 1966).

—— *Romans and Barbarians* (Madison, Wis., 1982).

—— *Who was St. Patrick?* (Woodbridge, 1985).

Todd, M., *The Barbarians* (London, 1972).

—— *The Walls of Rome* (London, 1978).

Todd, M., *The Northern Barbarians*² (Oxford, 1987).

Tomlin, R. S. O., '*Seniores-Iuniores* in the Late Roman Field Army', *AJP* 93 (1972), 253–78.

—— 'The Emperor Valentinian I', D. Phil. thesis (Oxford, 1975).

—— 'Notitia Dignitatum omnium quam civilium tam militarium', in R. Goodburn and P. Bartholomew, eds., *Aspects of the Notitia Dignitatum*, *BAR* S15, (Oxford, 1976), 189–209.

—— 'Meanwhile in North Italy and Cyrenaica', in P. J. Casey, ed., *The End of Roman Britain*, *BAR* 71 (Oxford, 1979), 263–70.

—— 'The Army of the Late Empire', in J. Wacher, ed., *The Roman World* (London, 1987), 107–33.

Trigger, B. G., *Time and Traditions* (Edinburgh, 1978).

Tsangadas, B. C. P., *The Fortifications and Defence of Constantinople* (New York, 1980).

Van Berchem, D., *L'Armée de Dioclétien et la Réforme Constantinienne* (Paris, 1952).

Van Creveld, M., *Supplying War* (Cambridge, 1977).

—— *Command in War* (London, 1985).

Van Es, W. A., 'Wijster: A Native Village beyond the Imperial Frontier', *Palaeohistoria*, 11 (1967).

Van Giffen, A. E., 'Der Warf in Ezinge Prov. Groningen und seine westgermanische Haüser', *Germania*, 20 (1936), 40–7.

Vickers, M., 'The late Roman Walls of Thessalonica', *LIMES* 8, ed. E. Birley *et al.* (Cardiff, 1974), 249–55.

Visy, Z., *Der pannonische Limes in Ungarn* (Stuttgart, 1988).

Von Petrikovits, H., 'Fortifications in the Northwestern Roman Empire from the Third to the Fifth Centuries AD', *JRS* 61 (1971), 178–218.

Waas, M., *Germanen im römischen Dienst* (Bonn, 1965).

Wallace-Hadrill, J. M., *The Long-Haired Kings* (London, 1962).

—— *Early Germanic Kingship* (Oxford, 1971).

Wardman, A. E., 'Usurpations and Internal Conflicts in the Fourth Century AD', *Historia*, 33 (1984), 220–37.

Watkins, T., 'Where were the Picts ?', in J. G. P. Friell and W. G. Watson, eds., *Pictish Studies*, *BAR* 125 (Oxford, 1984), 63–86.

Watson, R., 'Documentation in the Roman Army', *ANRW* 2/1 (Berlin, 1974), 493–507.

Webster, G., 'The Function and Organisation of Late Roman Civil Defences in Britain', in J. Hobley and B. Maloney, eds., *Roman Urban Defences in the West*, *CBA* 51 (London, 1983), 118–20.

Weitzmann, K., ed., *Age of Spirituality* (New York, 1979).

Welsby, D., *The Roman Military Defence of the British Provinces in its Later Phases*, *BAR* 101 (Oxford, 1982).

Werner, J., 'Pfeilspitzen aus Silber und Bronz in germanischen Adelsgräbern der Kaiserzeit', *Historisches Jahrbuch*, 74 (1955), 38–41.

—— *Beiträge des Attila–Reiches* (Munich, 1956).

—— 'Zu den alamannischen Burgen', in W. Müller, ed., *Zur Geschichte der Alamannen* (Darmstadt, 1975), 67–90.

—— 'Dančeny und Brangstrup', *BJ* 188 (1988), 241–86.

Wheeler, E. L., 'The Occasion of Arrian's *Tactica*', *GRBS* 19 (1978), 351–65.

Whitehouse, D., 'Raiders and Invaders, the Roman Campania in the first Millennium AD', in C. Malone and S. Stoddart, eds., *Papers in Italian Archaeology*, 4/4, *BAR* S246 (Oxford, 1985), 207–13.

Whittaker, C. R., 'Inflation and the Economy in the Fourth Century AD', in C. E. King, ed., *Imperial Revenue, Expenditure and Monetary Policy*, *BAR* S76 (Oxford, 1980).

—— 'Labour Supply in the Late Roman Empire', *Opus* 1 (1982), 171–9.

Wightman, E., *Roman Trier and the Treviri* (London, 1970).

Wolfram, H., *History of the Goths*[2] (London, 1988).

—— and Schwarz, A., eds., *Annerkennung und Integration* (Vienna, 1988).

Wood, I. N., 'Kings, Kingdoms and Consent', in P. H. Sawyer and I. N. Wood, eds., *Early Medieval Kingship* (Leeds, 1977), 6–29.

Zaharia, E., 'Données sur l'archéologie des IVe–XIe siècles sur le territoire de la Roumanie', *Dacia*, NS 15 (1971), 269–88.

Zöllner, E., *Geschichte der Franken* (Munich, 1970).

Zuckermann, C., 'Legio V Macedonica in Egypt', *Tyche*, 3 (1988), 279–87.

—— 'The Military Compendium of Syrianus Magister', *Jahrbuch der Öster-reichische Byzantinistik* 40 (1990), 209–24.

INDEX

All names follow conventions of PLRE. For individual army regiments, see under their names and Appendix 2. No references are included to individuals mentioned only in footnotes.

Acontisma 231
Adrianople 79, 80, 81, 82, 83, 85, 143, 170 n., 218, 248, 250, 251, 254, 255, 266, 268
Aetius 12, 198, 238
Africa 56, 86, 87, 120, 121–2, 132, 178, 179, 182, 190, 194, 195–6, 200, 201, 207, 210, 211, 214, 220, 228, 229, 233, 240, 246, 247, 267
Agathias 64, 65, 70, 234, 251, 270
agentes in rebus 152, 242
agriculture, barbarian 22, 23, 26, 28–9, 42, 54–5, 223–4, 280, 288
  destruction of 223–4
Aioulfus 35
Akatiri 35
  see also Huns
Alamanni 15, 17, 20, 21–2, 30, 31, 32, 33, 34, 36, 38–9, 40, 41, 46, 49, 50, 51, 52, 53, 54, 59, 69, 72–3, 75, 76, 77, 79, 131–2, 140, 177, 179, 180, 185, 188, 206, 211, 216–18, 221, 222–3, 224, 228, 229, 239, 246, 248, 249, 252, 254–6, 262
  see also Brisigavi, Bucinobantes, Iuthungi, Laeti, Lentienses
Alamannia 21, 65
Alans 15, 25–6, 38, 39, 41, 46, 55, 56, 58, 59, 63, 68, 74, 92, 94, 132, 188, 191
Alaric 7–10, 35, 41, 42, 51, 56, 74, 75, 77, 85–5, 96, 103, 135, 143, 177, 186, 219, 237, 266
Alatheus 6, 34
allies, Roman 91–2, 96–7, 107, 118, 124, 188–9, 228–9, 266
Alps:
  Cottian 230, 231
  Julian 74, 157, 230, 231, 233
ambassadors:

barbarian 56
  Roman external 182, 242 n.
  Roman internal 193–4, 195
Ambrose 142, 194, 228
ambushes:
  by barbarians 75, 79, 82, 236, 248, 256
  by Romans 79, 216, 233, 254
Amida 90, 171
Ammianus Marcellinus 17, 20, 24–5, 27, 30–1, 32, 33, 34, 37, 47–8, 70, 95 n., 137, 139, 175, 201, 234, 242, 251, 256, 258, 266, 270
Ampsivarii 39
  see also Franks
Anaolsus 43
Anastasius 144
Andragathius 7, 197
angons 65–7
annonae 121, 123, 124, 228
Anthemius 143, 239
Apollinaris, Sidonius 27, 205
Aquileia 83, 84, 98, 170, 171, 173, 230–1, 262–3
Araharius 2, 39, 40, 191
Arbogastes 7, 180, 192, 197, 236
Arcadiopolis 85
Arcadius 8, 9, 142, 185
arcani 242
  see also spies
archers, Roman 94, 104, 107, 170, 259, 263
Ardabur 12, 229, 247
Argentaria 52, 75, 218, 240
Arles 43, 98, 209, 254
Armenians 134
armour:
  barbarian 25, 57, 61–2, 69–71, 82
  horse 109 n., 114
  Roman 107, 110–14, 257, 264

army sizes:
  barbarian 58–9, 72–3
  Roman 105–6, 120, 210–11, 244–5
Arras 86
artillery:
  on ships 98, 100, 257
  Roman 105, 116, 124, 238, 252, 259–63
Aspar 12, 98, 129, 176, 212, 214, 231
assassination 192, 195, 242
Asterius 11
Ataulf 10, 11, 35, 42, 46, 47, 79
Athanaric 222, 226
Atrans 233
Attacotti 20
Attalus 10, 11, 197, 239
Atthuarii 17
  see also Franks
Aurelianus 8, 142, 143
autumn, effects 22, 79, 238
auxilia palatina 72, 89, 99, 104, 150–1
Avars 18, 84
axes 57, 60, 61, 65, 67, 68, 103 n., 110, 257

Bacurius 96
balistarii 105
barbarization 136–52, 265, 267, 272
Barbatio 2, 211, 218, 221
Basiliscus 125
Batavia 21
Bauto 6, 142, 224
Bazas 39, 191
bishops 85, 103, 142, 182, 193–4, 197
Bithynia 103, 130, 178, 194
blockades:
  by barbarians 76, 84, 85, 215
  by Romans 77, 191, 216, 218–19, 220, 258, 259, 263
boats:
  barbarian 24, 25, 79
  Roman 100, 124, 206 n., 207, 238, 245, 246, 257, 260, 263
Bonifatius 12, 94, 194, 212, 240
Botoşana 280
Boulogne 204
bows 57, 59, 60, 62, 63–4, 68, 103, 104, 106, 108, 116, 280
Braga 43
Bratei 28, 280
brigades 3, 72, 91, 101, 105, 208, 211
Brigetio 158

Brisigavi 32, 33, 132, 139
  see also Alamanni
Britain 20, 53, 54, 65, 86, 87, 140, 167, 178–9, 189, 196, 200, 201, 203–4, 210, 214, 220, 229, 230, 242, 246–7
Bructeri 15, 17, 39
  see also Franks
Brumath 52, 252
bucellarii 102
Bucinobantes 17, 35, 132, 140, 192
  see also Alamanni
Bulgars 108
burgi 158
Burgundians 22, 34, 40, 43, 51, 56, 182, 188, 220, 242

caltrops 161, 247, 262
campaign preparations:
  barbarian 22, 43
  Roman 96, 125, 130, 153, 180, 188–9, 209, 221–2, 226, 227–9, 235–9
candidati 96, 115, 195
cantons 32–3, 35, 37–9, 40, 41, 48, 58, 73, 138, 185–6, 224
capitus 122–4
Carnuntum 237
Castinus 11, 12, 240
Catalaunian Plains 82, 132, 218
cataphracts 106–7, 114, 116
cattle 22–3, 27, 53, 77, 223, 237, 278
cavalry:
  barbarian 24–5, 28–9, 57–9, 60, 68, 72, 78, 79, 80, 81, 250, 255
  Roman 89, 91, 94, 95, 96, 98–9, 103, 104, 108, 109, 110, 114, 115, 116, 122–4, 211, 233, 234, 237, 238, 243–5, 251–2, 255–6, 263, 266
  see also cataphracts; *scholae*
Celtae 91, 208, 211
cemeteries 61–3, 71, 278–80
Chalons-sur-Marne 52
Chamavi 17, 39–40
  see also Franks
Charietto 179, 217
Chariobaudes 213
chariots 59, 135
Chatti 15, 17, 39
  see also Franks
Chersonese 157
Cherusci 17
  see also Franks
Childeric 70

Index

Chnodomarius 1, 2, 32, 36, 38, 69, 74, 192, 256
Cibalae 233
cities:
defences, *see* fortifications
garrisons 47, 84, 86, 94, 99–100, 105, 171, 173, 203, 230
suburbanus 167–8, 173, 263
civilian leadership 102–3, 173–4, 176, 200, 240
Claudian 17, 27
Clermont 85, 173
clibanarii, see cataphracts
client kings 185–6
Clovis 35, 42, 43
coloni 130, 132, 153
column, monumental 25, 112–13, 115, 145, 151, 239
comes (rei militaris) 91, 96, 123, 147, 149, 176, 179, 182, 201, 204, 205, 210, 213, 214, 217, 239, 241, 243, 262
comes domesticorum 101, 240
comes stabuli 116, 147
comitatenses 50, 75, 89–99, 101, 103, 105–7, 131, 134, 137, 179, 188–9, 200, 204, 206, 207, 208–20, 234, 235, 239, 242, 250, 266
comitatus, barbarian 36, 72, 82
Comites (regt.) 93, 94
Como 98
confederations, barbarian 1, 5, 11, 15, 35, 43, 47, 50
Roman efforts vs 191–2
conscripts, Roman 128–9, 132, 134, 135, 138
consistorium 176
Constans (Aug., 337–50) 1, 208, 209 n.
Constans (Aug., 409–11) 9, 10
Constans (*comes Africae*, 409/10) 10
Constantine I 1, 90, 160, 175, 265
Constantine III 9–10, 51, 156, 177, 194, 228, 229–30, 239
Constantius (MUM) 97
Constantius I 130, 132
Constantius II 1–3, 21, 48, 87, 104, 121, 131, 135, 139, 152–3, 176, 180, 191, 193, 194, 195, 196, 197, 208, 211–12, 215, 224, 228, 229, 230, 231, 233, 237, 247, 252, 262
Constantius III 10–11, 77, 191, 220
co-operation between barbarians 38–40
see also confederations

Cornuti 95, 274
costs, Roman army 120–5, 127, 189
court:
Roman 17, 137, 141, 144, 168, 213
barbarian 42, 43
crossbows 105, 108
Cyrenaica 103
Cyzicus 98, 229, 258

Dacia 155, 177, 231, 243
Dagalaifus 217
Dalmatae 106–7, 158
Danube 25, 28, 30, 78–9, 181, 201, 226, 236, 238–9, 245–6
de Rebus Bellicis 118, 137, 200, 269
Decentiaci 228
Decentius 1, 196, 197, 198, 208, 218
deception operations 75, 230, 243
dediticii 129–30, 135
defence-in-depth 157, 203–4
deserters, Roman 41, 75, 84, 85, 101, 128, 140, 205, 230, 255, 266
deterrence 172, 187, 188, 193, 206
Dexippus 174
Diocletian 94, 123, 165
domestici 10, 101, 123, 147, 240, 242, 272
see also *protectores*
donatives 120, 121, 123, 125, 140
Dravus 233
Dura Europos 114, 115
dux 96, 123, 135, 139, 147, 155, 167, 179, 182, 201, 205, 210, 213, 239, 241, 243

Edobichus 254
Egypt 119, 121, 201, 213, 267, 272
Ellac 35
emperor 56, 94–6, 101, 115, 121, 125, 126, 152–3, 169, 176–8, 180, 182, 183, 185, 193–9, 200, 205, 208, 214, 221, 228, 239, 242–3
ethnicity 132–3, 141–5
Eudoxius 41
Eugenius 7, 45, 96, 197, 228, 229, 266
Eugippius 173, 201, 207
Eunapius 27, 110, 139
Eutropius 8, 143
excubitores 128
execution 186, 192, 197
exploratores 104, 248

fabricae 112, 115, 116–17, 168, 186, 240
field army:
  bases 95, 155, 203, 209, 219, 231, 235
  praesental 94, 179, 200, 208
  structure 208–14
  see also *comitatenses*
field battle 102, 107, 108, 216–18, 219, 222, 227, 250–6
field fortifications 82, 233, 252
finance, Roman 118–27
fireships 257 n.
Firmus 98, 210
fleet, Roman 97–9, 204, 220, 227, 230, 238, 257
flotillas, Roman 100, 201, 246
foederati 68, 91–4, 96, 107, 128, 132, 140, 143, 144, 253
  see also allies
fortifications:
  artillery 105, 161, 165, 171, 259–60, 261, 262–3
  barbarian 30–1, 78, 82
  construction/repair 155–6, 164–7, 171
  crenellations 163, 170, 172
  ditches 83, 157, 158, 161–2, 165, 166–7, 169, 171, 172, 259–61
  effectiveness 82–6, 165, 173–4, 203, 215
  fore-walls 162, 170
  functions 157–61, 172, 203–4
  gates 83, 85, 164, 167, 170–1, 259–60
  interior buildings 116–17, 164, 168–9, 173
  linear 157, 203
  placement 156, 157, 160–1, 203–4
  posterns 164, 171, 263
  storage 164, 185, 258
  towers 100, 155, 156, 157, 158–60, 163–4, 165–6, 170–1, 201, 259, 260
  walls 86, 162–3, 166, 168, 169–70, 259
forts:
  detachment 158, 160, 164
  garrison 158, 203–4
  landing places 100, 158, 160, 246
  watchtowers 158–60, 163, 164, 201, 203, 204
Francia 21, 61, 236

francisca 61, 62, 65–6
Franks 15, 17, 20–1, 30, 36, 37, 39–41, 42, 43, 45, 48, 50, 51, 52, 53–5, 60, 64, 65, 70, 72, 73, 75, 76, 80, 86, 130, 133, 141, 175, 180, 183, 189, 192, 206, 215, 216, 218, 228, 231, 236, 239, 240, 250, 258
  see also Ampsivarii, Atthuarii, Bructeri, Chamavi, Chatti, Cherusci, Merovingians, Salii, Sugambri
Fraomarius 35, 140, 192
Fravitta 98, 142, 143
Frigeridus 213, 216
Frigidus 197, 252, 255
Fritigern 83

Gabinius 51, 192
Gainas 8, 96, 142–3, 229
Galicia 56
Gaul 17, 38, 39, 42, 50–4, 56, 65, 73, 75, 86, 106, 120, 132–3, 135, 139, 168, 169, 178, 181, 191, 196, 200, 204, 208–9, 210, 211–12, 213, 220, 229, 231, 233, 236, 240, 267–8
Geiseric 267
gentiles 129, 132
Gepids 19
Germans 15, 17, 37, 60, 141, 144–5, 151
  see also Alamanni, Franks, Saxons, Suevi
Gerontius 9–10
gift-giving 36, 189
Gildo 8, 194
Glycerius 197
Goar 10
Gothia 25–6, 46, 61
Goths 18–19, 23, 25–6, 29, 34, 35, 39–40, 42, 46, 51, 55, 56, 58, 59, 68, 74, 77, 80, 82, 83, 92, 96, 102, 110, 120, 134, 142–4, 153, 177, 180, 189–91, 217, 219, 220, 226–7, 228–9, 253, 266–7
  see also Greuthungi, Ostrogoths, Tervingi, Visi, Visigoths
Gratian (Aug., 367–83) 5–6, 75, 93, 110, 114, 144, 145, 218, 224, 230, 239, 240, 266
Gratian (Aug., 406) 9, 196
greaves 115
Gregory of Tours 133, 271
Greuthungi 55, 75, 79, 222, 226
  see also Goths

guides, used by:
  barbarians 79
  Romans 243
Gundomadus 33, 35
Guntiarius 10

Haemus Mountains 219, 231
Hariobaudes 213, 242
harvest 22
Hellespont 98, 143, 229
helmets:
  barbarian 57, 61, 62, 69–70, 71
  Roman 110, 111, 113, 114–15, 249
Heraclianus 10, 97, 229, 230
Heruli 41, 50, 52, 86–7
Honorius 8–12, 56, 126, 145, 153–4,
  175, 177, 194, 237
horses 17, 23–5, 27–9, 58–9, 68, 85, 87,
  105, 109, 116, 122, 124, 135, 177,
  235, 237, 247, 258
Hortarius 140
hostages 186–7, 225
Housesteads 104
Huneric 186
Huns 15, 17, 18, 25, 26–9, 31, 35, 45,
  50, 58, 59, 63–4, 68, 69, 74, 82–5,
  86, 92, 94, 96, 107, 108, 173, 185,
  189, 190, 198, 205, 228, 253, 270,
  280
  see also Akatiri

Iazyges 18
  see also Sarmatians
Illyricum 48, 75, 133, 142, 178, 186,
  194, 200, 208, 209–10, 229, 231
Immo 262
income, imperial 119–20, 125–6
infantry:
  barbarian 57–8, 59, 60, 67, 72, 81,
    107, 256
  Roman, 89, 91, 94, 98, 99, 103–5, 107,
    108–10, 111, 112, 113, 115, 123–4,
    211, 244, 251–2, 256, 264, 271
information:
  control 230, 249
  transmission 75, 138, 140, 177–8, 205,
    241, 242–3
intelligence:
  barbarian 73–6, 79–80
  Roman strategic 204–6, 226, 234,
    240–3
  Roman tactical 191, 248–50, 266
Intercisa 158, 165, 166

interpreters 182 n., 242 n.
Ioannes (John) 12, 198, 228, 229, 231,
  247
Ioviani 95
Iovii 95
Ireland 20, 59, 190
Isauria 201, 210
Isaurians 133, 144, 182
Italy 30, 51, 56, 77, 86, 94, 121, 135,
  154, 168, 195, 201, 208–10, 219,
  229, 231, 233, 236, 240
iudices 34, 222
iuniores 94–5, 101
Iuthungi 17
  see also Alamanni

javelins 57, 60, 62, 64, 68, 72, 104, 108–
  9, 117
Jerome 17, 27, 86, 141
Jordanes 34 n., 132
Jovian 3, 185
Jovinus (Aug., 411–13) 10, 35, 196
Jovinus (MUM 361–9) 178, 179, 217,
  244, 249
Jovius 249
Julian 2–3, 38–9, 74–5, 76, 87, 100, 106,
  120, 130, 131, 135, 139, 140, 156,
  157, 160, 177, 180, 185, 189, 193,
  195, 196, 209, 210–11, 216, 218–
  19, 222, 226, 229, 230, 231, 236,
  237, 244–5, 246, 249, 254–5, 262–3
Justin 128

kingdoms, barbarian 33, 36, 41, 42–4,
  51, 55–7, 87, 181, 188, 220
kings 18, 20, 32–7, 38–9, 41, 42, 43, 56,
  69–70, 72–3, 74, 139, 175, 185–6,
  190, 192, 199
  Roman efforts vs 35, 40–1, 51, 175,
    185, 192, 221

Laeti 129–33
Lancearii 104
lances 68, 106, 109
lassoes 68, 110
Latin language 138 n., 140
leadership, barbarian 26, 34–5, 38, 42–
  3, 46–7, 185, 219, 224
legions 89–90, 95, 99–100, 101, 103,
  104, 105, 117, 128, 203 n., 217
Lentienses 17, 72, 75
  see also Alamanni
Letçani 63

Libanius 142
Liberi 40
  see also Sarmatians
light-armed troops 104–5, 251, 254
Limigantes 40, 152, 180, 222
  see also Sarmatians
limitanei 89, 95, 99–101, 103, 105, 106,
    107, 126, 128, 131, 139, 200–1, 211,
    220, 234, 246, 248, 250, 272
  deployment 158, 201–4
  effectiveness 179, 206, 207–8, 212
  functions 204–6
literary stereotypes, barbarian 17–18, 25
Litorius 90, 238
Lombards 18, 60, 216
Lupicinus 247
Lychidnus 78

Macrianus 4, 35, 46, 140, 184, 192
magister militum 95, 97, 101, 123, 131,
    147, 149, 176, 179, 180, 183, 187,
    197, 201, 205, 208–10, 213, 214,
    216, 217, 221, 239, 243, 271
magister officiorum 52, 240, 242
Magnentiaci 228
Magnentius 1, 21, 38, 51, 54, 139, 194,
    196, 197, 198, 208, 215, 228, 229,
    230, 231–3, 240
Magnus Maximus 6–7, 97, 194, 196,
    197, 209, 224, 228–9, 230, 266
Mainz 73–4, 100
Majorian 72, 98, 206, 239, 267
Manadus 104
manpower shortages 152–4, 229, 267
maps 243, 248
Marcellinus (*Mag. off.*, 350) 240
Marcellinus (MUM 461–8) 267
Marcellus 4, 196
march order:
  barbarian 78
  Roman 244–5
marching camps, Roman 247–8, 251,
    252, 271
Marcian 190, 212 n.
Marcianopolis 209, 225
Marcomanni 18, 21
Marcomere 39, 40, 192
Marcus 9, 196
Margus 85
Marinus 11
Martin, St 129
Mascezel 8, 194, 211
massacres of barbarians 143–4

Mauretania 119, 121, 267
Mauri 106–7
Mauricius 18, 60, 78, 91, 137, 234, 236,
    252, 254, 269–71
Maximinus 28
Maximus (Aug., 409–11) 10–11
Mederichus 186
Mediterranean 220, 229, 247
Menander 184, 234
Merobaudes 230
Merovingians 59, 133
  see also Franks
Metz 168
military effectiveness:
  barbarian 29, 50, 67, 80, 83, 85–6
  Roman 104, 145, 165, 173–4, 188,
    190, 206, 216, 219–20, 222, 227,
    237–8, 248, 250, 265–8
militias 102–3
Misenum 98
missile combat 80, 81, 104, 105, 114,
    161, 163, 165, 252, 253, 257, 259,
    260, 261, 263
Modares 110, 142
Moesia 100, 111
Moldavia 22, 26–7, 29, 31, 278–80
Moors 18, 134, 138 n., 146
Mursa 197, 230, 231–3

Naissus 84, 231
Narbonne 238
Natesio 263
naval activity, barbarian 50, 52–3, 59,
    86–7, 206
naval battles, Roman 257
naval construction 98–9, 230
naval transport 97–8, 207, 220, 238,
    245, 247
Nepotianus 1, 196, 231, 240
Nevitta 249
Nicaea 3, 139
night combat 82, 218, 243, 246, 254,
    262
nobility, see *optimates*
Noricum 50, 126, 207
Notitia Dignitatum 38, 89, 91, 93, 94,
    98–9, 101, 111–12, 115 n., 116, 131–
    2, 158, 160, 163, 201, 203 n., 204,
    209–10, 211, 220 n., 271
Numidia 119, 121

Odovacer 262
Olympius 8, 9, 240

optimates 26, 32, 34, 35–6, 37, 42, 57, 58, 70, 73, 82, 183, 186, 241, 256
Orosius 141
Ostrogoths 41, 43, 58, 59, 70, 77, 83, 85
see also Goths

pagus, see canton
palatini 94
passes 157, 216, 231, 233
pastoralism 17, 24, 26, 27–9, 280
patricius 193
Peri Strategikes 234, 270
Persians 18, 134, 135, 146, 185 n., 208, 226, 253, 258
Petulantes 91, 208, 211
Philippopolis 83, 231
Picts 20, 30
Pitzias 58
planning:
    barbarian 73–4
    Roman 41, 101, 181, 221, 235, 237–8, 240–5
plumbatae 108
plunder 48, 52–4
Poetovio 168, 233
Poitou 132
Pollentia 218
praefecti 97, 101, 131, 147, 149, 272
praepositi 90, 101, 123, 131, 147, 149, 154
praesental army 94, 179, 200, 208–11, 219, 246
    see also field army
praetorian prefect 131, 171, 176, 193–4, 209, 236, 238, 240
precedence 94–5, 100, 103, 212
Priarius 5, 75
Priscus 84 n.
prisoners:
    of barbarians 53, 84, 185
    of Romans 56, 129–30, 133, 134, 135, 223, 248
probatoriae 90
Procopius (historian) 18–19, 60, 88, 137, 234, 251, 270
Procopius (usurper, 365–6) 3–4, 104, 139, 177, 178, 196, 214, 225, 228, 229, 243, 258
procursatores 248
Promoti 106
Promotus 6, 75, 213
protectores 101, 147, 149, 242, 272
    see also *domestici*

provocation of barbarians, Roman 51
pseudocomitatenses 95, 103, 105, 212
Pusaeus 135
Pyrenees 231

Quadi 18, 22, 30, 34, 37, 39, 40, 51, 191–2, 221, 224, 237, 239
Quintinus 80, 239

Radagaisus 9, 42, 50, 51, 77, 85, 135, 154, 192, 211, 215, 219
Raetia 50, 51, 207, 224
rams 83, 84, 161, 163, 166, 260, 261, 262
Rando 73–4
Ravenna 43, 56, 83, 98, 145, 168–9, 175, 258, 262
rebels 182, 193–8, 228
recruiting:
    before campaigning 153–4, 227–8, 235
    Roman 122, 128–54
recruits, barbarian origins 92, 94, 129–31, 185, 228–9
refuges, civilian 172, 214–15
Reihengräberzivilisation 133
Rheims 209
Rhine 37, 40, 47–8, 51, 52, 78–9, 156, 157, 160–1, 181, 184, 201, 245–6
Richomeres 142, 240
Ricimer 97, 143, 258, 267
river crossing:
    barbarian 78–9
    Roman 160, 203, 245–6, 252
river transport 178, 207, 238, 245
Roman territory, loss of 119–20, 156, 181–2, 196, 204, 267
Romulus 197
royalty, barbarian 32–8, 58, 73, 183, 241
Rufinus 8
Rugi 41
Rutilius Namatianus 141–2

Saba, St 32
Sabinianus (MUM 479–81) 243
Sabinianus (MUM 505) 58
Salices 82, 218, 240
Salii 17, 40, 54, 55, 130
    see also Franks
Salona 231
Saphrax 6, 34

Sapor II 139
Sarmatians 23–5, 29, 31, 38, 39, 40, 58, 63, 68, 70, 104, 131, 132, 183, 188, 191–2
see also Iazyges, Liberi, Limigantes
Sarus 9, 34, 35, 47, 134
Sassanids, *see* Persians
Savus 231–3
saxes 62, 65–7
Saxon Shore 201, 204
Saxons 15, 19, 21, 48, 52–3, 59, 65, 86–7, 175, 189, 206, 228, 231
Scarponne 52
scholae 91, 94, 95, 96, 107, 151–2, 208, 240
Sciri 130, 132
Scotti 20, 87, 189
Scutarii 46, 106, 140
Scythia, Roman province 100
Scythians 18, 151, 189, 270
see also Alans, Goths, Huns
Sebastianus 213, 215, 217, 235
Segericus (Singeric) 11, 34, 35
seniores 94, 95, 101, 132
Sens 74–5, 76, 83, 262
Serapio 32, 38
Serdica 231
Serri 226
settlements of barbarians 42–3, 54–6, 96, 130–3, 228–9, 265
Severus (MUM 357–8) 75
Severus (MUM 367–72) 178, 244
sheep 22, 23, 27, 53, 77, 237, 278
shields 57, 60, 62, 63, 69, 71, 110, 114, 115, 161, 184, 243
ships:
 barbarians 50, 86–7
 Roman 98, 124, 257, 270
siege:
 artillery 105, 161, 171
 by barbarians 39, 74–5, 76, 82–6, 191, 215
 blockades 76, 218–19
 equipment, barbarian 83–4
 mining 150, 163, 166, 259, 260, 262
 rams 259, 260, 261, 262
 towers 238, 259–60, 261–2, 263
 warfare 108, 161, 173–4, 212–13, 230–1, 257–63
Sigisvultus 12
Silvanus 2, 51, 129, 146, 176, 195–6, 210, 230, 233
Singeric, *see* Segericus

Sîntana de Mures–Chernjakhov culture 63, 278–81
Sirmium 2, 168, 171, 173, 209, 230, 231–3
Siscia 233
slaves 41, 53, 102, 103, 145, 153–4, 223, 249
slings 64, 103, 105, 108
Solicinium 4, 79, 222, 244, 249, 254
Somme 52, 98
Sozomen 130
Spain 38, 42, 56, 139, 182, 188, 196, 200, 210, 220 n.
spatha 62, 67, 68, 70, 110
speculatores 248
Speyer 86
spies:
 barbarian 18, 75, 205
 Roman 187, 242
spring, effects 22, 79, 236–7, 247
Stablesiani 106
Stilicho 7–9, 39, 51, 97, 129, 135, 141–2, 144, 146, 176, 183, 192, 211, 213, 219, 266
stipendium 120–1
stirrups 109
Strasbourg 52, 59, 69, 72, 79, 81, 82, 106, 140, 157, 216, 237, 251, 255–6
Strategikon 18, 60, 78, 138, 254, 269–71
strategy 57, 181, 199–233, 234, 235–9
 blockade 218–19
 field battle 217–18
 harrassing 216–17
suborning troops 230
subsidies 36, 51–2, 189–90, 241
suburbanus 168–9, 173, 263
Suevi 17, 18, 35, 40, 42, 43, 50, 51, 55, 56, 74, 182, 188
see also Alamanni
Sugambri 17, 21, 38
see also Franks
Sulpicius Alexander 30
summer, effects 22, 79, 236, 238
Sunno 39, 40, 192
Suomarius 38–9
supply system:
 barbarian 18, 53, 74, 76–7, 84
 Roman 125, 209, 235, 236
surprise attacks:
 by Romans 53, 72, 75–6, 79, 194, 217, 245, 254–5
 by barbarians 78–9, 85, 206, 247, 250

Sutton Hoo 87
swords 57, 60, 62, 67, 68, 70, 71, 103,
    107, 110, 116
  see also *spatha*
Symmachus 142
Synesius 103, 137, 138, 142–3, 151
Syrianus 270

tactics:
  barbarian 80–2, 87–8
  Roman 87–8, 107, 109, 250–5
Taifali 40, 132–3, 188
tents 18, 28, 77, 115, 247
Tervingi 73, 222
  see also Goths
testudo 253, 260
Themistius 144
Theoderic (Amal) 77, 83, 85, 96, 101,
    258
Theoderic (Triarius) 85
Theoderic I 35, 43
Theodosius (the Elder) 4, 98, 190
Theodosius I 6–7, 28, 75, 118, 141, 144,
    145, 183, 185, 194, 228–9, 231, 265,
    269
Theodosius II 9, 12, 37, 98, 212
Thermopylae 231, 265
Thessalonica 83, 170
Thrace 178, 200, 209, 211, 216, 229
Tingitania 201
Toulouse 43, 90
Toxandria 52, 54
Tractus Argentoratensis 201, 217 n.
Tractus Armoricanus 204
trade restrictions 187, 191, 205
training 81, 103, 104, 108, 140, 212–13,
    235, 242, 254, 266
transfers:
  officers 140, 213
  troops 94, 95, 198, 199, 207, 209,
    211–12, 237, 246
Trapezus 83
treachery:
  by barbarians 138, 140
  by Romans 85–6, 173, 230, 231, 251
treaties with barbarians 18, 36, 38, 45,
    53, 57, 96, 134, 135, 139, 182–7,
    188–9, 194, 221, 224, 241
Tribigildus 8, 94
tribunes 90, 94, 101, 104, 116, 135, 140,
    147, 149, 154, 176, 177, 198, 213,
    243, 256, 266, 272
tributarii 129, 135

Uldin 8, 9
Ulfilas 10
Unnigardae 92–4, 95, 107
Urbicius 234, 269–71
Ursicinus 2, 208
Usafer 191–2
usurpation 193–8
  effects of 51, 124, 177, 179–80, 224,
    227–33, 266
usurpers:
  recognition 177, 193–5
  supporters' treatment 197–8
  treatment 175, 195, 196–7

Vadomarius 32, 33, 46, 135, 138–9, 186,
    192, 241
Valens 3–6, 139, 143 n., 144, 153, 177,
    213, 218, 222, 226, 235, 236, 266
Valentinian I 3–6, 35, 39, 41, 91, 140,
    144, 145, 153, 155, 156, 160, 167,
    177, 178, 180, 183, 184, 192, 208,
    209, 213, 221, 222, 230, 237, 239,
    242–4, 249, 254
Valentinian II 6–7, 194, 230
Valentinian III 12, 37, 118, 120–1, 125,
    168, 194, 196, 198, 269
Valentinus 4
Valeria 158–9
Vallia 11, 34, 42
Vandals 18, 19, 22, 38, 40, 41, 42, 50,
    51, 55, 74, 87, 120, 141, 182, 247,
    267, 268
Varanes 213
Vegetius 59, 104, 110–11, 114, 137,
    269
Vetranio 1, 194, 195, 197, 208
vexillationes 89, 94, 101, 103, 128,
    199
Victores 150
victory titles 37
Viderichus 34
villages, barbarian 16, 30–1, 32
  destruction of 221, 223
villas:
  barbarian 30, 43
  fortified 172
Visi 38
  see also Goths
Visigoths 19, 35, 40, 41, 42–3, 52, 56,
    57, 77, 134, 181–2, 188, 205, 220,
    238, 267
  see also Goths
Vithicabius 32, 34, 139, 192, 242

volunteers, Roman 92, 128, 134–5, 143
wagons:
   barbarian 26, 27, 28, 31, 42, 77–8, 82
   Roman 124, 238, 245, 252
warcries 81, 144, 253
watchtowers, *see* fortifications

winter, effects 22, 73, 74, 76, 77, 78,
   226, 235–7, 245, 247

Zeno 95, 118, 144, 211, 239
Zizais 38
Zosimus 27, 110, 142